D1052820

Democracy,
If We Can Keep It

ALSO BY ELLIS COSE

The End of Anger: A New Generation's Take on Race and Rage
Colorblind: Seeing Beyond Race in a Race-Obsessed World
The Best Defense
Bone to Pick: Of Forgiveness, Reconciliation, Reparation, and Revenge
The Envy of the World: On Being a Black Man in America
A Man's World: How Real Is Male Privilege—and How High Is Its Price?
The Press: Inside America's Most Powerful Newspaper Empires
The Rage of a Privileged Class: Why Are Middle-Class Blacks Angry? Why Should America Care?
A Nation of Strangers: Prejudice, Politics, and the Populating of America

Democracy, If We Can Keep It

The ACLU's 100-Year Fight for Rights
in America

Ellis Cose

NEW YORK
LONDON

Requests for permission to reproduce selections from this book should be made
through our website: https://thenewpress.com/contact.

Published in the United States by The New Press, New York, 2020
Distributed by Two Rivers Distribution

ISBN 978-1-62097-383-7 (hc)
ISBN 978-1-62097-384-4 (ebook)
CIP data is available

The New Press publishes books that promote and enrich public discussion and understanding
of the issues vital to our democracy and to a more equitable world. These books are made possible
by the enthusiasm of our readers; the support of a committed group of donors, large and small;
the collaboration of our many partners in the independent media and the not-for-profit sector;
booksellers, who often hand-sell New Press books; librarians; and above all by our authors.

www.thenewpress.com

Composition by Westchester Book Composition
This book was set in Adobe Caslon

Printed in the United States of America

2   4   6   8   10   9   7   5   3   1

For Peter Kougasian, whose intellect, talent, integrity
and wit will always be an inspiration

Contents

Introduction

I had not planned to write this book. When I became the writer in residence at the American Civil Liberties Union (ACLU) at the invitation of Executive Director Anthony Romero, he mentioned the ACLU's upcoming centennial; but that was not to be my focus.

We had agreed that it might be an interesting experiment to embed a journalist with total editorial independence within the ACLU. I would not formally be part of the ACLU, but would be granted access to the organization's resources to inform my writing on issues related to its civil liberties mission. I had two book projects in mind. One would look at the evolving movement for criminal justice reform. The other would examine American entitlements—to privacy and social mobility, among other things—and how technology affected them.

After Donald J. Trump's election, my focus began to shift. I couldn't imagine a coherent, constructive dialogue on criminal justice taking place with Trump in the White House. Also, Trump was threatening an unprecedented assault on civil liberties.

For months before he took office, Trump had promoted anti-Muslim travel restrictions. He regularly attacked the press—so distressing the Committee to Protect Journalists that the organization called out his betrayal of "First Amendment values." The ACLU also was alarmed. The summer before his election, the ACLU released a study calling Trump a "one-man constitutional crisis." It was clear that a clash of epic proportions loomed between the incoming president and the nation's preeminent civil liberties organization. At that point, a book about the ACLU struck me as something worth doing.

As my focus shifted, I realized I would need to change my status. Writing a book about the ACLU while under the ACLU's roof (even with a signed promise of editorial independence) was journalistically fraught. After consulting with family and friends, I stepped down from that wonderfully privileged appointment to pursue this book as a fully independent project.

Democracy, If We Can Keep It is the result. I realized early on that writing a history of the ACLU would necessarily mean telling a story about the evolution of America itself.

The ACLU sprung out of a core promise that America made to its citizens. That promise, embodied in the Bill of Rights, was that America would always stand for freedom of conscience, freedom of speech, and freedom of dissent.

In the days when the republic was born, many questioned whether we even needed a Bill of Rights. Delegates to the Philadelphia Convention of 1787 explicitly voted against including one in the body of the Constitution. Why, many wondered, would Americans need protection from the institutions they themselves had created? As historian Gordon Wood put it, the "adoption of the Bill of Rights . . . was so fortuitous, so confused, and so inadvertent that it can only be regarded as a striking example of those many historical events whose monumental significance comes to transcend their petty and haphazard origins."[1]

As a concession to certain founders—among them George Mason and Thomas Jefferson—James Madison shepherded the Bill of Rights through the House. It was ratified in 1791. Not that anyone took the amendments very seriously at the time.

In the late 1790s, when American ships were being attacked by the French and fear of the conflict expanding was palpable, the promised rights became eminently disposable. One result was the Alien and Sedition Acts of 1798.

Those laws made it easier to deport foreign dissidents—"dangerous to the peace and safety of the United States"—and increased the waiting period for citizenship. They also made it a crime for journalists and others to publish writings that were "false, scandalous, and malicious" or that alienated people's affections from the government. At the time, all branches of the government were controlled by Federalists. And the laws, as administered, effectively criminalized criticism of the Federalist government or of President John Adams.

Democratic-Republican Clubs, essentially debating societies, were disbanded. A number of writers and publishers were imprisoned. One pamphleteer was prosecuted for calling President Adams a monarchist and a "toady" to British interests.

As Robert and Marilyn Aiken describe the era: "Federalist judges did not require the government to prove statements false. . . . Malice was presumed and intent to defame was inferred from words that had a 'bad tendency.'"[2]

When Thomas Jefferson took office in 1801, he pardoned those convicted under the Sedition Act and explained in a letter to former first lady Abigail Adams, "I discharged every person under punishment or prosecution under the Sedition law, because I considered, and now consider, that law to be a nullity as absolute and as palpable as if Congress had ordered us to fall down and worship a golden image."

For the next century, many of the rights guaranteed by the Constitution were like precious heirlooms: things to be admired but not necessarily put to use. It was not until World War I that gross violations of the Bill of Rights by the federal government were seriously challenged. At that point, a movement of civil libertarians arose to insist that America obey its own Constitution.

Despite over a century's effort devoted to cementing, codifying, and protecting those rights, today many Americans remain uncertain what those rights are and whether they should apply to all. National opinion polls routinely find that more than one-third of Americans have no idea what the Bill of Rights is or what the First Amendment protects. And to make matters even more surreal, America put in office a forty-fifth president who seems to believe much in the Bill of Rights is optional. He believes that dissent from his views is an act of treason and endorses tossing citizens out of the country for publicly criticizing him.

The year in which the ACLU celebrates its first century of existence seemed the proper time in which to publish a book that looks back on some of America's history and that reminds us how difficult, and yet important, it has been to protect those who have the courage to stand up to the raucous, righteous, unthinking mob.

I am duty-bound to add that this is not the definitive story of the ACLU. I doubt that such a story could be contained in one volume. This book does not, for instance, tell in detail the story of the ACLU chapters and affiliates—some of which became influential enough to change national ACLU policy. Every ACLU leader since Roger Baldwin, its first executive director, has attempted to strengthen those affiliates. And over the years, the affiliates have grown from a rag-tag band of idiosyncratic, underfinanced cousins to become a force onto themselves. It would take a book just to tell their story. This is not that book.

Nor do I attempt to catalog and explain every important legal case that has involved the ACLU. I delve into a great many of them. But to write a litigation history of the ACLU would be to write an encyclopedia.

This book focuses largely on events and cases of national significance and follows closely the activities of the national office. The early material is drawn largely from archival research, including board minutes and correspondence and congressional and legal records, and from contemporaneous books, journals, and news accounts. Once the narrative moves into the middle of the twentieth century, the historical source material is supplemented by interviews.

This book is lightly sourced. For the most part, the only citations are to books and major journal articles. My editor and I decided that there was little point in publishing hundreds of pages of footnotes, particularly from contemporaneous news reports.

Long ago, before much of journalism was integrated into various internet-accessible databases, footnoting every news account might have served a purpose. But we no longer live in the days when checking most newspaper references requires the precise citations that would lead to the proper roll of microfilm.

I hope that you, dear reader, will find this material as engrossing as I have. I also hope that it helps to make clear why the defense of civil liberties is the responsibility of all Americans—not just of an organization with civil liberties in its name.

1

Preaching Peace to a World at War

World War I redefined the world and forever changed America's place in it. In the early years of the twentieth century, America was an isolated island of possibility, far from the superpower it was to become. President Woodrow Wilson, while eager to play international mediator, was reluctant to become democracy's guardian. World War I changed that. As historian Robert Zieger has observed, it "drove home the fact that America was Europe's offspring and successor."[1] It set off a battle for the nation's soul that rages to this day. And it ignited a battle over civil liberties that eventually spawned the American Civil Liberties Union.

Americans initially believed, along with their president, that the nation could avoid entanglement in Europe's war. No one believed that more strongly than the eclectic group who came together to combat the "militarism" of the times. The war ultimately proved them wrong. Valiantly though they fought, they could not turn America away from the unrelenting call of war.

In the summer of 1914, after a Serbian militant assassinated Austro-Hungarian Archduke Franz Ferdinand, Austria-Hungary declared war on Serbia. The war quickly spread through much of Europe, as the United States watched in dismay. President Wilson opted for neutrality during that first phase of conflict. Taking sides, he believed, could prevent America from serving as mediator once peace again seemed possible.

The following January, some of America's most socially prominent progressives formed the Woman's Peace Party to bolster Wilson's commitment to neutrality. They named Jane Addams as president. A social work pioneer, suffragette, and cofounder of America's first settlement house, Addams was unrelenting in her devotion to the cause. "I do not assert that women are better than men . . . but we would all admit . . . women are more sensitive than men" in terms of "treasuring" life, she told her fellow party members. She felt the commitment of American women of peace might embolden women "in the very countries which are now at war."

A cadre of prominent women coalesced around Addams's crusade. Gertrude Minturn Pinchot, wife of a politically connected lawyer, became chair of the New York State branch of the Woman's Peace Party. Pinchot presided over the second of two standing-room-only organizing meetings for the local chapter convened in the Blue Room of the McApin Hotel. The announced purpose of the party was "to enlist all American women in arousing the nations to respect the sacredness of human life and to abolish war."

Of the women who answered the call, none was more committed than Crystal Eastman Benedict, a dark-haired feminist who had earned a bachelor's degree from Vassar, a master's in sociology from Columbia, and a law degree from New York University. Her brother, Max Eastman, described her as "not the kind of girl around whom men gather like flies around a honey pot, but she had a joy in life and a genius for friendship." Her British second husband-to-be described her as "a very striking, attractive person . . . very American—in the New York sense of the word—no respecter of person—no sentimentality—no European refinement." Eastman Benedict, named to the executive committee, became the chapter's *de facto* day-to-day leader and its most effective strategist.

Many equally prominent women emphatically disapproved of the peace crusaders. Elizabeth Lowell Putnam, a conservative activist, anti-suffragist, poet, and philanthropist, slammed Addams's organization, in a *Boston Herald* commentary, as "one of the most dangerous movements which has threatened our emotional people for a long time." She attacked Addams's flock as "several emotional women whose hearts are so large that many people have mistaken them for heads." Many of the "most prominent," she wrote, were "childless," yet they "were lined up together and photographed as 'mothers of men,' and no one saw the absurdity of it all."

Former president Theodore Roosevelt was equally dismissive. In a letter in the *Chicago Herald*, he called the group's platform "both silly and base" and compared the organizers to nineteenth-century Copperheads: "to a man they voted against Abraham Lincoln. They did all they could to break up the Union and to secure the triumph of slavery because they put peace as the highest of all gods."

The next month brought a disaster that threatened peacemaking efforts across the board. On May 7, a German submarine torpedoed a luxury British ocean liner, the *Lusitania*, off the coast of Ireland. The ship quickly vanished beneath the waves, carrying 1,198 people, including 128 Americans, to their deaths. Germany claimed (justifiably) that the ship carried weaponry, but American and British citizens were outraged.

Wilson responded with a series of requests that Germany commit to safeguarding American "lives and ships," which critics found woefully inadequate. They also disapproved of Wilson's speech to newly naturalized citizens three days after the *Lusitania* sunk. In that speech, at Philadelphia's Convention Hall, Wilson recommitted himself to neutrality and nonaggression. "The example of America must be the example not merely of peace because it will not fight, but of peace because peace is the healing and elevating influence of the world," he declared. "There is such a thing as a nation being so right that it does not need to convince others by force that it is right."

Roosevelt, who had run against Wilson in 1912 as a third party (Bull Moose) candidate, told reporters that to act on Wilson's ideas would be to relinquish "the position won for it by the men who fought under Washington and by the men who, in the days of Abraham Lincoln, wore the blue under Grant and the gray under Lee." Americans "will do well to remember there are things worse than war," concluded Roosevelt.

Germany eventually assured Wilson that its submarine commanders would try to give fair warning to passenger ships. Still, pressure on Wilson to abandon neutrality increased.

The National Security League, a nonpartisan group of leading Americans organized by Wall Street lawyer Solomon Stanwood Menken, held a two-day conference on peace and preparedness at the Hotel Astor in June 1915. Attendees were treated to a show of armaments, including a twenty-one-foot torpedo. The first evening concluded with a rally at Carnegie Hall, where Henry L. Stimson, a former war secretary, argued that the Germans would be more responsive to Wilson "if it were known that our navy was in readiness and . . . our free people . . . disciplined and trained in arms." Jacob M. Dickinson, also a former war secretary, ridiculed pacifists: "It would be but little consolation to us if proceeding on such a theory and suffering disaster, we could commend ourselves for being guided by humanitarian views in advance of our time," he said.

Crystal Eastman Benedict attended the rally with other members of the Woman's Peace Party and sent up a note asking whether the Security League was "getting any money from the ammunition makers." Her questions "went unanswered," reported the *New York Times*.

The following evening, Eastman Benedict and the Woman's Peace Party held its own meeting in Cooper Union—long a sanctuary for radical thought—and critiqued the National Security League event. "It was one of those very large meetings full of empty seats," said Eastman Benedict. "As I understand their line or reasoning, it is this: All Europe is at war: we may be involved; the only way to be safe is to get ready; the only way to get ready is to be stronger than anyone else, or stronger than all the rest put together, if possible.

"Now that seems to my poor feminine intellect like high school boy logic, fist logic. All those men were grown men, however. Some of them were old men. . . . Their slogan, Peace by Preparedness, sounds sensible at first glance. You have to think a little before you realize they want to talk peace and get ready to fight."

Eastman noted that, during the event, she had sent up a question asking whether the organizers thought Europe represented "peace by preparedness." While they waited for an answer, "the chairman, who saw people leaving by tens and twenties, advanced and said, 'Ladies and gentlemen, I can promise you, if you will wait, [you will get] a treat after the present speaker gets through.' We thought that might mean the answering of our question, so we waited. But we soon gave up. As we started to go a hopeful woman said to us, 'Aren't you going to wait for the ice cream?' That was her idea of the treat."

Meyer London, the sole Socialist in Congress at the time, took a more somber tone: "How are we to prevent the mass of people being swept off its feet?" he asked. "If half a dozen of the great Metropolitan dailies come out for a few days with headlines urging that national honor demands that we fight somebody for something, we will fight."

Few of his colleagues were ready to concede the battle. Many looked to Addams to lead the way. Addams, who had recently served as president of the Conference of Women at The Hague, appeared at Carnegie Hall on the evening of Friday, July 9. In the five weeks after the conference, Addams and a small delegation had visited government officials and ordinary people in several countries. Her talks had convinced her that neutral parties held the key to peace: "They said in all of the foreign offices that . . . if neutral people may be gotten together, people who will command the respect of the foreign offices . . . if they finally find something upon which negotiations might commence," all warring nations would gladly "receive such service."

In a *New York Times* interview, Addams said she thought "the European peoples, as a whole, are ready and anxious for peace. This is not true of the belligerent Governments." She suggested a "conference of neutrals" guided by America, which she called "our really great opportunity and our undeniable duty."

Lillian D. Wald was among the many activists who attended Addams's Carnegie Hall talk. A trained nurse born to wealthy German-Jewish parents in Cincinnati, Wald had founded the Henry Street Settlement House in 1893 and devoted her life to the poor on New York's Lower East Side. Her settlement house, one of the oldest and most respected in the nation, steadily grew into a full-service social reform operation, serving people of all races and ages.

A stalwart peace activist, Wald had been among the leaders of a women's anti-war march down Fifth Avenue in August 1914. (The *Evening World* reported that all women who participated "wore some badge of mourning, either a band of black around her sleeve or a bit of crepe fluttering at her breast, as a token of the black death . . . hovering over the European battlefields.") Also present was Paul Kellogg, editor of *The Survey*, the leading social work journal of the day.

After hearing Addam's hopeful message, Kellogg and Addams convened a small group at Henry Street Settlement. They saw the roundtable "as a means by which in humbleness and quiet some of us who deal with the social fabric may come together to clarify our minds," recalled Wald in her memoir. After a day of deliberation, they formed an informal committee, chaired by Wald, to figure out a plan.

As the pacifists pondered how to engage a larger public, a hawkish coalition promoting "preparedness" preempted much of public discourse. That August, Rear Admiral Robert E. Peary gave a rousing speech to a multistate gathering of Rotarians in Portland, Maine. "[We] need aeroplanes—the modern eyes of war—submarines, and battle cruisers of the largest, swiftest and heaviest armed type. . . . There is no defense so effective as a vigorous offensive," he declared.

That October, the Conference Committee on National Preparedness urged ministers to make preparedness the subject of their Thanksgiving sermons. Meanwhile, the National Security League released a survey that found members of both houses of Congress in favor of preparedness.

The same month, Jane Addams and other officers of the Woman's Peace Party wrote a letter beseeching Wilson to hold fast to his anti-interventionist views. "We believe in real defense against real dangers, but not in a preposterous 'preparedness' against hypothetic dangers."

Wilson did not respond directly. But on November 4, he laid out his evolving position in a speech marking the Manhattan Club's fiftieth anniversary. "We do want to feel that there is a great body of citizens who have received at least the most rudimentary and necessary forms of military training; that they will be ready to form themselves into a fighting force at the call of the nation," said Wilson.

The *New York Times* observed: "While the diners gave plenty of evidence that they were with the President on the topic of preparedness the greatest applause came when he denounced hyphenated-Americanism and said it was high time that the small groups who held the interests of other countries first were called to a reckoning."

The speech—and its apparent embrace of a more hawkish policy—alarmed Eastman Benedict and her Woman's Peace Party colleagues. Several days later, at a party forum, she urged attendees to "do something besides talk peace. Now we must present a program."

"It is a dangerous time for us, and every morning we face a new crisis," added Eastman Benedict. "A fire as big as that with only the ocean between us is bound to scorch us. It is only by keeping cool, by playing the hose on our roofs all the time, and stowing all inflammables and combustibles out of sight that we can keep from catching fire."

Although Wilson continued to embrace the concept of neutrality in his annual address that December, he also endorsed the War Department plan for a troop increase and the training of a "citizen force" of 400,000.

"If our citizens are ever to fight effectively upon a sudden summons, they must know how modern fighting is done," he argued. He also addressed the danger within: "There are citizens of the United States . . . born under other flags . . . who have poured the poison of disloyalty into the very arteries of our national life." He appealed to Congress to "enact such laws" as could contain that threat: "Such creatures of passion, disloyalty, and anarchy must be crushed out."

Alarmed by the ever-more bellicose rhetoric, Crystal Eastman Benedict, Lillian Wald, Paul Kellogg, and their associates came together at year's end to form a new organization. Christening itself the American Union Against Militarism (AUAM), it was also known as the Anti-Preparedness Committee and the Anti-Militarism Committee. Its founding roster included Unitarian minister John Haynes Holmes; Rabbi Stephen S. Wise, an outspoken Zionist and civil rights leader; Florence Kelley, a child labor reformer and general secretary of the National Consumers' League; George Kirchwey, a former dean of Columbia Law School and co-founder of the New York Peace Society; L. Hollingsworth Wood, a Quaker attorney and peace activist; and Allan Benson, a leading Socialist and journalist. Wald was named chair.

Three days before Christmas in 1915, the *New York Times* announced the existence of the Anti-Militarism Committee and its "nationwide fight against the huge war budget and the "cult of preparedness." Crystal Eastman Benedict was named secretary "in charge of the organization work."

The *Times* explained that the committee aspired to "raise a budget which will permit it to put speakers into the field to meet the propaganda" of the preparedness organizations. The group "asserts specifically that Henry Ford is not financing it," added the paper.

The automobile mogul's anti-war activism, including his launching of a roundly ridiculed "Peace Ship" on a mission of peace to Europe, had made him a controversial and polarizing figure. Two days after Christmas, the *Chicago Daily Tribune* reported, "Only a miracle now can save the expedition from total disintegration," noting that one of Ford's top managers had "hinted that Mr. Ford would not return unless he could persuade representative Americans like William Jennings Bryan and Jane Addams to accompany him."

The newly minted organization immediately went on the offensive. At an Anti-Preparedness Committee rally shortly after the New Year, Oswald Garrison Villard, editor of the *New York Evening Post*, excoriated Wilson for his turn toward militarism. Wilson, he said, had proposed "the greatest naval program ever planned in a single year since Christendom began, with one possible exception, but also asks for military forces of such size that, by 1918, we should have actually in service, afloat and ashore, 740,000 men, exclusive of citizens and students in camps. This is 100,000 more than the entire German Regular Army at the outbreak of the war." Villard suggested the president was engaged in a blatant re-election ploy.

Days later, the committee released a statement attacking compulsory enlistment, calling it "the oldest Instrument of tyranny. It would place our entire democracy in the hands of a military caste."

Meanwhile, Wilson and other preparedness proponents drummed up support. That February, in a speech at the St. Louis Coliseum, Wilson argued, "the peace of the world . . . depends upon the aroused passion of other nations and not upon the motives of the United States. It is for that reason that I have come to call you to a consciousness of the necessity for preparing this country for anything that may happen." The United States, he concluded, was resolved "to do whatever it is adequate and necessary to do in order that no man might question the honor or invade the integrity or disregard the rights of the United States of America."

With a Carnegie Hall rally in April, Lillian Wald and her fellow AUAM activists took the battle to the masses. Before a crowd of four thousand, Wald spoke emotionally of the "uneasiness, nay the sorrow and unhappiness, of men and women who see in the military propagandas of the day a great peril" to America. Because of the military preparedness campaign, she said, "fear has dethroned reason."

James H. Maurer, head of the Pennsylvania State Federation of Labor, said he would not fight in the war "because I have nothing to fight for." Laborers, he added, would not "fight for the military capitalists." Other equally fiery speakers left the audience roaring. "It is doubtful if a more demonstrative audience ever jammed Carnegie Hall," reported the *Times*.

That rally kicked off a campaign that took members of the anti-preparedness movement to Buffalo, Cleveland, Detroit, Chicago, Minneapolis, Des Moines, Kansas City, St. Louis, and Cincinnati, as they essentially shadowed Wilson's nationwide preparedness tour.

At the end of April, Lillian Wald formally requested a meeting with President Wilson on behalf of the anti-preparedness group. In a statement explaining the rationale, Charles T. Hallinan wrote, "We believe that Mr. Wilson has been misled by the apparent unanimity of the press on the subject of so-called preparedness, and that some of the things which we learned on our trip may be of value to him."

That meeting took place on Monday, May 8, exactly a year and day after the sinking of the *Lusitania*. Americans were still talking about the incident, in part because new provocations kept occurring. On March 24, a German sub torpedoed the *Sussex*, a French steamer. Although the *Sussex* did not sink, more than fifty were killed. The day of the meeting, three German torpedoes (fired by the same sub that had downed the *Lusitania*) hit the SS *Cymric*, a British cargo ship.

Before Wald's group showed up at the White House, Germany sent Wilson word that the government would "do its utmost to confine the operations of war . . . to the fighting forces of the belligerents"—temporarily defusing tensions with Germany.

The delegation to see Wilson was led by Lillian Wald and Crystal Eastman (who had dropped Benedict from her name following her divorce). They told Wilson that support of the preparedness movement was tantamount to supporting militarism. He strongly disagreed, declaring himself "as much opposed to militarism as any man living."

The president's tone was just short of patronizing as he explained to the group of peaceniks how reality looked from his point of view. "When things are at sixes and sevens in a neighboring country, as in Mexico, and everybody apparently a law unto himself, there are not men enough to safeguard that border," he said. There was a big difference, argued Wilson, "between reasonable preparation and militarism."

"[This] is a year of madness. It is a year of excitement, more profound than the world has ever known before. . . . No standard we have ever had obtains any longer," said Wilson. "In the circumstance it is America's duty to . . . know the facts of the world and to act on those facts with restraint. . . .

All that I am maintaining is this: that we must take such steps as are necessary for our own safety. . . . In the last analysis the peace of a society is obtained by force."

New York City's preparedness parade was on Saturday, May 13, a cool day made for fluttering flags. The parade featured roughly eight thousand National Guardsmen, two hundred bands, fifty drum and bugle corps, and an American flag, said to be the largest in the country, strung between the St. Regis and Gotham hotels. By the *New York Times*' count, some 136,683 people marched, making it the "the greatest civilian marching demonstration in the history of the world." The procession took eleven hours. The last group passed the reviewing stand at 9:40 in the evening, trailed by a field gun on wheels, which was fired at the end.

Chicago's parade was just as grand. It took place on Saturday, June 3, and was also blessed with a beautiful day, as temperatures hovered in the 60s and 70s. The *Chicago Sunday Tribune* counted 130,214 marchers—including 107,475 civilian men, 4,194 soldiers, and 18,545 women—who passed before the reviewing stand at the Art Institute, a majestic building on Michigan Avenue guarded by two bronze lions.

The parade went past 7 p.m. After the first phase ended, Battalion C of the Illinois National Guard, which had pitched tents in Grant Park the previous night, showed their stuff. The men rose, saddled their horses, and stood rigidly at attention, waiting for a bugle call. "A moment later," reported the *Chicago Sunday Tribune*, "the troops fled across the high ground, their forms sharply outlined against the sky by the setting sun," and were followed by a marching band, soldiers, and cadets in war gear.

The *Tribune* proclaimed the event the "greatest parade in Chicago's history" and the "largest in the history of America." Army Major General T.H. Barry wrote a bylined piece in which he gushed, "This is the greatest burst of patriotism since the civil war—shows us a united country against any foe whatsoever."

The only sign of dissent—reported by the *Tribune* under a headline titled "Treason?"—was a banner on an apartment building: "There are 100,000 of you. You are not the Only Patriots. Two million farmers, half a million mine workers, and organized labor throughout AMERICA are AGAINST what you are marching for. Are you SURE you're right?"

A police captain ordered two patrolmen to tear the streamer down. They obeyed and booked two men on disorderly conduct charges. It turned out that one of the men, Captain Horace Wild, was a former member of the Aerial Reserve Corps of the U.S. Army. He explained that the banner had been sent to him from New York by the National Woman's Peace Party. The author, not coincidentally, of that poster art was Walter Fuller, a British national, editor, and art enthusiast who had come to America to manage his folk singer sisters. Crystal Eastman had asked him to work on Woman's Peace Party and AUAM projects.

Others also marched that day, thousands of them, in Hartford, Connecticut; Lima, Ohio; Nashville, Tennessee; Springfield, Illinois; New Orleans, Louisiana; Providence, Rhode Island: St. Louis, Missouri; Salt Lake City, Utah; and elsewhere as people across America turned out to show support for patriotism and preparedness.

Wilson proclaimed June 14 to be Flag Day—coinciding with the beginning of the Democratic Convention, which was in the process of nominating Wilson for re-election. As the Democratic delegates assembled in St. Louis, Wilson was in Washington, DC, leading a preparedness parade of some sixty thousand people down Pennsylvania Avenue.

He delivered a speech at the base of the Washington Monument on what had become a familiar subject: the disloyalty of certain foreign-born residents. "There is disloyalty active in the United States, and it must be absolutely crushed. It proceeds from a minority, a very small minority, but a very active and subtle minority." Americans, he pledged, "will teach these gentlemen once [and] for all that loyalty to this flag is the first test of tolerance in the United States."

The *Times* reported Wilson's comments were instigated by "editorials in some foreign language newspapers . . . supporting the Republican nominee." After learning that supposed fact, Wilson demanded that the "Americanism" plank in the party platform be "direct and unequivocal." The platform reflected his wishes, denouncing anyone who, under the influence of a foreign power, endeavored to "injure this government . . . or cripple or destroy its industries at home."

Delegates accepted Wilson's Americanism plank by acclamation. Indeed, they were consistently rapturous in their approval, responding at one point to the mere mention of his name with a floor demonstration that went on for nearly an hour. But Democratic leaders were uncertain, as was the president himself, of how to simultaneously project a resolve to fight along with a fervor for peace—of how to embrace the campaign slogan, "he kept us out of war," while rejecting the notion he was for peace at any price.

During his nominating speech for Wilson, New Jersey Attorney General John Wesley Wescott appealed for intervention in Mexico. "Help Mexico or over the graves of the dead will be sown the dragon's teeth of our own destruction," he said. But William Jennings Bryan (who had resigned as secretary of state because he felt Wilson was too confrontational with Germany after the sinking of the *Lusitania*) took a different tack. "I join the people in thanking God that we have a President who does not want the nation to fight. . . . For, my friends, annexation is the next step after intervention has been undertaken. And if we invaded Mexico, these same men would say, 'On to Panama!'"

But, in a sense, the United States had already invaded Mexico. Angered by America's recognition of the government of Mexican leader Venustiano Carranza, Francisco "Pancho" Villa had responded by attacking Americans. In January 1916, Villa's men had executed eighteen Americans traveling through Mexico by train. On March 9, Villa led an assault by 1,500 soldiers on Columbus, New Mexico, killing nineteen people, including several soldiers. Troops from the Thirteenth Calvary, stationed in Columbus, followed him into Mexico, where they killed several of Villa's men and lost one of their own.

Several days after Villa's raid, the United States dispatched Brigadier General John J. Pershing on a punitive expedition into Mexico. After several weeks of futile pursuit, Pershing remained resolute. "I don't care how Villa dies. As long as we get him, I'm satisfied," he declared.

As America fretted over the situation to the south, Eastman saw an opportunity for the AUAM to assert itself. She threw herself into the mission of keeping America out of war with Mexico.

AUAM convened a commission of Mexican and American citizens to negotiate peace. It also raised money to publicize the cause. And it worked to defuse anger over an incident involving American soldiers in Carrizal, Mexico, that June.

The battle between an African American regiment in pursuit of Villa and the Mexican Army had resulted in multiple casualties on both sides.

The U.S. Army blamed the Mexicans for the debacle. In the army's version of the story, the Americans were lured into a trap by a promise of a meeting with the head of the Mexican garrison and were ambushed by machine-gun fire. Many Americans, including General Pershing, were demanding that the United States retaliate. The AUAM received a telegram from the governor of Chihuahua giving a very different story. In that version, as the *New York Tribune* put it, "the Americans refused to wait . . . until a wire could be sent to Juarez asking permission [for them] to enter the village." Instead, they advanced on the town.

AUAM seized on a statement from an American captain at the scene—written as he lay wounded, expecting to die—that backed up the Mexicans' account.

Captain Lewis Morey's letter, as published in the *Atlanta Constitution*, described a confusing scene: "I came under Captain Boyd's command and marched my troop in rear for Carrizal at 4:15 a. m. Reached open field to southeast of town at 6:30 a. m.

"Captain Boyd sent in a note requesting permission to pass through the town. This was refused."

Instead, the Mexican general invited Boyd to bring his troops in town and chat. Fearing an ambush, Boyd prepared to attack. "We formed C troop on the left in line of skirmishers, one platoon of K troop on right of line and another K troop platoon on extreme right and a little to the rear," wrote Morey.

When the Americans were about three hundred yards out, the Mexicans opened fire, which the Americans returned. In the ensuing battle, "I was slightly wounded. Captain Boyd, a man told me, was killed. Nothing was seen of Lieutenant Adair after the fight started. . . . I am hiding in a hole 2000 yards from field and have one wounded man and three men with me," wrote Morey.

For the AUAM, Morey's letter was a godsend. "This clearly was a situation very different from the 'ambush' and 'unprovoked attack' of the front pages, and a declaration of war could hardly be based on the occurrence if the public knew the facts," recalled Lillian Wald in *Windows on Henry Street*.[2]

The committee "gathered together hurriedly, met until midnight, and the next morning paid for [full-page] advertisements of Captain Morey's report of the incident," recalled Wald.

"The press was generous in terms, and several papers on the Border, where the heat was dangerous, copied these four-column advertisements without charge," wrote Wald in her memoir.

Although it was originally assumed that Morey had died, he survived; and he had a poignant story to tell. The *Baltimore Sun*, relying on Morey's account, reported on the heroic "negro troopers" who "faced almost certain death at Carrizal with smiles on their lips" and songs in their throats as they "fought their grim fight against odds."

"For 45 minutes the men fought, joking among themselves all the while, even though they realized we had been trapped and had little chance of getting out alive," said Morey.

After helping to defuse the incident, the AUAM convened an unofficial border conference between Mexican and American representatives.

Historian Roland Marchand attributes the AUAM's activism with sparking a flood of telegrams to the White House that may well have pulled Wilson back from war. Shortly thereafter, an official Mexican-American Commission was named, which, in effect, took over the work of the AUAM.

G. Peter Winnington, the biographer of Walter Fuller, Crystal Eastman's second husband, sums up Eastman's contribution with, "By organizing private mediation and a publicity campaign in Mexico (funded largely by the AUAM), she was personally responsible for averting a war. It was a major triumph for the AUAM, and certainly her greatest."[3]

Whether the AUAM's activities were really that pivotal is impossible to say, but the events constituted a major victory for Eastman and her colleagues and established the AUAM as a political force. Eastman was determined to keep the momentum going.

In a memorandum to the AUAM that October, she laid out a pacifistic call to arms of breathtaking audaciousness. She urged her colleagues to make the most of the Mexican campaign: "We must make it known to everybody that the *people* acting directly—not through governments or diplomats or armies—stopped that war, and can stop all wars if enough of them will act together and act quickly."

She suggested that the AUAM "get in touch with organizations like ours in other countries—especially those countries expected to be our enemies" and organize what she called "peace forces." At the sign of an encroaching conflict, peace force members would shower enemy governments with messages of "good-will to stave off war . . . Imagine it! a thousand cables from 'enemy' to 'enemy' stating the firm friendliness of the people and their determination not to fight. . . . There never could be a war if our peace forces could mobilize like that in 48 hours."

Eastman's dreams of pacifistic glory crashed into harsh realities that steadily, inexorably moved America toward war.

Meanwhile, Eastman's marital status got an update. In November 1916, the *New York Times* reported, "friends of Crystal Eastman and Walter Fuller learned only yesterday that they were married some time ago, although they were reluctant to disclose the date and the place the ceremony was performed. The bride obtained a divorce last winter from Wallace J. Benedict, an insurance man, whom she married in 1911. . . . Mr. Fuller is a manager of concert artists." The couple had been married by Crystal's father, a Congregationalist minister, in September.

In January 1917, Germany suddenly withdrew its pledge to give fair warning to noncombatant ships. At the end of January, the German ambassador, Count Johann von Bernstorff, personally presented U.S. Secretary of State Robert Lansing with a note explaining that English forces were attempting to push "Germany into submission by starvation," forcing the German government to fight "with the full employment of all the weapons which are at its disposal." Therefore, beginning the next day, "sea traffic will be stopped with every available weapon and without further notice in [various] blockade zones around Great Britain, France, Italy, and in the Eastern Mediterranean." In short, Americans ships might be sunk by German subs.

When Wilson's private secretary, Joseph Patrick "Joe" Tumulty, hit him with the news, the president responded with disbelief. He spent the evening alone in his study and issued no immediate public statement.

Determined to steer the president away from war, Wald, Eastman, and other peace activists placed newspaper ads, identifying themselves as a "Committee of American Citizens," arguing that America "should refuse to allow herself to be dragooned into the war at the very end by acts of desperation committed by any of the belligerents."

William Jennings Bryan also appealed for peace. "If we go in, we step down from that high position as the world's greatest neutral and turn over to some other nation the greatest opportunity since the beginning of time," Bryan told a hastily convened crowd of five thousand people at Madison Square Garden on the evening of February 2.

The next afternoon, before a joint session of Congress, Wilson claimed the middle ground. He immediately broke off diplomatic relations with Germany but made no explicit move toward war. "I refuse to believe that it is the intention of the German authorities to do . . . what they have warned us they will feel at liberty to do. I cannot bring myself to believe that they will indeed . . . destroy American ships and take the lives of American citizens in the willful prosecution of the ruthless naval program they have announced their intention to adopt," said Wilson.

He also warned that "if this inveterate confidence on my part in the sobriety and prudent foresight of their purpose should unhappily prove unfounded," he would ask Congress for authority "to use any means that may be necessary for the protection of our seamen and our people in the prosecution of their peaceful and legitimate errands on the high seas."

Advocates across the ideological spectrum jockeyed for the president's ear. The quickly created Emergency Peace Federation organized a peace rally in Washington, DC, on Abraham Lincoln's birthday. The AUAM announced it was conducting a nationwide referendum (via postcards) of 100,000 Americans on two questions: whether the United States "should enter this war zone to uphold our legal right to go into the war zone regardless of these conditions," and whether people "should be consulted by referendum before Congress declares war—except in case of threatened invasion."

On February 18, 1917, the *Times* published a letter from Anna Ruth Weeks, a self-declared "feminist, suffragist, and socialist" and writer on economics, taking issue with Eastman's call for a referendum. "I am not asking my Congressman to tie the hands of this Government during the long time required for a national referendum. The hour of action has already struck. . . . If human life is to continue at all on this planet, Prussianism must be put down," wrote Weeks.

Even adolescent girls were asked to play their part by shunning pacifistic men. On February 24, the *New York Times* reported on the visit of Elizabeth Wood, national secretary of a war relief organization called the National Special Aid Society, to the posh, private Tewksbury School for

Girls in Scarsdale, New York. Mrs. Woods warned the young women about the threat pacifistic men represented to a happy home. "Always throughout life remember that the man who will not defend his country will not defend his wife, his child, his home," said Mrs. Wood. "Do not marry such a man. Do not have such among your friends. . . . No man who is not a patriot is to be trusted with a woman's welfare."

Meanwhile, the American Rights League fervently fanned the flames with newspaper ads asserting, "IT IS NO LONGER A QUESTION AS TO WHETHER THERE SHALL BE WAR WITH GERMANY. THERE IS WAR WITH GERMANY. The only question is whether our Government shall submit at Germany's dictation to the outrages of her submarine warfare, or whether it shall forcibly defend American sovereignty."

As Wilson struggled to find a path to peace, he was hit by a second shock. On February 26, a telegram decoded by British intelligence landed on his desk. The telegram, sent January 11 from German Foreign Secretary Arthur Zimmermann to the German ambassador to Mexico, proposed an alliance between Mexico and Germany and promised Mexico the return of lands lost during the Mexican-American war.

Wilson released the text on February 28, generating headlines across the nation detailing the "German plot" and urging America toward war.

On February 28, President Wilson met with two separate delegations of pacifists—including William Jennings Bryan, Jane Addams, Paul Kellogg, and Crystal's brother, Max Eastman, founder and editor of *The Masses*, a Socialist political and literary magazine. Participants promised not to reveal what was said, although afterward Bryan commented, "I am sure that . . . the President correctly interpreted the hope of the people. The people desire peace, but we have a war element in the country who are doing all in their power to manufacture war sentiment."

Addams subsequently recalled that Wilson "used one phrase . . . stuck firmly in my memory . . . to the effect that, as head of a nation participating in the war, the President of the United States would have a seat at the Peace Table, but that if he remained the representative of a neutral country he could at best only 'call through a crack in the door.'"

The comment infuriated her: "Was it a result of my bitter disappointment that I hotly and no doubt unfairly asked myself whether any man had the right to rate his moral leadership so high that he could consider the sacrifice of the lives of thousands of his young countrymen a necessity?"[4]

At the time of the peace delegation's visit to Washington, Crystal Eastman was pregnant with her first child, who would be born prematurely less than three weeks after the meeting.

That March 18, the peace movement's women garnered a profile in the *New York Tribune* titled "WITH THE PACIFISTS AT 70 FIFTH AVENUE: IMPRESSIONS IN TYPE AND PICTURE BY LOUISE BRYANT."

"Any group of persons who can arouse the editorial ire of all the leading newspapers about five times a week . . . ought to be deep-dyed enough in their villainy to be entertaining. I refer to the Pacifists," wrote Bryant, a progressive journalist married to fellow writer John Reed.

It was a sympathetic yet occasionally piercing portrait of high-society dames going radical chic (as Tom Wolfe would later call it): "Some are so lukewarm about their cause that they could truthfully be called 'mild militarists,' and some have the fervor of saints or of Irish revolutionists." The article was illustrated with drawings of attractive women in long tailored coats, striking sophisticated poses, sporting fashionable hats, and commenting on apparel: "What an adorable hat you are wearing." "Would you mind telling me where you got those shoes?"

Meanwhile Eastman, who was prominently mentioned in the text but conspicuously absent from Bryant's interviews, was weathering a difficult pregnancy. Her doctor was so concerned that he ordered her not to work until after the child was born. On March 16, suffering from convulsions, Eastman was rushed to the hospital. Three days later, she gave birth to her son.

On that day, March 19, 1917, front pages across America told of the sinking, without warning, of three American ships. The *Chicago Daily Tribune* reported, "Three American steamers, flying the American flag and manned mostly by Americans, have been destroyed by German submarines in the last twenty-four hours."

The *New York Times* editorialized, "By the repeated acts of Germany a state of war exists between that country and the United States. . . . It lacks only legal recognition to establish its existence."

As Eastman nursed her child, regained her health, and pondered the implications of the inevitable U.S. entry into war, the AUAM contemplated a major personnel change.

In February, Roger Nash Baldwin, an activist in St. Louis, had written the AUAM urging it to become more involved in protests against U.S. involvement in the war. Baldwin, who had served as the AUAM regional representative in St. Louis, had been sounded out in 1915 about running the AUAM, then in the process of formation. Doubting the organization's potential, Baldwin demurred, and the position went to Crystal Eastman Benedict.

A native of Wellesley, Massachusetts, Baldwin was the oldest of six children born to Frank Feno Baldwin, an affluent leather merchant, and Lucy Cushing Nash, his artsy, intellectual, suffragette wife. He had always known he would go to Harvard. A profile in the *American Mercury* notes that he was "handsome, gay and well-born; he could sing, play the piano, draw and paint in better than mediocre fashion, balance a tea cup gracefully; he was admired alike by beautiful girls and nice old ladies; and he was also able to mingle on comradely terms with all sorts and conditions of men. He belonged to the Hasty Pudding Club." He also had impeccable manners: "The best manners, probably, to be found anywhere in America; manners so simple and yet so classic as to be a fine art."

Baldwin had earned his baccalaureate in 1904 and a master's degree at Harvard in anthropology in 1905 before moving to St. Louis in 1906 to become a social worker and teach sociology at Washington University. He subsequently became chief probation officer of the St. Louis Juvenile Court and executive secretary of the St. Louis Civic League. He co-authored a book, *Juvenile Courts and Probation*, which explored, among other things, "the new idea" in juvenile justice. The new idea was that the state's mission was to save the child, not punish it.

By early 1917, Baldwin's doubts about AUAM's effectiveness had vanished. When he received a telegram from AUAM leaders inviting him to New York to assume many of Eastman's duties, he accepted, suggesting that he work only for expenses: "I had some old Puritan notion that I should not make money out of war service, so I settled for one hundred twenty-five dollars a month. I had no family obligations and could afford the luxury of a conscience."

Baldwin was told he would spend a lot of his time in the Washington office, which he would share with ex-newspaperman Charles Hallinan.

Although he was eager to enter the fray at a new, elevated level, it was difficult leaving St. Louis, "where I had first tested myself, where I had first learned the sociology I taught and where I had so many friends and associates," confided Baldwin to a biographer. "From a domestic reformer I became almost an instant internationalist, concerned with the fate of the universe."

On April 2, 1917, Wilson went before Congress expressing outrage and disbelief that the German government would "put aside all restraints of law or of humanity and use its submarines to sink every vessel" in waters it controlled.

That evening at Carnegie Hall, pacifists took a final stand against the war machine. Winter Russell, a New York lawyer speaking on behalf of the AUAM, brought a crowd of several thousand to cheers when he screamed, "We've got to start a revolution to prevent war. . . . Let's go to jail. . . . Make it necessary for Bethlehem Steel to cease making shrapnel to make bars to hold us. . . . Give me liberty to say that I will not kill my fellow man. Give me this liberty or give me death. If that be treason, then make the most of it."

Four days later, Wilson formally announced a "state of war between the United States and the Imperial German Government." Thus America, in the words of one headline writer, unsheathed "its sword in defense of humanity."

No genius was required to realize Wilson had had the last word, and that neither America—nor the groups that had doggedly fought to keep it out of war—would ever be remotely the same.

2

The War on Dangerous Speech

When the nation was young and its rights untested, America did not fully trust its Constitution; so, when war with France threatened in 1798, the fledging republic turned on immigrants and muzzled the press with the Alien and Sedition Acts. Thomas Jefferson, elected in 1800, gambled on free expression; but with World War I, the nation discovered that old tendencies die hard.

When Roger Baldwin arrived in New York at the age of thirty-three, he had no idea how much a declaration of war could darken a country's mood. "Apparently I was very naïve, but I couldn't believe it would instantly produce such savage attitudes," he recalled.

Days after Congress declared war, a scene erupted in a posh midtown hotel over the national anthem. Frederick Boyd, a British national, and his two female companions rejected diners' demands that they stand. Angered patrons surrounded the table and pummeled Boyd. Management turned him over to police, who charged him with disorderly conduct. Boyd told the night court magistrate that no law required him to stand during the playing of the anthem. The judge scolded Boyd for being insolent "in these tense times," found him guilty, and suspended the sentence.

Wartime tensions, Baldwin learned, brought out the ugly side of commerce. Employers, in his view, hid behind the pretext of patriotism to silence and subdue labor—often violently.

The closer American troops moved to foreign battlefields, the shorter America's patience with dissent became. Within months of America's

entry into the conflict, practically the entire nation was humming and dancing to "Over There," George Cohan's summons to young Americans to "get
your gun" and "go today" to war.

"Over There" was the biggest hit of the year and the number one song of
the war. It became "the manifestation of a perdurable American theme," a
tribute to "the euphoric confidence that the coming of the Yanks was the
march of the good guys to effect infamy's overthrow," wrote Cohan's
biographer John McCabe.

Prior to Wilson's declaration of war, the AUAM had focused primarily
on two things: keeping the United States out of war and beating back the
militaristic mindset. But with America preparing to put troops in the field,
the focus shifted to those young men likely to be called to serve.

Baldwin wondered whether the war might yet be fought with a volunteer force, sparing conscientious objectors the ordeal of being taken for enemies of the state. America, after all, had no real tradition of anything
remotely resembling universal service. During the Civil War, the Union
draft had been extremely porous. A draftee could have someone else serve
in his stead or pay a fee and avoid the obligation.

President Wilson personally favored a volunteer army. Historian John
Whiteclay Chambers believes that Wilson ultimately adopted the draft
because of pressure from Theodore Roosevelt.

Former President Roosevelt had split from the Republican Party in 1912
(which had renominated President William Howard Taft) to run as the
Progressive Party's candidate for president against Democrat Wilson. Wilson prevailed over the split Republican Party; but Roosevelt had never
embraced his leadership. Indeed, as the war proceeded, Roosevelt's attacks
on Wilson grew increasingly heated. He consistently slammed Wilson for
avoiding the European war, blamed him for the conflict with Mexico, and
suggested the president was a coward.

Rejecting the 1916 nomination of the Progressive Party for president,
Roosevelt instead endorsed Republican Charles E. Hughes, saying, "it
would be a grave detriment to the country to re-elect Mr. Wilson." Roosevelt, who believed in universal training and service, lambasted Wilson
for not properly preparing for war. In an October 1916 speech in Louisville, Roosevelt groused that "instead of speaking softly and carrying a big
stick, President Wilson spoke bombastically and carried a dish rag," adding,

"At the murder of 1,894 men, women and children on the Lusitania, his corpuscles did not shout; they did not even whisper. Apparently, all they did was to suggest to him that it was a happy occasion for a remark about being 'too proud to fight.'"

In an effort, no doubt, intended to get under Wilson's skin, the former president asked Wilson's administration in early 1917 for permission "to get ready a division for immediate use in the first expeditionary force sent over." Rather than deal with the embarrassment of Roosevelt riding to glory at the head of a division of volunteers, Wilson turned to the draft, argues Whiteclay: "The old Rough Rider paradoxically dragged down the entire United States Volunteer system with him."

Also, Wilson realized that only a draft would supply the numbers of soldiers he required while keeping people needed at home in place. In an April 19 letter to Democratic Congressman Guy Helvering, Wilson argued that a volunteer system does not mobilize all "productive and active forces of the nation" in the most efficient way: "When men choose themselves they sometimes choose without due regard to their other responsibilities." Farmers, miners, factory workers, he reasoned, might be better used at home.

Congressman Julius Kahn of California, a former Shakespearean actor, led the fight for the draft in the House. He invoked the name of Lydia Parker Bixby, who famously had lost five sons in the Civil War. "Why should she give five sons, and another, a nearby neighbor, perhaps give none? Why should any mother be called upon to give her all?" asked a visibly emotional Kahn, adding, "Under the selective draft such things will be impossible."

Senator William Calder, a New York Republican, took the Senate floor to declare that a volunteer army was "nonsense." Over a twenty-day period, he pointed out, the regular army had gained only 25,842 men. The army required nearly 184,000 to be at full authorized strength. The difference, he noted, could only be made up with a draft.

As popular sentiment against the draft collapsed, AUAM's focus shifted toward getting "a decent law for conscientious objectors" and keeping domestic restrictions on speech "reasonable," as Baldwin put it. In those tasks, he was aided not just by his considerable charm and fancy pedigree, but by a board that had easy access to the highest levels of government. "Our people had such high standing that they could go right in to see [President] Wilson," Baldwin recalled.

When "the negotiations began in April 1917 to try to get provision for conscientious objectors, Jane Addams came from Chicago and she and Lillian Wald and Emily Balch [an economist, sociologist, and future Nobel Peace Prize winner] went together to see Wilson," recalled Baldwin.[1]

Jane Addams also personally made the argument to Secretary of War Newton Baker. Meanwhile Baldwin, along with board member Norman Thomas, worked potential allies in Congress. The AUAM wanted conscientious objector provisions that went beyond members of well-recognized anti-war religious sects, and sympathetic legislators offered amendments exempting those with "conscientious scruples" against war. But no such amendments made it into the bill. Instead, the bill exempted ministers, ministry students, and those who belonged to "any well-recognized religious sect or organization" whose convictions forbade participation in war.

Congress also pondered the question of Negroes and the military. Congressman George Samuel Huddleston, an Alabama Democratic Congressman, assured his colleagues that Negroes were trustworthy. "These reports about the possibility of a Negro insurrection are almost traitorous. I have grown up with the Negros. . . . They are loyal, brave, and if called to the colors they will fight like men," vouched Huddleston. Asked by a colleague, why, if Negros were so estimable, he would not "give them the vote," Huddleston replied, "The gentleman doesn't understand the race question in the South."

The conscription bill, which cleared the Senate 65 to 8, authorized Wilson to raise regular army enlistment up to 287,000 men and to draft up to an additional 500,000, plus another 500,000 at his discretion. All males age twenty-one through thirty were required to register. Some legislators were concerned that the measure would not automatically expire at the end of the year. Many were critical of the "Roosevelt amendment," which authorized four divisions of volunteer infantry troops.

Senator William J. Stone argued that a "personal" and "political amendment" designed to accommodate one man—Roosevelt—didn't belong in the bill. Moreover, he questioned Roosevelt's "experience, training . . . temperament" and competence. During the Spanish-America War, Roosevelt led his Rough Riders "into a hole, and they would have been decimated and cut to pieces but for a Negro regiment," added Stone. Senator Hiram Johnson defended the amendment, saying of Roosevelt, "He wants to go out as he has done before to fight the battle of his country. When was this ever denied to any man?"

On May 17, 1917, Congress approved the draft bill, which authorized but did not compel approval for Roosevelt's regiment. The next evening, in signing the measure, Wilson made clear that Roosevelt would not be shipping out.

"I shall not avail myself . . . at the present stage of war, of the authorization conferred by the act to organize volunteer divisions," said Wilson, adding that such a force "would contribute practically nothing to the effective strength of the armies now engaged against Germany."

In a separate proclamation, Wilson defended the draft as "in no sense a conscription of the unwilling," but rather "selection from a nation which has volunteered in mass." AUAM chair Lillian Wald did not altogether disagree, though she saw the law's passage as more tragic than celebratory: "There was grieving in the homes of the neighborhood when the Selective Service Act went into effect, but by that time the young men had been stirred by war propaganda. They wanted to go," recalled Wald.[2]

With young men on notice that Uncle Sam soon would be coming for them, AUAM prepared to reinvent itself. "A Union Against Militarism becomes, during war time, inevitably a Union for the Defense of Civil Liberty," observed Eastman.

In May 1917, AUAM published a pamphlet titled, "Constitutional Rights in War-time." The publication, a full-throated defense of the right to free speech and assembly, observed, "Constitutional rights are being seriously invaded throughout the United States under pressure of war. Men are arrested and fined for criticizing the Government or the President. Halls are refused for meetings . . . pamphlets and literature opposing war are confiscated and the authors hauled into court."

Baldwin proposed that AUAM form a "Bureau for Conscientious Objectors." He imagined that the new bureau, working hand in hand with Secretary of War Newton Baker, would come up with mutually palatable options for conscientious objectors.

On May 30, 1917, the *New York Tribune* announced the opening of the bureau within the AUAM. Baldwin claimed the AUAM already had the names of fifteen thousand men intent on becoming conscientious objectors: "Our purpose is to give legal aid to them and also to urge the War Department to make provision for their exemption on grounds other than religion," he said.

Meanwhile, the crackdown against dissenters commenced. On May 18, 1917, a thirty-year-old pharmacy student affiliated with the Manhattan Anti-Conscription League was arrested on a "disorderly conduct" charge for speaking against the draft. The night court magistrate let him off with a suspended sentence but warned, "on Friday night you didn't know and I didn't know that the conscription bill had been signed; otherwise you would be guilty of treason. You must warn other members of the league that a repetition of such remarks will be considered treason. You have the right of speech, but not the right to attack the law."

The *New York Tribune* reported that the No-Conscription League was disseminating literature with "the direct object of discouraging registration." "Within a day or so," speculated the *Tribune*, authorities would start arresting "any agitator of this sort."

After spotting anti-conscription posters in a Milford, Massachusetts, neighborhood, police ordered a search of every person on the street. The unmistakable message was that passage of the draft law signaled a new day, that actions and words previously tolerated might now land one in jail.

Nonetheless, Baldwin continued to see War Secretary Baker and his men as potential allies. On June 15, 1917, Baldwin wrote Baker, "We are entirely at the service of the War Department in rendering any assistance that you think lies in our power to give." Less than a week later, Baldwin and (AUAM board member and *New York Evening Post* heir) Oswald Villard met with Joe Tumulty, President Wilson's private secretary, to promote a broader definition of conscientious objectors. Though Tumulty seemed uninformed on the subject, Baldwin reported that he was "entirely sympathetic" and had asked for briefing material to share with the president.

On the very day Baldwin and Villard met with his secretary, President Wilson signed the Espionage Act. The Justice Department called it "one of the most important pieces of legislation" enacted since the declaration of war and predicted numerous prosecutions "under its provisions."

The bill initially agreed upon by the House-Senate conference committee imposed serious censorship provisions on the press, making it a crime to publish various types of information deemed useful to the enemy. That provision was rejected by a 184 to 144 vote in the House after opponents concluded it would be unfair to assume newspapers were unpatriotic.

That same level of faith was not extended to ordinary citizens. Much in the new law was specific, comprehensible, and straightforward, dealing with such things as trafficking in information about sensitive documents, codebooks, and naval stations, or with the location of submarines or interfering with military forces. But the section covering speech was extremely vague, prohibiting "false statements with intent to interfere with the operation or success of the military . . . or to promote the success of its enemies" or willfully causing or attempting to cause "insubordination, disloyalty, mutiny, refusal of duty." The measure also targeted anyone who willfully obstructed "the recruiting or enlistment" of soldiers. Punishment included fines of up to $10,000 and imprisonment for twenty years.

The Civil Liberties Bureau considered the provision so troubling that it issued a second edition of "Constitutional Rights in War-time," which warned that "almost any activity in favor of peace or in criticism of the Government's war policies" might be seen as violations of law.

That July, a mob comprised of uniformed soldiers and bystanders violently attacked a peace parade organized in Boston by Socialists, labor unions, and others. The violence raged for an hour and a half before the police moved in. They arrested scores of protestors, but none of the attackers. Federal agents also arrested bystanders "alleged to have made unpatriotic remarks in the heat of the conflict."

As the *New York Times* reported the incident, "the ranks of the marchers were broken up by self-organized squads of uniformed soldiers and sailors. Red flags and banners bearing Socialistic mottoes were trampled on, and literature and furnishings in the Socialist headquarters in Park Square were thrown into the street and burned. . . . Blows were exchanged and flags were snatched from the hands of the marchers, while women in the line screamed in fright."

The assailants seized the marchers' American flag and forced the band to play the National Anthem. As speakers tried to address the crowd at the Boston Common, another near-riot broke out, at which point the police commissioner revoked the organizers' permit, forcing cancellation of the event.

The public mood also manifested itself in less violent ways. That July, Wald's settlement house planned to produce *Black 'Ell*, an anti-war play by Miles Malleson. City officials told her the play could not go on. Only after she personally appealed to the police commissioner was the production allowed to proceed.

With the nation in turmoil, Wald became increasingly ambivalent about the direction in which Baldwin and Eastman (who had returned from maternity leave in the summer of 1917) were taking AUAM. The embrace of civil liberties and of conscientious objectors would inevitably bring AUAM into conflict with administration policy—and with many of the wealthy donors who supported Wald's work.

There was also the matter of style. Baldwin and Eastman were stubborn, outspoken, and relatively young. Wald had just turned fifty, and Jane Addams, with whom she was often aligned, was close to sixty. Wald regarded the twosome with a combination of pride and consternation. She considered them "brilliant and courageous" but sometimes "extreme," and temperamentally opposed to non-radical measures that "failed to meet their eager urge for action."[3]

Baldwin and Eastman devoted much of the summer of 1917 to recruiting attorneys for the Civil Liberties Bureau. The term "civil liberties" was then uncommon in the United States. It most likely was adopted from the British National Council for Civil Liberties, an organization with which Eastman's British husband was closely affiliated. In his standard letter, Baldwin pledged the bureau would be "a clearing house for complaints of injustice" putting those whose rights were violated "in touch with good legal advice."

Scores of attorneys offered words of praise for the effort and agreed to participate or to allow themselves to be contacted by people looking for help. But Baldwin and Eastman also got some harsh responses, such as the one from attorney J.M. Broughton Jr. of Raleigh, North Carolina, who wrote, "I am in favor of preserving our civil liberties but I do not believe it is necessary to stab our country in the back in order to do this."

On July 3, 1917, the *New York Times* announced the birth of the National Civil Liberties Bureau (NCLB), describing its mission as "the defense of men who refuse to fight on the ground that they are 'conscientious objectors.'" The article quoted Crystal Eastman declaring, "It is high time that all honest liberals in this country, whether for or against war, realize that all that is real in American democracy is in danger today. Yesterday's outrage in Boston is the most extreme example of what we mean by the danger of militarism." The new bureau, she added, would not oppose the "competent prosecution" of the war: "We are not obstructionists or troublemakers."

A *New York Times* editorial published the next day, the Fourth of July, denounced the effort. "Jails Are Waiting for Them," read the headline. The *Times* agreed that freedom of speech was "a fine thing" but argued, "Inevitably there must be restriction on speech." That fact, said the *Times*, was "entirely ignored by the little group of malcontents who for present purposes have chosen to call themselves 'The National Civil Liberties Bureau.'"

"The freedom of speech wanted by these troublesome folk is that of talking sedition and of lending aid and comfort to our enemies," said the *Times*, which reassured readers by adding, "but they are an unimportant and minute minority—noisy out of all proportion to their numbers, and gaining attention just as crimes and accidents do, merely because they are abnormal and therefore 'news.'"

Eustace Seligman, a volunteer lawyer for the bureau, wrote the *Times* in response, "the function of this organization is to allay the fears of those who believe that our Government has temporarily suspended the right of free speech by opposing all cases of unauthorized interference with such rights. . . . Surely no fair-minded person can call such a purpose 'seditious.'"

A week after the bureau's official launch, Max Eastman, Crystal Eastman's brother, made news. He and others affiliated with *The Masses* magazine set out to test the new Espionage Act by suing Solicitor William Lamar for blocking distribution of their publication.

The post office had refused to mail the August 1917 issue because it appeared to violate Postal Solicitor William H. Lamar's order barring all publications that might be deemed "seditious." Several other "radical" publications also were prohibited. Business manager Merrill Rogers had met with authorities to seek direction on how to bring the magazine into compliance but received no clear guidance on what in the magazine was seditious. Arguing that the Espionage Act was hopelessly vague, rendering decisions made in its name arbitrary, *The Masses* convinced Judge Learned Hand to issue an injunction ordering the government to allow distribution.

Hand reasoned that since nothing in the magazine was "willfully false" or an incitement to insubordination or mutiny, it did not violate the act. An appellate court judge stayed Hand's injunction. Three months later, the appellate court reversed his decision.

In the interim, the government identified the specific offending items. Among them were an article called "Knit a Straitjacket for Your Soldier Boy," a poem, and several cartoons—including one of a skeleton taking the measurements of a drafted soldier, and another of a boy tied to the mouth of a cannon with figures representing labor and democracy chained to the gun carriage.

The government charged Max Eastman, Merrill Rogers, and several other staffers with seeking to "unlawfully and willfully . . . obstruct the recruiting and enlistment" of the army. Eastman and his alleged co-conspirators faced fines up to 10,000 dollars and twenty years of imprisonment.

But the government had already killed the magazine. In refusing to circulate the August edition, the post office destroyed the publication's circulation schedule, which allowed the government to rule that *The Masses* was not a regularly mailed magazine and therefore ineligible for second-class postage, rendering the enterprise financially unviable.

Meanwhile, Wald continued to struggle with her role in the AUAM and fretted over supporters withdrawing funding that "enabled the nurses to care for the families of the soldiers no less than the other sick." Horace Harding, chairman of the American Railway Express, was among the donors who abandoned her. He informed Wald that he was "concerned about your activities and association with the group described as 'Pacifists' or the 'American Union Against Militarism.'" And he regretted that she was associated "with such characters as Max Eastman, Crystal Eastman . . . and others of the same ilk." If Wald was "really in sympathy with such agitators as it appears to be the case from public print," wrote Harding, "I feel that I am so out of sympathy with your views and associates that I prefer to extend my financial aid to works that you are not connected with and will discontinue my contributions to the Henry Street Settlement."

By late August, Wald and Paul Kellogg had left the AUAM. As Wald put it in her memoir, she finally concluded "that my effort to hold together so divided an organization was no longer justified."[4] In an October 12 letter explaining her resignation to Baldwin, Wald wrote, "I did not resign at all because of my other responsibilities . . . it was because of the difficulties of administration of the American Union as it developed."

AUAM continued to draw hostile fire from the press. On August 27, it was the focus of "Enemies Within," a standing column in the *New York Tribune* that typically attacked radical publications, the Socialist party, foreign-language newspapers, and similar targets. The *Tribune* accused the AUAM of preaching "revolution."

Baldwin responded with a letter to the editor, observing, "your attack is entirely confined to the publication of extracts from magazines of various radical organizations with which you say the Civil Liberties Bureau is associated. . . . When men stand for freedom of speech they do not necessarily uphold everything that every speaker says."

That September, *Life* magazine also took disapproving notice of Baldwin and his work with a short piece titled "Nothing to be Proud of":

There is grave doubt whether, after the war is over, a membership in this society will be sought as eagerly as is membership in the Order of the Cincinnati, the Society of Colonial Dames, or the Sons and Daughters of the American Revolution—all of them societies made possible by men who fought to free this nation from the torturing talons of autocracy. In fact, it is highly probable that the descendants of the founders of the American Union Against Militarism will be bitterly ashamed of having known that any of their relatives belonged to that organization.

Even more controversial than the bureau's support of pacifism, free speech, conscientious objectors, and Socialist intellectuals was its support of the Industrial Workers of the World (IWW), which in certain high circles was seen as a violent group of wild-eyed anarchists.

The IWW, widely known as "Wobblies," had a controversial history long before America entered World War I. Founded in 1905, the IWW was a radical alternative to the American Federation of Labor. Unlike other unions of the time, it aggressively reached out to blacks and new immigrants. America's growing industrialization offered the IWW a potentially fertile field for recruits. That was especially true in such places as Colorado, Montana, and Arizona, where new industrial areas springing into existence attracted workers to the logging industry and the mines.

In an era when violence, on both sides, was not uncommon during labor disputes—when Pinkerton detectives and other outsiders were sometimes hired to spy on and break unions—the IWW did not shy away from the rhetoric of confrontation and strategic sabotage. Nor did it shy away from the language of socialism, which—particularly following the eruption of the Russian Revolution and consequent rise of Bolshevism in 1917—greatly agitated employers, political leaders, and the establishment press.

In June 1917, a sheriff's posse and vigilantes seized an estimated 1,200 striking IWW copper mine workers in Bisbee, Arizona, and illegally deported them to New Mexico. That August—in response to a call for a general strike of crop harvesters and construction workers—federal troops raided the IWW office in Spokane, Washington, and arrested local leaders for conspiracy. Numerous other conflicts broke out between the IWW and local or federal authorities, but no government action was as audacious or ambitious as the raids on IWW offices on September 5, 1917.

In a coordinated strike at 2 p.m. central time, Justice Department agents and local police stormed IWW offices across the country and scooped up any evidence they believed implicated the IWW in anti-war activities. They also raided the office of the Socialist Party in Chicago.

The *New York Times* reported the alarming story behind the raids, which "follows the revelation of a country-wide plot, the purpose of which included not only the destruction . . . of the wheat and corn crops of the West and the disorganization of the mining industry . . . but the commission of a multitude of crimes, all intended to hamper the successful prosecution of the war against Germany."

The *Times* reported that federal officials had "no doubt" that "German spies have figured in the working out of details of the conspiracy against the Government and people of the United States."

The Justice Department also blamed the IWW for strikes or labor problems in Minnesota, Montana, Idaho, and Arizona and implicated the organization in impeding the movement of timber "for the construction of airplanes." Reporters were told that among the items seized in Detroit was a bomb small enough to fit in a pocket yet capable of sinking a battleship.

On Friday, September 28, 1917, the Justice Department got federal indictments against 166 members of the IWW, including its top leaders. The indictments—for interfering with the war effort—were handed down in Chicago, where the IWW was headquartered.

A statement released by the U.S. District Attorney's office in Chicago gave its take on the IWW, which it said openly advocated "the most vicious forms of sabotage, particularly in industries engaged in furnishing war munitions." The government went on to slam the IWW for its "pronounced opposition to the support of the war in which this country is enlisted."

The government alleged that the IWW had blown up ammunition factories, tried to foment armed resistance, and torched forests and lumber mills (none of those claims would ever be proved). It also claimed (without proof) that German money was behind the IWW—and pointed out that many of those indicted claimed German ancestry.

Immediately after the indictments were announced, detectives piled into cars owned and driven by female socialites (from the Navy Relief Society) and headed to the IWW headquarters office on Madison Street in Chicago. There, they took thirty-five men into custody. Across America, other law enforcement officials were similarly occupied.

IWW leader William "Big Bill" Haywood was held on $25,000 bond. Bail for his lieutenants was set at $10,000. Not one was able to come up with the money, and all were eventually carted over to the county jail.

At the federal building, "Haywood, admittedly the great chief of the IWW, was quite the central figure," reported the *Chicago Daily Tribune*. "In charge of a deputy United States marshal, he was passed back and forth through the corridors of the federal building several times [as] he and his associates were put through severe questioning." Across the street from the federal building, a movie marquee reportedly advertised "The Menace of the IWW."

On October 28, 1917, precisely a month after the IWW indictments, a bizarre incident occurred that bewildered those involved with the NCLB. Herbert Bigelow, a well-known minister who had worked with the AUAM, was kidnapped and horsewhipped by nightriders in Kentucky.

That evening he had left Cincinnati and boarded a streetcar bound for Newport, Kentucky, where he was scheduled to address a Socialist meeting. As Bigelow approached the hall where he was to speak, several men handcuffed him and threw him into a car. They pulled a bag over his head and drove him to an isolated clearing where he was tied to a tree and surrounded by men in white masks and matching cloaks.

"[My] arms were released sufficiently to enable them to take off my overcoat coat, coat and vest and suspenders. Then a man with what appeared to be a black snake whip . . . stepped forward and took position to strike. He awaited the word of the leaders, who said 'In the name of the women and children of Belgium and France lay on,'" recalled Bigelow, in an account published by the NCLB.

"How many more times I was cut I am not sure, but not many, perhaps ten or twelve in all," said Bigelow, who was ordered to abandon his Cincinnati home within thirty-six hours and stay away for the duration of the war.

At a meeting at New York's Liberty Theater arranged by the NCLB, Bigelow scorned the notion that his attackers were misguided patriots. Instead, he insisted, "The assault was an act of revenge, perpetrated by the public utility interests of Cincinnati and the Kentucky cities across the river" to punish him for speaking against them.

An even wilder episode nearly two weeks later in Tulsa gave the NCLB reason to believe that Bigelow was right. A local judge had found nine men guilty of vagrancy and fined them $100 apiece; but he promised to suspend the sentence if, after a night in jail, they would all leave the city. Later that night, police abducted the men from their cells. At that point, things took a horrific turn.

As James S. Hirsch relates in *Riot and Remembrance*, shortly after the prisoners were taken, "a group of men wearing black cowls and black masks jumped from behind a pile of bricks with leveled rifles and revolvers and ordered the drivers to stop." The black-robed kidnappers tied the prisoners hands and feet and drove them "to a lonely ravine northwest of Tulsa, which was illuminated by a fire and the headlights of automobiles drawn in a circle. One by one the ropes were taken from the prisoners' wrists, which were then tied to a big tree."[5]

The captives were beaten with ropes until each was deemed to have had enough. At that point, each prisoner was coated in tar and smeared with feathers as a voice gravely intoned, "In the name of the women and children of Belgium!"

As one of the victims told it, "After they had satisfied themselves that our bodies were well abused, our clothing was thrown into a pile, gasoline poured on it, and a match applied. By the light of our earthly possessions, we were ordered to leave Tulsa, and leave running and never come back."

The NCLB argued that the attack, carried out with such brazenness, precision, and impunity, was more likely the work of anti-union employers than of overzealous patriots; and its report quoted from a *Tulsa World* editorial that had appeared prior to the attack as evidence the assault was planned by oil industry war profiteers: "The attempt of the I.W.W. or any other organization to decrease . . . the oil supply of the government should be sternly repressed. . . . If the I.W.W. or its twin brother, the Oil Workers Union, gets busy in your neighborhood, kindly take occasion to decrease the supply of hemp. A knowledge of how to tie a knot that will stick might come in handy in a few days."

To the NCLB, the episode represented "the lengths of violence to which business interests will go in their attempt to crush labor organization. No evidence has been produced to prove any violence on the part of the IWW on the Oklahoma oil field."

In the midst of dealing with the attacks, Baldwin sent out a statement to all AUAM members promising them that the NCLB—officially reborn as a separate organization, with Baldwin at its head, on October 1, 1917—would stay on mission: "The Bureau as an independent agency is maintaining exactly the same work in behalf of constitutional liberties and the conscientious objector as was made possible by the interest, co-operation and support of the Members of the Union during the past five months," he wrote. The NCLB, he also revealed, was processing some 125 cases a week where the rights of pacifists, conscientious objectors, and labor activists were being "violated at the hands of officials acting under war hysteria." He assured AUAM members that the bureau was in "constant" communications with the War Department, which was "showing a liberal and sympathetic attitude."

Baldwin's assessment of his relationship with the War Department secretary notwithstanding, President Wilson made it clear, in a November 12 speech to the American Federation of Labor, that his administration was not at all sympathetic. Wilson made plain his disdain for peaceniks: "My heart is with them, but my mind has a contempt for them. I want peace, but I know how to get it, and they do not." Wilson also implicitly attacked the IWW: "Nobody has a right to stop the processes of labor until all the methods of conciliation and settlement have been exhausted," he said.

Wilson's contempt was widely shared by the establishment media. On December 23, the *New York Times* ran a lengthy article—"Ebb of Pacifism in America"—celebrating the demise of the peace movement. "The plight of the idealist who, his eyes in the stars, is rudely brought back to earth by stumbling over a reality, is strikingly shown by the present condition of the pacifist party in this country," opined the writer George MacAdam. He added: "Some of the altruists are still in the party, but they are 'singing low,' to quote one of the most influential who, accordingly, insists upon the anonymity of this quotation. And such flabby activity of the peace movement as exists today is being stimulated by the Socialist, the anarchist, the alien propagandist, or 'the professional gasbag element.'"

A massive amount of Baldwin's time in late 1917 and early 1918 was devoted to the IWW, first in trying to get the administration to drop the prosecution, and then in arranging financial and other support for the defense. He exchanged countless letters with George Vanderveer, the IWW's lead attorney, advising him how to communicate with the administration, coordinating funds for bail and other legal costs, and acting generally as coach, confessor, and behind-the-scenes cheerleader.

Vanderveer, an Iowa native, Columbia Law School graduate, and former King County, Washington, chief prosecutor, wrote Baldwin a series of letters in early 1918 anguishing over difficulties with bondsmen, the firing of IWW supporters from jobs, and the arrests of people for simply carrying an IWW card. Nonetheless, Vanderveer expressed confidence that the government would either lose the case or dismiss it once it realized that it had no case.

In early 1918, Baldwin wrote to John Graham Brooks, an activist and author who was helping to raise money for the IWW defense, to tell him that he had "engaged a first rate newspaperman to go to Chicago" to organize publicity for the trial. Although the NCLB was guaranteeing the first two weeks of newsman Paul Hanna's salary and expenses, "it is undesirable for us to be publicly connected with him," wrote Baldwin, who possibly fretted that an open acknowledgment of the relationship might damage

Hanna's credibility. Baldwin was certainly concerned about the reputation of the NCLB. As he confided in a memo to biographer Peggy Lamson, "we held off full support of the defense until we saw what the trial evidence produced. But we were anyhow committed to a fair trial, which required defense funds and a nonpartisan appeal for support."

That April, Baldwin sent Hanna an NCLB publication on the IWW to help him get up to speed for the job. Hanna was charged with producing a daily report of the trial for circulation. Shortly thereafter, Hanna was replaced by another journalist, Charles Stern, who was soon drafted into the army. Baldwin replaced him with local newsman Samuel Kaplan, who was drafted as well. He replaced Kaplan with David Karsner, who worked for the *New York Call*, a Socialist newspaper, after Karsner offered his services for $25 a week. "My time is taken up all day in the courtroom. In addition to writing my story each night for *The Call*, so you see I would be cramped for time in which to do your work. However, I have the will to do it," Karsner told him.

Baldwin also endeavored to engage the larger legal community. He invited several lawyers to a meeting in Washington, DC, with famed attorney Clarence Darrow in January 1918 to explore how to disseminate the message that the IWW case was "probably the most important labor case in history."

Baldwin also corresponded with Elizabeth Gurley Flynn, the sole woman among those charged. Flynn's supposed crime was having written a diatribe called *Sabotage* before America entered the war, which the IWW had published without her knowledge. Nonetheless, prosecutors had concluded that she was part of the conspiracy to undermine the war effort.

Several months before the trial opened, Baldwin wrote President Wilson a letter requesting his intervention. He argued that prosecuting the IWW was not stopping "labor agitation" but "had exactly the contrary effect." Moreover, he pointed out, the prosecution—ostensibly brought because of interference with the conduct of the war—was really a tactic "directed against the essential operations of the IWW as a labor organization." The problem, concluded Baldwin, "is an administrative matter which should in our opinion be handled by the Department of Labor. It cannot be successfully solved by prosecution."

Wilson opted not to intervene. Indeed, in the time since Baldwin's arrival in New York, an important shift had occurred in the government's attitude toward Baldwin and his work. Though Baldwin continued to see Secretary of War Newton Baker as a potential friend, the administration was increasingly coming to view Baldwin as a troublesome firebrand.

In February 1918, Assistant War Secretary Frederick Paul Keppel had written Baldwin telling him their communications might have to stop. Baldwin's access was being curtailed, and he and his NCLB increasingly were seen as potential federal targets.

The IWW trial officially began April 1, 1918, but it took a month to impanel a jury. Opening arguments began on July 2 with 113 defendants in the dock. Of the 166 indicted, one had died, one had been dismissed, four had been severed from the trial, and others had vanished. Still, as the *New York Times* observed, "more men were under indictment than in any other case in the history of American criminal jurisprudence."

During his opening argument, Special Prosecutor Frank Nebeker promised to use the defendants' own words to make his conspiracy case. He introduced a book written by union leader Haywood that suggested restaurants workers could "get even" by contaminating food; and he spoke of workers told to plant trees upside down or to hoe vines instead of weeds.

Prosecutors spent over a week introducing documents from the raid. One particularly odd bit of evidence was a missive recounting a defendant's dreamlike vision of President Wilson and his cabinet fleeing the world as the IWW rose up as saviors. Prosecutors interpreted the vision as evidence of IWW's intent to commit sabotage. Prosecutors also introduced a draft union resolution opposing war, though they had no evidence the resolution was adopted. And they presented an array of witnesses who testified to various statements by IWW members that could be interpreted as opposing the war, favoring strikes, or endorsing violence. Essentially nothing was heard of the German spies, industry assaults, mass crop destruction, or tiny superbombs about which the Justice Department previously had regaled the press.

Defense attorney George Vanderveer denied that the IWW had tried to attack the government but was prevented from presenting a key element of his defense. A Federal Industrial Relations Commission report, he said, would show the strikes had nothing to do with sabotaging the war effort but were motivated by concern for worker safety. Judge Kenesaw Mountain Landis refused to allow the document to be introduced. Conversely, when

Vanderveer objected to the prosecution introducing pamphlets written by members but not approved by the union, Landis overruled the objection. Landis also allowed the government to introduce other materials prosecutors considered seditious—even if written before the Espionage Act was passed.

Baldwin occasionally showed up to observe the trial firsthand, as he noted in one of his confidential memos: "Every man had to be in court every day. It happened one day when I was there that one of the men wasn't in court when the hour came; he had been on a drunk and everybody knew it, including the judge, who sat on the bench waiting. An hour late he wobbled in, grinned at the judge and winked. The judge just watched him take his seat and opened court."

As the trial proceeded, politicians worked on a bill to effectively outlaw the IWW. On May 6, 1918, the Senate passed an anti-sedition bill that would make it a crime for an organization to attempt to bring about, through force or violence, "any governmental, social, industrial or economic change" during the war. It also criminalized belonging to an organization that advocated such things. (Senators disagreed over whether the measure would, unintentionally, outlaw lynching.)

On May 7, the House passed the Sedition Act, which was enacted into law on May 16. The new law, an amendment to the Espionage Act, made it a crime to "willfully utter, print, write, or publish any disloyal, profane, scurrilous, or abusive language about the form of government of the United States, or the Constitution of the United States, or the military or naval forces of the United States, or the flag" or to use language intended to bring "the United States into contempt, scorn, contumely, or disrepute." Such behavior was punishable by fines of $10,000 and imprisonment of up to twenty years.

On August 4, 1918, as the marathon trial moved toward a conclusion, the *New York Times* published a wrap-up that read more like a prosecution brief than a news report. It lauded Judge Landis as "one of the more able judicial officers on the Federal Bench" and portrayed the IWW as a band of dangerous outlaws reeking of the ideas of the "American Bolsheviki" and "at all times defiant of the court." The report condemned the IWW for its "unceasing warfare to exterminate the wage system and seize the industries of the nation."

David Karsner, the reporter hired by Baldwin, published a considerably more balanced analysis in the *New York Call*. He observed that the heart of the government case consisted of thousands of letters written by defendants, which, at worst, showed "among certain individuals of the IWW a dislike of the war . . . and of the conscription act."

Nonetheless, he pointed out, the government had charged those men with conspiracy, which meant proving that "two or more of these defendants entered into an agreement, a compact, a conspiracy, to oppose the war and the draft, and to tie up Industries upon which the government relied for basic war supplies." Such a conspiracy, argued Karsner, "has not been proven."

Vanderveer agreed with that view. Indeed, he was so confident that he declined to make a closing argument after the prosecution rested on Saturday, August 17.

One hour and five minutes after receiving the judge's instructions, the jury sent notice that it had arrived at a verdict after one ballot. The remaining one hundred defendants were brought into the courtroom and told they had been found guilty on all counts.

As the *Chicago Sunday Tribune* described the scene: "Haywood, seated at his attorneys' table was fiddling with a toothpick when the verdict was read . . . his face became ashen, the toothpick fell in bits, crushed by the grip of his fat fingers. . . . It had been feared . . . that were the 100 convicted, there might be a riot in court. Instead there was a dead, almost breathless silence."

"I can't understand how some of us were not acquitted at a moment's notice," said Haywood. Vanderveer was also stunned. "I can conceive of some of the defendants being found guilty, but that all of them should be is astounding," he said.

Baldwin saw the verdict as "a foregone conclusion. No jury hearing such evidence of opposition to the war could be moved to consider constitutional liberties."

Prior to delivering sentence on Friday, August 30, Judge Landis ripped into the defendants: "I do not mean to say that this organization deliberately started out to organize in the United States to help Germany," he said, but concluded: "The jury could not have done anything else on this evidence but find a verdict of guilty. When a country is at peace it is a legal right of free speech to oppose going to war . . . but when once war is declared, this right ceases."

Haywood and his fourteen top lieutenants were given twenty years. Thirty-three defendants were given ten years, thirty-three more were given five, and twelve were given one year and a day. Two got off with ten-day sentences. The *Chicago Daily Tribune* calculated the total fines at $2.3 million, with each defendant assessed from $20,000 to $30,000. Total prison time was put at 807 years.

Hours after Landis sentenced the IWW defendants, the Justice Department raided the offices of the New York Bureau for Legal Services—which was on the floor just above Baldwin's NCLB office. Guards were left in the building, presumably to ensure that no papers were removed overnight. The next morning, agents raided NCLB's office, where they confiscated pamphlets and correspondence.

That same afternoon, August 31, President Wilson signed an amendment to the Selective Service Act raising the age limit of potential draftees to forty-five—which made Baldwin, who was thirty-four, eligible for the draft.

On Friday, September 6, 1918, the IWW defendants were taken from Chicago County Jail in ten police patrol vans and driven to the La Salle Street Station for transport to Leavenworth Federal Penitentiary. They were accompanied by some sixty federal marshals and city detectives. The procession attracted a crowd of several hundred onlookers who bore witness in silence as prisoners were handcuffed together in pairs and put aboard a special train.

On September 12, after registering for the draft, Baldwin wrote a letter to his draft board. "I am opposed to the use of force to accomplish any ends, however good. I am, therefore, opposed to participation in this or any other war," declared Baldwin, who added, "I will decline to perform any service under compulsion, regardless of its character."

At the September 30 meeting of the NCLB Directing Committee, Baldwin offered his resignation. He was told his resignation "would be accepted only upon event of actual action under the draft act."

As Baldwin wrestled with the IWW case and its aftermath, another high-profile prosecution of particular interest had moved forward. If convicted of conspiring to violate the Espionage Act, Max Eastman and his six colleagues risked prison terms of twenty years and $10,000 fines.

At the time of the trial, which began on April 16, 1918, two of the seven charged were not available. The writer John Reed was in Russia, and cartoonist Hendrik J. Glintenkamp had mysteriously disappeared. On April 25, after nearly two weeks of testimony, the jury began deliberating. On three separate occasions, the jury asked the judge for further instructions. On Sunday, April 28, the foreman told the judge that it was "absolutely impossible" for the jury to agree on a verdict. A new trial was ordered for later that year.

On May 10, 1918, *The Masses* defendants were honored at a testimonial dinner for 1,400 attendees at the Central Opera House on East Seventy-Sixth Street. Sheltered by a large American flag overhead, their lawyer, Morris Hillquit, harshly critiqued the Sedition Act then on the verge of passage: "By the provisions of this law, which forbids criticism of the Constitution, the army or navy . . . I shall be unable to explain this law, as I am now doing."

Max Eastman was equally critical: "I can't figure out why these espionage laws don't get some of the 150,000 German spies that are said to be at large, instead of American citizens."

The retrial began on Monday, September 31. It was distinguished by the hour-long statement Eastman was allowed to deliver and his introduction into evidence of a letter from President Wilson. The letter resulted from Eastman's visits with Wilson to discuss neutrality and terms of a possible peace and seemed to show Wilson's ambivalence toward his administration's policy on sedition. "I think that [during] a time of war . . . it is legitimate to regard things which in ordinary circumstances be innocent as very dangerous to the public welfare, but the line is manifestly exceedingly hard to draw, and I cannot say that I have any confidence that I know how to draw it," wrote Wilson.

In his address to the jury, Eastman declared, "the District Attorney has never produced one letter that shows that any of us ever met together for any purpose whatever in all the time that was described in this indictment." Eastman pointed out that crimes with which he and associates were charged were not even crimes at the time. "The only thing that these articles prove," he concluded, "is that I was one of the citizens . . . violently opposed to [the law] and that I chose to talk at least until the day of the passage of the law in question."

The defense rested on Friday, October 4.

A day later the jury sent word that it was hopelessly deadlocked [8 to 4]. The judge discharged the jury at 10:10 that night. The government dismissed the indictment on January 10, 1919, two months after the November 11 armistice had ended hostilities in World War I.

"It must be recognized that the war is now over in all except the formalities of conclusion of peace" and that "no additional evidence has come into the Government's possession to warrant a belief that a third trial would produce a result different from that reached in the two trials," noted assistant U.S. attorney Earl Barnes's *nolle prosequi* (or dismissal declaration).

Even as the war wound to a close, Roger Baldwin's struggle against conscription was getting increasingly personal. In October 1918, Baldwin received notice from his draft board to appear for his physical examination, to which he responded with a letter requesting a speedy trial. "I shall of course plead guilty." A few days later, he was arrested at his aunt's home on West Eighty-Third Street, where he was then living.

The police officer took Baldwin to the basement of the American Museum of Natural History, where the local draft board was housed. There the chairman, Julius Henry Cohen, suggested that Baldwin think things over while in custody for the night. After feeding Baldwin, taking him for a haircut, and allowing him to call his girlfriend, the policeman led Baldwin to a cell.

The next day, Rayme Finch, the Bureau of Investigation agent who had led the raid on the NCLB office, stopped by Baldwin's cell and told him, "Come on out to breakfast. You're going to have the fanciest little arrest you ever heard of."

Virtually nothing followed the normal course in Baldwin's case. In part his special handling was due to his prominence, but it was also because the Bureau of Investigation had bungled the raid on his office in September. During that search, Finch had been assisted by the Propaganda League— an offshoot of the elite and prestigious New York Union League Club, whose members got draft deferments for their work with the Justice Department. The league's men had made a mess of the confiscated NCLB materials, and Finch desperately needed help sorting them out. Finch sought Baldwin's assistance; and Baldwin, having nothing to hide, agreed.

As author Curt Gentry tells the story: "Each morning, for the next month, an agent would check Baldwin out of the Tombs [so called because the original structure seemed reminiscent of an Egyptian mausoleum] and take him to the Bureau offices . . . where he'd work on the records. . . . At mealtimes he insisted on taking Baldwin to the better restaurants. Once . . . he even treated him to a burlesque show." At one point, said Baldwin, Finch "showed me his telephone-tapping equipment and asked if I wanted to listen in on any conversation. . . . I declined."[6]

At the end of twenty days, Baldwin appeared before U.S. District Court Judge Julius M. Mayer. Mayer accepted his guilty plea, listened to his prepared statement ("I cannot consistently, with self-respect, do other than I have") and sentenced him to the maximum of a year in prison, minus the twenty days he had already served.

After sentence was pronounced, a number of people—Socialist candidate for Congress Scott Nearing, the Reverend Norman Thomas, Rabbi Judah Magnes, and others—rose to "congratulate Baldwin on his stand," reported the *New York Tribune*.

Less than two weeks later, the fighting ended. On Monday, November 11, the front page of the *New York Times* proclaimed: "ARMISTICE SIGNED, END OF THE WAR! BERLIN SEIZED BY REVOLUTIONISTS; NEW CHANCELLOR BEGS FOR ORDER; OUSTED KAISER FLEES TO HOLLAND."

It would take several months for the war to officially end with the signing of the Treaty of Versailles on June 28, 1919. But in every meaningful sense, the war was over, and the world was profoundly changed. More than 17 million had died. Europe had been remade. Empires had fallen. And America had taken a huge first step toward becoming a superpower.

It had also taken a huge step away from some of the core ideas embedded in its Constitution. Between 1917 and 1919, more than two thousand individuals were indicted under the new wartime laws, and more than a thousand were convicted—generally on no real evidence of wrongdoing. Many of the defendants were ordinary people who had expressed personal opinions that were no longer considered legal. Indeed, most were arguably better patriots than the mobs who pummeled them and the prosecutors and magistrates who imprisoned them for the crime of speaking their minds.

Historian Robert Zieger credits the Great War with the rise of the national security state, arguing that "for the first time in U.S. history, government forged powerful instruments of coercion and repression in the service of military and foreign policy goals."[7] America, in short, had shown how easily the Constitution was flung aside, how weak were the protections that many of its citizens had accepted on faith. Americans, it turned out, could not depend on the government and powerful private interests alone to keep America true to herself. The Great War had shown, in other words, that the modest work started by Wald, Kellogg, Eastman, and their friends at the Henry Street Settlement might not yet be at its end.

3

The Year That Shook America and Spawned the ACLU

President Wilson had pledged "the whole force of the nation" to make the world "safe for democracy." No one could say exactly how safe the world was—but America definitely was on the rise. The emerging superpower had won a great military victory and replaced Great Britain as the world's dominant economy.

On November 11, 1918, as Germany acknowledged defeat, the *Atlanta Constitution* captured the euphoric mood: "For the first time since the dawn of civilization the peoples of all the great nations of the world are free."

"To conquer the world by earning its esteem is to make permanent conquest," Wilson told a joint session of Congress on that day of victory. The victors, he pledged, would "make conquest of the world by the sheer power of example and of friendly helpfulness."

The Sunday following the armistice, virtually every church in New York City celebrated the military triumph. Trinity Church's organist played anthems of the allied nations and a detachment from the Ninth Coast Artillery carrying allied nations' flags marched in formation around the church. Louisville celebrated with nearly a hundred floats and ten thousand soldiers, who put on the "most spectacular pageant ever witnessed in Louisville," claimed the *Courier Journal.* Fort Devens, in Massachusetts, scheduled three days of the "Biggest of All Military Shows," reported the *Boston Globe.* In Atlanta, blacks came together for "the largest parade ever staged in the city by negroes," reported the *Atlanta Constitution*, which encouraged employers to release colored workers wishing to celebrate "the splendid service rendered by the colored troops."

The day after Christmas, hundreds of thousands of New Yorkers turned out to welcome the arriving victory fleet: ten battleships escorted by twenty-one airplanes. The ships made their way, through snow and biting winds, up the New York Harbor to the Statue of Liberty, each firing off a nineteen-gun salute, as Secretary of the Navy Josephus Daniels, War Secretary Newton Baker, and other notables stood in review on the USS *Mayflower.*

But as the thrill of victory waned, along with wartime's spirit of shared sacrifice, America's fragile unity fragmented. Xenophobia, racism, and the war between management and labor resurged, making 1919 one of the most turbulent and divisive years in American history. Out of that turbulence rose the American Civil Liberties Union.

Samuel Gompers, president of the American Federation of Labor (AFL), foreshadowed the trouble ahead. After the head of an anti-union employers' group suggested wages would drop now that the wartime need for labor had eased, Gompers replied in a speech in December 1918: the "working people of the United States will resist and make any sacrifice," he said, "to prevent the industrial baron riding on horseback over the masses of the people."

As the New Year dawned, Gompers's prophecy raced toward reality. Some 35,000 shipyard workers in Seattle, free of the wartime no-strike pledge, walked off the job on January 21. The city's Central Labor Council backed them, overwhelmingly approving a general strike. By early February an estimated 77,000 workers were out, driving local politicians and the national press mad. The *Los Angeles Times* pronounced the strike "the beginning of the Bolshevik revolution in America." Mayor Ole Hanson encouraged guards "to shoot to kill at first sign of rioting" and requested federal troops, whom he personally escorted into the city.

Facing a belligerent mayor and a hostile public, the strikers ended their protest on February 11, teaching employers, politicians, and the press that anti-radical hysteria was a useful weapon against unionism.[1]

The Seattle strike was little more than a warm-up for the orgy of hysteria to follow. On February 19, a would-be assassin shot French prime minister Georges Clemenceau in Paris. None of the wounds was fatal. The assailant, Louis Émile Cottin, was tackled by a barber's assistant as he fled after tossing his gun. Initially rumored to be Russian, Cottin turned out to be a homegrown anarchist.

Two days after the shooting (on the same front page updating Clemenceau's condition) the *Philadelphia Inquirer* assured readers that the city was well protected against a "'Bolsheviki' or IWW 'uprising.'" A "secret service police force . . . stands ready to meet any emergency, and a heavily armed soldiery is being maintained at all times at the Philadelphia Navy Yard," reported the *Inquirer.* Days later, New York police picked up fourteen men they claimed were members of the Spanish branch of the IWW cooking up a terrorist plot to kill Allied and American officials.

In late April, the postal service received several small packages addressed to prominent Americans. One went to the home of Seattle mayor Ole Hanson. The box started leaking acid and was discovered to be a bomb. An identical package showed up at the Atlanta home of former Senator Thomas Hardwick. The bomb exploded, injuring his maid, provoking the *Atlanta Constitution* to run an editorial insisting, "TIME TO STOP IT."

More "infernal machines" were quickly discovered—sixteen in the New York City post office and others in post offices elsewhere. In all, thirty-six turned up, addressed to prominent men, all primed to explode on May 1 (May Day: otherwise known as International Workers Day). Among those targeted were Attorney General Alexander Mitchell Palmer, Secretary of Labor William B. Wilson, Associate Supreme Court Justice Oliver Wendell Holmes Jr., and John D. Rockefeller, the tycoon.

No bomb reached its intended target. Still, in the following weeks, newspapers ran countless stories warning about the "red menace" and the need to deport radical immigrants. The press also warned about various unions (the IWW most prominently) supposedly under the sway of Bolsheviks. Blacks were also targeted. Black men were torched in Arkansas, Florida, Georgia, Mississippi, and Texas—for supposed crimes ranging from attacking white women to resisting arrest. ("White Heathens Burn Man's Body to Ashes," screamed the *Chicago Defender* in recounting a particularly gruesome death in Mississippi.) Endless alarm sounded about possible uprisings of blacks and Bolsheviks, separately or together.

In a May Day speech in Topeka, Kansas, Mayor Hanson of Seattle challenged Washington to "either hang or incarcerate for life all the anarchists in the country." Two days later, the *Christian Science Monitor* observed, "the time for leniency and tolerance is past and . . . force must be answered with force."

Even random citizens risked abuse if they failed to meet the demands of public patriotism. One of the more bizarre incidents took place early that May during the playing of the national anthem at an American victory celebration in Chicago's Grant Park. Joseph Goddard, an unemployed tinsmith, refused to stand. When a woman demanded that he rise, Goddard replied that he stood "for no man, flag or music." A sailor on guard urged the crowd, "Get that man, fill him full of holes." As Goddard sprinted across the field, the sailor aimed his rife and fired. Two bullets went into the dirt, a third went into Goddard's arm, and the fourth hit and exploded a pistol cartridge he was carrying on his hip.

Goddard ended up in the hospital "with his left arm torn to shreds . . . and his hip wounded," reported the *Chicago Tribune*. Witnesses' claims that Goddard had fired his gun turned out to be untrue. Still, he was charged with carrying a concealed weapon. The shooter was not charged.

On Monday evening, June 2, bombs exploded in eight American cities along the East Coast. Among those targeted were the mayor of Cleveland, a federal judge in Pittsburgh, and Attorney General A. Mitchell Palmer. The bomb exploded outside Palmer's home in northwest Washington, DC, shortly before midnight. Palmer and his wife escaped injury, as did Franklin D. Roosevelt, assistant secretary of the navy, and his wife Eleanor, who lived across the street and reportedly had walked by shortly before the explosion.

Palmer had been preparing for bed when he heard "a crash downstairs as if something had been thrown against the front door. It was followed immediately by an explosion, which blew in the front of the house," said Palmer, in an interview published in the *Chicago Daily Tribune*.

A man's scalp, covered with dark, curly hair, was found in the debris. Police also found a worn Italian-American dictionary, parts of two guns, and blood-stained fragments of clothing. From a train ticket stub found in a man's hatband, investigators deduced the bomber had arrived from

Philadelphia earlier that evening. Anarchist handbills entitled "Plain Words" were found at the scene, as they were near several of the other bombings that took place that night.

Anyone with radical connections became a focus of scrutiny. In Pittsburg, detectives stormed the office of John Johnson, the local IWW president. As they confronted Johnson, he fired at an officer, missed, and was quickly overpowered. Police also arrested suspects in Boston, Philadelphia, Detroit, and Cleveland. Following a bomb explosion on Chicago's Northwest Side, authorities raided several print shops and residences, arresting a printer they believed might be linked to the literature found near the bombing in Washington, DC.

"More than sixty suspects have been taken into custody . . . but no indications have been received here that would indicate the capture of the actual plotters," reported the *Atlanta Constitution* on June 5. In the end, the bombings remained unsolved, though the perpetrators ultimately were widely presumed to be followers of the Italian-born anarchist Luigi Galleani.

A. Mitchell Palmer, a Quaker and former liberal Pennsylvania congressman, was profoundly affected by the attacks. In early 1919, Palmer had stepped up from his position as alien property custodian (charged with safeguarding the seized belongings of so-called enemy aliens). At his March 5 swearing-in ceremony, Palmer pledged, "the policy of the Department of Justice will be the same as heretofore."

After the bombings, his tone changed. In a statement on June 3, Palmer predicted the bombing attacks would increase and declared war on the "anarchistic element in the population" out to "terrorize the country."

Frank Morrison, secretary of the AFL, blamed immigrants for the violence: "I can understand why the nihilists of Russia used bombs. . . . They do not even understand our language."

On June 13, Louisiana congressman James Benjamin Aswell introduced four separate bills to deal with the terrorist threat. He aimed to subject bombers to the death penalty, halt all immigration for three years, and deport anti-government immigrants and those who had rejected citizenship rather than serve in the U.S. military during the war.

That same day, Palmer requested $500,000 from the House Appropriations Committee (in addition to $1,500,000 he had already requested) to take on anarchists.

Palmer told Congress: "It has come to be accepted as fact that on a certain day in the future . . . there will be another serious and probably much larger effort . . . a proposition to rise up and destroy the government at one fell swoop."

Soon thereafter, the Justice Department announced plans to round up and deport or imprison some two thousand suspected radicals, as speculation grew that Palmer might be preparing to run for president.

As the press extolled Palmer's virtues and his crackdown on alleged radicals, America was bumping up against an unfortunate reality: the war to make the world safe for democracy had not made America safe for equality.

Some civil rights proponents had dreamed that America's racial caste system might be ending, that the war had allowed blacks to prove their worth and devotion, and that America would respond with gratitude and acceptance. In a speech in San Francisco in early July, James Weldon Johnson, the poet, novelist, and field secretary of the National Association for the Advancement of Colored People (NAACP)—founded in 1909 to promote equality and abolish racial discrimination—said America appreciated the loyalty and courage blacks had demonstrated.

But evidence of that appreciation was difficult to find. For whatever the war had taught white America about black potential and worth, it had also fueled rampant fear about black demands for equality.

The Washington, DC, riot began on July 19, 1919. It was a rainy Saturday night, with the temperature rising to 85 degrees. Rumor had it that a black man had attacked the white wife of a navy veteran; and white veterans were out to exact revenge. Armed with clubs, lead pipes, and lumber, the gangs marched on a predominantly black neighborhood in southwest DC, beating random blacks they encountered.

The rioters were egged on by an irresponsible press, which lashed out against "attacks on white women by negroes," as the *Atlanta Constitution* put it. The *Baltimore Sun* similarly attributed the violence to "a vicious attempt on the part of a negro to criminally assault" a white mother of two. The rampage went on for several days before troops from Camp Meade and Quantico contained it.

A writer from Camp Meade wrote a letter to the *Sun* explaining that he was "not prejudiced toward the negro race, but when our women . . . are assaulted here in our own country it boils the blood in our veins, and if the police department [is] incapable of protecting our women then our service men who crossed the sea to protect them will."

Congressman Frank Clark, a Florida Democrat born in Alabama, introduced a resolution condemning the city for "utterly" failing to "bring to justice the cowardly and inhuman beasts who are guilty of ravishing innocent and defenseless women."

The black press saw the riot differently. The *Philadelphia Tribune* blamed "Southern white hoodlums dressed as soldiers or sailors" determined to "create race friction in any city" where blacks enjoyed a modicum of respect.

The narrative of sexually insatiable blacks preying on innocent white women was a popular justification for anti-black violence in the aftermath of World War I, as was the presumption that whites were justified in murdering blacks who demanded fair pay or otherwise stepped outside their assigned place. A riot in Chicago, the week following the violence in Washington, DC, offered a case study in the war over public space.

It was one of the hottest weekends of the year. Temperatures on Sunday, July 27, peaked at 96 degrees. Thousands of Chicagoans sought relief on the beaches ringing Lake Michigan. An invisible wall separated the all-white Twenty-Ninth Street Beach from the Twenty-Fifth Street Beach, which allowed blacks.

That Sunday, Eugene Williams's raft drifted into the forbidden zone. White sun worshippers pelted the black teen with rocks, knocking him into the water, where he drowned. The *Chicago Defender* reported accusations that a white policeman, Daniel Callahan, "not only refused to make an arrest, but kept expert swimmers from reaching Williams."

When black beachgoers heard of the tragedy, some marched over to confront the whites. Accusations flew, tempers flared, and chaos reigned. For the next several days, blacks were dragged from cars and beaten, and gunshots were exchanged. By Tuesday night, much of Chicago was a battlefield. "The first pitched battle of the night" climaxed when an automobile filled with whites, "each armed with a pistol and firing indiscriminately at blacks, crashed into a patrol wagon" at the intersection of Thirty-Fifth and State Streets, reported the *New York Tribune*.

Meanwhile, a white mob attacked a black hospital, only to be "beaten off by policemen," reported the *Louisville Courier Journal*. Police also rescued two families attacked by a mob in their North Side home. And a black teen survived being stabbed and tossed into the Chicago River.

"For five days it raged. . . . Thirty-eight people died—23 blacks and 15 whites. By the time the National Guard and a rainstorm brought the riots to an end, more than 500 people had been injured, wounded blacks outnumbering whites by a ratio of about 2-1," a *Chicago Tribune* writer noted.[2]

After the riot, a *Tribune* editorialist put forth the paper's vision of interracial harmony. "[So] long as this city is dominated by whites . . . there will be limitations placed upon the black people," predicted the *Tribune*, which made an impassioned argument for the status quo. Neither the "radicalism, expressed in the IWW propaganda among Negroes" would help, nor would "thuggery," or a "rebellion by the Negroes against facts which exist and will persist." Instead, "the situation in Chicago" must be "handled in the fashion it always has been handled."

Shortly after the riot, the *New York Tribune* brought its wisdom to bear on the recent outbreaks. It attributed the riots to six things: black men attacking white women, "hoodlumism" by soldiers, insufficient police protection, easy access to firearms, hysterical press coverage, and the dissemination "among the negro population of this country of dangerous race propaganda growing out of the war."

The *Tribune* also lambasted the black press for spreading propaganda about racial equality, concluding "this type of propaganda is most generally ascribed to two causes: The presence of negro soldiers in France, where French women of the lower classes accepted them as equals, and the presence of an increasing number of agitators among negroes."

The very radical idea of equality was indeed spreading through black communities in the wake of the war; and, for many whites, that was just as scary as the idea of bomb-throwing Bolsheviks.

That August the *Atlanta Constitution* reported that in Eastman, Georgia, the "charred body of Eli Cooper, an aged Laurens County negro" was found "in the ashes of Petway's Gift Church, which was burned by incendiaries at an early hour. . . . Three other negro churches and a negro lodge near Cadwell" were also burned. Cooper, the paper reported, lately had been talking 'in a manner offensive to White people," and fueling rumors of an "uprising of negroes."

On the evening of September 28, several thousand whites stormed the county jail in Omaha, Nebraska, to lynch a black man suspected of assaulting a white woman. The mob set the jail aflame and attempted to lynch the mayor after he tried to calm the crowd. Police officers cut the rope, pulling the mayor into a car and rushing him to a doctor's office.

Meanwhile, the mob surrounded the county courthouse where William Brown, the black suspect, was being held. The crowd pummeled two black policemen who rushed to the scene and attacked black civilians unfortunate enough to be downtown. After some nine hours of resistance, with the lives of his men and a hundred prisoners at stake, the sheriff gave up the fight. Around eleven o'clock that night, the mob dragged Brown through the flames and hung him from an electric light pole. Only then were the firemen allowed to work.

Arkansas was also the site of racial warfare. That October 1, Americans learned that some five hundred soldiers from Camp Pike were headed to the small town of Elaine to put down a "negro uprising."

On October 3, the *Arkansas Democrat* reported that the "uprising" had been contained: "With military control established at Elaine . . . center of the negro disorders which for 48 hours have thrown Helena and Phillips County in turmoil . . . the task of pacification was declared well under way."

The *Democrat* explained that the "trouble . . . is not a race riot in the strict sense of the word. It is rather a negro uprising nipped in the bud by prompt and vigorous action." The paper assured its readers that "absolutely no violence has been done to law abiding negroes."

Historians have a distinctly different view. *The Encyclopedia of Arkansas History & Culture* describes the conflict as "by far the deadliest racial confrontation in Arkansas history and possibly the bloodiest racial conflict in the history of the United States . . . [Estimates] of the number of African Americans killed by whites range into the hundreds; five white people lost their lives."

Although local newspapers were filled with stories of blacks mobilizing to murder whites, in fact the riot grew out of an attempt by black sharecroppers to get fair pay for their work. Among items found during a police raid on a local white attorney's office, the police "found contracts with negro share croppers, showing that each of 12 negroes had paid $50 down and each was to pay an additional sum later in return for legal advice," reported the *Arkansas Democrat*.

Ida Wells-Barnett, a well-known black journalist, investigated the incident and concluded, "the terrible crime these men had committed was to organize their members into a union for the purpose of getting the market price for their cotton, to buy land of their own and to employ a lawyer to get settlements of their accounts with their white landlords."[3]

In the aftermath of the violence, scores of blacks were arrested, and eventually twelve were sentenced to death. Several years later, after numerous legal proceedings, the men were released, several after being forced to confess to lesser crimes.

The events in Washington, Chicago, Arkansas, Georgia, and Nebraska were not exceptions. Violence was so pervasive in 1919 that the period became known as "Red Summer."

James Weldon Johnson was not alone in hoping the post-war period would usher in an era of opportunity and brotherhood. Instead, a "tocsin of anti-black riots and lynchings" swept the country, in the words of author Cameron McWhirter. Before the year was over, notes McWhirter, "at least 25 major riots and mob actions erupted and at least 52 black people were lynched. . . . Hundreds of people—most of them black—were killed and thousands more were injured. . . . In almost every case, white mobs— whether sailors on leave, immigrant slaughterhouse workers, or southern farmers—initiated the violence."[4]

Afterward, James Weldon Johnson seemed resigned to a dark reality. During a fact-finding visit to Washington, DC, just before Chicago exploded, Johnson told the *Washington Post* that more riots were in the offing: "When they come, they will be serious. The colored men will not run away and hide as they have done on previous occasions. . . . The experience here has demonstrated clearly that the colored man will no longer submit to being beaten without cause."

The Crisis, the NAACP's magazine, embraced Johnson's new perspective: "One of the greatest surprises to many of those who came down to 'clean out the niggers' is that these same 'niggers' fought back. Colored men saw their own kind being killed, heard of many more and believed that their lives and liberty were at stake," wrote NAACP Assistant Secretary Walter F. White.[5]

Poet Claude McKay captured the new attitude in his poem "If We must Die," published in *The Liberator*. "If we must die, let it not be like hogs," he wrote, urging instead that blacks die "fighting back." McKay later described the words as having "exploded out of me."[6]

Unable to understand such thinking, hostile journalists and politicians assumed that only left-wing propaganda could account for the new black mood. So official America made war on both leftists and blacks.

On August 1, 1919, Attorney General Palmer established within the Department's Bureau of Investigation a so-called General Intelligence—or anti-radical—division. He named John Edgar Hoover, then twenty-four years old, to head it. Hoover was tasked with identifying radicals across America. In a matter of months, notes author Curt Gentry, Hoover "had amassed 150,000 names . . . cross-indexed by localities, so when a strike broke out . . . all the local 'agitators' could be quickly identified."[7]

Even as fear of foreigners and radicalized blacks spread throughout America, a few voices of moderation rose in their defense. An editorial in the July issue of *Current Opinion* argued that the remedy to radicalism was not "to suppress, imprison and deport active supporters of Bolshevist doctrines" but a rededication to "social democracy."[8]

William Bayard Hale, a journalist, former Episcopal priest, and Woodrow Wilson biographer (tainted in many eyes because of his work as a German propagandist before the war), argued that the nation was in the throes of an irrational rush to judgment. "The sober common sense of our countrymen must be shown that neither the violent folly of a few anarchists, nor the 'filming' of it by interested reactionaries, affords any reason or justification for sitting upon that safety-valve of democratic emotion, namely, the opportunity of free speech," wrote Hale.[9]

Few Americans were in a mood to entertain such arguments. The mood became even uglier in August as labor again went on the warpath—this time in Boston, where policemen were fed up with long workdays and low wages.

In defiance of police Commissioner Edwin Curtis's orders, the Boston police joined the AFL. In response, on August 26, Curtis suspended nineteen leaders of the rebellion but deferred firing them until a mayorally appointed citizen's committee could weigh in.

On September 7, the committee agreed that policemen "should not affiliate or be connected with any labor organization." But the members also recommended a "material adjustment" in the men's "wages, hours and working conditions." Curtis responded the next day by summarily firing the nineteen leaders.

The policemen voted, 1,134 to 2, to walk off their jobs the afternoon of September 9. Only thirty policemen showed up for work that night. Just after midnight, reported the *Boston Globe*, a crowd of three hundred people went berserk in downtown Boston: "They smashed window after window, robbing the place each time. A single policeman remonstrated with them, but they laughed at him."

The second day was just as bad. The mobs "swept along the city streets and broke into stores and smashed valuable plate-glass windows almost at will. It was not until daylight yesterday that the work of looting ended. But trouble was resumed early in the day and storekeepers and peaceable citizens generally were at the Mob's mercy," reported the *Globe*.

Four regiments of the state militia arrived Wednesday evening. The troops ended up firing into a crowd, leaving two dead and three wounded. "A shower of stones so endangered the soldiers that the machine gun crew was ordered to fire," reported the *New York Tribune* on Thursday. The next day's paper put the death toll at seven. One man was shot and killed by state guardsmen during a raid on a dice game, another was killed during a riot in South Boston, and a third—a striking policeman—was shot and killed "by a storekeeper who thought his place was about to be looted."

That Friday, AFL head Samuel Gompers asked the policemen to return to work until after a meeting already scheduled for October between President Wilson and labor leaders. He hoped the meeting would lead to an amicable solution. The policemen agreed to return, but Wilson nonetheless denounced them, calling the strike an "intolerable crime against civilization." Meanwhile, Governor Calvin Coolidge, also condemned the police. "The present situation should not be called a strike. . . . These men are public officials, not employees," Coolidge told the *Globe*, and pronounced them guilty of "desertion of duty."

Gompers pleaded with Governor Coolidge to intercede, but Coolidge refused. "Your assertion that the commissioner was wrong cannot justify the wrong of leaving the city unguarded. . . . There is no right to strike against the public safety by anybody, anywhere, any time," said Coolidge.

Meanwhile, Curtis fired all striking policemen and ordered division captains to banish any policemen who had "failed to report for duty on Sept. 9, 1919 or since that time."

Whatever the merits of their wage and work hours demands, the union had lost the battle, thanks not just to hostile politicians but to an aggressively hostile press. The *Nashville Tennessean*, in labeling the strike "a form of civil treason," was typical.

On Friday, September 19, the *Globe* reported that streets were "back to normal" and the *Christian Science Monitor* announced that advertising had begun "for the recruiting of a new police force to replace the men locked out." Three months later, the *Globe* reported that the total number of cops was "about 1560, or more than were in the department when members . . . went on strike."

As the Boston police strike ended, the Great Steel Strike of 1919 was about to begin. For months, the AFL and Amalgamated Association of Iron, Steel, and Tin Workers had struggled to organize steelworkers. The corporations had fought them at every turn, firing organizers and disrupting meetings.

The conflict ultimately served up two martyrs. On August 26, Fannie Sellins, a union organizer in Pennsylvania known as Mother Jones, reportedly intervened in the beating of striker Joseph Starzeleski by so-called special deputies. The deputies shot and killed both Sellins and Starzeleski. The United Mine Workers called the killings (for which no one was ever held to account) "the most shocking double murder ever committed in Allegheny County."

The deaths fueled the anger of the unions (twenty-four separate ones were involved), who scheduled a general strike of the nation's 500,000 steelworkers for September 22 unless numerous demands were met, including formal recognition of unions, reinstatement of men fired for organizing, an eight-hour workday (twelve-hour shifts were common), and higher wages.

The *Chicago Daily Tribune* called the strike "a general union war on capital." The *Nashville Tennessean* proclaimed it "the first Battle of Manassas," an allusion to the first big clash of the Civil War. The "unions place themselves in the position of disregarding the desires of the President, of opposing the sentiment of the country, and of over-riding the anti-radical conservatism within their own ranks," warned the *Wall Street Journal*.

The strike commenced with scattered violence. In Newcastle, Pennsylvania, mill guards wounded seven people while fighting through a crowd of four hundred strikers. In North Clairton, Pennsylvania, state troopers stormed into and broke up a union meeting. In East Chicago, Indiana, strikers physically attacked workers who crossed picket lines. Riots erupted in Newcastle and in Buffalo, New York. But, for the most part, the strike proceeded peacefully.

At the end of the first day, union leaders said 284,000 men had walked out, but steel executives claimed the strike was having little effect. Management spokesmen also insisted that most of those striking were foreigners. "American-born workers did not respond," they told the Associated Press. At the end of the first week, union spokesman William Z. Foster claimed the strikers had gained "about 60,000 men since the first day."

As the nation reeled from the steel strike, coal workers leapt into the fray. Like steelworkers, they wanted to make up ground lost during the wartime salary freeze. In late September, the United Coal Workers announced that its 400,000 members would strike on November 1 unless they got a 60 percent increase, a six-hour day, and a five-day workweek. The National Coal Association insisted that such a huge raise would cost the public a billion dollars a year. Acting United Mine Workers president John L. Lewis called that response "preposterous." The Coal Association also insisted that miners were still bound by their wartime agreement "until the treaty of peace is ratified and proclaimed."

Amid rumors that the attorney general might seek a restraining order, President Wilson urged the unions to resume negotiations. Union leader Lewis refused, denouncing the administration for attacking "mine workers without even suggesting that mine operators may have brought about this unhappy situation."

On October 31, thirteen hours before the strike was to begin, federal judge A.B. Anderson issued an injunction at Attorney General Palmer's request. John Lewis called the strike prohibition "the most dramatic abrogation of [constitutional] rights . . . that has ever been issued by any federal court." Lewis sent a telegram to strike leaders informing them: "Our position remains unchanged. Strike order issued October 15 becomes effective tonight." The union later claimed the message was not technically in violation of the injunction as it had been sent before Anderson issued his order.

At midnight, the miners walked out—nearly 436,000 of them according to the union, although thousands of non-union miners were at work in scattered districts, reported the *Chicago Daily Tribune*.

Public outrage was loud and unyielding, fueled by management talk of a "Bolshevik revolution" and by "wholly untrue reports which claimed the coal strike was being undertaken on direct orders from Lenin and Trotsky and that Moscow gold was financing the whole project," observed author Robert Murray.[10]

In a speech at Carnegie Hall the Monday after the coal strike began, former Seattle mayor Ole Hanson repeated the claim that Lenin and Trotsky were behind the strikes. He also called for deporting seditious immigrants and using force against strikers.

Meanwhile, Bethlehem Steel president Charles M. Schwab struck a public tone of moderation. "There has been too much calling of names between the opposing forces in the steel strike, the miners' strike and other industrial revolts," said Schwab, stirring up people "to the point where some are expressing fears of a revolution or civil war."

At that point, Schwab surely realized that he and his fellow tycoons had already won, given that the unions never garnered the support of the courts, the president, the press, or much of the public.

The coal strike ended December 10. The United Mine Workers accepted President Wilson's settlement plan, which gave them a 14 percent wage increase. Wilson agreed to appoint a three-person commission to fashion the basis for a new agreement within sixty days. The union leadership accepted the agreement with only one dissenting vote and issued a statement declaring, "the action taken today should demonstrate to the people of our country that the United Mine Workers of America are loyal to our country and believe in the perpetuity of our democratic institutions."

A month later, on January 8, the steelworkers capitulated. William Z. Foster, described by the *New York Times* as "the storm center of the strike," immediately resigned as secretary-treasurer of the National Committee of the Steel Workers Union.

The union released a statement lashing out at "the press, the courts, the Federal troops, State police and many public officials" who "denied the steel workers their rights of free speech, free assemblage and the right to organize."

As the strikes collapsed, America bore witness to a strange deportation scene: the sailing of what came to be called the "Soviet Ark," a 5,000-ton army transport ship named *Buford*, on which famed anarchist Emma Goldman and 240 immigrants labeled criminal revolutionaries were dispatched to their supposedly beloved Russia. The steaming away of the Soviet Ark, which ended the first phase of Palmer's crusade against radicalism, took place on December 21, 1919.

The previous month, on November 7—the second anniversary of Russia's Bolshevik Coup—federal agents fanned out to a dozen cities in the Midwest and on the East Coast to arrest "alien revolutionists," as the *New York Tribune* put it.

The Russian People's House in New York yielded a bonanza: 142 suspects deemed worthy of interrogation. Of those taken, forty-eight men and two women were charged with being "alien criminal anarchists." The total number arrested nationwide that night was put at nearly 1,000, of which 239 were among the 249 passengers destined for the *Buford*.

Goldman, who came to American from Russia in 1885 at the age of fifteen, was not among those arrested in the raid. Her one-way ticket came at the end of a long struggle she had finally relinquished. Authorities had discovered that Goldman's long-divorced husband had not met the requirements for U.S. citizenship when he was naturalized. His citizenship was revoked in 1909, placing Goldman, whose status was linked to his, in danger of deportation.

In July 1917, she and longtime lover Alexander Berkman, a native of St. Petersburg, were convicted of organizing against the draft. Berkman had previously served hard time for the attempted assassination of Carnegie Steel Company chairman Henry Clay Frick. Federal Judge Julius Mayer sentenced the couple to two-year terms (the maximum for the offense). Prior to their release, the Department of Justice initiated deportation proceedings against both Goldman and Berkman. Goldman initially fought deportation, but ultimately waived her right to appeal, opting to accompany Berkman to Russia.

So it was that, four days before Christmas, America's most celebrated radical couple was set, along with 247 others, to start a new life in Russia. The *Buford* launched at 6:13 that Sunday morning "just as the first rays of the sun illumined the murky gray of the harbor," recalled the *New York Tribune*. Chants of "Long live the revolution in America!" carried back to shore. Only when the ship "steamed out of the narrows between Forts Hamilton and Wadsworth did the din cease," reported the Associated Press.

The exact destination was unknown. That information was contained in sealed orders the captain was to open twenty-four hours after the *Buford* set to sea. Goldman and Berkman left behind a statement thanking the American government for the honor of showing Russia the "cruelties practiced upon American men and women because of their opinions."

On January 2, Palmer ushered in the new year by presiding over simultaneous late-night raids in over thirty cities across the country. Press reports proclaimed it the "greatest roundup of radicals in the nation's history." By midnight, reported the *Detroit Free Press*, some 2,500 suspects were in custody, with another 1,000 arrests expected before daylight.

Along with supposedly plotting to overthrow the government, the radicals also stood accused of attempting "to organize Negroes in support of plans to overthrow the present political and economic system," reported the *Free Press*.

Meanwhile, Cook County State's Attorney Maclay Hoyne was so pumped up that he had arrested two hundred alleged radicals in Chicago before Palmer could act—even though Palmer had requested that he wait. Hoyne accused Palmer of "pursuing a pussyfoot policy."

The January 4 *New York Tribune* reported that radicals had intended to turn the recent steel and coal strikes "into a general industrial tie-up, and ultimately into a revolution to overthrow the United States government." Happily, said government officials, the raids "nipped the most menacing revolutionary plot yet unearthed."

As America was ripped apart, Roger Baldwin sat in jail: a perfect place, he discovered, to contemplate his future. He later called his confinement a state-sponsored "vacation."

After being sentenced by Judge Julius M. Mayer (the very judge who had presided over the trial of Emma Goldman), Baldwin returned to the Tombs while arrangements were made to send him to the Essex County Jail in Newark.

The transfer occurred on November 11, Armistice day. A marshal escorted Baldwin, handcuff-free, out of the Tombs, to a city celebrating the end of the war. As he walked along lower Broadway, confetti fell around him. Baldwin chatted with the marshal all the way to the subway, becoming so chummy they stopped in a bar for a drink before Baldwin was delivered to his new home.

The jail, he immediately realized, "was the better sort, small, a few hundred men, many awaiting trial, informal, easy-going. I knew I would feel at home."

It turned out that the warden, an Irishman, was something of a rebel himself. He had been "against England's war." The two instantly took to each other, and the warden assigned Baldwin to help prepare food and work in the greenhouse taking care of plants. When he learned that Baldwin played the piano, he invited the new prisoner to play for his family sing-alongs, which took place in the warden's residence in the jail.

Shortly after Baldwin arrived, Caroline Bayard Dod Colgate stopped by. Colgate's ancestors had settled in the area prior to the American revolution. Her husband, Sidney Colgate, was a grandson of the founder of the Colgate-Palmolive Company and president of Colgate Palmolive-Peet.

As Baldwin recalled, "Mrs. Colgate was a specialist in helping prisoners." With her help, he "in no time had the most complete set of services in that jail I had ever heard of—public library books, family service, classes with volunteer teachers, a piano and a glee club, and . . . free legal services by a lawyer who later became district attorney." Everything went wonderfully well until the sheriff realized what was going on.

Sheriff John Flavell informed Baldwin that jail's function was not to "spoil" inmates and "saw to it that our experiment in self-help ended." That May, the *New York Tribune* asked Sheriff Flavell about shutting down Baldwin's Prisoners Welfare League.

Flavell explained that he had no idea of the lengths to which Baldwin would take things, but Baldwin, "being a man of brains," assumed "too much authority" and had been granted "too many privileges."

Flavell had Baldwin transferred to the Essex County Penitentiary in Caldwell, New Jersey, which Baldwin took in stride. "Mrs. Colgate knew the place well, run by a warden who was, with both of us, a member of the National Conference of Social Welfare. . . . I was put to work in the gardens just where I wanted to be in spring. . . . [The] atmosphere was easygoing and friendly."

Baldwin was set free Saturday morning, July 19, as race riots broke out in Washington, DC. Lucille Milner, a longtime volunteer with the NCLB and a graduate of the New York School of Philanthropy, organized the welcome home party. It was held at Norman Thomas's East Village home. In a memoir, Milner described the scene: "'There's not going to be any public stuff tonight,' Albert DeSilver announced, 'this is just a chance for you to say howdy to Roger upon his return from, shall we say, his vacation? . . . Make a few remarks on the state of the nation, Rog; you can say anything you doggone please from Gesundheit to the Ten Commandments.' . . . 'I feel like a deb at a coming-out party,' Roger quipped as his admirers joyously greeted him.'"[11]

The *New York Tribune* article that ran the next day reported that Baldwin considered his time behind bars "the most profitable year I have ever spent. It . . . has brought me in contact with a great stream of men going in and out of the penitentiary in a way that no reformer or social worker can possibly obtain."

He also said that jail had made him more physically fit, allowed him to catch up on his reading, and made him question his previous brand of activism. Over the next several months, he hoped to attach himself to "the revolutionary labor movement." He was going to "aid in the struggle of the workers to control society in the interest of the mass."

His subsequent actions were considerably more modest than his grandiose plans. Baldwin's initial focus had nothing to do with social activism. His priority was his fiancée, Madeleine Zabriskie Doty, a well-known feminist pacifist and writer with degrees from Smith College and New York University's law school, who had been among the small group greeting him when he emerged from the penitentiary.

The two had met some years earlier at a national meeting of social workers. "She was like me essentially a reformer. I was attracted by her gayety and humor, clear blue eyes, her trim figure and her professional style of dressing," wrote Baldwin, in a memo prepared for the Doty papers at Smith College.

After Baldwin moved to New York, they re-encountered each other at a party hosted by a friend of Crystal Eastman and began seriously dating. "We were married . . . a month after I got out of prison, at her parents' home in Sparta, N.J. by my friend Norman Thomas, at a simple ceremony beside a rushing brook." A "prison friend" served as "sort of a best man."

The couple honeymooned in the Adirondacks at Caroline Bayard Dod Colgate's summer home, which Baldwin recalled as "not an entirely happy arrangement among the distractions" of Colgate's ménage, "though we had a tent away on another lake."

"Roger Baldwin, Draft Dodger, Weds Writer," is how the *New York Tribune* announced the August 8 marriage.

Baldwin moved into his bride's Greenwich Village apartment. As he later recalled, "I didn't settle down long because I had to be off on an experiment I had determined on in jail."

That experiment, Baldwin explained, was "to study the industrial unrest at first hand." His plan was to acquire a union card, which would allow him—assuming he encountered pro-union conductors—to ride the rails for free in search of short-term work at various enterprises in the heart of the industrial Midwest.

IWW head Bill Haywood sponsored his membership in the IWW. Baldwin also joined the AFL Cooks and Waiters Union in Chicago. Through much of October and November, Baldwin found several short-term jobs. He joined steelworkers on picket lines in Gary, Indiana, and South Chicago, worked in a brickyard and shoveled lead ore in southern Missouri, and joined a railroad construction crew in Youngstown, Ohio. A reporter caught up with him in St. Louis and filed a report that ran that October in the *Nashville Tennessean*. It noted that he had come down from Peoria in a "gondola car, loaded with sand," traveling on his cooks' union card. "When the trainmen found that I was a union man in search of a job . . . they were perfectly willing to let me ride," Baldwin told the reporter.

He spied for AFL leader William Z. Foster while working as a strikebreaker in Pennsylvania's Homestead steel mills. He was fired after a few days and returned to his hotel room to find it had been searched and his notes stolen by persons unknown.

"Brief and perhaps superficial as he admitted his experiences had been," Baldwin finally experienced firsthand "what he had previously only known academically," observed Baldwin biographer Peggy Lamson.[12]

Despite Baldwin's embrace of a laboring life and Socialist-sounding rhetoric ("Once workers have control of production, they will work more willingly, and production will increase," he told a reporter), he had no job and no concrete sense of what he wanted to do.

The Civil Liberties Bureau had become a part-time operation run by Albert DeSilver. "It was evident the Bureau was either going to fold or someone had to rescue it," he later observed—at the very time America seemed desperately in need of an organization to fight suppression of free speech and threats to civil liberties. And he did not think the Free Speech League was up to the job.

The League had been intermittently active since shortly after the turn of the century. In 1903, it opposed the deportation of English anarchist John Turner under the Anarchist Exclusion Act and was a longtime defender of the IWW and a range of unpopular causes. It backed William Sanger in 1915 when he was convicted of distributing a birth control pamphlet authored by his wife, Margaret Sanger. It supported Upton Sinclair in 1914, when he was arrested for protesting the deaths of men, women, and children during a mining strike in Colorado. And it stood with union activist Elizabeth Gurley Flynn when she was barred from speaking in Paterson, New Jersey, and had stood with women arrested for demonstrating for Emma Goldman in 1917.

But Theodore Schroeder, a wealthy lawyer who was the public face of the League when Baldwin came to New York, was not Baldwin's sort: "He was the scholar who wrote briefs and argued a few cases on principle. He was not a man engaged in court battles or eager to advise clients," surmised Baldwin.

The Civil Liberties Bureau, on the other hand, was made up of "high-minded and well-known people . . . with the courage and backing" to take on the task of defending the rights "of speech, press and conscience."

His ex-colleagues asked him to take over from DeSilver, but Baldwin hesitated, thinking it might be tough for a convicted man to generate public support. He agreed to take the job only if everyone agreed it was a good idea. "There wasn't a single dissent," recalled Baldwin.

That January 12, at the Civic Club on West Twelfth Street in lower Manhattan, Baldwin and his colleagues convened the "conference to reorganize the work of the National Civil Liberties Bureau." At that meeting, they named the new organization the American Civil Liberties Union. Baldwin raised the question of whether his and Elizabeth Gurley Flynn's notoriety and jail records might be a problem but was assured their attributes outweighed their liabilities. The committee thereupon took on the task of organizing a campaign against the sedition legislation then pending in the House of Representatives.

A smaller group met the next day and agreed that the Reverend Harry F. Ward would chair the new organization and Baldwin would serve as secretary. The following Monday, the organizing committee reviewed its finances. Some $3,300 was already pledged, mostly from committee members. They agreed to a goal of at least $4,500 to sustain the work over its first three months, and Baldwin agreed to get out a release announcing the new organization.

The following Sunday, Ward officially unveiled the new organization. The ACLU, reported the *Washington Post*, would "champion in the highest courts the civil liberties of persons and organizations." It also would fight to ensure "industrial struggles" were "in conformity with the constitution of the United States and of the several states of the Union."

The Sunday before the ACLU's announcement, the *New York Tribune* ran a page-one story about a new ruling by Secretary of Labor William Wilson. The ruling, explained the *Tribune*, "is based on the finding . . . that the Communist party was created for the avowed purpose of overthrowing the United States by force." Upwards of three thousand suspects already caught up in Palmer's net were at risk of deportation.

That same Sunday, the *Los Angeles Times* reported that a sedition bill making its way through the House might have to be modified because of free speech concerns raised at Rules Committee hearings over the weekend. Jackson Ralston, counsel for the AFL, argued that hardliners should have confidence "in American traditions." But Thomas Blanton, a Democratic congressman from Texas, rejected that argument, saying it was Congress's duty to "squelch anarchy," not just in the union movement but in the Labor Department.

As Congress debated the limits of free speech, the *Buford* reached its destination. The ship arrived in Hanko, Finland, on January 16. A special train took the passengers to the Russian frontier. When a reporter asked Goldman whether she was for the overthrow of the American government, she responded, "You need a new government and I hope the election will provide it."

On January 19, the group reached the border town of Terijoki, Finland. A member of the All-Soviets Executive Committee was among the greeters. "There is no question they will be welcomed in Russia," he told the Associated Press. "We will give them work according to their professions and trades, but first we must provide them with comfortable homes and feed them well." After a brief conference with Berkman, the Russians agreed to allow the party into the country. A few who could not walk across the ice were transported by sleigh.

"The deportees, laden with suitcases and boxes, trudged through the deep snow, laughing and singing revolutionary songs as they neared the border" to the tune of the Soviet national anthem played by a military band, reported the AP. Russians cheered the exiled Americans as they crossed the frozen Systerbak River; and when they reached the other side, they shared food and cigarettes. Goldman (as reported by the *Baltimore Sun*), declared, "This is the greatest day of my life. Once I found political freedom in America. Now, with the doors closed there, free-thinkers and enemies of capitalism find once more sanctuary in Russia. Send my greetings to the proletariat of America. Tell them to keep a stout heart, for the day of freedom is coming. I shall return to America someday—for I love America as no other land, but not the American Government. I shall return to American when it is once more a free land."

4

Setting Fire to Wisdom
and the Origin of Man

The Great War demolished the notion that America was immune to Europe's troubles. Instead, it left many Americans afraid—of foreign ideologies, domestic collaborators, homegrown violence, and newly emboldened blacks. And that fear led to repression. "Never before were the civil rights guaranteed by constitutional provision so generally ignored and violated," wrote Roger Baldwin and Albert DeSilver in the ACLU's first annual report.

Lucille Milner, an ACLU co-founder and long-serving executive secretary, remembered the era as one in which the "future of democracy, we thought, was at stake." The government had "turned wrathfully" on the IWW and other dissidents, "destroying their property and arresting them wholesale with or without warrants."[1] States were also adopting repressive tactics.

By the end of 1919, some twenty states had passed laws against "criminal syndicalism," making it illegal to belong to organizations deemed to promote revolution. In such an environment, juries "see red because . . . the very air they breathe is surcharged with the red hysteria," complained a contributor to the *Central Law Journal*.

Radicalism was not the only thing preoccupying Americans in early 1920. Thanks to the Eighteenth Amendment, the United States was on the verge of becoming officially dry. Many Americans were taking a break to mourn the death of John Barleycorn.

On January 19, the first workday of America's new sobriety, Roger Baldwin reported on outreach efforts to various states, and Albert DeSilver spoke of his work against a sedition bill pending in Congress. But the fledging ACLU was severely limited in what it could do. What it mostly could do was make noise—with publications, statements (about political prisoners, the free press, and sedition laws), and attention-grabbing stunts.

In March 1920, the ACLU and the Amalgamated Textile Workers took aim at a rule prohibiting public meetings without a permit in Passaic, New Jersey. The ACLU scheduled a public meeting without asking the public safety commissioner for permission. Harry Ward and the Reverend Norman Thomas were featured speakers. The owners of the hired hall, under police orders, refused to unlock the door. Having arranged for that possibility, they proceeded to another small hall nearly a mile away. There, Thomas took the stage and started reading the New Jersey State Constitution.

Detective captain Benjamin Turner ordered Thomas to stop. When Thomas ignored him, he ordered the lights extinguished. As the hall plunged into darkness, some people left. Holding a candle in one hand, Albert DeSilver took over the constitution reading. After he finished, Frank Laitovick, a Polish union representative, took the stage and began to read the constitution in Polish. After much commotion, the police allowed him to finish—as a bilingual officer monitored the situation to make sure Laitovick did not utter anything seditious.

Over the next several months, the ACLU participated in or facilitated several similar pranks. That May, ACLU members were arrested along with iron and steelworkers in Duquesne, Pennsylvania, after attempting to hold an open-air meeting. That October, the ACLU sent a three-person team to Mount Vernon, New York, to test a law that allowed the mayor to bar street-corner speakers.

A week and a half later, the ACLU sent another three-person team to Mount Vernon. At around 8:30 p.m. their car—which had been decorated with the American flag—stopped in front of a theater where a large crowd had assembled. Unitarian minister John Haynes Holmes stepped out and tried to read the U.S. Constitution, but police ordered him to move on. He circled the block—three times, according to the *New York Times*—and then "dashed up and down the street, followed by the police and 2,000 men and women." The police quickly caught up with Holmes and arrested him, along with Rose Schneiderman, president of the Women's Trade Union League of New York, and Norman Thomas.

The ACLU prevailed. Two days after the second arrests, the New York State Supreme Court declared the ordinance unconstitutional.

Looking back on the year, Baldwin and DeSilver singled out their free speech victories as hugely significant, noting that they had succeeded not only in eliminating the Mount Vernon law but in having similar measures struck down in Passaic and in the Connecticut towns of Waterbury, New London, Meriden, and Norwich.

While the ACLU was raising its profile fighting for free speech through political performance art, an epic battle was playing out in Washington between Attorney General Palmer and a most unlikely foe. Palmer, reveling in public acclaim, was gearing up to run for president. Louis Freeland Post, a bewhiskered, bespectacled seventy-year-old lawyer and assistant secretary of labor, was to become a major stumbling block.

Post had not set out to become Palmer's nemesis. But events had placed him in Palmer's path. Labor Secretary William Bauchop Wilson was ailing, and John William Abercrombie, acting secretary, had left to run (unsuccessfully) for Alabama's open Senate seat. Responsibility for signing off on deportations fell to the most senior Labor Department official around: Louis Freeland Post.

Post was okay with deporting Communists but was a stickler for due process, which Palmer's agents routinely violated. As author Stanley Coben notes, "By April 10, Post had decided 1,600 cases, canceling arrest warrants in 1,141 or 71 percent of them."[2] Post also denounced the attorney general's "drastic proceedings on flimsy proof to deport aliens who are not conspiring against our laws."

The press was vehemently critical of Post—as were congressmen from both major parties. The *San Francisco Chronicle* accused him of coddling radicals. Ohio Congressman Martin Davey suggested he was conspiring with "enemies of our Government." Congressman Homer Hoch of Kansas introduced a resolution ordering a House Judiciary Committee investigation. "A general feeling . . . has sprung up to the effect that the Assistant Secretary of Labor . . . is not in sympathy with the law," reported the *Washington Post*.

Post was flabbergasted by all the negative attention he attracted for "deporting only such aliens as were proved guilty and releasing the others."[3]

With the House investigation looming, Post was obliged to mount a defense, and he fretted about the potential cost. An unexpected benefactor emerged: E.T. Gundlach, a wealthy, Chicago-based, Harvard-educated advertising executive, was no radical, but he abhorred social injustice. Gundlach told Post, "in these circumstances, you will need money, need it bad. And I am here to tell you to draw on me . . . for ten thousand dollars.'"

Post, stunned at the gesture, accepted immediately. He retained Jackson H. Ralston, who had practiced before the Supreme Court and claimed the AFL as a client.

The Rules Committee hearings began on April 27, 1920. Albert Johnson, chairman of the House Committee on Immigration and Naturalization, presented a report that was essentially an indictment charging Post with pampering aliens who were "trying to overthrow" America.

Three days later, appearing before the Rules Committee, Post's attorney ridiculed the "confused mess which has been submitted here." The report, he added, contained "no straightforward, distinct charge of any wrongdoing on the part of Mr. Post."

When committee chairman Philip Campbell asked him to elaborate, Ralston charged government agents with acting as provocateurs. "I don't know why this Red agitation goes on," he said. "I don't know whose ambition is served by its being kept up, but [the] country has been terrified."

In many cases, he said, agents had forged "the alien's signature to the supposed examination—absolute forgery, straight out," said Ralston, who accused the attorney general of acting in "absolute ignorance of American principles or of the rights of . . . citizens."

A week later, Post spoke in his own defense. He accused Palmer's minions of targeting innocent people and coercing admissions of guilt. He also suggested the meager results—in terms of dangerous revolutionaries or wrongdoers caught—were not worth the monumental effort. In "all these sweeping raids over the country, in which men were arrested at midnight and taken out of their beds at 3 o'clock in the morning . . . there have been three pistols, I think it is, brought to our attention. . . . Three pistols, two of them .22 caliber."

Palmer appeared before the committee on the first day of June. He spent two days defending his tactics and attacking Post. He also delved into Post's past, suggesting Post was a radical who, along with his wife, had edited a "liberal" magazine some thirteen years previous, "when the anarchists of this country were especially active."

In responding to charges of wrongdoing by agents conducting raids, Palmer acknowledged he was not always aware of the details of their activities but expressed confidence in their work.

After Palmer's testimony, Chairman Philip Campbell announced that no formal action would be taken on the impeachment resolution, effectively ending the process.

The *New York Evening Post* applauded the decision: "The simple truth is that Louis F. Post deserves the gratitude of every American for his courageous and determined stand in behalf of our fundamental rights. It is too bad that in making this stand he found himself at cross-purposes with the Attorney General, but Mr. Palmer's complaint lies against the Constitution and not against Mr. Post."

The *Evening Post* did not point out that in the time between the proceedings beginning and end, some important events had taken place.

First, despite Palmer's prophecies of widespread anarchistic violence, May Day had passed without incident, even though New York put its eleven thousand policemen on emergency alert. "The revolution scheduled to come to America yesterday must have missed the boat," observed the *New York Tribune*, which put the "sum total" of the "Reds'" activities of the day at the arrest of one Mollie Steimer for violating the Espionage Act.

Second, Secretary of Labor William Wilson ruled on May 5—over Palmer's objections—that simply belonging to the Communist Party was not grounds for deportation, nullifying the rationale for most of the expulsions. Although Wilson saw Communists as radicals, he did not agree that they necessarily supported the violent overthrow of the government.

Third, on May 27, a highly respected group of lawyers distributed a paper denouncing Palmer's tactics. The group of twelve, which called itself the National Popular Government League, included the deans of Harvard, Washington University, and other leading law schools.

The "Twelve Lawyers' Report," as it came to be called, lashed out at the Justice Department for ongoing illegal acts and accused the Justice

Department of creating "a propaganda bureau . . . to excite public opinion against radicals, all at the expense of the government and outside the scope of the Attorney General's duties."

Post had no idea, when he took on Palmer, that the tide was turning or that some of society's most prominent thinkers would rally to his side. Nonetheless, he took his stand as a matter of principle.

After the impeachment effort collapsed, the American Legion made a formal request to President Wilson to dismiss Post. Instead, the White House released a letter from Labor Secretary William Wilson, which read, in part, "Louis F. Post is one of the truest Americans I have ever come in contact with. . . . He has no sympathy with an alien or American who believes in, advocates, or teaches the use of force to overthrow the Government of the United States. He has, however, a profound belief in and reverence for the Constitution of the United States."[4]

Post retired quietly in 1921.

Post's victory and associated events went a long way toward defanging the Deportation Act of 1918, but the Espionage Act—with its punishing wartime amendments—was still in force. As the ACLU pointed out in a letter to President Wilson, hundreds of people remained in prison because of it.

The letter was sent in response to a June 1920 interview with President Wilson by *New York World* reporter Louis Siebold, in which Wilson vigorously defended his wartime treatment of citizens and denied "any man has been punished for expressing his opinion."

The ACLU shot back that "established constitutional rights of American citizens have been violated by the wholesale during and since the war by the responsible officers of your administration." Six hundred citizens "whose only crime was the expression of the truth as they saw it" were still in prison or out pending appeal, pointed out the letter, signed by DeSilver and three ACLU national committee members.

It eventually came to light (well after Siebold won a Pulitzer Prize for the interview) that the article was largely a White House concoction orchestrated by Wilson's wife, Edith, at a time when the president was too ill to sit for a proper interview. The interview's publication was timed for maximum political impact: between the Republican Convention (which had nominated Warren G. Harding) and the Democratic convention. The idea was to pass off a seriously ill president (who thought he might yet garner a third term) as vibrant and vital.

President Wilson had collapsed from "nervous exhaustion" on September 26, 1919, in Wichita, Kansas, during the final stages of a whistle-stop train tour. He had scheduled speeches in over twenty midwestern and western states promoting the League of Nations and ratification of the Paris peace treaty. By the time the presidential train reached Wichita, he had already made forty speeches in seventeen states. A few days later, in Washington, Wilson had experienced a devastating stroke—one of several strokes he suffered that were kept secret—and vanished from view for months.

The Siebold interview gave Wilson another chance to roar on the international stage. And it provided the fledging ACLU with an opportunity to remind America that the fight for those jailed for speaking up was not yet won.

The ACLU co-sponsored four large rallies in New York on Labor Day in 1920 on behalf of "political prisoners." All were keynoted by William "Big Bill" Haywood, who remained under the shadow of a twenty-year sentence.

Later that month, in response to pressure from the ACLU and others, Attorney General Palmer hosted two separate delegations (representing labor and Socialists) requesting a general amnesty for "political prisoners." Palmer refused but pointed out that he had pursued no prosecutions under the Espionage Act since the armistice.

On December 9, the Seventh Circuit Court of Appeals upheld Haywood's conviction (and that of his ninety-three co-defendants) but gave him a stay to seek relief from the Supreme Court. The following April, the Supreme Court denied the appeal. Those who had not already served their time were ordered to report to Leavenworth penitentiary within three weeks. Shortly thereafter, the press reported that Haywood had fled to Russia.

On April 21, the ACLU confirmed that Haywood was "on his way to Moscow to attend the international conference of the Federation of Trade Unions." Haywood "intends to serve sentence immediately after the conference," added the ACLU statement.

In fact, Haywood was gone for good. As Lucille Milner explained many years later, Haywood "had been a person of indefatigable energy but he was old and tired and he was not well. . . . Given to understand there was little hope for a favorable decision on his case in the Supreme Court, he grasped at the suggestion that he go to Russia."[5]

Baldwin had much the same take. "One dose of prison was enough for him and he couldn't face going back if we lost the appeal. He's no Communist but Russia is a workers' country and he knows he'll be safe there," wrote Baldwin in a memo obtained by his biographer, Peggy Lamson.

Six years after Haywood left, the *New York Times* took note of his marriage, reporting, "His wife is described as a woman of 'about 37, of attractive and sympathetic personality,' while Haywood is 53. She speaks no English and he speaks no Russian." Two years later, Haywood was dead, never having returned.

The 1920 election gave new impetus to ACLU efforts to free America's remaining domestic prisoners of war. It also was the first election in which women across America could vote. The Nineteenth Amendment, forbidding states from denying women that right, was ratified that year. On August 18, the Tennessee House voted 49-47 in favor of the amendment, thus becoming the final vote needed for ratification. Passage added an estimated 12 million possible voters to the 15 million already empowered under various state laws. That news seemed to favor James Cox, the Democratic candidate, who supported the Treaty of Versailles and American membership in the League of Nations. After hearing of the Tennessee vote, Cox was ecstatic: "The mothers of America will stay the hand of war and repudiate those who trifle with a great principle," he predicted. In the end, however, the women's vote did not help him.

Warren Harding's theme—"return to normalcy"—played well with an American public weary of the social upheaval of war. Harding garnered 60 percent of the ballots and more than 16 million votes, winning by just over 7 million—the largest popular vote margin up to that point in history. In his first speech as president-elect—on November 4, in Marion, Ohio—Harding pronounced the League of Nations "now deceased."

Although his election signaled an end to Wilsonian ideals on foreign policy, it was unclear what it meant for America's political prisoners—the most prominent of whom was Eugene Debs. The Socialist candidate for president, Debs, had received nearly a million votes from his prison cell in Atlanta.

In January 1920, the *New York World* suggested that Wilson would commute Deb's sentence and release him on February 12, Abraham's Lincoln's birthday. Attorney General Palmer recommended that he do so, but Wilson rejected the advice.

Debs responded to Wilson's inaction with defiance. "I hope Mr. Wilson sleeps as easily and with as clear a conscience in the White House as I do in the penitentiary," said Debs.

The same day Wilson rejected Palmer's clemency recommendation, the Supreme Court set aside the conviction of former Wisconsin congressman Victor Berger. Like Debs, Berger had opposed the war. The federal indictment accused him and four other presumed Socialists of willingly causing "insubordination, disloyalty, and the refusal of duty." Their crime was distributing pamphlets with such titles as "Down with War" and "Why You Should Fight." Berger had been kicked out of Congress and sentenced, in February 1919, to twenty-two years in Leavenworth. His judge was Kenesaw Mountain Landis, who had also presided over the IWW trial. The Supreme Court threw out Berger's conviction after his lawyers impugned Landis's impartiality by highlighting his anti-German comments.

On March 1, three days before Wilson's term was to end, Congress repealed the war amendments used to imprison so many war critics. Three days later, Warren Harding was sworn in as the nation's twenty-ninth president.

Finally free to tell the truth about Wilson, the Associated Press reported that he left office "frail in health, with his body racked by 18 months of illness." While in office, reported the news service, Wilson had suffered thrombosis in a leg and was "practically sightless in one of his eyes." He could barely control his left arm and leg and had an array of other maladies that had been hidden from the public.

During the first several months of Harding's presidency, the ACLU and other advocates kept Debs's name before the new administration. Attorney General Harry Dougherty responded by inviting Debs to visit him that March. Debs left prison—in civilian garb and unescorted—for a two-and-a-half hour meeting with Dougherty in Washington.

Over the next several weeks, a seemingly unending succession of visitors came to Washington to speak on Debs's behalf. On April 13, Harding received a delegation that included Norman Thomas, Jackson Ralston, and other civil libertarians. They urged freedom not just for Debs but for all those imprisoned for opposing the war. Other delegations made the argument to Vice President Coolidge, House Speaker Frederick Gillett, and Attorney General Daugherty. As the delegations met with Washington's political leadership, a larger group, estimated at roughly 200 people, paraded down Pennsylvania Avenue with a petition urging amnesty.

The protestors were told that a general amnesty was not in the cards while the United States was still officially at war. But Attorney General Daugherty promised "that in the meantime I would carefully consider any individual cases presented to me and, where the record showed it to be one of merit, I would be inclined to be lenient in reaching a decision."

In commenting on what it called "Debs Day at Washington," the *New York Times* counseled against a general amnesty: "The proposal to turn lose on the community dangerous criminals, who did their worst to help Germany and clog the United States in the war, is almost fantastically preposterous."

Although freedom of political prisoners was the preeminent crusade of American civil libertarians of the day, they were forced to focus on the status of American blacks after Tulsa experienced one of the worst racial slaughters in American history.

The violence started on the evening of May 31, 1921, after rumors raced through Tulsa that a black delivery boy had assaulted a seventeen-year-old white elevator girl. "Nab Negro for Attacking Girl in Elevator" read a *Tulsa Tribune* headline.

Talk of lynching quickly took root. A mob gathered around the county courthouse where the black teen, Dick Rowland, was being held. The mob screamed for Rowland to be brought out. A small group of black men armed with guns went to the courthouse in hopes of protecting him.

Angry words were exchanged, shots were fired, and people lay dead in the street. The mob became an avenging army intent on destroying the Greenwood District, the most prosperous black community in America.

When the mob was done, a thirty-five-block area had been destroyed and some ten thousand blacks were homeless. The Red Cross, which conducted a major relief operation in the aftermath, estimated the death toll at perhaps three hundred.

Newspapers of the time attributed the outbreak to the usual suspects. "Negro Reds Started Riots," shouted the *Los Angeles Times*. The *San Francisco Chronicle* blamed "Bolshevik Propaganda." In a generally sympathetic commentary, the *Philadelphia Inquirer* pointed out that blacks "fought for their country, just as the whites did. . . . But it should not be forgotten that the strain of savagery in the race is not yet eliminated."

The black-owned *Philadelphia Tribune* had a different view: "Once again has the attention of the world . . . been called to the inhuman and brutal side of the American white man in his dealing with the colored people of this country."

Roger Baldwin took the occasion to make a broader point about racial violence and Southern economics. That July, the ACLU published a small pamphlet entitled "Lynching and Debt Slavery." The text was written by William Pickens, field secretary of the NAACP. Pickens argued that slavery had not ended with the Thirteenth Amendment, but that white Southerners instead concocted a system to keep blacks in economic bondage— and that mob violence erupted when whites suspected blacks were trying to escape that system.

Because whites were so intent on maintaining economic dominance, argued Pickens, "when race riots break out, the prosperous and well-to-do colored men who own business and property . . . are the ones most likely to be forced to leave the community." Pickens blamed that "evil system" for "all the massacres of Colored people and for nearly all the horrible lynchings and burnings of individuals that have lately taken place in this region."

Baldwin pointed to the mob violence in Tulsa—where economically successful blacks were, indeed, resented and ultimately driven out—as evidence of the truth of Pickens's observations.

In reissuing Pickens's NAACP report under the ACLU's imprimatur, Baldwin was not only giving that report new life; he was publicly working out his ideas of the class struggle he believed had the potential to reshape the nation. By attaching the ACLU's name to one of the biggest news stories of the summer, he also was providing the ACLU with yet another burst of attention.

Much of the public activity around Debs was generated by the ACLU, which that November allocated a $5,000 budget for a Washington office devoted to Debs and the issue of political prisoners. That office supported Bertha Hale White of the Debs amnesty committee. White appeared in Washington on November 9 bearing petitions for Debs's freedom. She announced that a delegation of war veterans—including congressional Medal of Honor winners—would follow in support of the campaign for general amnesty. Their arrival would coincide with the meetings of the international Conference on the Limitation of Armament.

The conference, which brought together the principle Allied powers and others to consider possible paths to disarmament and peace, opened Saturday morning, November 12. President Harding set the tone, declaring in the opening session that the United States was seeking a commitment to "less preparation for war and more enjoyment of fortunate peace." Secretary of State Charles Evans Hughes shocked the assembled diplomats by proposing cuts in the British, American, and Japanese fleets and suggesting that "for a period of not less than ten years there should be no further construction of capital ships." As Harding and Hughes spoke inside, women just outside Continental Hall held banners demanding the release of America's political prisoners.

That Monday, Harding formally proclaimed peace between Germany and the United States. In fact, he declared, the war had actually ended July 2, upon congressional approval and presidential acceptance of the joint peace resolution. The press speculated that Harding's announcement may have brought the president one step closer to granting amnesty for Debs.

The soldiers' delegation arrived on Tuesday. As the *Baltimore Sun* reported the morning's events, "at 10 o'clock sharp the amnesty picket line formed in front of Continental Memorial Hall. Two strong, husky ex-service men, Carl O. Parsons, of Minneapolis, commander of the World War Veterans, and 'Sailor Jim' White, of New York, known as the 'Hercules of the Navy,' led the procession, bearing two flags—one the American flag, and the other one declaring that, 'soldiers who fought the World War demand the release of the political prisoners.' They were followed by women carrying banners bearing various declarations."

Over the next weeks the ACLU and its allies kept the pressure on— periodically sending delegations to petition top administration officials. On December 19, Harding received yet another group of women seeking Debs's release.

On Christmas Day, 1921, President Harding commuted Deb's sentence. At the same time, he commuted the sentences of twenty-three other political prisoners and gave full pardons to five former soldiers who had been court-martialed for murdering a British officer.

That day, shortly before noon, Debs left the penitentiary. He raised his hat in one hand and his cane in the other as he waved at the men cheering him. He continued to wave, and they continued to cheer, until he reached the prison gates. After passing through, reported the *Atlanta Constitution*, Debs "gripped hands fervently and kissed the women and men alike who gathered to welcome him to liberty."

Debs announced that his first stop would be Washington, where he would "confer with Attorney General Daugherty, which was a condition of my release." After that, he said, "I am going to my dear little wife in Terre Haute as fast as the train will take me."

His wife was sorry he would not be home that Christmas Day, she confided to a United Press International reporter, but "what is a day or two more when I've waited for over two years." Meanwhile, she was slow-roasting a goose.

The government gave Debs money for a sleeping car, but he opted for a day coach. He would donate the cost difference, he said, to a Russian relief fund. He was donating the $5 in second-chance money received from the federal government to a defense fund for Nicola Sacco and Bartolomeo Vanzetti, anarchists accused of murder during an armed robbery.

Three days later, Debs returned to Terre Haute, Indiana, and was greeted with "red fire and blaring bands," reported the *New York Times*. "Fully 50,000 men, women, and children made a demonstration such as probably never hitherto greeted the return of a man from a Federal prison."

Admirers lifted Debs onto a truck, and a marching band—led by men carrying "Welcome home, Comrade Debs" streamers—serenaded the beloved felon with "Hail, Hail, the Gang's All Here."

"You have secured my liberation, but I am not free," Debs told his well-wishers. "My job was not completed because I was compelled to leave behind me in prison at Atlanta others . . . who are no more guilty than I was."

Some weeks later, Baldwin visited the Socialist hero at his home in Terre Haute. Although he had not previously met Debs, he had long admired him from afar. Debs picked Baldwin up at the train station and took him to breakfast. "What struck me most . . . was the intensity with which he concentrated on every person, every detail of our doings," said Baldwin.

Over breakfast, the men bonded over their common prison experiences. Baldwin shared a letter Emma Goldman had written him while he was in jail. After thoughtfully reading the letter, Debs said, "I admire her spirit, though you know I do not agree with her ideas."

After lunch, they walked to Debs's home, where Baldwin met his brother and wife and "sat down for a long chat over . . . issues of the day." Years later, reflecting on that visit, Baldwin wrote, "I had the sense of a red-letter day spent with a man of intense feeling both for people and a cause."

Over the next several months, Baldwin continued to argue against the Harding administration's policy of considering clemency for political prisoners on a case-by-case basis. Baldwin pointed out that the imprisoned IWW members "refused to make applications for clemency on the ground that their trials and sentences were unjust." He asked that Harding consider releasing them on the same "legal or moral grounds" as Debs.

Harding refused to relent. His intransigence precipitated a reversal in the union policy of expelling members who made individual clemency requests. As a result, IWW members applied for amnesty.

On June 20, 1923, Harding again took out his pardon pen. Harding commuted forty-four sentences, granted one full pardon, restored civil rights to twenty-seven former prisoners, and denied eighty-four petitions. Of the forty-eight petitions concerning crimes under the war statutes, Harding commuted twenty-seven convictions. These included all the remaining IWW members convicted in Chicago and three from Wichita.

A month and a half later, Harding was dead. On August 2, at approximately 7:30 p.m., as his wife read the newspaper to him in their room in San Francisco's Palace Hotel, Harding trembled and collapsed. He had been ailing the past week from complications attributed to poisoning from a tainted Alaskan crab.

The official statement read, "The president died instantaneously, and without warning. . . . Death was apparently due to some brain evolvement, probably apoplexy."

In the 1923 ACLU report, Baldwin observed that although Harding "had not seen fit to oppose the American Legion and reactionary officials . . . by releasing the political prisoners, President Coolidge at once showed a different attitude, and set about finding a method of releasing the prisoners which would have the least possible political come-back."

Cover was provided by an official report prepared by former Secretary of War Newton Baker, Bishop Charles Brent, and retired Army Major-General James G. Harbord. Baker and Brent recommended unconditional release, which Harbord opposed. The president accepted the majority recommendation.

On December 15, some four months after taking office, Coolidge unconditionally commuted the sentences of thirty-one persons still imprisoned for violating the so-called war laws. The one person he did not release was Mexican national Nicholas Zogg who was serving a ten-year sentence for taking an American to Mexico to evade the draft. Zogg had not been on the list of any of the groups advocating for amnesty.

Senator William Borah of Idaho released a statement pronouncing himself "delighted that a President of the United States has discovered the First Amendment to the Constitution and has had the courage to announce the discovery."

Baldwin was not at all sure that other government officials and jurists shared the president's insight. In a speech in March 1922 at Madison Avenue Temple in New York, Baldwin complained that the Supreme Court had "wiped out the Bill of Rights, free speech and a free press."

In the ACLU's 1922 report, Ward, Baldwin, and DeSilver pointed to a disturbing change in government's treatment of labor: "[We] have faced in the past year an unprecedented array of force through troops and constabularies, sweeping injunctions aimed at every means of expression, and a series of Supreme Court decisions which have seriously impaired the rights to organize, strike and picket."

The court decisions Baldwin found disturbing ran the gamut, including *Schenck v. United States* (in which the Supreme Court decided that the speech of anti-war activists could be restricted if their speech constituted a "clear and present danger"); *Abrams v. United States* (which upheld legislation criminalizing the distribution of leaflets denouncing American war efforts); and *American Steel v. Tri-City Trades Council* (where the court protected employers against picketers using threats, intimidation, or offensively aggressive argumentation to stop workers from entering the workplace).

Confronted with a hostile judiciary, an inward-looking conservative Congress, and a tentative president, Baldwin was not inclined to see government—including the courts—as the preeminent engine of progressive change. Baldwin instead favored direct action: pamphleting, speech-making, street theater, under-the-radar diplomacy, and tools of what is now called civil society. In the early 1920s he found a perfect collaborator and disciple in Charles Garland, a young Harvard dropout and heir to a small fortune.

Garland had created quite a stir when, in 1920, at the age of twenty-one, he and his wife announced that they had no intention of accepting a $1,000,000 inheritance from his father. "I would no more accept the inheritance of my father than you would stolen cattle. It is against the teachings of Christ and against my moral belief," he told reporters.

His wife, with whom he had an infant daughter, seemed perfectly aligned. "If my family in Dedham leaves me any money—they have plenty of it—I will turn it down myself," said his bride.

Garland, who had rowed for Harvard and considered himself a pacifist but not a Socialist, had settled with his wife and infant daughter on his mother's farm in Massachusetts. The *Nashville Tennessean* from June 1921 features a photograph of him atop a tractor: a handsome, dark-haired, slim, young man with a mustache. The caption reads: "No sports car for Charles Garland, Harvard graduate and farmer of Buzzards Bay Mass. No shoes. No fancy clothes. He prefers a tractor, corduroy and bare feet."

In 1922, the Associated Press reported that Garland and his wife were no longer together. He accepted his fortune and gave $200,000 of it to her. The rest, he would donate to a new charity, which Baldwin, apparently, had persuaded him to launch, and which Baldwin and his colleagues would control.

The American Fund for Public Service, as Garland's foundation was named, elected Norman Thomas as president, Roger Baldwin as secretary, and other ACLU people to key positions. In a statement, Garland said the funds would be used "to the benefit of mankind—to the benefit of poor as much as rich, of black as much as white, of foreigners as much as citizens, of so-called criminals as much as the uncondemned."

One of the first grants, announced in July 1922, went to striking mine workers in Pennsylvania. Money also went toward establishing a National Bail Fund for cases involving free speech and other civil liberties. "All applications for bail came to my desk. I examined them, secured the necessary guarantees against loss and with the Board's authorization recommended to the surety company the writing of the bail," recalled Lucille Milner.[6]

Over the years, money from Garland went to a variety of organizations and causes, including the AFL, the NAACP, and New York City's teachers' union. It helped fund the Vanguard Press and *New Masses* magazine and helped consolidate Baldwin's role as a person of influence in the larger progressive universe. In the end, Baldwin saw the money as a mixed blessing. "We yielded too often to friendship and passing pressures," he told Peggy Lamson.[7]

For Baldwin, the early 1920s was an exhilarating period—a period of intense activity and equally intense reflection. He had left prison with big ideas about the nature of societal change—ideas that drew inspiration from America's union movement and the Russian Revolution, ideas that screamed for action.

In addition to taking charge of the ACLU and the Garland inheritance, Baldwin started the Mutual Aid Society. There "was a good deal of pressure on me personally to help radicals who were in trouble. . . . So we formed a society based on [Peter] Kropotkin's [the Russian philosopher's] principle of mutual aid: 'from each according to his means, to each according to his need.' Each person who was capable put in whatever money he could and the people who were in need took out what they had to have."[8]

Baldwin also organized the International Committee for Political Prisoners—a response to the Palmer deportations. "Many times the husband would be deported, and not always to Russia either. They were sent to other countries . . . and the wives would be put in the position of . . . following them to a place where they didn't know the language," Baldwin told Lamson. Baldwin's committee raised money for them and put them in touch with foreign agencies that might help.

Both of those projects plunged Baldwin into issues central to the Russian "experiment." *Letters from Russian Prisons*, published in 1925, was a result of the International Committee's work. In his introduction to the book, a collection of writings by Russian political prisoners, Baldwin observed, "many of the members of the [International] Committee [for Political Prisoners] as individuals regard the Russian Revolution as the greatest and most daring experiment yet undertaken to recreate society in the interests of the producers and in terms of human values, however faulty its course may have been and however discouraging its many compromises."[9]

Baldwin later acknowledged his essay, which reflected his hopefulness that the Russian Revolution would eventually fulfill its promise, was "somewhat naïve."[10]

Despite his fascination with Russia, Baldwin rejected any suggestion that he was a Marxist. Indeed, when the *Chicago Daily Tribune* ran a three-part investigative series in 1924 naming the ACLU as a Communist front organization, the ACLU quickly demanded a retraction.

The *Tribune* series claimed that twelve "chief organizations" were "backing the pacifist move in American churches, colleges and public schools." It named the ACLU as first among them, adding that "its list of officials contains known Russian Communist agents and . . . is the guiding hand in spreading propaganda to other organizations."

The following month, the *Tribune* ran what Baldwin called a retraction. It was not a formal retraction—although the article merited one—but a story about the Bureau of Investigation (later renamed the FBI), which was the main source for the original *Tribune* story, and the bureau's request for additional funding.

The ACLU opposed the funding, which it charged was intended for a misinformation campaign of the sort that had produced the *Tribune* report. So the *Tribune* wrote about the ACLU's objection, as opposed to focusing on its own misleading reporting.

"Charges that the Bureau of Investigation of the Department of Justice has spread misleading propaganda concerning Communist activities in the United States, 'In order to maintain secret service men in their jobs and to get increased appropriations from Congress,' were contained today in a statement issued by the American Civil Liberties union," reported the *Tribune*.

The *Tribune* duly reported the portion of the ACLU statement that attacked its previous story: "'It was even stated, for instance, to a representative of The CHICAGO TRIBUNE that the American Civil Liberties union was part of the Communist movement and was subsidized by money received from Moscow through a New York lawyer. This TRIBUNE representative so reported in his articles on the Reds. Such a statement is wholly false.'"

Baldwin evidently saw the *Tribune's* decision to publish the statement without challenge or comment as the equivalent of a retraction.

The next year, 1925, saw the ACLU at the center of two hugely important court battles. The first was *Gitlow v. New York*.

On the evening of November 8, 1919, Benjamin Gitlow, a former Bronx assemblyman, had been arrested along with James "Big Jim" Larkin, former head of the Irish Transport Workers Union. Both were Communist Labor Party members. Their Communist affiliation made them a target of the Lusk Committee, an organ of the state legislature charged with investigating and countering radical activities, which had ordered a raid of the New York Communist Party's headquarters.

The raids ensnared hundreds of suspected radicals, including Gitlow and Larkin. Both were involved with a newspaper called *The Revolutionary Age*, which ran a "Left Wing Manifesto." That manifesto, in the eyes of authorities, advocated America's overthrow, which put Gitlow and Larkin on the wrong side of the law. As fate would have it, two days after their arrest, the Supreme Court (in *Abrams v. United States*) upheld the 1918 Amendments to the Espionage Act.

NCLB attorneys Walter Nelles and Charles Recht represented both men. Clarence Darrow, an internationally famed attorney and ACLU friend, joined the defense team for the trial.

Gitlow's trial (which was separate from Larkin's) began in late January, with Darrow arguing that the charges were invalid. Gitlow had not called for a violent revolution, he insisted, and his conviction would be a violation of his constitutional rights.

Justice Bartow Weeks instructed jurors that free speech was not at issue. The only question before them was whether Gitlow had supported the violent overthrow of the government. The jury took two and a half hours to find him guilty.

Larkin, who acted as his own lawyer, was tried two months later. His dramatic summation quoted presidents Lincoln, Washington, and Wilson; he spoke movingly of his dream of fostering the "brotherhood of man." The speech so touched those in the courtroom that "several women" sobbed, reported the *New York Tribune*. On April 27, hundreds awaited the verdict outside the courtroom. After the jury found Larkin guilty, "One young woman began to cry aloud," noted the *Tribune*.

Both men were sentenced to five to ten years. On July 12, 1922, the New York Court of Appeals affirmed the verdicts.

Several months later, in January 1923, Governor Al Smith pardoned Larkin, who by that point had been behind bars for more than two years. "There is no evidence that Larkin ever endeavored to incite any specific act of violence or lawlessness," said Smith. Smith was prepared to pardon Gitlow as well, but the ACLU asked him to put that plan on hold.

In a letter to John Hastings, a friendly state senator, Baldwin explained, "We do not want the Governor to act on his case at this time because it is important to get a decision from the Supreme Court on the constitutional question involved. Gitlow, who would prefer personally to withdraw his appeal and take a pardon, is willing to subordinate his personal interests to the larger issue involved."

Walter Nelles, joined by Walter Pollak, argued before the Supreme Court that the law was an unjustified restraint on speech and violated the Fourteenth Amendment right to due process. On June 8, 1925, the court ruled against them.

Writing for the 7–2 majority, Justice Edward Terry Sanford concluded that the criminal anarchy law was valid. Freedom of speech and the press, he wrote, was not an "absolute right." And "utterances inciting to the overthrow of government by unlawful means present a sufficient danger of substantive evil to bring their punishment within the range of legislative discretion."

In dissenting, Justices Oliver Wendell Holmes Jr. and Louis Brandeis referenced the *Schenck v U.S.* standard requiring a "clear and present danger" before the government clamped down on speech. "If the publication of this document had been made as an attempt to induce an uprising against government at once and not at some indefinite time in the future, it would have presented a different question," they wrote, pointing out that, in some sense, every "idea is an incitement. . . . Eloquence may set fire to reason." But words alone were not a fuse. The "only meaning of free speech" in a democracy is that even distasteful opinions "should be given their chance and have their way."

The ACLU worried that the decision might make it harder to fight sedition and criminal syndicalism laws. But the decision also moved the court to make an incredibly important point that was far from obvious: "Freedom of speech and of the press . . . are among the fundamental personal rights and 'liberties' protected by the due process clause of the Fourteenth Amendment from impairment by the States." Before that decision, the prevailing presumption (enunciated in the 1833 case *Barron v. Baltimore*) was that the Bill of Rights pertained only to the federal government. Gitlow changed that forever.

On December 11, Governor Al Smith gave Gitlow a full pardon and issued a statement: "Gitlow's record in prison . . . has been good . . . I am satisfied that the ends of justice have been met and no additional punishment would act as a deterrent to those who would preach an erroneous doctrine of government."

Gitlow had been ordered back to Sing Sing following the Supreme Court decision. In total, he had served thirty-four months. Upon receiving the pardon, Gitlow, "smiling broadly . . . boarded a train for New York alone," reported the *New York Tribune*.

Albert DeSilver, who had played a major role in the Gitlow case, did not live to see its end. He died on December 7, 1924. A product of Yale University and Harvard Law, DeSilver was not just a loyal lieutenant and forceful advocate, he was also the ACLU's largest individual donor and a true believer who had held things together when Baldwin was in jail. He died at age thirty-six on an express train from New York City to New Haven. While passing through Rye, New York, DeSilver had left his wife and son and headed for the smoking car, where he intended to read a book and smoke a cigar. As he was maneuvering between cars, the train hit a curve. DeSilver fell through a vestibule door and onto the track, fracturing his skull. More than $1,000 in bills fell from his pockets and scattered across the tracks. His colleagues and family said goodbye at a small ceremony in his Brooklyn home led by Norman Thomas. DeSilver's ashes were scattered over New York Harbor.

The ACLU's other big case that year was its defense of a high school science teacher.

In 1925, Tennessee passed a bill barring the teaching of evolution in public schools. The statute, known as the Butler Act (for John Washington Butler, the Democratic legislator who introduced it), prohibited "any of the universities, normals [or teaching-training colleges] and all other public schools of the state" from teaching "any theory that denies the story of the Divine creation" or asserts that "man has descended from a lower order of animals." Famed evangelist Billy Sunday had come to Memphis to support the measure, which passed 71 to 5 in the House and 24 to 6 in the Senate.

On signing the legislation, Governor Austin Peay pronounced evolution "at variance with man's creation as related in the Bible." The law was a "distinct protest against an irreligious tendency to exalt" such misguided science.

Baldwin routinely checked press reports for civil liberties violations. After reading about the new legislation, he sent press releases to Tennessee newspapers offering to defend any teacher who defied the law. Shortly thereafter, he got a call from George Rappleyea, PhD, manager of the Cumberland Coal and Iron Company in Dayton, Tennessee.

Rappleyea thought Dayton could benefit from the publicity of a big trial. He also had a personal motive. His pastor, H.G. Bird, had convinced Rappleyea there was no conflict between the Bible and science. The bill attacked the beliefs of a minister whom "I had learned to respect greatly," he told the press. A trial would be Bird's defense.

"Do you really mean what you offered in the papers?" Rappleyea asked Baldwin. "Would you furnish lawyers and costs if a teacher is willing to risk his job and livelihood? If [so], I have one, a young biology teacher in the high school here named Scopes."

"Of course we mean it," said Baldwin.

Baldwin heard that William Jennings Bryan—a former Democratic presidential candidate, former secretary of state, and devout proselytizer affectionately called "The Great Commoner"—was interested in defending the bill. Baldwin called the great man to confirm it, and Bryan replied that he was indeed interested, particularly if Clarence Darrow argued the other side.

Darrow, an ACLU stalwart, was America's most celebrated criminal defense attorney. He had participated in numerous famous and controversial cases, among them the successful defense of William "Big Bill" Haywood for supposedly ordering the bombing and assassination of former Idaho governor Frank Steunenberg.

Darrow immediately accepted. "I've always wanted to put Bryan in his place," he subsequently told Baldwin.

In addition to Darrow, the ACLU team included ACLU counsel Arthur Hays; Dudley Field Malone, a liberal attorney who had unsuccessfully run for governor of New York; and John Randolph Neal Jr., a former Tennessee state senator and former University of Tennessee Law professor, who served as chief counsel.

John Thomas Scopes was a twenty-four-year-old from Paducah, Kentucky, and a 1924 graduate of the University of Kentucky, where he had studied law and geology. Rhea County High School had hired him in 1924 to coach football and teach science. A slim, soft-spoken young man who wore glasses, he agreed over sodas in Robinson's Drugstore to be the sacrificial lamb. Rappleyea had invited two prosecutors (Wallace Haggard and Sue Hicks) to the drugstore meeting. They saw to it that Scopes was properly indicted.

Baldwin was ecstatic. "Had we sought to find a defendant to present the issue, we could not have improved upon" Scopes, said Baldwin. He was popular, athletic, literate in science, "clean-cut, typically American."

Scopes came to New York City in June for meetings with the ACLU. He candidly told the press he was quite prepared to lose: "It's pretty hard in Tennessee to find twelve men who wouldn't want to convict me."

Along with senior counsel John Neal, Scopes visited Henry Fairfield Osborn, president of the American Museum of Natural History. Osborn declined an invitation to be an expert witness but agreed to be on an advisory board. He confided that he was dedicating a new book to Scopes, lauding him as a "courageous teacher who . . . taught the truths of nature and the fact that these truths are consistent with the highest ideas of religion and conduct."

Osborn added—prophetically, as it would turn out—"Williams Jennings Bryan is the man on trial."

Scopes lunched at the Civic Club with several ACLU members, including Baldwin and Elizabeth Gurley Flynn. Some argued that Darrow's agnostic or atheist religious beliefs (they were not quite sure what he believed) could become an issue and counseled Scopes to select a more mainstream lawyer. But Scopes held out for Darrow, whom he felt was agnostic but also fair-minded. The next day's *New York Tribune* reported, "John T. Scopes, boyish science teacher from Dayton, Tenn., showed yesterday that he intends to command the legal fight . . . over evolution in the classroom."

Later that week, Scopes visited the Library of Congress in Washington, DC, where he gazed upon the U.S. Constitution. While there, he explained to reporters, "I was brought up in a religious atmosphere, to be exact, of the Presbyterian Church and, while I am not a member of any church, I have, and have always had, a deep religious feeling."

That same day, the AP reported that, according to an unnamed friend, Scopes had been offered a fortune for his story: "One motion-picture corporation offered Scopes $50,000 for the rights to the trial and for him to appear in a production. Other offers for rights to syndicates brought the sum beyond $150,000."

Scopes, reportedly, turned down the money.

For tiny Dayton, with a population of fewer than two thousand, the trial was a truly fantastical event. Bryan, who arrived Tuesday, July 7, 1925, was greeted with the awe due a Biblical prophet, and he responded in character.

At a dinner in his honor at in dining room of the Hotel Aqua, he called the contest between evolution and Christianity "a duel to the death," adding, "it has been in the past a death grapple in the dark. From this time on it will be a death grapple in the light."

The next day, defense attorney Dudley Field Malone redefined the battle. It was a struggle, he said, "between true religion and science on one side and Mr. Bryan and ignorance on the other. Nether religion nor science will be dead when this thing is over, but Mr. Bryan's influence as a teacher will be gone."

In the days leading up to trial, Scopes received a great deal of attention. The *Knoxville Journal* reported that he had recently taken up with a pretty employee of the W.A. Ault Department store, but "all the girls like him. He is big and blond and 24 years old. He has abandoned his horn-rimmed spectacles since his pictures began to flash into the first pages of the country."

For Arthur Hays, visiting Dayton was like visiting an alien planet. "Had anyone suggested that there were millions of people who believe it possible to build a theocracy in the United States under the leadership of Bryan, I should have thought the statement that of a madman—that is, before I went to Dayton," he said.

Journalists treated the affair like a huge festival. "Roman holiday at hand. . . . The day of days had arrived," gushed the *Knoxville Journal*, noting that townspeople had "thrown their homes open to visitors and here and there along the principal thoroughfares hot dog and soft drinks stands, religious literature and evolutionary tract stands were in operation."

The Memphis *Commercial Appeal* peered into the mind of presiding judge John T. Raulston, who, it reported, "sees the trial as an inquiry into the mysteries of God and he asks the help of a higher power in all his judicial acts."

On Friday, July 10, the *Chattanooga Daily Times* announced that "Dayton's big show has opened." What was ordinarily "a beautiful cool, green lawn" housing the courthouse had gained the trappings of an amusement park. "A regular hot dog stand of enormous size, and a barbeque pit are in evidence. Blind street singers and players each gather a knot of people, who stand around in a silent circle listening to the melodies."

Hays soaked in the atmosphere as he approached the courthouse on the opening day of the trial: "Our attention was first caught by a sign on the fence reading, 'Sweethearts, come to Jesus,' and conveying other advice of like kind. . . . At the entrance to the building was a large sign 'Read your Bible daily for one week.' I never passed that sign without mentally transposing the words, 'Read your Bible weakly for one day.'"

Spectators sat silent as Scopes, in rolled-up shirtsleeves, entered the court, but applauded fifteen minutes later as Bryan entered.

The Reverend L.M. Cartwright opened the session with a prayer praising God as "the source of our wisdom and of our power." Hays later observed that Cartwright's prayer was "not just an ordinary prayer, but an argumentative one, directed straight at the defense. We were told that 'every perfect gift comes from God, the Father of Lights.'"

A grand jury promptly re-indicted Scopes, to deal with possible technical issues around his original indictment, and the trial proceeded. The court quickly impaneled a jury comprised of twelve men—eleven of whom were religious fundamentalists. As the *New York Tribune* described them, "not one of the jurors is an educated man; none has read a book on evolution. . . . Eleven are farmers, the twelfth a shipping clerk."

Prior to opening arguments, Attorney General A.T. Stewart declared there was no need for scientists to testify since Scopes would "not deny that he taught students . . . that men descended from a lower order of animals. If that is true, he is guilty of violation of the law and all the evidence of scientists within his reach cannot save him."

In his own prepared statement, Darrow argued that Dayton seemed on the verge of blowing an opportunity to educate the world about both science and religion: "Men have debated a long time as to the meaning of much in the Bible and especially of the account of creation, and yet a Tennessee jury that has given no attention to evolution is supposed to know first, what evolution is, and secondly, what the Bible teaches with references to the creation and man and, third, whether these theories and the account in the Bible are in conflict. . . . The effort to keep the defense from offering evidence in this case is a plain effort to run away from the facts."

In its preview of the trial, the *New York Herald* concluded, "If Darrow wins [the argument over introduction of scientific evidence] . . . geologists from Harvard, biologists from Yale and theologians from Chicago will come to Dayton . . . to testify that one can be both a Christian and an evolutionist and that the natural theory of man's descent does not clash with the Mosaic record . . . [If] Bryan persuades Judge Raulston that evolution . . . is inimical to God's word . . . the trial will degenerate into an ordinary misdemeanor hearing."

That Monday, during arguments over an unsuccessful motion to quash Scopes's indictment, Darrow forcefully critiqued the law. The state, he argued, "has no more right to teach the Bible as a divine book than that the Koran is one, or the book of Mormon, the book of Confucius or Buddha." One shocked observer protested, "They ought to put him out." But Darrow pressed on. The Bible, he thundered, was "not a work on evolution . . . It is not a work on astronomy."

That Tuesday, as the AP reported that Tennessee biology textbooks would be delayed as publishers eliminated sections describing the descent of man, the courtroom battles continued.

Darrow accused Bryan of being a "religious bigot." And Hays objected to each court session opening with prayer. Hays's objection was overruled, but he won the concession that non-fundamentalist preachers would be permitted to lead the prayer.

That Friday, Judge Raulston sided with the prosecution, agreeing to exclude scientific testimony. Instead, said the judge, the defense could provide affidavits from the scientists, which would not be shared with the jury (but might presumably be read by an appeals court).

In that case, said Bryan, he would like to cross-examine the experts. Raulston agreed that he could, and Darrow exploded.

"I don't understand why every request of the state is granted and our merest suggestion overruled," he complained.

"I hope you do not mean to reflect on the court," said Judge Raulston.

"Well, Your Honor has the right to hope," Darrow shot back.

"I have a right to do something else," said the judge.

"All right. All right," muttered Darrow, igniting speculation that Raulston would cite him for contempt.

The heavily credentialed experts brought into town to testify were dismayed to learn they could not. Some left, but eight scientists and two clergymen settled down to the task Raulston had set them and produced a sixty-thousand-word document expressing their views.

To accommodate the huge crowd (the courtroom floor "sagged under the weight of sweating hundreds," observed the *Philadelphia Inquirer*), Judge Raulston held Monday's court session in the open air. The participants were on a high wooden platform next to the courthouse, shaded by two large maple trees.

Judge Raulston demanded that Darrow explain why he should not be cited for contempt and be required to post a $5,000 bond for his comments on Friday.

Darrow instead apologized: "I have been practicing law for forty-seven years and I have been pretty busy most of the time in court, and I have many a case where I have had to do what I have been doing here, fighting the public opinion of people in the community . . . and I have never yet [been criticized] for anything I have done in court . . . I certainly meant nothing against the State of Tennessee . . . I want to apologize to the Court for it."

The judge forgave him. "The man that . . . came into the world to save men from sin . . . taught that it was godly to forgive. . . . I believe in those principles. I accept Colonel Darrow's apology," he said.

Asked whether the defense had more evidence to present, Hays (without consulting with Darrow) piped up that they wished to call Bryan. "We . . . want to take Mr. Bryan's testimony for the purposes of our record even if Your Honor thinks it is not admissible in general," explained Hays.

Hays later admitted that he had no idea whether Darrow anticipated the gambit, but it seems to have caught him off-guard. Darrow turned to Malone, indicating that perhaps Malone should be the interlocutor. But Malone waved him away. Hays also declined.

Warming to the idea, Darrow suggested that he and Bryan cross-examine each other. Malone suggested Bryan was afraid. Supremely confident in his abilities, and over the loud objections of others at the prosecutors' table, Bryan agreed to be questioned provided he could examine the defense counsel in turn.

The judge said he would allow it, provided the jury was excluded. The testimony presumably would become part of the record that a higher court might eventually consider. As the lawyers and judge debated the rules of engagement, anticipation grew. Bryan had come to town promising a battle of mythical proportions, a "duel to the death," a "grapple in the light." And it looked as if the trial might finally deliver.

In reporting the episode, the *Commercial Appeal* spared no superlative. "Never before in the recorded history of world jurisprudence . . . has anything occurred that surpassed the proceedings here today. . . . There was pathos beyond the power of words to depict and humor that would have astounded Aristophanes. There was grandeur and Lilliputian buffoonery."

Bryan asked why Darrow was so hellbent on having him testify. Darrow replied, "I am examining you to show the world what it means for bigots and ignoramuses to control the educational system of Tennessee."

"I answer the questions of this agnostic in order to shut his mouth," roared Bryan. "I want the world to know I am not afraid to take the stand and defend the Bible against the attacks of the greatest atheist—agnostic—in the United States."

It immediately became clear that Darrow meant to do precisely what he had promised: to reveal Bryan as a man ignorant not only of science but of religion.

Looming over Bryan, he demanded to know whether the Bible was to be taken literally. Bryan responded that not everything could be. The phrase that man is "the salt of the earth" did not mean people were composed of salt.

"Do you believe that the whale swallowed Jonah?" asked Darrow.

Bryan replied that it was a "big fish," not a whale.

So did the big fish swallow Jonah?

"I believe in a God who can make a whale and can make a man and can make both do what He pleases," Bryan answered.

Was that fish "made specially to swallow a man or not?"

The Bible didn't say, responded Bryan.

"But you believe He made . . . such a fish . . . big enough to swallow Jonah?"

Stewart objected that the questions were argumentative. Darrow replied that the witness was at fault for arguing with him. The interrogation went on.

A question about Joshua making the sun stand still provoked another objection from Stewart. Bryan nonetheless tried to answer.

"I believe that the Bible is inspired, and whether the inspired author . . . understood the things he was writing about, I do not know."

"Do you think whoever inspired it believed that the sun went around the earth?" demanded Darrow.

"I believe it was inspired by the Almighty and he may have used language that could be understood at that time, instead of using language that could not be understood until Darrow was born," replied Bryan.

Asked again whether the earth would have stood still to lengthen the day, Bryan attempted to deflect. He noted that he could overcome gravity by lifting a glass of water. "If my puny hand can overcome the law of gravitation . . . I would not deny power to the hand of Almighty God that made the universe," he said.

But Darrow pressed on: "Can you answer my question directly? If the day was lengthened by stopping either the earth or the sun, it must have been the earth?"

"Well, I should say so."

Asked whether he believed God made the serpent go on its belly after he tempted Eve, Bryan said he did.

"Have you any idea how the snake went before that time?" asked Darrow.

"No, sir."

And so it went for nearly two hours, with Darrow hitting Bryan with one example after another in which a literal interpretation of the Bible defied scientific theory and facts. What would be the physical consequences of the world standing still? What was the date of Noah's flood? What happened to the fish? Were they on the ark too? And what about civilizations, such as China, that date their existence to a time before the flood? Was Eve really created from a rib? Where did Cain find his wife? Was the story of the tower of Babel literally true?

Asked about other religions, Bryan admitted he was not interested in what other religions had to say. Asked whether everything in the Bible was literally true, he replied, "I believe that everything in the Bible should be accepted as it is given there."

Darrow asked about the rainbow God had put in the heavens after the flood. Bryan, who was sweating, had had enough. He rose and faced the judge. "Your Honor, I think I can shorten this testimony. The only purpose Mr. Darrow has is to slur at the Bible. This man does not believe in God; this agnostic is trying to break down revealed religion, and to use the courts of Tennessee to make fools and idiots of Christian people—"

Darrow shot back, "I object to your statement. I am examining you on your fool ideas that no intelligent Christian on earth believes."

Judge Raulston adjourned the court and made it known that tomorrow's session would be held inside.

The *Philadelphia Inquirer* summed up the encounter with, "at the end the man who has loomed in leadership of American public life for nearly a third of a century was near hysterics. . . . Darrow, arch unbeliever, put the arch fundamentalist on the rock and tortured from him admissions that will be discussed over breakfast tables around the globe."

The *Boston Daily Globe* called the day's proceedings an "appalling and tragic thing," an ordeal "the Commoner stood . . . as long as he could."

The managing editor of Science Service Inc. had a distinctly different view. "Bryan's pitiful exhibition of ignorance under the skillful examination by Darrow was quite the most important evidence for the defense introduced today" and had "brought out the poor foundation upon which his campaign for fundamentalism is erected."

Judge Raulston announced the next day that he had made a mistake in allowing Darrow to question Jennings and ordered the testimony expunged.

On Tuesday, the jury took only nine minutes to find Scopes guilty. He was fined $100.

Judge Raulston invited Scopes, who had not been called during the trial, to speak.

"Your Honor, I feel that I have been convicted of violating an unjust statute," he said, and promised to "continue in the future as I have in the past to oppose this law in any way I can." Afterward, the students of Dayton High held a dance in Darrow's honor. "He attended, danced and even smoked cigarettes with them. They seemed to recognize that this was their battle," observed Hays.

After the trail, Scopes reportedly turned down thousands for lectures and movie appearances. His "only expressed wish was for educational opportunity," said Hays, and "through the efforts of the scientists at the trial, a fund was raised to provide him with a scholarship at the University of Chicago."

Bryan died on July 26, less than a week after the trial. "He died fighting for the Word of God, as he understood it," reported the *Atlanta Constitution*. "His last public pronouncements were declarations of faith in the 'Revealed Word of God,' faith in the hereafter, faith in the literal interpretation of the Bible. . . . There was none to see his passing as his soul was carried away."

He was still in Dayton when his chauffeur entered his room to awaken him from a nap. The examining physician concluded that Bryan had been dead for perhaps thirty to forty minutes. The official cause of death was apoplexy.

In 1927, Scope's conviction was set aside on the technicality that the judge, not the jury, had determined the fine. Forty years later, the Tennessee legislature repealed the law that had made teaching evolution a crime.

That decision was driven by the firing of another twenty-four-year-old science teacher, Gary Lindle Scott, who was dismissed for teaching evolution.

The American Civil Liberties Union and the National Education Association hired William Kunstler to defend him. Under legal pressure the school board reinstated Scott, who nonetheless filed to have the statute ruled unconstitutional. Faced with the prospect—and potential embarrassment—of another Scopes trial, the state legislature voted to repeal the law. On May 18, 1967, Governor Buford Ellington signed the bill.

5

Phony Rapes and a Righteous Purge

The Scopes trial—with its made for Hollywood moments and clash of titans—catapulted the ACLU onto the national stage, cementing its status as something infinitely more consequential than a group of guerilla theater activists enamored with the Bill of Rights. The irony is that, judged strictly on the judicial result, Scopes was a failure. It did not open schools to teaching about the theory of evolution. And although Scopes's conviction was reversed, that reversal "left no grounds for appeal to the U.S. Supreme Court, for which we had hoped," complained the ACLU in its annual review. But it burnished the ACLU's prestige and certified its growing influence. Like the Gitlow case, which the ACLU also lost, it was a failure that was also a triumph.

The year 1925 also brought Baldwin a new level of exposure. That August, *The American Mercury* treated the ACLU leader to a celebrity profile of over five thousand words. "Roger Baldwin's ancestry is of a sort to bring tears of envy to the ordinary Colonial Dame or Son of the American Revolution. Compared with the Baldwins, those austere creatures, the Lowells and the Cabots, are rank parvenus. It is not impossible that Roger's family comes direct from Balder, the son of Odin and Frigga, the god of Summer sunlight," wrote Robert L. Duffus.

Baldwin, as rendered by Duffus, is "an imagined portrait of the average American as he would have been if America had listened to Thoreau instead of Barnum. . . . He is the Puritan whose strain kept sound. He is the individualist who learned to respect individualism in others."

A feature by the *Boston Globe* that year hit many of the same notes, portraying Baldwin as a revolutionary, well-connected blue blood far afield from where he'd begun: "This was the Roger N. Baldwin of 1905: pleasure-loving in the good sense, good-looking, popular, musical. All the cards seemed to be stacked in his favor. All his friends supposed that he would graduate and step into a well-paid position which would enable him to marry some pretty girl of his own class and settle down on his lot to enjoy his wife, family and friends." Now, Baldwin's former classmates were wondering how it came about that Baldwin, "formerly of Wellesley Hills, gets six months in jail for holding an unlawful meeting during a silk workers' strike in Paterson, N.J."

The answer was simple: Baldwin was in Paterson doing what the ACLU had done from the beginning—engaging in civil disobedience on behalf of free speech. In this case, Baldwin was on the side of striking silk workers. On their behalf, Baldwin had convened a meeting in October 1924 without procuring a permit. Police chief John Tracey broke up that meeting. Undeterred, the group marched to the steps of City Hall, where they reconvened.

Again, the police intervened, pummeling protestors with batons. They also pulled down an American flag that two female demonstrators held aloft. Baldwin and nine others were charged with violating a 1798 statute against "assaults, batteries, false imprisonments, affrays, riots, unlawful assemblies, nuisances, cheats, deceits, and all other offenses of an indictable nature."

In a written statement Baldwin was not allowed to read at trial, he said the demonstration was aimed at ending "the intolerable police dictatorship over freedom of speech."

Baldwin had tried unsuccessfully to get a restraining order against the police, leaving him with no recourse, he said, "but to submit, or to protest by a meeting in a public place." The disorder, said Baldwin, "was caused solely by the police in violently dispersing a peaceful meeting held to protest against their high-handed abuse of power."

Judge Joseph Delaney was not persuaded. He dismissed the charges against two defendants and found the remaining eight guilty. Upon pronouncing sentence in April 1925, he explained that since Baldwin was "primarily at fault," he would be dealt with "more severely than . . . the others."

He sentenced Baldwin to six months behind bars and the other defendants to a fine of $50 each.

The day after the city hall arrests, the ACLU had announced another unsanctioned meeting and dared the police chief to interfere. Only two policemen showed up, and no one got arrested. "From that time on during the strike there was no police interference with freedom of speech and assemblage. . . . Our practical purpose was accomplished," declared an ACLU pamphlet issued after Baldwin's conviction.

As the ACLU flourished and Baldwin's fame spread, he became increasingly unhappy with his life. His marriage (negotiated as a partnership of liberated equals—marriage "on a 50/50 basis") had never lived up to the ideal.

"We had conflict from the start over our different ways of life," Baldwin recalled some years later. "Madeleine expected me to stay home evenings, while I was always going out to some meeting. . . . There was no question of our love and devotion, but our ways could not be reconciled, nor could she accept, despite her views on sexual freedom, my women friends, even my elderly aunt Ruth to whom I was devoted. . . . We did not talk of divorce; we talked of a trial separation."

Madeleine Doty had much the same recollection. Her uncompleted memoir quotes from a letter Baldwin sent her in July 1925: "You are unhappy with me most of the time, and I am unhappy with your unhappiness."

She was working in the New York branch of the Women's International League for Peace and Freedom and heard of an opening for the international secretary's position in Geneva. She applied and was immediately hired: "It was as though God had offered me a solution. . . . I hoped that after a year's separation Roger would be willing to give up some personal freedom for the sake of the home. And he hoped I would begin to take things more easily and not get upset."[1] She left that October.

In the year after Doty left New York, Baldwin fell into a slump. He tried to shake the blues by camping in a tent on the upper Hackensack River, seeing a psychiatrist, and traveling to California and St. Louis. Still, as Peggy Lamson describes it, he was enveloped by "a strange and . . . uncharacteristic lassitude" and felt both "restless and purposeless."[2]

He toyed with taking a sabbatical but worried about leaving the ACLU in the hands of associate director Forrest Bailey, DeSilver's replacement. A native of San Jose, California, and a former high school English teacher, Bailey had worked in Europe preparing naval officers to return to civilian life. Baldwin questioned Bailey's temperament, passion, and intellect, but ultimately decided that he had to leave. He set sail for Europe on Christmas Eve, 1926.

Madeleine joined him in Paris and the couple traveled together to Geneva, where she lived. Over the next several months, Baldwin and various companions meandered through Great Britain, the Netherlands, Czechoslovakia, Hungary, Italy, Bulgaria, Romania, and Turkey. His last major stop was Russia, where he spent three months researching his book *Liberty Under the Soviets*.

While Baldwin was in Europe, two cases closely watched by the ACLU made their way through the courts. One was about criminal syndicalism. The other centered on two Italian immigrants, Nicola Sacco and Bartolomeo Vanzetti.

Charlotte Anita Whitney, a California aristocrat born in 1867, was at the center of the syndicalism case. California's statute took effect in the spring of 1919. It was one of more than twenty such state laws that outlawed advocating sabotage or violence in the service of industrial or political change—or associating with those who did. The vagueness of the laws was intentional, providing prosecutors with a potent legal weapon that required neither evidence nor actual intent or harm. In the first year the law was in effect, California indicted more than one hundred individuals for violating it. Whitney was the most prominent.

After graduating from Wellesley, Whitney had moved to New York City to work in a settlement house. That job inspired her to dedicate her life to public service. She returned to the West Coast and became active in the suffrage movement. She also became a Socialist and, later, a Communist.

In 1919, when America was in the throes of the Red Scare, a roundup of suspected radicals eventually led authorities to Whitney. She was arrested that November 29 in Oakland, following a talk she had given on "The Negro Problem in America," and charged with violating five counts of the criminal syndicalism law.

Whitney was not accused of any specific treasonous act. Instead, she was connected, through innuendo, with dangerous attitudes and supposed Communist and IWW plots. The alleged draping of a red flag over a case containing an American flag was an important piece of evidence against her, as were sympathetic letters she had written to the IWW. On February 7, little more than a week into the trial, Whitney's principal attorney died. Prosecutors refused her request for a delay. They convicted Whitney on one of the five counts and sentenced her to one to fourteen years in prison at the state penitentiary in San Quentin.

"The only time when she lost her gentle composure, during all the strain and stress of her trial, was in an interview with an old suffragist associate, when she broke into sobs, declaring that the one thing she could not bear was that her friends should believe her disloyal to her country," observed Miriam Michelson, an author who had worked with Whitney for women's rights.

As Whitney's case shambled through the courts, the ACLU announced a campaign against criminal syndicalism laws. The ACLU, along with others, argued for a pardon—which California Governor Friend William Richardson opposed on principle. "Other violators of this law, who have lacked this influence, have been serving time in prison," he responded.

In 1925, the Supreme Court rejected Whitney's case because no constitutional issue was at stake. Whitney's attorneys countered that the law violated the Fourteenth Amendment, which led the court to take a second look.

In May 16, 1927, in a unanimous opinion written by Justice Edward Terry Sanford, the Supreme Court ruled against Whitney, arguing that the law did not discriminate because "it affects all alike, no matter what their business associations or callings, who come within its terms."

In a concurring opinion joined by Oliver Wendell Holmes, Louis Brandeis waxed poetic on the founders' hopes and the value of free speech: "Those who won our independence . . . valued liberty both as an end and as a means. . . . They believed that freedom to think as you will and to speak as you think are means indispensable to the discovery and spread of political truth. . . . Fear of serious injury cannot alone justify suppression of free speech and assembly. Men feared witches and burnt women. It is the function of speech to free men from the bondage of irrational fears. To justify suppression of free speech there must be reasonable ground to fear that serious evil will result if free speech is practiced. There must be reasonable ground to believe that the danger apprehended is imminent. There must be reasonable ground to believe that the evil to be prevented is a serious one."

Brandeis's opinion inevitably raised questions as to why he had voted against Whitney given that his sympathies seemed to place him on her side.

Her supporters accepted the loss and continued to fight for a pardon; and on June 21, 1927, California Governor Clement Calhoun Young granted their request, observing, "I do not believe that under ordinary circumstances this case would ever have been brought to trial. . . . I feel that the criminal syndicalism act was primarily intended to apply to organizations actually known as advocates of violence, terrorism or sabotage, rather than to such organizations as a Communist Labor Party."

While Baldwin was in Europe, the Sacco and Vanzetti case also came to a head. Nicola Sacco and Bartolomeo Vanzetti, both admitted anarchists, had been convicted of murders in which they claimed no involvement. Although the ACLU had no formal role in defending them, it championed their claims of innocence and rallied support to their cause.

Their saga began in 1920, with the killing of Frederick Parmenter and Alessandro Berardelli, the paymaster and bodyguard for the Slater and Morrill Shoe Company in South Braintree, Massachusetts. On the afternoon of April 15, Parmenter and Berardelli were carrying boxes containing $15,776.51 in company cash when they were killed by two pistol-packing assailants. As the victims lay dead or dying, a car pulled up and the killers jumped in, escaping with the cash.

Three weeks later, Vanzetti, a self-employed fish peddler, and Sacco, who worked in a shoe factory, were arrested and charged with the crimes. No physical evidence linked them to the scene, but they were Italian-born anarchists friendly with a man whose car, cops surmised, may have been used in the crime. They were indicted for murder that September.

On July 14, 1921, the jury found Sacco and Vanzetti each guilty of two counts of first-degree murder. Over the next several years, the conviction was upheld through numerous appeals—even though a man (Celistino Madeiros) who claimed to have been in the getaway car confessed in a 1925 note to Sacco that he and his associates were responsible for the crimes.

In an exhaustive review of the case published in the *Atlantic Monthly* in March 1927, Harvard professor and ACLU national committee member Felix Frankfurter argued that Sacco and Vanzetti were victims of prejudice run amok. Frankfurter (a future associate justice of the U.S. Supreme Court) accused the prosecutor of using tainted eyewitness testimony and of knowingly eliciting misleading statements from an expert witness. "By systematic exploitation of the defendants' alien blood, their imperfect knowledge of English, their unpopular social views, and their opposition to the war, the District Attorney invoked against them a riot of political passion and patriotic sentiment; and the trial judge connived," concluded Frankfurter.

In April 1927, following the denial of a new trial, the two men came before Superior Court Judge Webster Thayer for sentencing. Thayer told the men the proceeding "has absolutely nothing to do with the question of guilt. . . . There is only one thing the court can do—to pronounce sentence." Thayer gave them the opportunity to speak, which they did—emotionally, accusingly—for roughly three-quarters of an hour.

"I never knew or heard or read in history of anything so cruel as this court," said Sacco. "I am here today because I am of the oppressed class. . . . After seven years and despite my poor wife and family, you sentence me to death. . . . I have never been guilty, not today, or ever."

Vanzetti spoke even more fervently: "In all my life, I did never steal, kill or spill blood. . . . I can live by these two arms and live well . . . What we have suffered for seven years, no human tongue can tell. . . . You know in your heart that you have been against us from the beginning. You knew we were radical underdogs and we were against the institutions. We know you have spoken of your despisement of us with your friends in Boston and at the golf club in Worcester."

He accused the judge of doing all in his power to "agitate . . . the passion of the juror, the prejudice of the juror, against us. . . . I have suffered more for my family and for my beloved than for myself, but . . . if you could execute me two times, and if I could be reborn two other times, I would live again to do what I have done already."

Thayer sentenced both to die in the electric chair.

The condemned men's defenders mobilized to save them, with massive demonstrations in America and around the world. The ACLU won assurances from the Department of Labor that immigrants would not be deported for participating in the protests. There were bombings—in New York, Philadelphia, Baltimore, and Buenos Aires—and countless appeals for clemency. Albert Einstein signed a letter to President Calvin Coolidge requesting the prisoners' "liberation."

On August 3, Governor Fuller rejected calls for clemency, saying he believed the men were guilty.

On August 19, the Supreme Court of Massachusetts dismissed the final petition for a new trial, and the federal courts declined to intervene. Four days later, just after midnight, they were delivered to the execution chamber at State Prison in Charlestown, Massachusetts. Celistino Madeiros, who had confessed to involvement in the killings in hopes of saving Sacco and Vanzetti, accompanied them. Though Madeiros's confession was never seriously considered, he had been convicted of another murder. He was executed first. Sacco followed. "Long live anarchy," he shouted in Italian. Moments before the electricity sizzled, he murmured, "Farewell, mother." Vanzetti shook hands with the warden before walking to the chair. Once seated, he spoke: "I never committed any crime, but sometimes some sin." He thanked the warden for his kindness and then delivered his benediction: "I wish to forgive some people for what they are now doing to me." Moments later he was dead.

The executions set off protests across much of Europe, Latin America, and the United States.

Baldwin had maintained a warm and supportive correspondence with both men during their seven-year ordeal and had frequently visited them in prison. He recalled Vanzetti as something of a philosopher who "sent me pages of translation of the French anarchist Proudhon in usable English." After the execution, he became trustee for French funds given for Sacco's children's education. He was in Moscow when they were executed, but "received from each man a letter of farewell written just after all hope of commutation had gone."

In early November, Baldwin, then in Paris, learned that the New Jersey Supreme Court had upheld his conviction for unlawful assembly in Paterson. He pronounced himself ready to go to jail whenever ordered to do so.

In May 1928, a few months after Baldwin returned to New York, the New Jersey Court of Errors and Appeals set aside the Paterson convictions, having concluded that the defendants were lawfully exercising their right to protest and had "no intention of disturbing the public peace."

Even before the courts relieved him of the imminent burden of jail time, Baldwin's focus had shifted away from Paterson and toward the lessons of Russia. In October 1927, while still in Paris, he praised Russia to reporters as a place where citizens enjoyed more liberty than ever before. Baldwin was eager to spread that message at home.

During a speech in January 1928, Baldwin attacked fascism in Italy and dictatorships in Poland, Spain, and Turkey; but he spoke warmly of the Soviet Union, where he said he had found a "youthful" spirit and a government-friendly press. Later that month, during a talk before the Labor Institute Forum in Philadelphia, Baldwin again sharply criticized Mussolini's Italy and pointed to communism as an alternative.

That February, at the Hippodrome Theater in Baltimore, Baldwin praised Europe's relative lack of racism and Russia's treatment of workers and peasants.

In *Liberty Under the Soviets*, Baldwin defended and expanded on such points, noting that "Communists everywhere see Soviet Russia as the greatest hope for the freedom of the masses." He defended the book's title with praise for "the basic economic freedom of workers and peasants and the abolition of privileged classes based on wealth" and for "the new freedom of women, the revolution in education—and, if one count it as significant, liberty for religion—and anti-religion."[3]

He concluded, "The fairest test by which to judge the Soviet experiment in relation to 'liberty' is not by Western standards of political or civil liberties, but by the effects of the dictatorship's controls and repression on its own avowed object of creating a 'free and classless society.'"

Reviewers noted the seeming contradictions in his viewpoint. As a reviewer in *The Bookman* put it, "Mr. Baldwin, whose fight for civil liberties in his own country has made him a national figure, relapses into apologies when it comes to the dictatorship of the proletariat."

Joseph Shalom Shubow, writing in the *Jewish Advocate*, observed, "the author urges upon us the thought that compared with Czarism, Bolshevism allows much more political freedom. It is as if one were to say: compared with death a life of torture, though admittedly bad, still shows some life and so is good."

Even as Baldwin struggled to reconcile his belief in civil liberties with his admiration of Soviet Communism, the Communist movement at home presented challenges. Indeed, a Communist-led textile mill strike in 1929 led to a major rupture between the party and the ACLU.

North Carolina was the capital of America's textile industry, and Gaston County—with an estimated one hundred cotton mills—was its hub. The Loray Mill of the Manville-Jenckes Company in Gastonia, some twenty-three miles west of Charlotte, was the largest plant in the state.

Company officials had fired and ejected from company housing some sixty workers who had joined the union. When a thousand workers gathered on March 30 for their first open-air union meeting, they authorized the National Textile Workers Union to proceed with strike preparations. The *Daily Worker*, the Communist-affiliated daily that closely followed the dispute, saw the conflict as a potential milestone: "the first open struggle of enslaved mill workers under real union leadership."

The workers in Gastonia were not just angry at the company's attempt to break the union, but at low wages, long hours, and a new so-called "stretch-out" efficiency system that seemed nothing more than a way to make them work harder and faster with no increase in pay. They were also upset about company housing: a complex of vermin-ridden hovels, with no sidewalks, no baths, and paperboard walls. The leaders, Fred Beal and Ellen Dawson, both Communists, were veterans of the months-long and bitterly fought New Bedford, Massachusetts, textile strike of 1928.

On April 2, workers demanded immediate recognition for their local of the National Textile Workers Union, as some 2,500 employees went out on strike. The next day, police tried to rope off picketing strikers. Workers responded by wrestling the ropes from the police. Governor Oliver Max Gardner mobilized five companies of national guardsmen. Department of Labor conciliator Charles Wood arrived shortly thereafter and promptly denounced the strike leaders as Communists intent on fomenting a "form of revolution." Workers across the region joined the strike in droves.

The *Baltimore Sun*, one of the few mainstream newspapers sympathetic to the strikers, accused the Labor Department's Wood of "trying to obscure the real issue of long hours and low wages by raising a scare about Communism." Correspondent M. Farmer Murphy argued that the strikers were not radicals, but were "composed of that old American stock which fears and dislikes 'foreigners.'" But they had been so mistreated that they overcame "their instinctive distrust" and joined the union. He cited examples that he claimed to have verified of the pay workers had been forced to accept: $24.05 for a fifty-five-hour workweek, $13.75 for a thirty-eight-hour week.

On the morning of April 18, a mob of masked men packing sledgehammers and crowbars raided the local union headquarters and relief office. Meanwhile, Gastonia police officers and deputy sheriffs, wielding bayonets and batons, clubbed strikers they claimed were parading illegally, injuring a female reporter for the *Charlotte Observer.*

On the night of June 7, prompted by a supposed tip that workers intended to shut down the Loray Mill, police confronted strikers at the tent city they had organized after being kicked out of company housing. Guns were fired. Police chief Orville Aderholt was wounded—as were three of his men and a union organizer.

Aderholt died at 10:20 the next morning. The city council ordered the tent city destroyed. Strike leader Beal was arrested for inciting the workers to murder, although he had not been at the scene.

The *Gastonia Gazette* screamed for blood. The "electric chair should claim every one of the number who participated in the shooting," editorialized the paper.

On October 21, after deliberating for slightly less than an hour, the jury convicted Fred Beal and six co-defendants of second-degree murder. International Labor Defense (ILD), the newly organized legal arm of the Communist Party which had represented the defendants, issued a statement on their behalf: "only by appealing to the prejudice, religious, racial, and political, of the jury were the mill owner's lawyers able to obtain a conviction." Roger Baldwin called the verdict "amazing and unjust" and accused the judge of "transforming a murder trial into one for heresy." Using funds from the Garland inheritance, the ACLU put up bail as the convicted men appealed.

For several months, at least three of the men were missing. In August 1930, the *New York Times* reported that Beal and perhaps two others had fled to either Germany or Russia. The ILD refused to produce any of the defendants unless all were found.

America was in the grip of the Great Depression, and the ACLU stood to lose tens of thousands of dollars committed to bail-jumping strikers.

Worse, the men's flight was an embarrassment to the ACLU, which had guaranteed they would appear in court.

That imbroglio led to the exchange of several testy letters between Baldwin and John Louis Engdahl, national secretary of the ILD. Engdahl accused Baldwin of making the "reactionary and absurd" demand that he "obtain from the Soviet government an agreement that refugees from American boss class justice" be refused admission to Russia.

Baldwin rejected that characterization, saying all he was requesting was that the ILD and the party condemn bail-jumping. In the end, Communist Party official William Z. Foster resigned from the ACLU's National Committee. The ACLU adopted a new policy regarding its Communist friends, which Baldwin spelled out in a memo in October 1930: "In view of the forfeiture of bail in the Gastonia, N.C., cases and in the case against Fred E. Beal in Michigan due to bail-jumping [the ACLU] hereby resolves to discontinue writing and recommending the writing of all bail for members of the Communist Party."

His Communist conundrums and confusions notwithstanding, Baldwin had shaken his pre-sabbatical slump. He was both professionally renewed and institutionally ambitious. In a memorandum to the ACLU national committee on Valentine's Day 1929, Baldwin outlined his ideas for expansion.

Traditionally, the ACLU's mission had "been to protect the civil liberties described as 'freedom of speech, press and assemblage,'" he wrote in a memo to his national committee. Occasionally, the ACLU had also fought for the right to be free from "unreasonable searches and seizures," he added, but the constitution covered plenty of other rights that should probably be under the ACLU umbrella, and whose defense would help the organization build "a far larger and more effective constituency." It was time, he suggested, for the ACLU to become a less New York–centric, truly national organization with more local chapters and more sweeping ambitions.

The future ACLU, he wrote, should work more emphatically for "Negroes in their fight for civil rights," for immigrants facing discrimination, for criminal defendants facing police abuse or infringement on their constitutional rights, and for the rights of American Indians. It should fight against unlawful searches and seizures, censorship, compulsive military training, and all discrimination based on race, religion, or political views. And it should oppose American imperialism—or, as Baldwin put it, "control of weaker nations by the United States."

The proposal provoked an animated response among committee members. John Nevin Sayre, an Episcopal minister active in the Fellowship of Reconciliation, doubted the ACLU's capacity to take on American imperialism. And Harvard professor Felix Frankfurter was leery of expansion altogether, saying, "the resources with which our purposes have been pursued are piteously meager." Norman Thomas, on the other hand, was eager to discuss "how to work it out."

In the end, and over the decades, Baldwin's vision largely prevailed. In part that was because, as author Samuel Walker observed, the ACLU was "remarkably undemocratic." Other than Frankfurter, few members of the national committee were actively engaged in its day-to-day activities, leaving an essentially autocratic Baldwin to do as he pleased.[4]

But Baldwin also prevailed because the ACLU had outgrown its role as an organization of free speech pranksters baiting officials into sometimes hilarious displays of intolerance. As the ACLU wrestled with its core mission of defending civil liberties, it became clear that mission creep was inevitable and that the ACLU inevitably would be drawn into areas that Baldwin had not even thought to put on his list. The ACLU also grappled with the need to change its structure. It was then a voluntary association. Donors interested in tax deductions would be more inclined to give to a nonprofit corporation.

In March 1929, Forrest Bailey shared with general counsel Morris Ernst what he called "another bequest problem." Two elderly Philadelphia women were eager to give $30,000 to be divided among the ACLU, NAACP, and ILD. The ladies had confided that "in the absence of incorporation there would be difficulties."

The ACLU incorporated and scheduled its first annual board meeting for June. Active members of the National Committee would become members of the board, which would be required to consult the National Committee on all matters of general policy.

The institutional transformation coincided with the ACLU engagement in an area—freedom of sexual expression—missing from Baldwin's list. Not that Baldwin had ever shied away from sexual and reproductive issues.

He had a long and warm relationship with pioneering birth control advocate Margaret Sanger, whom he credited for his first serious burst of free speech activism. In 1912, after police shut down a Sanger lecture in St. Louis, Baldwin convinced her to take her speech outside to the steps of the lecture hall. Baldwin later recalled that act of public disobedience as his "first free speech meeting."[5]

The ACLU also had spoken in defense of Carlo Tresca, convicted in 1923 of mailing obscene materials. Tresca had published an advertisement for a birth control pamphlet in his newspaper, *Il Martello*; but he claimed to have been unaware the ad was in his newspaper. The ACLU successfully appealed to Calvin Coolidge for a presidential commutation, which cut two-thirds of the time off the year-and-a-day sentence Tresca began serving in January 1925.

The most recent sexual expression case came courtesy of Mary Ware Dennett, who had authored a pamphlet titled *The Sex Side of Life*. A native of Worcester, Massachusetts, and a graduate of Boston's School of the Museum of Fine Arts, Dennett was a prominent anti-war activist, feminist, and birth control advocate. Her pamphlet grew out of her desire to sexually enlighten her two adolescent sons. "[After] reading sixty or so pamphlets . . . and finding them deficient," she wrote her own. She shared it with other parents "until it was literally in tatters," she testified during her trial. The *Medical Review of Reviews* published it in its February 1918 edition. Dennett reprinted the article as a pamphlet, which she sold for 25 cents apiece.

The pamphlet begins with the observation, "When boys and girls get into their 'teens,' a side of them begins to wake up. . . . That is the sex side of them. It is the most wonderful and interesting part of growing up."

The booklet explores the process of reproduction in organisms ranging from amoebae to human beings, extols the beauty of committed love, and features one (notably non-erotic) drawing apiece of nude male and female torsos. It also warns readers not to "stimulate your sex organs into action *intentionally* [emphasis in original]."

The postal service targeted Dennett, ordering her pamphlet for a nonexistent person at a fictitious address in Grottoes, Virginia. On April 23, 1929, Dennett was found guilty of sending the pamphlet through the mail.

She "seemed stunned" when the verdict was read: "Clubwomen and social workers who had filled the courtroom to overflowing rushed up to Mrs. Dennett, who is a silver-haired grandmother, and assured her of their sympathy and support," reported the *New York Herald Tribune.*

Five days after she was found guilty, Baldwin announced that the ACLU was organizing a defense committee. Members would be asked to sign a copy of her pamphlet which they would send through the mail to President Hoover. The next morning, Judge Warren Burrows sentenced Dennett to a $300 fine. The *New York Herald Tribune* reported that orders for *The Sex Side of Life* were "pouring in to Mrs. Dennett from all parts of the country."

The National Defense Committee created by the ACLU was not the only group formed to fight for Dennett. Some thirty-two clergymen, calling themselves the Conference of Younger Churchmen, released a statement asserting that "the moral education demanded of the churches will be seriously retarded" by Dennett's conviction.

Dennett announced that she would go to jail rather than pay the fine. That proved unnecessary. On March 3, 1930, the U.S. Court of Appeals unanimously exonerated Dennett. The opinion by Justice Augustus Hand declared, "The statute . . . was never thought to bar from mails everything which might stimulate sexual impulses." Hand lauded Dennett for her "sincerity of feeling" and her "idealization" of marriage and "sex emotion."

The victory caught the Mary Ware Dennett Defense Committee by surprise, as the committee was already raising funds to go to the Supreme Court. The committee donated the $1,265 surplus to the ACLU "to be administered in its discretion as a fund to resist censorship tending to limit freedom of sex education."

Between Baldwin's arrival from Europe and Dennett winning her case, America's economy had taken an unexpected turn. When accepting the Republican nomination for president in August 1928, Commerce Secretary Herbert Hoover had declared, "we in America today are nearer to the final triumph over poverty than ever before in the history of this land." A year later, a catastrophic worldwide economic depression hit.

Initially, most experts thought it was nothing more than a temporary decline. Indeed, when markets rallied in November, a *New York Times* headline declared, "Stock Market Crisis Appears to be Ended." Just after

Christmas, President Hoover pointed out that Christmas shopping was on pace with the previous year. A year later, such optimism had evaporated. A "spirit of absolute hopelessness began to prevail," observed *New York Times* financial editor Alexander Dana Noyes.

Congressman Hamilton Fish Jr. decided, during that already highly anxious time, to wage war on the Communist menace. He introduced a House resolution proposing creation of what became the Special Committee to Investigate Communist Activities in the United States. In a series of hearings in late 1930, Chairman Fish and his fellow committee members repeatedly linked the ACLU to the Communist conspiracy.

In a hearing in Chattanooga that November, the committee turned the questioning of John Randolph Neal, a pro bono lawyer for the striking workers in Gastonia, into an inquiry about Communist influence on the labor movement and the ACLU.

In response to Chairman Fish's observation that the Trade Union Unity League was "organized by Communists and founded as a Communist revolutionary union," Neal replied that "practically all of those workers that participated in that strike," including those on trial, "told me personally that they were not Communists and did not share Communist views and were simply struggling . . . against the introduction of what is called the stretch-out system in that particular mill."

Neal also made clear that he was not hired by Communists; and he acknowledged being dismayed at the ACLU's deference to the ILD: "I was actually there at the request [of] and representing, you might say, the American Civil Liberties Union" but was "notified that I must be the lawyer of the International Labor Defense—an organization of which I had never heard."

Neal wired the ACLU demanding an explanation: "They then wired me [that] the International Labor Defense had insisted . . . that they must be held out to the world as conducting the defense of these prisoners, these defendants, down there."

At that point, Neal faced an agonizing decision: "Here I was, the lawyer representing ten defendants on trial for murder in the first degree, which is mandatory electrocution in North Carolina; and it was a question of possibly severing my connection with the cases that might harm the defendants, or the choice of staying by the lawsuit and trying to get [justice] to sixteen human beings. . . . I chose to remain in the lawsuit and chose to continue to defend those sixteen human beings, held out to the world as a lawyer for the International Labor Defense."

He added, "I always resented the situation that the American Civil Liberties Union and the Garland Fund put the lawyers in in connection with the defense, by practically financing the case but allowing the International Labor Defense to hold themselves out as financing it."

Baldwin appeared—"under protest," as he put it—as a reluctant witness before Fish's committee that December. It was the final day of a series of hearings that had featured several people accusing the ACLU of complicity in America's planned destruction. Prominent among them was the Reverend Father Edmund Walsh, president of Georgetown University. Walsh accused the ACLU of various sins, including working to "enable the communists to have an easier time in the civil war they hope to bring about."

In a prepared statement, Baldwin denounced the committee on the ACLU's behalf. "We see no occasion for its formation, for its expense, nor . . . for its stirring up the prejudices and passions which have inevitably accompanied the publicity attending your inquiry," he told Fish. He denied the ACLU was conspiring in any Communist plot, or that communism represented a serious threat. The committee would be better served, he lectured, investigating "those conditions which bring about protests and demands for change in our economic and political life."

Fish read a report from New York State's Lusk Committee (a body charged with investigating sedition) pronouncing the ACLU "a supporter of all subversive movements." Baldwin shot back, "That report was likely to say anything." The author's "conception of patriotism and mine differ very markedly," he explained.

In the annual report for 1931, Baldwin observed that however "ridiculous" the Fish committee's work "seemed to intelligent people, it was taken seriously by police and prosecutors all over the country. . . . While the Committee's recommendations for dealing with Communists have no chance of adoption, still its effect in stirring up prejudice, breaking up meetings, and causing arrests, was tremendous."

In 1931, with the release of its *Black Justice* report, the ACLU stepped into another contentious area. The ACLU called the study the "only survey of all discrimination against citizens on account of color." The report's conclusion was emblazoned on the cover: "Of all minorities in the United States, the 15,000,000 Negroes suffer most violations of their civil rights."

The slender pamphlet explored the contradiction between the promises of the American Constitution and the "galling limitations put upon" black Americans. It criticized laws and policies barring blacks from enjoying a decent education, a fair wage, trial by their peers, the right to vote, and the right to marry outside the race—pointing out the "incongruity of the two phrases: 'All men are created equal' and 'it shall be unlawful for any white person to intermarry with any Negro.'"

The report was astonishingly blunt for the era and a clear reflection of Baldwin's intent to expand the ACLU's agenda—as was the ACLU's deep involvement in one of the most explosive racial dramas of the day.

That drama revolved around nine black youths charged with raping two white girls on a freight train in Alabama. The youths came to be known as the Scottsboro Boys, and the case became a window into the South's unremittingly brutal system of justice, in which blacks had no rights that whites were bound to respect. Their treatment shocked much of the world—though the abuses and attitudes laid bare were normal practice for the South.

As *Baltimore Afro-American* correspondent Paul Peters summed it up in 1932: "At first the South looked upon Scottsboro as just another 'Negro rape' case. This one was slightly more thrilling than most, because here were nine victims [referring to the accused boys] instead of one, and all of them younger than usual. They called the boys 'black fiends' and 'Negro brutes' and clamored for 'quick justice'—meaning wholesale slaughter."

But as the world focused "upon that one little self-satisfied town in Alabama," people "began to read the court records, to gather information, to ask embarrassing questions. 'This isn't a trial,' they cried. 'This is a lynching. This is murder!'"

The South, added Peters, "did not like this. Nobody before had dared tell them 'how to treat our niggers?' Nobody before had dared to question the verdicts of their courts. It was a new and terrible thing for the South to be caught red-handed before the whole world like this: to find itself fought tooth and nail by a powerful, organized movement of colored as well as white. Who ever before had dared to stand up in the South for poor, unknown, uneducated colored boys?"

The case unfolded with astounding rapidity. It was less than a week from the arrest of the suspects on March 25, 1931, to the grand jury indictment, which took place on March 30. The trial was set for April 6. The indictment rested on the testimony of the two alleged victims. They claimed that the nine blacks came upon them and several white male companions in a freight car, whereupon the blacks ejected the males and raped the females. The black youths were taken to the jail in Scottsboro, but they had to be removed, under the protection of a hundred national guardsmen, when a mob threatened to lynch them. They were held some sixty miles away in Gasden and delivered to Scottsboro the morning of April 6 for their trials.

Some ten thousand visitors crowded into tiny Scottsboro—whose normal population was two thousand—on the first day of the trials, which proceeded at a lightning pace. The first two convictions—of Charlie Weems and Clarence Norris—came on April 7, the second day of trial. Two days later, eight of the nine stood convicted and sentenced to death, with their executions scheduled for July 10. Jurors had deadlocked on the fate of the ninth defendant, fourteen-year-old Roy Wright. Seven jurors were holding out for the death penalty, although prosecutors, because of his age, had only requested a life sentence.

Immediately following the trials, George Mauer of the ILD sent a telegram to Alabama Governor Benjamin M. Miller charging the young men had been framed. The boys' court-appointed lawyers, wrote Mauer, were "only interested in catering to prejudices of mob. In the name of hundreds of thousands of workers, we protest this legal lynching. Sending attorney to make motion for new trial or appeal. Demand stay of execution."

The trial judge emphatically disagreed with that assessment. The defendants "were given every opportunity to provide themselves with counsel and I appointed able members of the Jackson County bar to represent them," said Judge Alfred E. Hawkins. Stephen Roddy, speaking for the six defense attorneys, said that he and his colleagues had fought to see that the defendants got "the fairest trial."

William Pickens, field secretary for the NAACP, also condemned the proceedings. "The 'Massacre of Gadsden'! That is what it will be called in the indifferent future, if the State of Alabama proceeds to put to death eight Negro boys on the ostensible charge that they 'assaulted' two white girls, but really out of revenge because they licked the mischief out of a gang of white youths,' he wrote in a letter to the *New York Herald Tribune*.

The ACLU was not initially involved. But as the case attracted increasing attention, Forrest Bailey dispatched Hollace Ransdell, a young Columbia-educated journalist, to take a closer look. After spending a week and a half in Alabama, Ransdell produced a detailed and nuanced report. It challenged the tale of the two white "mill girls" from Huntsville, Alabama—Victoria Price and Ruby Bates, twenty-one and seventeen, respectively—who had dressed up in overalls and "hoboed their way by freight train" to Chattanooga supposedly to seek work.

According to Price, she and Bates spent the night in Chattanooga with a friendly woman (whom investigators could not locate). Unable to find jobs at various mills (which they never specifically identified), the girls decided to return home the next morning. They boarded an oil tanker and later climbed into an open freight car where they met seven friendly white boys, whom Price said she joined in laughter and song. When the two females were roughly halfway home, testified Price, twelve black boys, one waving a pistol, invaded the car and forced all but one of the white boys to leap from the fast-moving train.

She claimed six of the black youths raped her and six raped her companion. Three of the alleged assailants left the train. Meanwhile, the whites, who supposedly had been forced from the train, notified the station master. The nine young black men who remained on the train were seized by an armed posse at Paint Rock, a town roughly twenty miles outside of Scottsboro. Neither girl showed evidence of rough treatment, although they did show signs of sexual intercourse, testified a doctor at the trial.

George Chamlee, an attorney for the ILD, told Ransdell that Price and Bates originally said nothing about rape; that those allegations were only made after the girls had assessed "the spirit of the armed men that came to meet the train and catch the Negroes." In other words, "they were swept into making their wholesale accusation."

Ransdell's conversations with the two girls convinced her that Chamlee might be right. Victoria Price, she concluded "was the type who welcomes attention and publicity at any price." She also had "no notions of shame connected with sexual intercourse in any form and was quite unbothered in alleging that she went through such an experience as the charges against the nine Negro lads imply. Having been in direct contact from the cradle with the institution of prostitution as a side-line necessary to make the meager wages of a mill worker pay the rent and buy the groceries, she has no feeling of revulsion against promiscuous sexual intercourse. . . . It is very much a matter of the ordinary routine of life to her, known in both Huntsville and Chattanooga as a prostitute herself."

Price lived in a small, unpainted shack in Huntsville with her elderly, infirm mother "for whom she insistently professes such flamboyant devotion, that one immediately distrusts her sincerity" reported Ransdell. Although Price's age "was variously reported in Scottsboro as 19, 20, and 21," her mother "gave it as 24, and neighbors and social workers said she was 27." She also had a reputation. The chief deputy in Huntsville told a social worker that he left her alone because she was a "quiet prostitute, and didn't go rarin' around cuttin' up in public and walkin' the streets solicitin', but just took men quiet-like." The sheriff thought she might be "running a speakeasy on the side with a married man named Teller." He had not yet succeeded in catching the couple with liquor on them.

Ransdell also visited Bates, whom she described as a "large, fresh, good-looking girl, shy, but a fluent enough talker when encouraged." The younger girl was "pushed into the background by the more bubbling, pert personality of Victoria. . . . When I talked with her alone she showed resentment against the position into which Victoria had forced her, but did not seem to know what to do except to keep silent and let Victoria do the talking," concluded Ransdell.

Bates's home—"a bare but clean unpainted shack"—was in a rundown section of Huntsville. Like Price, Bates lived with her mother. "They are the only white family in the block. Of the five children in the family, two are married and three are living at home. . . . The social service worker who accompanied me on the visit sniffed when she came in and said to Mrs. Bates: 'Niggers lived here before you, I smell them. You can't get rid of that Nigger smell.' Mrs. Bates looked apologetic and murmured that she had scrubbed the place down with soap. The house looked clean and orderly to me. I smelled nothing, but then I have only a northern nose."

As Ransdell and Bates talked out front, the younger children in the household played with their black neighbors: "Yet here was Ruby saying earnestly—as she sat in a Negro house, surrounded by Negro families, while the younger members of her family played in the street with Negro children—that the Scottsboro authorities had promised her she could see the execution of the 'Niggers'—the nine black lads who were to be killed merely for being Negroes," wrote Ransdell.

Ransdell also wrote about the conflict between the ILD and the NAACP. Both organizations had sent representatives to Scottsboro. Both had engaged lawyers. The NAACP apparently sent over Chattanooga lawyer Steve Roddy, who, as Ransdell put it, "represented himself in Scottsboro as sent by friends of the defendants in Chattanooga but refused to go on record as attorney in the case, saying that he had not been employed by any organization whatever." The ILD sent in attorney George Chamlee to work on the appeal.

"The two organizations differ so fundamentally on principles and tactics," concluded Ransdell, "that any hope of a compromise in the legal control of the case seems impossible." The ILD believed in mass demonstrations, bombastic propaganda, and other forms of public pressure. The NAACP believed in quietly working through the system. "They are most anxious to try to avoid antagonizing Southern prejudice," wrote Ransdell.

Ransdell reported that the NAACP's Walter White had gotten four of the defendants to agree to NAACP representation and warned the defendants' parents "that it meant electrocution for their sons to have anything to do with the ILD."

Ransdell's report, which was mimeographed and distributed by the ACLU (it sold for fifty cents a copy), quickly entered into the public dialogue.

Ransdell concluded that Alabama officials, including the trial judge, "all wanted the Negroes killed as quickly as possible in a way that would not bring disrepute upon the town. They therefore preferred a sentence of death by a judge, to a sentence of death by a mob, but they desired the same result."

The Ransdell narrative, in the words of Author James Miller, "had an electrifying impact upon the office of the American Civil Liberties Union, and its effect rippled outward, helping to shape northern liberal and mainstream opinion."[6]

The ACLU's direct involvement was complicated by its long history with the NAACP and the ILD. In the September following the boys' convictions, the NAACP signed up the ACLU's Arthur Hays and Clarence Darrow as volunteer counsel. Shortly after arriving in Alabama, the famous lawyers received a telegram from the ILD, informing them, on the boys' behalf, "we do not want you to come and fight the ILD and make trouble for [ILD lawyer James] Chamlee just to help the NAACP. If you want to save us and help us get a new trial, please help the ILD and Mr. Chamlee."

The ILD proposed that the two lawyers work for them instead of for the NAACP. Hays and Darrow instead offered to work on the case without formally affiliating themselves with either organization. The ILD balked, and Darrow and Hays withdrew, as did the NAACP (although the NAACP eventually found its way back to the case). The bickering, however, continued. In a March 1932 article in *The Crisis*, the NAACP's magazine, Darrow praised the NAACP and slammed the ILD for "seeking credit" in the case.

Meanwhile, a letter surfaced from Bates to a lover admitting the black youths had not attacked the women. Other information came out "proving that the girls are notorious prostitutes, one of them with a long and varied police record in Huntsville," reported the *Atlanta Daily World*.

The ILD lawyers asked the Alabama Supreme Court to overturn the verdicts on several grounds: that the defendants had neither been provided with adequate counsel nor received due process, that the atmosphere of fear and hysteria enveloping the case had made a fair trial impossible, and that one of the defendants—Eugene Williams—as a juvenile, should not have been tried in a court for adults.

That March, the state supreme court upheld all the convictions except Williams's, who was granted a new trial. The others were to be executed that May. The NAACP offered to reenter the case, simultaneously taking a poke at the ILD. Had Clarence Darrow and Arthur Hays been allowed to participate, said Walter White, "these famous lawyers might have achieved a different result."

Rejecting the NAACP's help, the ILD engaged Walter Pollak, a highly respected lawyer who had argued *Gitlow v. New York* before the U.S. Supreme Court for the ACLU.

Pollak made several points to the Supreme Court: that his clients had not received a fair and impartial trial; that they had been denied the right to counsel and an opportunity to prepare a defense; and that (because blacks were systematically excluded) they had not been tried by a jury of their peers. On November 7, the Supreme Court (*Powell v. Alabama*) sided with Pollak.

Writing for the majority, Justice George Sutherland pointed out the boys had never been asked whether their parents or friends might hire lawyers for them. "That it would not have been an idle ceremony . . . is demonstrated by the fact that, very soon after conviction, able counsel appeared in their behalf." The boys were entitled to new trials, concluded the court. That decision, author Samuel Walker later observed, "became the cornerstone of an eventual 'due process revolution,' by means of which the Court applied constitutional standards to virtually the entire criminal justice process."[7]

Baldwin hoped that decision would end the boys' ordeal, that Alabama would drop the case. But that was not to be.

Outraged by the Supreme Court's interference, Alabama again put the boys on trial. In April 1933, Haywood Patterson, the first of the Scottsboro defendants to be retried, was again found guilty. "A new set of verdicts of guilt, it is felt, would restore [the state supreme court's] prestige," observed the *New York Times*.

The surprise came in July. In what the *Norfolk Journal and Guide* called "a decision momentous in a Southern Court," Judge James E. Horton set aside the jury verdict.

Horton tore apart Price's testimony. She had claimed that the wounds from the assault left her lacerated and bleeding, with a gash on her head and her clothes saturated with semen and blood. Yet neither of the two doctors who treated her saw a head wound and no blood or semen was found on her clothes. Nor were the women overwrought when discovered, as would have been expected. And the only white boy put on the stand "contradicted her."

Horton questioned the likelihood of black boys choosing such an exposed place to rape white women: "The time and place and stage of this alleged act are such to make one wonder and question did such an act occur under such circumstances. . . . The place is upon a gondola or car without a top. . . . The whole performance necessarily being in plain view of any one observing the train as it passed."

Horton also noted that, in Chattanooga, the women had "falsely accused two negroes of insulting them," and concluded they were "pre-disposed to make false accusations upon any occasion whereby their selfish ends may be gained."

Defendants should not be convicted solely on the testimony that "bears on its face indications of unreliability or improbability and particularly when it is contradicted by other evidence," wrote Horton.

"It is therefore ordered and adjudged by the Court that the motion be granted; that the verdict of the jury in this case and the judgment of the Court sentencing this defendant to death be . . . hereby set aside and that a new trial . . . hereby ordered," concluded Horton.

Patterson's third trial was before Judge William Washington Callahan, who blithely assured prospective jurors that "belief in the Negro's inferiority does not disqualify you for jury service." Patterson again was found guilty. Days later, Clarence Norris also was found guilty and, like Patterson, sentenced by Callahan for execution.

In June 1934, Judge Horton lost his bid for re-election, which was attributed to his favorable ruling for the Scottsboro Boys.

On April Fools Day, 1935, the Supreme Court again weighed in on the Scottsboro cases (*Patterson v. Alabama* and *Norris v. Alabama*), this time focusing on the exclusion of blacks from juries in the counties where they were tried. Chief Justice Charles Hughes observed: "Within the memory of witnesses, long resident there, no negro had ever served on a jury in [Morgan] county or had been called for such service." This was despite abundant evidence "that there were a large number of negroes in the county who were qualified for jury service." Because of "this long-continued, unvarying, and wholesale exclusion of negroes from jury service," wrote Hughes, "the judgment must be reversed."

It was another landmark decision for the Scottsboro Boys, with profound implications for the American justice system. But, in the end, the Supreme Court decision brought neither vindication nor freedom. The Scottsboro boys had simply won the right to be retried.

Meanwhile—after weathering one setback after another, including charges against two ILD representatives for offering Victoria Price a bribe to change her testimony—the bickering defense organizations worked out a rapprochement. In December 1935, on the eve of yet another set of trials for the Scottsboro youths, the ACLU, NAACP, ILD, League for Industrial Democracy, and the Methodist Federation for Social Service came together as the Scottsboro Defense Committee. The first retrial, under Judge Callahan, was set for January 1936.

"The issues in the Scottsboro case are fundamental. If the lynching element of the South is permitted to murder these innocent boys, it will be the signal for the return of mob rule throughout the South on such a scale that it may rival the activities of the Klan during reconstruction," editorialized the *Cleveland Call and Post.*

This time, twelve blacks were included in the jury pool of one hundred. All were challenged by the state. The trials again took place before all-white juries. Again, the boys were found guilty.

Over the next several years, the Defense Committee repeatedly went to court, launched public campaigns, and sought pardons for their clients. In July 1937, they finally got a break. On July 24, 1937, Alabama released four of the original nine defendants: Olin Montgomery, Roy Wright, Willie Roberson, and Eugene Williams. In a prepared statement, the prosecutor pronounced Roberson and Montgomery innocent. Williams and Wright were shown clemency, he explained, because they were juveniles at the time of the alleged crime. The state also pronounced Ozie Powell innocent, but he remained in prison—under a twenty-year sentence—for attacking a guard.

The Defense Committee appealed to Governor Bibb Graves to free the remaining prisoners, arguing that since all had been convicted on the same evidence, some could not be innocent and the rest guilty. Committee members negotiated what they thought was an agreement with the governor to pardon the remaining four in October 1938; but the governor reneged, drawing a sharp rebuke from Defense Committee chairman Allan Chalmers, who accused Governor Graves of "such a betrayal of all honor and decency that it has shocked men of high standing who are acquainted with the facts."

On October 25, 1976, Alabama Governor George Wallace pardoned Clarence Norris at the request of the NAACP. Norris, sixty-four, had spent fifteen years behind bars, five of those on death row. He was released on parole in 1946. Fearful of being murdered if he remained in Alabama, Norris fled to Cleveland and eventually to New York. He had spent twenty years as a fugitive, subject to re-arrest for parole violation. At an NAACP-arranged event that December, Norris was asked how he would change things if he could relive his life. "I would not come back to this life at all," he replied.

At the time of Norris's pardon, Haywood Patterson, Charles Weems, and Andy Wright were presumed dead, and were therefore not eligible for pardons. In 2013, after the legislature passed a law permitting posthumous pardons, they received full and unconditional pardons.

In 1934, as the world weathered the Great Depression and the Scottsboro Boys fought for their lives, the Baldwins reconsidered their relationship. "I do not remember why [Madeleine Doty] left the job [in Geneva], surely not because of dissatisfaction on either side, but she'd had enough. She got her PhD . . . and came back to New York, where she hoped we might resume our life together," recalled Baldwin in a memo prepared years later. "She took a four-room apartment next to mine and we saw much of each other dropping in and out, but no intimacy developed. I was already interested elsewhere," added Baldwin.

The "elsewhere" was with Evelyn Preston, a wealthy Barnard College graduate and labor activist with a husband and two sons.

"In 1935 I went to Geneva to get a divorce, already arranged for," recalled Baldwin. "My father was living there in a villa on the lake and I stayed with him. . . . Our divorce was simply an appearance before an official, with a few questions about our intentions, then the signing of papers already prepared by our lawyers."

By then, Preston had gotten a divorce in Mexico. When Baldwin returned from Geneva, he moved into a townhouse Preston owned next to her own residence in the West Village "We waited a respectable time to make it official," Baldwin told biographer Lamson. The two married on March 6, 1936: "We had a Quaker-like ceremony on the lawn at Dellbrook [an estate Baldwin owned in New Jersey] one Sunday morning. We were married by Judge Dorothy Kenyon, Evie's great friend who was also her lawyer."

They later had a daughter together.

With its *Black Justice Report* and its Scottsboro Boys crusade, with its forays into sexual expression, academic freedom, censorship, and opposition to loyalty oaths, the ACLU was fulfilling Baldwin's expansionist vision. But ominous external challenges loomed.

By 1938, Japan and China were already at war, and dark clouds had gathered over Europe. Adolf Hitler was moving to annex Sudetenland, a part of Czechoslovakia occupied largely by ethnic Germans. On September 15,

1938, British prime minister Neville Chamberlain met Hitler in the German ruler's mountain retreat above the town of Berchtesgaden, Germany. Hitler personally greeted Chamberlain at the entrance of his chalet. After meeting for two hours and thirty-five minutes, the two leaders issued a joint communique claiming they'd had "a full and frank exchange of views on the situation," and Chamberlain was returning to England "to consult the British Cabinet."

Ten days later, the French and the British were asking the German Fuehrer to modify his demands. "But they were not optimistic," reported the *Baltimore Sun*. Europe seemed "closer to the abyss of a general European war than it has been at any time since July 28, 1914, when Austria opened hostilities against Serbia and touched off what became the World War," observed the *Sun*.

Hitler gave Czechoslovakia until Monday, October 31, to give up the Sudetenland. On August 27, Winston Churchill, then a private citizen, warned that the "whole state of Europe and of the world is moving steadily toward a climax which cannot long be delayed."

The immediate crisis was averted in the early morning hours of October 30 when Great Britain and Germany signed what came to be known as the Munich Agreement. The four-power pact (Great Britain and France on one side and Germany and Italy on the other), for which Chamberlain was widely praised, gave Hitler what he wanted. In a joint statement, Great Britain and Germany declared: "We regard the agreement signed last night . . . as symbolic of the desires of our two peoples never to go to war with one another again."

The *Christian Science Monitor* reported, "two feelings prevail throughout Britain today. One is of deep relief at lifting the dread of war which for tense moments appeared so imminent. The other is a firm resolve that— cost what it may—never again shall such a black shadow of impending conflict be allowed to deface the landscape of civilization."

As America anxiously watched the goings-on in Europe, the ACLU was feeling hostility from yet another House committee investigating radical activities. Formed in May 1938, the Committee on Un-American Activities, chaired by Martin Dies Jr., was the latest incarnation of the Fish Committee. And, like Hamilton Fish, Dies lost no time linking the ACLU to communism.

Dies not only accused the ACLU of supporting communism but Baldwin and other ACLU leaders of being Communists themselves. The ACLU and its allies fought back. Secretary of the Interior Harold Ickes called Dies a political "zany" and publicly dismissed the notion of the ACLU as a Communist threat. In January 1939, the ACLU sent Dies two affidavits—one signed by Baldwin and the other by members of the board—insisting the ACLU "has never been part of a united front for the Communist Party" and denying any "direct or indirect connection with any political movement."

The ACLU's anxiety about the taint of communism deepened as the role of Russia evolved.

In late August 1939, Russia and Germany signed a non-aggression pact. The agreement (later known as the Molotov-Ribbentrop Pact) committed the two nations to a ten-year period during which they would refrain from "every aggressive action and every attack against one another" and not associate "with any other grouping of powers which directly or indirectly is aimed at the other party."

The Supreme Soviet formally ratified the agreement on the evening of August 31. The next day, Germany invaded Poland. Great Britain and France warned Hitler to stand down. On September 3, the allies declared war.

President Franklin Roosevelt expressed "hope that the United States will keep out of this war" and promised "every effort of our government will be directed toward" that end.

On November 30, the Soviet Union invaded Finland. The American press, for the most part, was critical, but the *Daily Worker*—the Communist Party paper—praised the attack. "Finns Here Cheered Over Looming Freedom," read a typical headline. The *New York Herald Tribune* denounced the new "puppet" government of Finland and advised Americans to be "over-suspicious" of Communists.

In this atmosphere of growing paranoia and suspicion of American Communists, the ACLU chose to take on the issue of Communists in its ranks—one of the most controversial decisions in ACLU history.

Even before the invasion of Finland, the ACLU had contemplated taking a stand against non-democratic forms of government. After discussing the idea in May 1939, the board affirmed its traditional position of neutrality and of defending "without favoritism the rights of all comers, whatever their political or economic views."

As the war progressed, the board revisited that decision. Disturbed by the Soviet-Nazi pact, the apparent rise in anti-Communist sentiment, and Dies' attacks on the ACLU, a block of board members—led by Thomas Ernst, John Haynes Holmes, and Norman Thomas—pushed Harry Ward to step down as chair. They feared being associated with the American League for Peace and Democracy, which Ward also chaired, and which Dies called a Communist front group.

Ward, who been chair since the ACLU's founding and was apparently already weighing stepping down, gave up his chairmanship in January 1940, and vice-chair John Haynes Holmes moved up.

Ward's resignation did not put the issue to rest. Ernst and his allies demanded a clear statement disassociating the ACLU from Communists. In February, the national committee and board approved what came to be known as the February 5th resolution.

That resolution deemed it "inappropriate for any person to serve on the governing committees of the Union or on its staff, who is a member of any political organization which supports totalitarian dictatorship in any country, or who by his public declarations indicates his support of such a principle."

Among forbidden associations, the resolution named "organizations in the United States supporting the totalitarian governments of the Soviet Union and of the Fascist and Nazi countries (such as the Communist Party, the German-American Bund and others); as well as native organizations with obvious anti-democratic objectives or practices."

Through dressed up as a general resolution of principle, the resolution transparently targeted Elizabeth Gurley Flynn, an ACLU founder and the only Communist then on the board. As critics were quick to point out, no Fascists, Nazis, or members of the Bund had ever tried to join the ACLU board.

In an interview with the *Daily Worker*, Flynn made her position clear: "When I joined the Communist Party three years ago, I informed the directors of that fact and the ACLU chairman said they were glad to have a Communist on the board. I was re-elected to the board a year ago and my term has two years more to run. I am not quitting."

But Baldwin suggested that Flynn's days as a board member were numbered. "Any report that the resolution adopted by the union does not mean what it says is wholly incorrect," Baldwin told the *New York Post*.

Meanwhile, Harry Ward, who had remained on the board after leaving the chairmanship, quit altogether. He thought the February 5th resolution reeked of hypocrisy. In a letter that March, he disputed the board's insistence that the resolution simply affirmed long-standing ACLU policy. The board majority "acting under the pressure of wartime public opinion, tells the minority to confirm to its views or get out," wrote Ward. "What kind of civil liberties is this?"

On Monday, March 4, the board formally requested Flynn's resignation. She refused, leading board member Dorothy Dunbar Bromley, a prominent feminist and journalist, to formally request her expulsion.

Flynn responded with a defiant memo to the board declaring, "I refuse to resign my Directorship in the American Civil Liberties Union. . . . I will do all in my power to expunge the offending resolution from our records, and to make the ACLU a truly democratic organization so that such disgraceful compromise and red-baiting can never again occur."

Baldwin sought Arthur Hays's counsel on how to proceed. Hays advised him that the ACLU should "handle this matter in such a way as to be proof against successful attack in court," which to Hays meant giving Flynn written notice, granting her a fair hearing, and taking a "proper vote."

Hays added, "It seems to me that not only should we put in evidence that Elizabeth is a Communist, but we should also have the Constitution of the Communist Party, showing that the prescribed oath requires obedience and the following of direction."

In mid-March, Flynn declared open war on the ACLU. The fusillade began with an article titled, "I Am Expelled from Civil Liberties," in the March 17 issue of the *Daily Worker*. "When, unladylike, I refused [to resign], they brought charges against me and I am slated for expulsion. . . . I feel like an unwanted wife sent to Reno, after all these protestations of affection, except that I don't expect any alimony will be forthcoming," wrote Flynn.

Flynn admitted she had no expectation of winning but was fighting to ensure "the issue will be well aired." The ACLU, she added, once welcomed radicals and activists but had become a collection of old "capitalists" stuck in their outmoded ways.

She continued her assault in the *New Masses* with a March 19 article headlined, "Why I won't Resign from the ACLU." The ACLU, she pointed out, was born out of the last war. "Present indications are that it is likely to pass out during the present one."

How, she wondered, can ACLU leaders "defend Communists in the right to teach or to hold public office if they themselves exclude me solely as a Communist?" She concluded, "I don't mind being exposed by this kind of people. I don't belong with them anyhow."

The ACLU struggled over how to respond. On March 10, chairman John Haynes Holmes wrote Baldwin, "I don't relish the prospect of her going forth as a martyr . . . but I can swallow it a darned sight better than the prospect of her going forth as . . . a reborn Joan of Arc, flaunting us and taunting us with the charge that we took a stand and then didn't care to go through with it when we faced a Communist who had the nerve to call our bluff." That same day, Holmes wrote to Flynn asserting his belief that the articles "make impossible your further membership on our Board." He asked that she resign prior to the board meeting—where her hearing otherwise would take place—on Monday, March 25.

Before the meeting could occur, Flynn's twenty-nine-year-old son, Fred Flynn, was hospitalized. Fred, who was an activist in his own right and a member of the American Labor Party, was suffering from an advanced and aggressive form of cancer. Elizabeth Gurley Flynn's reckoning was postponed. On Friday, March 29, Fred Flynn died following surgery.

Elizabeth Flynn Gurley's hearing took place Tuesday, May 7, 1940, beginning at 8 p.m. at the City Club of New York, with John Haynes Holmes presiding.

Flynn was charged with three offenses. One was being a Communist. The other charges, which sprang from her two articles, were essentially two counts of insulting the ACLU.

Flynn's defended herself in a prepared statement that she read aloud— after apologizing for any deficiencies occasioned by her having to prepare it in the wake of her son's death.

She challenged "the validity of this entire procedure," even as she freely confessed membership in the Communist Party. She pointed out that the

ACLU had a long-standing policy against censoring the views of its members—that, indeed, the board had been proud of the diversity of opinions represented on the board. She also objected to board members who had brought charges against her also standing in judgment. "Mrs. Bromley, Mr. [Elmer] Rice, Mr. [Roger William] Riis and Dr. Holmes cannot surely qualify since they have assumed the roles of complainants." All four, she said, should recuse themselves (which they did not do, although the board interrupted her reading for a lengthy period during which members considered several procedural matters).

When Flynn resumed her statement, she essentially accused the board of lying when it claimed to have never knowingly admitted Communists to its board. She also accused Baldwin and Holmes of lying in claiming she had become an obstructionist: "I defy them to prove any change in my position on civil liberties or my conduct in defense of them for the past three years, since I became a member of the Communist Party."

The ACLU resolution, by abandoning the "honored traditional position of the ACLU," had created the very demoralization Holmes feared, charged Flynn. "I refuse to resign because I will not be a party to saving the face of this anti-civil-liberties majority nor to whitewashing their red-baiting," she said.

Following a series of exchanges, the board asked Flynn to wait outside the meeting room. The board concluded its deliberations at roughly 2:20 a.m. Hours later, it released an announcement: "After a lengthy hearing, a majority of the board sustained the charges and voted to remove Ms. Flynn from the board subject to approval by the members of the national committee of the union. . . . A vote of that body will be taken by mail."

Three decades later, in interviews with Peggy Lamson, Baldwin continued to defend the board's action. "The Nazi-Soviet Pact made a big difference. A communist was no longer a communist after the Nazi-Soviet Pact. A communist was an agent of the Soviet Union. . . . It made cooperation with communists inside the Civil Liberties Union impossible."

He did not address the calculation he and others at the ACLU were clearly making, a calculation about how much their credibility as patriots and Americans would be affected by association with Communists. Instead, he focused on the threat—more theoretical than real—of Flynn's foreign allegiance.

Many liberals were simply confused by the ACLU's actions. In March 1940, seventeen self-identified liberals—including I.F. Stone and Theodore Dreiser—signed an open letter in Flynn's defense. "We believe that by the purge resolution the American Civil Liberties Union encourages the very tendencies it was intended to fight," they wrote.

The ACLU, they pointed out, was "formed in 1920 to fight post-war hysteria. It would be a great pity if it were now to become the victim of pre-war hysteria."

"On the whole," argued Baldwin, "the result of the Elizabeth Gurley Flynn case was to increase our membership and our adherents, not to lose them." On a literal level, his statement seems defensible—albeit barely. In the fiscal year that ended on January 31, 1940, members' total contributions to the ACLU were $34,267, and membership stood at 5,272. The next fiscal year, after Flynn's trial, membership contributions stood at $34,381 and membership at 5,453. If the Flynn spectacle did not increase membership, neither did it decrease it.

But membership is a very narrow measure to try to measure the effect of the imbroglio on the soul of the organization. Author Samuel Walker pronounced the episode "a disaster for the ACLU. A breach of principle, it both failed to placate right-wing critics, who continued to vilify the ACLU as a Communist front, and outraged the left, many of whom never let the ACLU live down the 'trial.'"[8]

The Flynn affair was indeed a self-inflicted crisis that haunted the ACLU for decades. The organization survived. And, in some respects, it emerged stronger. But it had lost its innocence and some of its luster. It had traded principle for expediency and presumably gotten the Dies committee off its back.

If Chamberlain could sacrifice Czechoslovakia, surely the ACLU could sacrifice Flynn. There were, after all, more important things at stake. With the battle approaching America's shores, irrational hysteria would surely surge, and human rights would surely be trampled. What was unclear was whether this new, supposedly more tough-minded ACLU was better or worse prepared for the task.

6

A Yellow Menace, Red Fears, White Racism, and Assimilation

In October 1939, the ACLU celebrated the 150th anniversary of the date Congress sent the Bill of Rights to the states for ratification. Some 750 guests attended the ACLU's opening banquet at New York City's Hotel Biltmore. Attorney General Frank Murphy, a former Michigan governor and future Supreme Court justice, delivered the keynote. The United States would avoid the mistakes of World War I, promised Murphy. America would defend itself against "internal aggression" but would not violate constitutional rights: "Whether it be peacetime or wartime, there could be nothing more unpatriotic in this land of many peoples and many creeds than the persecution of minorities and the fomenting of hatred and strife on the bases of race or religion."

O. John Rogge, head of the newly named civil liberties unit at the Department of Justice, reinforced that message. The Roosevelt administration assumed "the United States will stay out of war," said Rogge. But whatever "espionage, propaganda and similar problems" arose, "I can give you assurance that [the administration's response] will be closely coordinated with the civil liberties union." The government would not "become an instrument of oppression."

It was a month and a half after Germany had invaded Poland, and a week after Germany and the Soviet Union had apportioned the country between them. Still, the group at the Biltmore was optimistic that America might yet avoid being drawn into the conflict. But even if the nation did go to war, the current administration was sworn to avoid the xenophobia and hysteria of World War I.

Still, the ACLU fretted. As the fighting intensified over the next two years, ACLU secretary Lucille Milner authored or co-authored a series of articles reminding readers of the excesses of the past. Writing in *Harpers*, Milner and co-author Groff Conklin warned that censorship "in a coming war" might be worse than in World War I. In the *New Republic*, Milner presented the British model as a standard: "England is demonstrating that democracy can defend itself and still uphold its guarantees."

In her article, Milner recalled the sad saga of Robert Goldstein, the producer of a silent movie titled "The Spirit of '76." After Goldstein premiered his Revolutionary War movie in 1917, the U.S. government prosecuted him for violating the Espionage Act. His crime? Portraying an ally (the British) as villains. Goldstein drew a ten-year prison sentence. Although President Wilson commuted his sentence to three years served, Goldstein left America in disgrace and never again worked in the film industry. "The lesson of 1917–23 must not be lost," insisted Milner.

When Germany had invaded Poland, Roosevelt had pledged "every effort" to avoid committing American troops. But in June 1940, as Italy entered the fight, he publicly recalibrated. Addressing the 1940 graduating class at the University of Virginia, he condemned Italy and rejected the "obvious delusion that we of the United States can safely permit the United States to become a . . . lone island in a world dominated by the philosophy of force." Roosevelt's declaration drew bipartisan support, but also prompted concerns. "The speech sounded to me like a prelude to a declaration of war," observed Congresswoman Edith Nourse Rogers, a Massachusetts Democrat.

An equally troubling omen for American doves was Congress's passage of the Alien Registration Act. The so-called Smith Act, signed by President Roosevelt on June 29, 1940, required registration and fingerprinting of all resident foreigners—estimated at 3.5 million—starting within sixty days.

The legislation also authorized expulsion for wrongs committed before the law was passed. It sanctioned deportation of any alien "who, at any time after entry, shall have on more than one occasion, knowingly and for gain, encouraged, induced, assisted, abetted, or aided any other alien or aliens to enter or to try to enter the United States in violation of law"; any alien "who, at any time after entry, shall have been convicted of possessing or carrying in violation of any law any weapon which shoots or is designed to shoot automatically or semi-automatically," along with various other weapons; and aliens who "at any time, shall be or shall have been a member" of various groups "excluded from admission into the United States."

"As enacted, the law is so sweeping in scope that it would call for mandatory deportation of even former members of organizations which advocate or taught the overthrow of this Government by force," observed the *Baltimore Sun*.

The bill's unusually expansive language was adopted not merely out of fear of so-called "fifth column" activities but to target one Harry Bridges— the Australian-born head of the West Coast longshoreman's union, whom many politicians thought of as a troublemaker and Communist sympathizer. Indeed, the House had overwhelmingly passed a bill targeting Bridges personally for deportation. That bill stalled in the Senate only after Attorney General Robert Jackson pronounced it probably unconstitutional and warned that passage would mark "the first time an Act of Congress has singled out a named individual for deportation." Alabama Representative Sam Hobbs predicted that the Smith Act would compel Bridge's deportation in a "perfectly legal and constitutional manner." Despite that prediction, Bridges had the last laugh when the Supreme Court blocked the years-long effort to deport him in 1945.

But even setting aside the Bridges melodrama, the law struck many observers as overbroad and fundamentally un-American. That America was adopting policies previously "scorned as out of line with the American way of life" was "indicative of the seriousness with which the government regards the threat . . . growing out of the National Socialist victories in Europe," observed the *New York Times*.

That September 16, the United States took another step toward war preparedness. The Selective Training and Service Act instituted America's first peacetime draft, setting October 16 as the date for all men between twenty-one and thirty-five to register for possible military service. "We cannot remain indifferent to the philosophy of force now rampant in the world," declared Roosevelt in his signing proclamation.

In a radio address delivered the evening the bill was signed, Army Chief of Staff General George C. Marshall recalled World War I: "The situation today is utterly different from that of 1917. Then we were at war—but we foresaw small possibility of military danger to this country. Today such a possibility trembles on the verge of becoming a probability." The next six months, he added, might be "the most critical period in the history of this nation."

As the Democratic administration embraced the seeming inevitability of war, the Republican Party repositioned itself. "The Republican party stands for Americanism, preparedness and peace," proclaimed the platform adopted at the national convention in late June. "The national defense plank of our party puts the Republican Party before the country as the peace party," declared Congressman Hamilton Fish during his seconding speech for the platform's adoption. Former President Herbert Hoover told the convention that America's president "should abate war, not stimulate it. "

With his opponent Wendell Willkie running on the dovish Republican platform, Roosevelt also emphasized his commitment to peace. "We will not participate in foreign wars and we will not send our army, naval or air forces to fight in foreign lands outside of the Americas except in case of attack. It is for peace that I have labored; and it is for peace that I shall labor all the days of my life," he declared at a campaign rally in Philadelphia that October 23—a month after Italy, Japan, and Germany signed the Tripartite Pact.

Even as Roosevelt moderated his language, Americans reluctantly accepted the possibility of war. A Gallup poll published in December 1940 found that 90 percent of Americans favored increased aid to Britain and that 60 percent favored giving aid "even at the risk of getting into war"—a sharp increase from the 36 percent who favored it in May.

Many blacks saw America's mobilization against fascism as a perfect occasion to highlight inequalities at home. In January 1941, A. Philip Randolph, president of the Brotherhood of Sleeping Car Porters, called for a ten-thousand-person march on Washington. "We Loyal Colored Americans Demand the Right to Work and Fight for Our Country" was his proposed slogan.

The march "would wake up and shock official Washington as it has never been shocked before," he said. "It is not enough," he added, "for us to want jobs in the factories, mills, mines and offices; we must diplomatically and undiplomatically, ceremoniously and unceremoniously, cry out in no uncertain terms our demand for work and our rightful places in every department of the army, navy and air corps, based, of course, upon recognized qualifications."

The *Chicago Defender* and other black newspaper endorsed the initiative. Enthusiasm among African Americans swelled. By summer, Randolph had increased his goal to 100,000 marchers and set July 1 as the protest date.

First Lady Eleanor Roosevelt wrote Randolph a letter saying that although she was "deeply concerned about the rights of Negro people," she strongly felt "that your group is making a very grave mistake at the present time to allow this march to take place. . . . I feel that if any incident occurs as a result of this, it may engender so much bitterness that it will create in Congress even more solid opposition from certain groups than we have had in the past." The president himself called the march a "grave mistake" and asked, "what would happen if Irish and Jewish people were to march on Washington?" Randolph replied: "There is no comparison between a march on Washington by Jews and Irish people, and the Negroes. The public knows that the Negroes have justification for bringing their grievances to the President and to present them to the American people."

To head off the looming public relations disaster, in early June Roosevelt urged the Office of Personnel Management to integrate blacks into the defense effort. He also appointed a committee to address discrimination. Randolph was unmoved. Only an executive order mandating real change, he vowed, would stop the march.

On June 25, following a meeting with Randolph and other march leaders, Roosevelt issued Executive Order 8802, prohibiting discrimination in the defense industries and creating the Fair Employment Practice Committee. A triumphant Randolph declared that the march was unnecessary "at this time." "This is the first executive order which has been issued by a President of the United States in behalf of Negroes since the immortal Abraham Lincoln issued the Emancipation Proclamation in 1863," Randolph proclaimed in an article published in the black press.

As Roosevelt put the troubles with Randolph behind him, even more daunting challenges loomed. In late July, Japanese bombers attacked Chungking, China, damaging the *Tutuila*, an American gunboat anchored in the Yangtze river. No Americans were injured, but bombers narrowly missed hitting the U.S. embassy. That September, the USS *Greer* took fire from a

German submarine in the North Atlantic. Again, no Americans died, and the incident was eventually chalked up to a misunderstanding. Nonetheless, Roosevelt announced a new policy.

"We have sought no shooting war with Hitler and do not seek it now," he said on September 11. "Neither do we want peace so much that we are willing to pay for it by permitting him to attack our naval and merchant ships while they are on legitimate business. . . . From now on, if German or Italian vessels enter the waters, the protection of which is necessary for American defense, they do so at their own peril."

A Gallup poll released that October showed that 62 percent of Americans supported the "shoot at sight" policy. Even so, the poll noted, 63 percent of Americans opposed declaring war on Germany.

Later that same month, an American merchant ship was sunk in the Red Sea—by an airplane of unknown nationality. All crew members were rescued. At that point, reported Gallup, 70 percent of Americans believed the nation should "take steps to keep Japan from becoming more powerful"—even if that meant risking war.

The fighter planes appeared Sunday morning shortly after sunrise. The attack, which began after 7:55 a.m., "broke with such suddenness that at first the identity of the planes was not definitely known. But observers soon could plainly see the Rising Sun insignia of Japan on the bomber's wings," reported United Press International.

Pearl Harbor, on Oahu island, housed the navy's largest fleet and the army's largest airfield. The damage was staggering. News outlets reported that two American warships—a battleship and a destroyer—were sunk and numerous planes destroyed or disabled. Officials estimated some 1,500 dead.

The *Syracuse Herald-Journal* called the attack "a piece of malevolent, brutal treachery unsurpassed in all the annals of international duplicity." "At the moment Japan's envoys in Washington were preparing to meet Secretary [of State Cordell] Hull again, to continue their peace masquerade, Japanese planes were bombing Pearl Harbor, ruthlessly slaughtering hundreds of American boys," the paper groused.

That Monday, at 12:30 p.m., President Roosevelt addressed Congress. "There is no blinking at the fact that our people, our territory, and our interests are in grave danger," he said. "With confidence in our armed forces—with the unbounding determination of our people—we will gain the inevitable triumph, so help us God. I ask that the Congress declare that since the unprovoked and dastardly attack by Japan on Sunday, December 7, 1941, a state of war has existed between the United States and the Japanese Empire."

The Senate vote, 82 to 0, concluded at 1:01 p.m. The House vote, 388 to 1, wrapped up ten minutes later. Jeannette Rankin, a Montana Republican and devout pacifist, was the only congressperson voting against war. "Thus the struggle for world conquest, which Adolf Hitler started on Sept. 1, 1939, became today a World War in fact as well as name," reported the *Christian Science Monitor.*

Tuesday evening, President Roosevelt broadcast a somber message: "We are now in this war. We are all in it—all the way. . . . So far, the news has been all bad. We have suffered a serious setback in Hawaii. Our forces in the Philippines . . . are taking punishment, but are defending themselves vigorously." He urged Americans to reject rumors and propaganda and expressed faith that America eventually would triumph.

The night before Roosevelt's fireside chat, the FBI arrested some 250 Japanese nationals throughout the United States and roughly the same number in Hawaii—with more arrests promised.

"The F.B.I. has for some time conducted a careful and detailed investigation into the activities of Japanese in the United States, and the detention of the persons now in custody represent the results of these investigations," Attorney General Francis Biddle told the press. Biddle cautioned that although those seized were considered dangerous, their arrests should not color opinions regarding all Japanese: "There are in the United States many persons of Japanese extraction whose loyalty to this country, even in the present emergency, is unquestioned." He urged state and local police to make arrests only after consulting the FBI.

The night after federal agents detained the first round of Japanese, they arrested scores of Germans and Italians. "The nation-wide arrests included a former German Consul in Los Angeles, German American Bund leaders, retired German businessmen, Italian bankers and German newspapermen," reported the *Herald Tribune.* On December 10, Attorney General

Biddle announced that 2,303 enemy aliens had been arrested in the previous few days—1,291 Japanese, 865 Germans, and 147 Italians. But it soon became clear that the Japanese were considered a class apart.

Even before the attack, reported, the *Herald Tribune*, the "loyalties of the Japanese in Hawaii" were suspect. Now, the backlash was unrelenting—and not just in Hawaii.

In San Francisco, "a Japanese was arrested while taking pictures in the Twin Peaks area," reported the *Austin American Statesman*. The paper also noted that police were investigating reports of signals "flashed from the ground in an attempt to guide hostile planes." All Japanese nationals in Georgia were ordered to stay in their homes. Sacramento forbid Japanese aliens to buy automobiles. Some retail stores in Los Angeles abruptly fired Japanese employees. Damon Runyon, writing in the *Austin American Statesman*, claimed the Chinese consul in Los Angeles was "going to issue buttons to his people to prevent the Caucasians getting the two nationalities confused." The Japanese American Citizens' League and other Japanese American groups responded to the outbreak of hostility by pledging their support to the American effort.

The 150th anniversary of the ratification of the Bill of Rights fell on December 15, 1941, a week and a day after the Pearl Harbor attack. The ACLU seized the occasion to promote the message that repression had no place in a free society—even during war.

In a letter to President Roosevelt, ACLU chairman John Haynes Holmes and national committee chair Edward Ross wrote that it was "gratifying" the anniversary celebration "has been made an official function of the Government through the Office of Civilian Defense. We trust that the continuing work of this civilian agency will include the protection of citizens' rights against the inevitable tendencies in war-time to curtail them."

Baldwin released a statement expressing optimism about the Roosevelt administration's approach to civil liberties: "The Administration is on the whole committed to the principle that civil liberties must not be subordinated in a war for democracy. . . . With this policy the Civil Liberties Union is of course in accord." The ACLU, he added, "which takes no position on any issue save the subject of civil liberties, will be on the alert to guard against their infringement."

Undersecretary of War Robert Patterson pledged that freedom of press, speech, and assembly "which have made this country a refuge from tyrants . . . will not be blacked out by this war." Wartime measures, he pledged, "will be approached free of any war hysteria."

At a sesquicentennial celebration at the federal court in Baltimore, Circuit Court Judge Morris A. Soper delivered a passionate defense of civil liberties. "[Let] us make one another a solemn promise," he said, "that even as we stand adamant in time of peace against oppressive action of the Government toward the individual citizen, so likewise we shall defend him against oppression amid the passions roused by war, whoever he may be, and whatever the offense with which he may be charged."

At countless Bill of Rights celebrations across America, the inclination was to contrast a democratic America against the authoritarian regimes it was fighting—and to swear fealty to civil liberties as America waged war. As New York City Mayor Fiorello La Guardia put it, "We can't preserve and protect the Bill of Rights any longer by oratory. . . . We must protect these rights with our very lives."

In a sense, Baldwin had it right. Thanks in large measure to the ACLU, World War II would not see a repeat of the civil liberties mistakes of World War I. This time around, the government was much less inclined to target Socialists, pacifists, or people who simply opposed the war. But this new appreciation for the Bill of Rights would not stop government from targeting people whose very identity was deemed offensive, and whose right to liberty—never mind free expression—was easily violated in deference to racialized fear.

The restrictions against so-called enemy aliens came in a steady stream. By Christmas, 2,971 enemy aliens were in custody, roughly half of whom were Japanese. On December 27, Attorney General Francis Biddle, worried about espionage, ordered all Japanese, Germans, and Italians in seven western states to turn in their cameras, radio transmitters, and shortwave sets. A week later, he extended the order to citizens of enemy countries anywhere in the United States—adding firearms to the list of items forbidden in enemy alien hands. Failure to turn in such items could result in imprisonment for the duration of the war. "The time for laughing at the foolish looking little Jap with his camera has passed," wrote journalist Damon Runyon.

January 5 was the deadline for turning in prohibited items. On that date, foreigners laden with cameras and guns swamped many police precinct stations. Crowds also gathered at the offices of local U.S. attorneys, as Biddle had barred enemy aliens from traveling outside their respective communities without first getting permission.

In mid-January 1942, Biddle announced that, between February 2 and 7, enemy aliens over fourteen in eight western states had to apply for identification cards that would carry their photograph, signature, and fingerprint. Registration was to be extended nationwide shortly thereafter.

In early February, Biddle announced yet more restrictions. To prevent sabotage of dams, hydroelectric plants, and other structures, he designated large parts of Oregon, Washington, and California as "restricted areas." In California, five hundred miles of coastline (extending thirty to fifty miles deep inland) were deemed "restricted," making enemy aliens subject to a 9 p.m. curfew. They were also ordered not to wander far from work or home. Meanwhile, the Federal Security Agency revealed it was making plans to relocate enemy aliens to presumably less vulnerable landlocked areas.

Politicians lobbied for stronger measures. California Attorney General Earl Warren and one hundred local district attorneys asked that all Japanese be moved inland. California Governor Culbert Olson suggested evacuating all persons of Japanese extraction unable to prove their loyalty. Numerous congressmen—particularly those out West—demanded drastic action against the Japanese. House Committee on Un-American Activities chairman Martin Dies proposed moving all Japanese on the Pacific Coast at least five hundred miles inland. California Congressman Leland Ford of California said his mail was running heavily in favor of evacuating and interning Japanese—citizens and aliens alike. If Japanese American citizens were truly patriotic, he argued, they would willingly submit to confinement in camps.

The "burden" of "every American-born Japanese," said Los Angeles Mayor Fletcher Bowron, was to demonstrate loyalty to America: "Every person of Japanese blood . . . should be made to understand that one single act of sabotage—anything that might assist the Japanese government in this time of war—will brand the entire Japanese population not only during the . . . war but for at least a generation."

Congressman Dies claimed to be completing a "yellow paper" that would expose some "8,000 Japanese secret agents in the United States and Hawaii." An early draft contained maps supposedly created by Japanese spies for an impending invasion. The information was widely criticized as both plagiarized and false.

At a Rules Committee hearing in February 1942, a representative of the Brotherhood of Railroad Trainmen denounced Dies's committee as a key information source for Axis propagandists. Federal Communications Commission Chairman James Fly backed up that complaint by quoting a draft FCC report: "Representative Dies, ardent supporter of Americanism and opponent of subversive propaganda, received as many favorable references in Axis propaganda to this country as any living American public figure."

"If what the Federal Communications Commission says is true, since Hitler is utilizing the statements of the Dies committee as part of his propaganda ammunition that is being used against the United States, naturally Hitler would vote 'aye' on the continuation of the Committee to Investigate Un-American Activities," pointed out New York Congressman Vito Marcantonio. Addressing Dies directly, Marcantonio added, "you will have to admit that the Nazis are using you against the United States Government."

Despite such occasional pushback, politicians continued to lash out against Japanese Americans. "Once a Jap, always a Jap. You can't any more regenerate a Jap than you can reverse the laws of nature," exclaimed Mississippi Congressman John Rankin. Rankin insisted that the West Coast and Hawaii were "teaming with spies and fifth columnists." California Congressman Harry Sheppard declared, "No one with any knowledge of Jap psychology" would allow Japanese American their civil liberties "because it represents a national hazard."

As congressmen hyped the threat from Japanese Americans, the army, State Department, and Justice Department reached agreement on a way forward. On February 18, 1942, the administration announced that army Lieutenant General John DeWitt would establish military zones from which both citizens and aliens could be banned whenever the military deemed necessary. "It is understood that the Attorney General is confident he can submit a proposed order to President Roosevelt . . . that does not invalidate any civil rights or liberties," reported the *Los Angeles Times*.

On February 19, President Roosevelt issued Executive Order 9066. It authorized the Secretary of War and select military commanders "to prescribe military areas . . . from which any or all persons may be excluded, and with respect to which, the right of any person to enter, remain in, or leave shall be subject to whatever restrictions the Secretary of War or the appropriate Military Commander may impose in his discretion."

The order was to take effect in California and other Pacific States "as rapidly as conditions permit. No other geographical sections of the country are at present included," reported the *Los Angeles Times*. The specific target, noted the *Times*, were people of Japanese ancestry: "Citizens of German and Italian descent will not be involved except for specific cause."

In announcing the order, Attorney General Biddle acknowledged there was no evidence of treacherous behavior on the part of Japanese Americans, but "people on the Coast have a very strong feeling that the Japanese situation is dangerous."

San Francisco mayor Angelo Rossi called the executive order "a wise decision." Roger Baldwin was not so sure. He called the executive order "unprecedented and founded on no specific evidence of need," but pledged the ACLU would not interfere "with any necessary moves to protect the West Coast areas."

On the Monday evening after signing the executive order, President Roosevelt broadcast a war update and rousing call to arms. He reported that some 2,340 had been killed in the Pearl Harbor attack and 940 wounded. "Of all of the combatant ships based on Pearl Harbor—battleships, heavy cruisers, light cruisers, aircraft carriers, destroyers and submarines—only three are permanently put out of commission."

He refused to say how many planes had been disabled, but assured his listeners that America had destroyed "considerably more Japanese planes" than vice versa and pledged: "We, not they, will win the final battles; and we, not they, will make the final peace."

As the president spoke, a submarine, presumed to be Japanese, surfaced and fired several shells at oil wells near Santa Barbara. No one was hurt and minimal damage was done. Benjamin Sumner Wells, acting secretary of state, called the attack a "stunt" aimed at creating turmoil in the wake of the president's radio address.

Two days later, shortly after 2 a.m., Los Angeles residents were startled when American troops fired thousands of anti-aircraft artillery rounds into the sky. The all-clear came five hours later. Frank Knox, Secretary of the Navy pronounced the incident a "false alarm." "There were no planes over Los Angeles last night," said Knox. The troops had been spooked by erroneous reports of a Japanese raid.

In the confusion, an air raid warden broke his leg chasing someone he apparently thought was Japanese, a woman died in a car crash; a sixty-three-year-old state guardsman died of a heart attack; a Long Beach policeman was killed in a traffic accident; and a pedestrian was mowed down by a car. That same night, in Venice, two Japanese men and one woman were seized on suspicion of using flashlights to signal to ships at sea.

Japanese Americans did what they could to allay suspicion. The United Citizens Federation, a group comprised of American-born Japanese from various organizations, presented a large parchment with five thousand signatures to the Board of Supervisors of California's Riverside County swearing allegiance to the United States. The Japanese American Citizens League promised the group would garner at least five hundred more signatures before delivering the document to the White House.

Still, pressure built to take strong action against Japanese on American soil. As Senator Tom Stewart, a Democrat from Tennessee, put it, "the time has arrived when we deal sternly with the Japanese in this country."

General DeWitt, a Nebraska native, World War I veteran, and a hardline advocate of Japanese evacuation, was preparing to do just that. In support of his plan, he cited as fact what later proved to be a hugely consequential lie: that American intelligence had found evidence of "the existence of hundreds of Japanese organizations in California, Washington, Oregon and Arizona which, prior to December 7, 1941, were actively engaged in advancing Japanese war aims." According to DeWitt's blatantly false information, "thousands of American-born Japanese had gone to Japan to receive their education and indoctrination there and had become rabidly pro-Japanese and then had returned to the United States."[1]

The great migration from Los Angeles began just over a month after Roosevelt signed the executive order. Those who were not evacuated straightaway were put under a strict curfew. Effective March 27, all persons of Japanese ancestry in seven western states would have to be in their residence between 8 p.m. and 6 a.m.

The government originally had planned to rely largely on "voluntary migration." But as DeWitt later explained, the "voluntary movement did not gain momentum because means had not been provided on the ground for aiding evacuees." In addition, Japanese migrants, for the most part, had no place to go and no reason to expect a warmer welcome elsewhere. Some who did move were met with violence. So very few—the number was put at roughly nine thousand—voluntarily moved to the interior.

The policy also made no sense. "If the Issei and Nisei were being excluded because they threatened sabotage and espionage, it is difficult to understand why they would be left at large in the interior," where there was plenty of stuff to sabotage, pointed out *Personal Justice Denied*, a report by the Commission on Wartime Relocation and Internment of Civilians.

Thousands began their involuntary journey to what essentially were prisons. All were instructed to bring bedrolls and water jugs—but no cameras or guns. One of the first places to receive the unwilling guests was the Owens Valley Reception Center in Manzanar, California—a former ranching town at the base of the Sierra Nevada mountains. Some eight hundred arrived on March 23, the first day of mass relocation.

As the *Austin Statesmen* reported it, "Five hundred came by special train. Three hundred drove their own cars, loaded with a few possessions, in a two-mile-long motorcade convoyed by 50 army cars." They would be housed in wooden barracks, only 38 of which were completed, with another 786 partially built. Nonetheless, according to the *Statesmen*'s reporter, at least one evacuee had an upbeat attitude. "You wait, we'll make a little heaven out of it," he supposedly said.

The white population responded with horror. "No Japanese had ever settled in the Owens Valley. None was wanted—let alone 50,000," observed the *Baltimore Sun*. One local restaurant owner vowed to "shoot the first . . . Jap who sticks his nose into my place." The next day, three Asian men walked into his restaurant and ordered steaks. "After they had gone, I looked into the cash register and I couldn't see any difference between their money and the other money in the drawer," the now-accepting restaurateur told the *Sun* reporter.

Once the Owens Valley camp was full, some twenty thousand families were to be moved into the Blythe Park area of the California Arizona border and sixteen thousand into the Santa Anita Racetrack in the Los Angeles area, reported the *Christian Science Monitor*. "Part of America stands transplanted today in a dramatic security measure, because no sure test was found for proving the loyalty of residents of Japanese extraction," observed the *Monitor*, which did not speculate on why no "sure test" was needed for Italians or Germans.

Over the next several months, more than 110,000 persons of Japanese extraction were moved into internment camps. Many lost virtually all their possessions. "[Forced] by sudden evacuation orders to dispose quickly of their goods . . . they disposed of their personal property for a mere fraction of its value. Secondhand dealers and plain opportunists swarmed into the areas where Japanese Americans lived, forced their way into homes, and grabbed what they wanted. New electric refrigerators were sold for five dollars, dining room suites for ten," recalled journalist Bradford Smith in a 1947 article published by the Common Council for America Unity.

The mainstream press typically described the internment camps with prose more appropriate for an exotic vacation paradise. The *New York Herald Tribune*, reporting on "Camp Harmony" in Puyallup, Washington, concluded, "Army authorities have taken every measure to ease the sting to the Japanese of herding them here. Careful attention is given to food, sanitation facilities, schooling and medical care."

A Camp Harmony resident disagreed, writing a letter describing the center as "a penitentiary—armed guards in towers with spotlights and deadly tommy guns, 15 feet of barbed-wire fences, everyone confined to quarters at 9, lights out at 10 o'clock. The guards are ordered to shoot anyone who approaches within 20 feet of the fences."

The ACLU was uncertain how to respond to Roosevelt's executive order and to the cascade of events that flowed from it. Although Baldwin and others disagreed with the order, the board majority had little appetite for attacking a key strategy of the popular war. Some board members— including co-counsel Morris Ernst—were opposed to taking any position on the executive order. Others supported internment and the concept of loyalty tests for "enemy aliens."[2] So Baldwin adopted a position which was essentially supportive of the government but also sympathetic to people being evacuated and interned.

As the ACLU explained its position in its annual report, "the Civil Liberties Union has co-operated with agencies endeavoring to resettle the Japanese-Americans . . . and has closely and sympathetically followed the activities of the Relocation Authority." But it also tried to mitigate the effects of anti-Japanese hysteria—filing a brief, for instance, opposing a group calling itself Native Sons of the Golden West that wanted to strip American-born Japanese Americans of their citizenship.

There were also differences between the national board and the affiliates—especially those out West, which were witnessing, firsthand, America's treatment of its Japanese American residents.

Anne Kunitani, a Japanese American secretary working in the Northern California ACLU affiliate office, was among those evacuated. Her boss, Ernest Besig, a Cornell University law graduate who had fought on behalf of San Francisco dock workers, had little patience for the national board's approach. Nor did his affiliate's board. As historian Judy Kutulas put it, "Besig's board did not embrace the national organization's enthusiasm for the government, nor was it very sympathetic to the Board's concerns."[3]

Eager to clarify the national board's position, Baldwin put forth competing resolutions on the issue of Japanese detention. The first resolution declared that, absent a declaration of martial law, it was unconstitutional to round up American citizens, deny them due process, and send them off to camps. It did not address the question of so-called enemy aliens. The second proposed resolution conceded the government's authority to remove both citizens and aliens from military zones—implicitly accepting the policy as constitutional. It asserted that such actions must be justified by military necessity, that basic civil liberties must be protected, and that civilians should be involved in the process.

By a two-thirds majority, the board chose the second, nonconfrontational approach, The resolution, adopted June 22, 1942, acknowledged the government's "constitutional right in the present war to establish military zones and to remove persons, either citizens or aliens, from such zones when their presence may endanger national security, even in the absence of the declaration of martial law." It included caveats about military necessity, civilian review, protection of rights, and access to hearings but avoided putting the ACLU in the position of opposing government policy.

The compromise left the ACLU in something of a bind. It was difficult to argue that government actions were legally wrong but also constitutionally permitted. Also, by taking constitutional challenges off the table, the resolution prohibited ACLU attorneys from making some of their most powerful arguments.

Nonetheless, the ACLU plunged ahead, looking for cases that would allow it to help the Japanese without angering the government. Besig was eager to test the evacuation policy. And when he read a newspaper story about Fred Toyosaburo Korematsu, a twenty-three-year-old American-born welder and son of plant nursery owners from Oakland, California, he wondered whether he might have found the ideal client.

The third of four boys, Korematsu had studied chemistry at (but not graduated from) Los Angeles City College. He had tried to enlist in the navy in 1940 but was rejected because of a gastric ulcer. Though he was later reclassified as draft eligible, Pearl Harbor made his status moot—the United States stopped inducting Japanese Americans.

With evacuation imminent, Korematsu opted to stay behind. He dreamed of settling down with Ida Boitano, his Italian America fiancée. Marriage in California was unlikely given a state statute declaring "marriages of white persons with Negroes, Mongolians, members of the Malay race or mulattoes" to be "illegal and void." But the couple figured they could work it out. Ida "was more important to me than anything else."[4]

Korematsu sold his car (at a loss) and rented a room in Oakland. Ida thought plastic surgery to disguise his Asian identity might increase their options. He had the surgery in March 1942 and immediately realized it was a failure. Nonetheless, he started using the name Clyde Sarah—thinking it sounded Spanish enough to help him pass as Spanish-Hawaiian. When his parents and brothers were sent away—initially to an "assembly center" (or temporary detention camp) in San Bruno—Korematsu stayed behind.

On Saturday, Memorial Day, 1942, Korematsu and his fiancée were strolling through San Leandro when they were stopped by a policeman. Korematsu initially claimed to be Clyde Sarah and produced his altered draft registration card to prove it; but he soon admitted he was Japanese American and therefore in violation of the exclusion order. He was arrested and transferred a day later to the Alameda County jail, where Ernest Besig visited him in his cell.

Besig explained that the ACLU was looking for a plaintiff to challenge the exclusion order—which was difficult, he pointed out, especially given the Japanese American Citizens League's opposition to fighting the government. Besig acknowledged the battle would be tough but promised the ACLU would bear the financial costs.

That June 18, the *New York Sun* reported that Korematsu had been released from jail after the ACLU posted a $1,000 bond. It also quoted A.J. Zirpoli, an assistant U.S. attorney, who said that military police would pick up Korematsu and send him into detention. He was arrested within minutes of his release and sent to the detention camp at Tanforan Racetrack, where his family was being held. He requested his own room—a place to think before reuniting with his family—and was put in a converted horse stall. "As I sat there . . . I said, boy, this is really a miserable place, no heat or anything. I mean, this was made for horses, not for human beings," he recalled.[5]

Roger Baldwin was not convinced Korematsu was the ideal plaintiff—in part because he had tried to pass as non-Asian instead of opposing the government outright. Baldwin also feared defending Korematsu might violate the policy against constitutional challenges. He suggested that Besig organize an independent committee to provide financial and public relations support, which would put some distance between the case and the ACLU.

Besig never fully distanced himself from the case, feeling it would be dishonorable to renege on his commitment to Korematsu. As Besig was not licensed to practice law in California, he brought on local attorney Wayne Collins to handle the case. That became yet another source of friction, as the national office was unimpressed with Collins's legal prowess.

As Collins prepared a case for the dismissal of charges again Korematsu, Baldwin reached out to the Roosevelt administration. In an August 28 letter to Edward Ennis, director of the Enemy Alien Control Division, Baldwin reiterated the ACLU's lack of interest in contesting "any cases involving enemy aliens. Our sole concern is with the evacuation of citizens and in those cases only where we are convinced that the order is unreasonable."

On September 1, Federal District Judge Martin Welsh of Sacramento ruled that the government was empowered to intern Japanese citizens and aliens alike and therefore had operated lawfully in confining Korematsu.

On September 8, the case landed in the courtroom of Federal District Judge Adolphus Frederic St. Sure. Korematsu told the judge he had hoped to earn enough money to take his fiancée to the Midwest, where he presumably would not be persecuted for being Japanese. When St. Sure asked whether he was willing to fight for his country, Korematsu replied that he had tried to enlist but been turned down. St. Sure found Korematsu guilty of illegally entering a military zone and sentenced him to five years—remitted to probation—and a fine of $5,000.

Collins filed an appeal three days later, citing error in the denial of all four motions to dismiss and insufficient evidence to justify the verdict. Korematsu was returned to the Tanforan Assembly Center in San Bruno.

Meanwhile, Wayne Collins prepared a brief for the appellate court in which he called internment a "statutory monstrosity" that "entails involuntary servitude" and violates the Thirteenth Amendment.

On December 2, the Ninth Circuit Court of Appeals sustained Korematsu's conviction. It was settled law, opined Judge Curtis Wilbur, that, in waging war, the government was empowered to temporarily encroach on individual liberties. That principle, said Wilbur, "clearly sustains the validity of the proclamation for evacuation." Besig planned to appeal.

The *Christian Science Monitor* applauded the decision and suggested that it might "help to reduce an inflamed condition of public opinion, made critical recently by rebellious acts of avowedly disloyal Japanese in the Tule Lake segregation center."

Around the time Besig sought out Korematsu, Mary Farquharson, a state senator and founder of the ACLU affiliate in Seattle, was also looking for potential plaintiffs. She found Gordon Kiyoshi Hirabayashi, a twenty-four-year-old Quaker and registered conscientious objector who had attended the University of Washington, of which Farquharson was an alumna.

Hirabayashi, the son of immigrant farmers, quit his college studies after the United States entered the war and worked with the American Friends Service Committee preparing prospective evacuees for internment. In May 1942, he took a public stand by surrendering to the U.S. Attorney's office and pronouncing himself "a conscientious objector to evacuation." Hirabayashi was charged with failure to register and refusal to leave Seattle in conformance with the deadline.

Farquharson committed the ACLU to his defense; but after the ACLU board passed its pro-administration resolution, she agreed, under protest, to step aside. Instead she would organize a defense fund for Hirabayashi, and non-ACLU lawyers would handle the case.

A.L. (Abraham Lincoln) Wirin, legal director of the Southern California ACLU affiliate, was also wrestling with how to fight the internment policy. In testimony before the House Select Committee on National Defense Migration, Wirin had publicly opposed the executive order authorizing that policy. "We must not, in the fighting, lose the freedoms for which we fight," he had told the committee.

That April, with Baldwin's backing, Wirin took up the cause of Ernest Kinzo Wakayama, a former postal worker and World War I veteran, and his wife, Toki. The Wakayamas, both American-born children of Japanese immigrants, were incarcerated in the Santa Anita Assembly Center. Wirin filed suit arguing that the military had no authority to exclude American citizens from military areas. Before a three-judge federal panel that October, Wirin argued that the overwhelming majority of Japanese Americans had proved their loyalty to America. "The evacuation order may have been justified by military necessity, but continued detention of Japanese-American citizens is not justified or warranted under the American system of justice," he said.

The following February, the judges issued a writ of habeas corpus empowering the Wakayamas to appear in court to argue the merits of their case. By then camp life had worn them down. Among other unpleasantries, Ernest had been arrested and held in the Los Angeles County Jail for conducting a meeting in the camp in Japanese. Disheartened, the Wakayamas gave up the fight and applied for repatriation to Japan.

In October 1942, the ACLU had passed yet another resolution that made the defense of evacuation cases even more difficult. The so-called Seymour resolution (authored by board member Whitney North Seymour) declared that—barring denial of fundamental due process—the ACLU would not defend individuals presumed to be "cooperating with or acting on behalf of the enemy," even if the case otherwise merited ACLU intervention.

That resolution affected the ACLU's treatment of Minoru Yasui, a twenty-five-year-old native of Hood River, Oregon, where his immigrant parents owned an apple orchard. Yasui had received both his baccalaureate and law degree from the University of Oregon. On the night of March 28, 1942, he walked into the Portland, Oregon, police station and demanded the police arrest him for violating the curfew order. After he was charged and released, he refused to be evacuated.

Yasui was, in many respects, the ideal ACLU plaintiff. He was a highly educated Christian (Methodist) who was in the U.S. Army Reserve. He had tried to sign up to serve numerous times but been rejected because of his ancestry. After Pearl Harbor, Yasui returned home with the intention of practicing law. Prior to that, he had worked as a speechwriter for the Japanese consulate in Chicago—which put him at odds with the Seymour resolution. With the ACLU barred from representing him, he went with a local attorney.

Yasui appeared before federal Judge James Alger Fee on November 16, 1942. Fee agreed that, in the absence of a declaration of martial law, the curfew and evacuation of American citizens of Japanese ancestry was likely illegal. A military commander, he said, did not have the power "to regulate the life and conduct of the ordinary citizen." Congress, alone, ruled Fee, could make laws that "govern the conduct of citizens, even in time of war."

It was stunning language. But the real stunner was to follow—in a passage in which Fee effectively stripped Yasui of his American citizenship. By working as a Japanese propagandist—and giving "his allegiance to the Emperor"—Yasui had forfeited his birthright. And as Yasui was no longer American, he had no standing to sue.

The ACLU board took note of Yasui's intention to appeal but voted, 10 to 4, not to participate, citing the Seymour resolution. But Wirin remained excited about the case, pointing out that if the higher courts followed Fee's reasoning, "all of General DeWitt's exclusion orders . . . will be set aside."

"Roger Baldwin found himself in an extraordinary situation," observed author Samuel Walker. "The ACLU was the only organization challenging the internment program, but he was besieged by attacks from two sides. . . . The conservative-liberal-left coalition on the Board thought he was doing too much, whereas his most vocal affiliate attacked him for not doing enough."[6]

Baldwin spent much of the next several months seeking a comfortable middle ground. In December, he wrote Gus Solomon, the Portland lawyer assisting the Yasui effort, explaining that the ACLU could not "participate officially" in any arguments about Yasui's citizenship but might nonetheless be "of some help" in his appeal.

Ultimately, the ACLU did participate in Yasui's appeal. Wirin was an attorney of record and several ACLU lawyers, including Arthur Garfield Hays and Osmond Fraenkel, signed on to an amicus brief.

Mitsuye Endo also caught the ACLU's eye. Born in Sacramento in 1920 and the daughter of Japanese immigrants, Endo had graduated from a local junior college and worked as a keypunch operator in California's department of employment—until she became a victim of anti-Japanese animus following the Pearl Harbor attack.

With politicians agitating for dismissal of all Japanese American workers, the California Personnel Board came up with a plan to "cleanse" them.

State Attorney General Earl Warren pushed back, arguing that "discriminating against people because of their forebears . . . will be absolutely disruptive of our war effort." Despite Warren's warning, the State Board of Equalization suspended thirteen employees with Japanese ancestry. The official responsible argued that the board, which handled certain taxes and fees, was particularly vulnerable to enemy infiltration. Other state agencies followed suit. Ultimately, the Personnel Board ordered a mass dismissal. "We were given a piece of paper saying we were suspended because we were of Japanese ancestry," Endo recalled.

Alarmed by the purge, the Japanese American Citizens League asked a white attorney, James Purcell, to intercede on the workers' behalf. As Purcell worked on a legal response, the fired employees, including Endo, were evacuated.

Endo ended up at the Tanforan Assembly Center, the same converted racetrack where Korematsu was held. Purcell, whose father had worked as a prison guard, was stunned when he visited Tanforan. "I know a prison when I see it, and Tanforan was a prison."[7]

Purcell was pleased when he discovered Endo. As a Christian woman (Methodist) who didn't read (though did speak) Japanese and had a brother serving in the army, she struck him as a perfect potential plaintiff. In July 1942, Purcell filed a habeas corpus petition on her behalf, seeking her appearance before a judge to make her case for freedom. Meanwhile, Endo was transferred to the Tule Lake internment camp in Newell, California.

The federal district court denied the petition, and Endo's lawyers kicked it up to the Ninth Circuit Court of Appeals, which sought clarification from the Supreme Court on whether the government could indefinitely confine, without due process or a hearing, citizens deemed loyal who had not committed any crime.

The ACLU closely followed the Endo case. Baldwin and Clifford Forster, an ACLU staff lawyer, regularly solicited updates from Purcell. Baldwin and others at the ACLU had doubts about the strength of the case and Purcell's strategy in pursuing it. Among other things, Baldwin fretted that Purcell's strategy would not advance the case to the Supreme Court in time for joint consideration with the other internment cases. Nonetheless, the board voted in August 1943 to consider weighing in on the appeal.

In December 1943, ACLU chairman John Haynes Holmes and Arthur Garfield Hays wrote to Secretary of War Henry Stimson: "Now that the segregation of the disloyal among the Japanese Americans has been completed, we desire to suggest that the time has come to resume the drafting of Japanese American citizens on precisely the same basis as others." They also wrote a letter complaining about restrictions placed on Japanese American scholars in universities, particularly those universities involved in research for the military.

Difficult as it was for the ACLU to build internal consensus, it ultimately played an important role in many of the cases that finally ended up before the Supreme Court. The first to be resolved were those of Gordon Hirabayashi and Minoru Yasui, which were decided June 21, 1943.

The court ruled unanimously against Hirabayashi, endorsing General DeWitt's decision to set a curfew for Japanese Americans. Chief Justice Harlan Stone authored the decision, which found that General Dewitt had acted neither unilaterally nor arbitrarily but was merely exercising authority Congress had granted him by ratifying Roosevelt's executive order.

He also concluded that Congress and President Roosevelt operated within their constitutional authority, writing that, in order to exercise war, the Constitution granted the president and Congress "wide scope for the exercise of judgment and discretion." Since the military had reasonably concluded that a curfew would minimize danger, they were justified in declaring and enforcing a curfew.

In a concurring opinion, Justice Frank Murphy acknowledged that the order was discriminatory: "Today is the first time, so far as I am aware, that we have sustained a substantial restriction of the personal liberty of citizens of the United States based upon the accident of race or ancestry . . . The result is the creation in this country of two classes of citizens. . . . In my opinion, this goes to the very brink of constitutional power."

Although Justice William Douglas supported the government's policy, his concurring opinion made clear his discomfort with implicitly endorsing discrimination: "Detention for reasonable cause is one thing. Detention on account of ancestry is another." The exigencies of war made the military's discriminatory policy justifiable, he concluded.

Legal scholar Jerry Kang argues that the justices' reasoning was both disturbingly disingenuous and innovative. "[As] a matter of theory, the Court waxed eloquent against racism, prejudice, and racial discrimination. Indeed . . . the Court poured the foundation of what we now call strict scrutiny for governmental racial classifications," he wrote. "On the other hand, as a matter of practice, the Court was extremely deferential to claims of military necessity. As Chief Justice Stone explained, 'reasonably prudent men' had 'ample ground' and a 'substantial basis' to believe that the Japanese in America might reasonably be expected to aid a threatened enemy invasion.

"Such reasoning conforms to what we now call racial profiling."[8]

The Supreme Court also ruled against Yasui, in another decision authored by Stone. Stone ruled that Yasui had not, in fact, surrendered his citizenship, but he also concluded that issue was irrelevant. Employing the same reasoning he had applied to the Hirabayashi case, Stone concluded the curfew—even for American citizens—was a legitimate response to the harms threatened by the war.

A year and a half later, on December 18, 1944, the court decided the two big remaining internment cases. The atmosphere was considerably different than had it been in the months following the Pearl Harbor bombing, when many Americans saw danger in virtually any Asian face.

In the closing days of 1944, six months after the D-Day invasion, Allied victory seemed not just plausible but imminent. In a story published on the third anniversary of the Pearl Harbor raid, Canada's *Globe and Mail* reported that production was "now eight times what it was in 1941. Planes are coming off assembly lines at nearly 14 times the 1941 rate." New York's *Herald Tribune* declared, "America's war machine is moving relentlessly ahead to eventual victory."

The day before the Supreme Court made public its decisions on the remaining internment cases, the War Department announced it was ending the practice. The War Department had concluded several weeks earlier that interment was no longer a military necessity but, wary of upsetting West Coast voters, the Roosevelt administration had delayed making its intentions clear until after the presidential election, in which Roosevelt defeated Republican challenger Thomas E. Dewey.

With the Supreme Court decision imminent and the election decided, the government could finally start shutting down what the ACLU termed the "most complete and tragic exhibition of race prejudice against a single minority in American history." (In making that sweeping assessment in its 1945 annual report, the ACLU apparently forgot about America's race-based slavery.)

"Since the evacuation, our armed forces steadily have pushed the enemy in the Pacific farther from our shores and closer to the Japanese home islands. Although hard fighting is ahead in the Pacific, it no longer can be said . . . that an enemy invasion of the west coast on a large scale is a substantial possibility," declared the War Department.

Beginning January 2, the remaining internees would gradually be freed: "Those persons of Japanese ancestry whose records have stood the test of Army scrutiny during the past two years will be permitted the same freedom of movement throughout the United States as other loyal citizens and law-abiding aliens," said the government.

The Japanese American Citizens League hailed the policy reversal as a "vindication of the loyalty of the Japanese-American population." League president Saburo Kido credited "the wonderful combat record" of American soldiers of Japanese ancestry.

The Supreme Court's decision in favor of Mitsuye Endo the day after the War Department's announcement was decidedly anticlimactic. The unanimous decision, authored by William O. Douglas, granted Endo a writ of habeas corpus—which theoretically would have allowed all Japanese Americans who could prove their loyalty to leave the camps. But, of course, the Roosevelt administration was already taking care of that.

Douglas did not dispute the government's right to imprison citizens who presented a threat, but noted that did not include Endo: "A citizen who is concededly loyal presents no problem of espionage or sabotage."

In his concurring opinion, Murphy went even further: "I am of the view that detention in Relocation Centers of persons of Japanese ancestry regardless of loyalty is not only unauthorized by Congress or the Executive but is another example of the unconstitutional resort to racism inherent in the entire evacuation program."

The high court split, 6 to 3, on Korematsu, upholding his conviction and detention. The decision, authored by Hugo Black, conceded the policy was a hardship on Japanese Americans, but "hardships are part of war, and war is an aggregation of hardships." Black rebuked those who called the facilities concentration camps, deeming it an "unjustifiable" term "with all the ugly connotations that term implies."

In dissenting, Justice Owen Roberts argued that the government's actions were a "clear violation" of the Constitution as they punished a citizen "solely because of his ancestry, without evidence or inquiry concerning his loyalty and good disposition towards the United States." Justice Frank Murphy's dissent declared that the internment policy went over "'the very brink of constitutional power" and tumbled into "the ugly abyss of racism."

Looking back on the cases from the vantage point of 1998, Chief Supreme Court Justice William Rehnquist, writing in *American Heritage*, observed, "There is a certain disingenuousness in this sequence of three opinions—Hirabayashi, Korematsu, and Endo. There was no reason to think that Gordon Hirabayashi and Fred Korematsu were any less loyal to the United States than was Mitsuye Endo. Presumably they would have been entitled to relief from detention upon the same showing as that made by Endo. But even had Hirabayashi tried to raise that question in his case, he would have failed, for the Court chose to confine itself to the curfew issue. It was not until we were clearly winning the war that the Court came around to this view in Endo. The process illustrates in a rough way the Latin maxim *Inter arma [enim] silent leges* (in time of war the laws are silent)."

Even as America abandoned the policy of warehousing loyal Japanese Americans, it could not admit that it had done anything fundamentally wrong or make amends in any serious way. When America finally decided

to free the captives, the major concern was not for those unjustly imprisoned but for white Americans wary of their presence.

Secretary of the Interior Harold Ickes promised the new policy "most
definitely does not mean that there will be a hasty mass movement back
into the coastal area."

California Governor Earl Warren, who had been among the first calling for their exclusion of Japanese, issued a statement asking his constitu-
ents to respect the constitutional rights of the returning Japanese. But others
made it clear they had no intention of welcoming the returning exiles. "We
believe the Japanese still are dangerous to the war effort. We see no reason
why they should be allowed to return to the coast, especially when they
are getting along all right where they are," said Benjamin Smith, president
of the Remember Pearl Harbor League based in Washington State.

The ACLU noted in its annual report that "although the Pacific coast
was again open to the return of most of the 115,000 evacuated, compara-
tively few went back. Reports of violence and of threatened violence, and
difficulties in reestablishing themselves in property occupied by others . . .
made resettlement a formidable task for people who had sacrificed so many
of their possessions and who had been living for almost three years as wards
of the government."

In time, anti-Japanese sentiment cooled. And the ACLU tried to help.
It filed suits on behalf of individuals the military still tried to exclude and
finally won a decision denying the military the power to enforce individual exclusion orders. But the divisions that had haunted the ACLU in the
early days of internment did not go away. As Walker notes, "The most urgent problem involved the so-called renunciants whom the government
had begun to deport. Many changed their minds and sought to regain their
American citizenship. . . . The ACLU offered to represent them, but this
only precipitated another bitter internal dispute." Eventually Wirin "managed to salvage an ACLU role by representing three clients," and the courts,
"in a series of cases that dragged on until 1951, ordered citizenship restored
to the renunciants."[9]

As America grudgingly reintegrated its Japanese American citizens, the war
marched grimly toward resolution. On April 11, 1945, American troops
liberated Buchenwald. Of an estimated 60,000 held there, roughly 21,000

were still alive. The liberators marched hundreds of the citizens of Weimar through the camps to bear witness.

The next day, Franklin Roosevelt died of a cerebral hemorrhage. Two and a half hours earlier he had complained of a severe headache. He was in Warm Spring, Georgia, at "the Little White House." Roosevelt was sixty-three and had spent more time as president than any of his predecessors. The new President, Harry Truman, proclaimed April 14 a national day of mourning.

Two weeks after Roosevelt's death, Americans freed some 32,000 captives from the Dachau concentration camp. Upon seeing the American vehicles in the distance, "There was one cry: 'Here are the Americans!'" reported the *New York Herald Tribune*. American General Henning Linden forced German captives to gaze upon the corpses of the dead. American soldiers were so angered and sickened by the cruelty and suffering that some retaliated by torturing and killing their German prisoners of war.

The next day, Adolf Hitler took his life. A few days later, on May 7, at 2:41 a.m. French time, Germany surrendered unconditionally to General Dwight D. Eisenhower's chief of staff, General Walter Bedell "Beetle" Smith, at the red schoolhouse Eisenhower used as headquarters in Reims, France.

Upon signing for Germany, Army Chief of Staff Jodl commented, "With this signature, the German people and armed forces are for better or worse delivered into the victor's hands. . . . I can only express the hope that the victor will treat them with generosity."

The official announcement of the end of the war came the next morning. In a radio address delivered from the White House, President Truman declared, "Our victory is but half won. The West is free, but the East is still in bondage to the treacherous tyranny of Japan. When the last Japanese division has surrendered unconditionally, then only will our fighting job be done."

Three months later, the war entered its final phase. It was preceded by the successful test of a new weapon at a U.S. Army facility in the Jornada del Muerto desert in New Mexico. On August 6, the War Department released an astonishing statement: "Mankind's successful transition to a new age, the atomic age, was ushered in July 16, 1945. . . . Here in a remote section of the Alamogordo Air Base, 120 miles southeast of Albuquerque, the first man-made atomic explosion, the outstanding achievement of nuclear science, was achieved at 5:30 a.m. of that day. Darkening heavens pouring forth rain and lightning immediately up to the zero hour heightened the drama." The new weapon, speculated the War Department, "may even be the instrumentality to end all major wars."

The day of that unexpected announcement, a bomb of unprecedented destructiveness went off in Hiroshima, Japan. "Japanese perished by uncounted thousands from the searing, crushing atomic blast that annihilated 60 percent of the 343,000 population center for Hiroshima," reported the Associated Press. The *New York Herald Tribune* reported, "it would be incorrect to say these victims were burned to death, because death-dealing rays generated at that incredible heat explode atoms. . . . What happened to the people of Hiroshima never happened to human beings before."

Three days later a bomb exploded in Nagasaki, population 253,000. The Associated Press reported that it destroyed 30 percent of the town, leaving the shipping and railway center completely covered with smoke and dust. The plutonium-239 Nagasaki bomb was substantially more powerful than the uranium-235 Hiroshima bomb. Brigadier General Thomas F. Farrell, who oversaw atomic bombing operations, said the new bomb was "so powerful it made obsolete the kind which blasted Hiroshima Monday." American pilots littered the landscape with leaflets warning that the "the awful fact" of atomic power "is one for you to ponder and we solemnly assure you it is grimly accurate."

Less than a week later, the war was over. On August 14, at 7 p.m., President Truman told reporters, "I have received this afternoon a message from the Japanese Government . . . a full acceptance of the Potsdam declaration which specifies the unconditional surrender of Japan." Truman also announced a two-day holiday for all federal employees. The peace agreement was signed on September 2.

On that day, the *Herald Tribune* observed that New York City was in a solemn mood, that on "the eve of the first peace-time Labor Day in four years," reminders abounded that "the battle against unemployment is yet to be won."

Also yet to be won was the battle against discrimination. Two weeks after V-J (Victory in Japan) Day, Charles Loeb, a correspondent for the

Baltimore Afro-American, watched as Supreme Allied Commander Douglas MacArthur ordered the American flag raised over the embassy in Tokyo. The journalist reflected on the status of black troops, who, for the most part, were relegated to non-combat and segregated positions in the military: "In reporting that these men are pessimistic about post-war race relations, I am not giving the opinions of illiterate, unlettered men, but of ex-collegians, clerks, newspapermen, businessmen, barbers, bakers, cooks, and laborers who are about to return to civil life. . . . They were hoping that V-J Day would also be FEPC [Fair Employment Practice Committee] Day and E-J (Equality Justice) Day. They're a little disappointed."

Still, in the wake of the victory against Nazism, Fascism, and Japanese imperialism, America had much to celebrate. And celebrate America did. On October 15, San Francisco welcomed Admiral William Halsey and some fourteen units of his Third Fleet. That afternoon, his USS *Dakota* led an armada of warships that swept through the fog and under the Golden Gate Bridge as thousands looked on from the bridge, the piers, and the San Francisco hills. Navy blimps bearing welcome banners hovered above and submarines trailed behind. "We have dreamed of, hoped for, fought for and prayed for [this day]. We are glad to be back," said the admiral in comments broadcast via radio.

On October 27, Navy Day celebrations were held across the nation. The biggest was in New York City, where forty-seven warships steamed into the Hudson River and honored President Harry Truman, who stood in review on the presidential destroyer, with a twenty-one-gun salute as carrier planes soared above. In an address in Central Park before a crowd estimated at one million, Truman declared, "We seek to use our military power solely to preserve the peace of the world. For we now know that that is the only sure way to make our own freedom secure."

Truman's articulation of his "Peace by Force" foreign policy (as the *Chicago Tribune* called it) underscored the world's and America's new reality. America had emerged from World War II as the world's only atomic power, its dominant economic power, and the undisputed leader of the free world.

In its first post-war annual report, the ACLU noted how effortlessly civil liberties were restored. The ACLU attributed the striking difference from the post–World War I era to a more tolerant government. "Only a few score persons had been prosecuted for speech or publication. Public debate and discussion had remained unrestricted. The rights of minorities, save for the Japanese, had not been curtailed. No war-time hysteria had marked the country. Organized labor had become too strongly entrenched to permit wholesale attacks upon the trade union movement."

But one huge area in which the country fell conspicuously short was race—a failing made even more conspicuous by the fact that it had used a Jim Crow army to fight a war against an enemy largely defined by anti-Semitism and racism. Roosevelt's military anti–Jim Crow executive order (issued in return for A. Philip Randolph calling off his march on Washington) papered over the problem instead of solving it.

In June 1942, roughly a year after Randolph called off his march on Washington, Winfred W. Lynn, a black landscape gardener from Jamaica, Queens, received his draft notice. Lynn, whose brother was a civil rights attorney, responded by writing the draft board a letter stating he was ready to serve but not in a segregated unit: "Unless I am assured that I can serve in a mixed regiment and that I will not be compelled to serve in a unit undemocratically selected as a Negro group, I will refuse to report for induction."

Lynn's ultimatum led to his arrest and thirteen days in jail, after which he went into the army on the advice of his brother, who told him he would only have standing to sue if he allowed himself to be inducted. The ACLU embraced Lynn, reasoning that a suit on his behalf—based on the 1940 Draft Act, which forbade racial discrimination—would be a perfect test of whether segregation constituted discrimination. It would also raise the issue of whether a war for democracy should be fought by a segregated army. Arthur Hays became the lead attorney on the case, and the ACLU formed the Lynn Committee to Abolish Segregation in the Armed Forces to help publicize and raise funds for the effort.

Lynn lost in both the district court and New York Circuit Court of appeals; and in May 1944, the Supreme Court refused to review the case because Lynn had been sent outside the country. The case was "moot, it appearing that the petitioner is no longer in the respondent's custody," said the high court.

Hays wrote to James Forrestal, secretary of the navy, to complain about the military's decision to remove Lynn beyond the court's jurisdiction.

Forrestal assured Hays that it was his policy "to assist, rather than impede, the determination of constitutional questions by the courts." But the ACLU had no other case ready to test the policy.

Lynn was honorably discharged after serving nineteen months in the South Pacific, having achieved the rank of sergeant. In an interview with the *Baltimore Afro-American*, he confided that "the Army wasn't half as bad for me as I expected because all of the men with me knew of my case and were watching out for any persecution. The Army knew that the Lynn Committee to Abolish Segregation in the Armed Forces back home in the states would raise hell if they'd tried anything."

Just before taking on the Lynn case, ACLU Chairman Holmes had invited novelist Pearl Buck to chair a conference on racial discrimination in the military. She accepted, suggesting that they limit invitations to "white people, although I think it would be all right, if you agree, to have a few Negro leaders of the caliber of Elmer Carter [editor of *Opportunity*, a National Urban League magazine billed as a "Journal of Negro Life"] to be there."

Buck launched her project with a luncheon on March 26, 1942, at New York's Hotel Commodore, which led to a standing committee focused on racial discrimination in the military. In its annual report, released in the summer of 1942, the ACLU noted that anger at "exclusion from many branches of the armed forces and from defense industries, coupled with segregation, flared in the Negro press and was vigorously voiced by Negro agencies."

In May 1943, Buck and the ACLU announced a continuing Conference Against Negro Discrimination: a "nationwide movement to do away with race discrimination in the war effort," as summed up by the *Atlanta Daily World*, coordinated by a nucleus of twenty-six national organizations. "The eyes of the world are upon us, to see how we work out our democracy here at home," declared Buck.

The world's eyes certainly focused on America over the next several weeks as race riots erupted across the country. Although the disturbances were not on the scale of the riots of World War I, they challenged any notion that the United States might be on the road to racial harmony.

In late May of 1943 in Mobile, Alabama, violence broke out at the Alabama Dry Dock and Shipbuilding Company after twelve blacks were upgraded to welding jobs. The promotions (ordered by the president's Committee on Fair Employment Practice) angered white workers, who recoiled at the idea of blacks working closely with whites—especially white women. The whites attacked their black co-workers with pipes and other tools of the trade. Troops from nearby Brookley Field restored order.

In early June, the-so-called Zoot Suit Riots erupted in Los Angeles. For nine days, American soldiers assaulted minorities, primarily Mexican Americans, for their fashion sense, suspected misconduct, non-Anglo heritage, and presumed lack of patriotism.

Beaumont, Texas, boiled over in mid-June. There, resentment toward black workers in the shipbuilding industry was heightened by reports of a black man raping a white woman. The suspect was wounded by police and only escaped mob vengeance by dying of wounds he had sustained in the shooting. Rumors of a second rape—never confirmed—reignited the anti-black violence.

A week later fighting broke out in Belle Isle Park, on the Detroit River, between blacks and whites trying to escape 90-degree heat. Rumors that whites had thrown a black woman and her baby into the river and that blacks were raping white women fed fuel to a riot that left 34 dead and more than 765 wounded before federal troops could quell the violence.

In the wake of that summer of violence, Pearl Buck's committee sent telegrams urging President Roosevelt to appoint a committee "of distinguished citizens" to investigate racial violence and to broadcast a radio appeal "to the American people to end these outrages and devote themselves to establishing racial understanding."

Other than highlighting racism in the military, Pearl Buck's committee seems not to have accomplished much, but its activities coincided with the ACLU's representation of several black Seabees. They were discharged from the navy—without trial—as "undesirables" in October 1943.

With the help of the ACLU, the NAACP, the National Citizens' Committee for Winfred Lynn (as it had been renamed), and the Congress of Industrial Organization's War Relief Committee, the men—nineteen in all—finally got a hearing in December 1944 before the Navy Board of Review.

They had been discharged within a few days of speaking out about discrimination in the Jim Crow military at a meeting called by a commanding officer at the base in Trinidad, West Indies. From the military's perspective, the men's candid comments were tantamount to sedition. One of the men, Isaac McNatt, told a radio interviewer: "We joined the Navy and we are paying and will pay for being Negroes."

Hays argued that the meeting could not have been seditious, since it was called by the men's superior officer. "The men were asked off the record what their complaints were. They spoke frankly. This was not a seditious meeting. . . . Yet they were discharged without honor, merely for obeying orders at this meeting."

In April 1945, the navy publicly reversed itself. Fourteen of the men had their discharge status upgraded to honorable. One was not upgraded because, according to the navy, he had violated various unspecified rules. The remaining four men had not petitioned for review.

Ultimately, the accomplishments by the few persons of color permitted to fight had more impact on public opinion, and perhaps on public policy, than the lawsuits brought in the name of equality.

Japanese Americans served, for the most part, in segregated units; but those units—most notably the 100th Infantry Battalion, the 442nd Infantry Regiment, and the 522nd Field Artillery Battalion—became legendary for their valor. The same is true of the black 92nd and 93rd infantry divisions and of the Tuskegee Airmen (formally known as the 332nd Fighter Group and the 477th Bombardment Group).

As scholars Andrea Hunter and Alethea Rollins noted, "in combat, the Tuskegee Airmen flew over 1,500 missions and over 15,000 sorties, and individual airmen were decorated [with] the Distinguished Flying Cross, Legion of Merit, Silver Star, and Bronze Star."

As one black aircraft and engine mechanic aircraft and engine mechanic put it, "we proved that black Americans were not ignorant, that we could fly airplanes just like any other ethnic group, if given the chance. We proved that we could excel. . . . [We] sank a destroyer with 50 caliber AP bullets. We could soldier, we were sharp dressers, and proud to be called the cream of the crop."[10]

In 1947, A. Philip Randolph and Grant Reynolds, a Harlem activist and member of the New York State Corrections Commission, co-founded the Committee Against Jim Crow in Military Service and Training. Joe Louis signed on as a member. The men were spurred to act by the introduction of a Universal Military Training Act in Congress that did not prohibit segregation. "The attempt by the armed forces to steam-roller conscription legislation through Congress without even a mention of equality for Negro youths has done more than anything to revive the wartime resentment of Negroes," said Reynolds, who had served as a chaplain with the 366th Infantry Regiment during the war.

In June 1948, Randolph and Reynolds formed yet another organization, the League for Non-Violent Civil Disobedience Against Military Segregation, and threatened to discourage blacks from registering from military service unless Truman issued an executive order barring discrimination in the military. "I believe that the enactment of this peace-time draft law with no provisions against the elimination of jimcrowism in it will set back the cause of civil rights a hundred years," said Randolph.

On July 26, 1948, President Truman signed an executive order prohibiting discrimination in the U.S. military. The executive order reversed Secretary of Defense James Forrestal and military leaders who, in a meeting with civil rights leaders at the end of April, had defended segregation.

Executive Order 9981 mandated "equality of treatment and opportunity for all persons in the Armed Services without regard to race, color, religion or national origin." The order created the president's Committee on Equality of Treatment and Opportunity in the Armed Services to help guide the process of integration.

Because the order mandated "equality of treatment" as opposed to an end to segregation, the reaction from civil rights leaders was mixed. The situation was confused further by a statement attributed to General Omar Bradley, army chief of staff, saying the army would eliminate segregation only "when the nation as a whole changes." At a press conference, President Truman said he believed Bradley had been misquoted and that he expected the order ultimately to end racial segregation. Shortly thereafter, Randolph endorsed the order: "We have been given assurances that segregation is unequivocally banned under the executive order," he said.

So concluded the drama that began before the war, when Randolph's 1941 threat of a march on Washington forced Roosevelt to sign Executive Order 8802. The era of colored regiments, Japanese American battalions, and whites-only leadership was finally at the beginning of an end.

The new executive order did not simply expand opportunities for minorities in the military. As legal scholar John L. Newby II observed, it "had implications in the fight for broader civil rights. The Executive Order was a presidential proclamation of the right to bear arms for one's country as a civil right. It also provided ammunition for advocates presenting subsequent challenges against discrimination in other contexts. . . . With discrimination on the ropes in the venue of federal government, it was only a matter of time before broader fights against societal injustice could be successfully raised and won."[11]

It was also a confirmation of Roger Baldwin's conviction that race would continue to be a dominant issue in American life. Beginning with its deep involvement in the Scottsboro Boys battle, the ACLU had signaled its intention to be a major player in the fight for racial justice—even as it largely deferred to organizations such as the NAACP.

The ACLU continued to play that role in the late 1940s, joining in a landmark amicus brief (*Shelley v. Kraemer*) where the NAACP's Thurgood Marshall took the lead. The case centered on a black couple who purchased a house in St. Louis covered by an exclusionary covenant. Although the covenant prohibited its sale to blacks or members of "Mongolian" races, Ethel and J.D. Shelley bought the duplex via a third party in 1945, unaware of the restriction. A local group filed suit to invalidate the sale. The trial judge refused to enforce the covenant because the restrictive agreement on which it was based had never been finalized, but the Missouri Supreme Court reversed him. On May 3, 1948, the case was decided unanimously by the Supreme Court. (Three justices had recused themselves, presumably for possible conflicts arising from their own involvement in restrictive covenants.)

The opinion was delivered by Chief Justice Fred M. Vinson, who reasoned that although private parties could make agreements restricted by race, they could not turn to the state, which was bound by the Fourteenth Amendment, to enforce such agreements.

Thurgood Marshall pronounced the decision the greatest blow yet against "the pattern of segregation existing within the United States." Roger Baldwin likely had that case in mind a few days later when, in a speech at Cooper Union, he declared, "The United States is alert as never before to the evils of race discrimination and segregation. . . . The southern revolt against the civil rights program is the last stand of those who know they are fighting a losing battle."

Baldwin was overly optimistic in his appraisal of the nation's progress on civil rights, but he was significantly more clear-eyed in his view of the incipient Red Scare, which loomed against the backdrop of increasing tension with the Soviet Union.

At a joint session of Congress on March 12, 1947, Truman had requested $400 million to push back against threats to Greece and Turkey from the Soviet Union. In that speech, he articulated what came to be known as the Truman Doctrine.

A stark choice faced nations in terms of what types of societies they would become, Truman said: "One way of life is based upon the will of the majority, and is distinguished by free institutions, representative government, free elections, guarantees of individual liberty, freedom of speech and religion, and freedom from political oppression. The second way of life is based upon the will of a minority forcibly imposed upon the majority. It relies upon terror and oppression, a controlled press and radio, fixed elections, and the suppression of personal freedoms."

America's policy, he said, was "to support free peoples who are resisting attempted subjugation by armed minorities or by outside pressures. [We] must assist free peoples to work out their own destinies in their own way."

It was the beginning of a major shift in foreign policy as the containment of communism became official American policy. For the ACLU, it was a time of distraction from progress in civil rights and civil liberties as the organization refocused on the Red hysteria.

In its 1947–1948 annual report, the ACLU observed: "The Republican-controlled Congress not only failed to enact any major bill for civil rights of any sort, but through the irresponsible antics of its House Committee on Un-American Activities contributed largely to the hysteria against everything conceived to be Communist. . . . The Administration under political pressure resorted to unprecedented moves against Communists."

That pressure resulted in the indictment of the twelve-member national board of the Communist Party for violating the Smith Act. That law, also known as the Alien Registration Act of 1940, prohibited advocating the violent overthrow of the government.

John Gates, editor of the *Daily Worker*, and William Z. Foster, national chairman of the Communist Party and a former member of the national committee of the ACLU, were among those arrested and charged in July 1948.

In an article in the *New Leader* that July, Baldwin made the case for defending Communist speech as part of a larger argument for supporting democracy and free speech generally. The concept of political democracy, he argued, meant "the extension of democracy on fronts where entrenched power and privilege resist. It is racial equality, anti-monopoly, public ownership, less for the big boys, more for the little fellows. It's what every progressive wants and must fight for if a free democracy is to be the instrument of advancing power against reaction and Communism alike."

The Communist Party leaders' trial began in January of 1949. Because of his heart problems, Foster's trial was separated from the others. The government's case relied largely on two FBI agents and nine informants who had joined the party to gather information.

Toward the end of the trial, the Soviet Union provided a major distraction. On August 29, 1949, at a test site in what is now Kazakhstan, the USSR detonated an atomic bomb. It was not until September 23 that President Truman confirmed the news. The "eventual development of this new force by other nations was to be expected. This probability has always been taken into account by us," he said.

Tass, the official Soviet news agency, released neither a denial nor a confirmation. Instead, its statement alluded to "large-scale blasting work" in the country that "might draw attention beyond the confines of the Soviet Union."

For a nation already prone to Red hysteria, the news was a gut-wrenching shock.

Three weeks after Truman's announcement, the nine-month trial of the Communist Party leaders ended. The jury needed only seven hours to find all eleven guilty. Since they had not been convicted of any overt act but merely of joining a widely reviled political organization, the verdict raised the question of whether every Communist Party member was subject to imprisonment.

Congressman Marcantonio called the verdict an attempt "to brand as a crime the basic American right of free political opinion and free political association." National Committeewoman Elizabeth Gurley Flynn vowed the party would continue to "operate as usual." William Foster, still await-ing trial, said the verdict would "injure American democratic prestige all over the world. The book burners, thought controllers, anti-Semites, Negro haters, union smashing and Fascist reactionaries may well rejoice at this victory over the democratic forces. This conviction is another big step on the road to fascism."

Baldwin responded with resignation. The convictions were "almost in-evitable," he said, given the language of the 1940 law—which the ACLU had always opposed.

In a lengthy article entitled "Free Speech Works Both Ways" published in the *New York Herald Tribune* two days after the verdict, Baldwin de-nounced American Communists as "servants of a police-state philosophy opposed to every principle of what we regard as liberty." But he harshly criticized the recent trial and the increasingly more repressive turn of gov-ernment policy: "To get at the Communists, we have adopted unprece-dented and sweeping loyalty tests, not only of all federal employees and workers in firms contracting with the government, but of teachers and public employees in many states and registrants for the draft," wrote Baldwin.

The attorney general, he noted, had declared more than 150 organ-izations to be subversive, "mostly for their Communist complexion." Other democracies had learned that political suppression doesn't work: "Free speech works both ways. Communists are entitled to speak. But they must expect to hear in return a chorus of voices against them and feel the im-pact of the democratic truths." The answer to abusive speech, he con-cluded, "is more free speech—with those of us who believe in democracy speaking out loud and clear."

It would take eight years for the Supreme Court to decide that defen-dants could not be prosecuted simply for their beliefs. In that 6 to 1 major-ity decision (*Yates v. United States*), Justice John Marshall Harlan wrote: "We are . . . faced with the question whether the Smith Act prohibits advocacy and teaching of forcible overthrow [of government] as an abstract princi-ple, divorced from any effort to instigate action to that end. . . . We hold that it does not."

In a concurring opinion, Justice Hugo Black wrote, "Unless there is com-plete freedom for expression of all ideas, whether we like them or not, concerning the way government should be run and who shall run it, I doubt if any views, in the long run, can be secured against the censor."

In late October 1949, on the eve of the ACLU's thirtieth anniversary, the ACLU announced that Roger Baldwin, at sixty-five, would be stepping down the following January. His replacement, Patrick Murphy Malin, had been an economics professor at Swarthmore College for twenty years.

The *Christian Science Monitor*'s weekly "appreciation," published on October 29, was a bouquet to Roger Baldwin.

"Justice Oliver Wendell Holmes, in a famous opinion, demanded 'freedom for the thought we hate.' Fighting for the freedom to express this or that thought somebody—usually the majority of Americans—hates has been the ACLU's and Mr. Baldwin's chief occupation. It is not always a popular pursuit. For the defense of the right to speak is sometimes confused with a defense of what is spoken. The battle to assure a criminal a 'speedy and public trial by an impartial jury' and the other guarantees of the Sixth Amendment sometimes has been strangely construed as sympathy with crime," observed the *Monitor*. "But the ACLU has hewed ahead and let the chips fall where they may."

Malin arrived at a contentious time for America and for the ACLU—at a time, not unlike when the ACLU was founded, when the world was realigning and the threat of presumably radical philosophies was being reconsidered. Major school desegregation cases were working their way through the courts, the State Department had effectively declared war on Communists, and America was experiencing "an atmosphere in which fear makes the maintenance of civil liberties precarious," in the reckoning of the ACLU.

In his letter to the National Committee in February 1929 laying out his vision for the future, Baldwin had focused, in part, on the organization's deficiencies: "We are in effect a highly centralized organization operating from New York on cases arising all over the country. We work by correspondence and through local attorneys and representatives. In only a few centers where issues are acute have we local committees. We have no membership as such. We have 3,000 contributors all over the country who only indirectly have any share in controlling policies or activities."

Twenty years later, many of the criticisms still applied; but the organization had grown in both size and stature. It had offices or local affiliates in northern and southern California, Connecticut, Illinois, Iowa, Maryland, Massachusetts, Michigan, Missouri, New York, Ohio, Pennsylvania, and Washington State. It counted correspondents in virtually all the states and had a roster of roughly a thousand lawyers it could call on for help. It was more powerful and more esteemed than ever. Still, judging by the language in its annual report, it felt immensely challenged: "Never in our thirty years were obligations so heavy, nor the stakes for the Union and all democratic forces so high."

During an interview, biographer Peggy Lamson asked Baldwin whether he considered the ACLU his "enduring cause." He agreed that he did—not just because, in her words, he "invented it," but because "no fight for civil liberties ever stays won. So I always had to stick with it."

7

McCarthy Crosses a Line and Eisenhower Sends Troops to Little Rock

Nineteen fifty found America in the throes of a Red Panic more chilling than the scare following World War I. Then, fear-mongering politicians warned of wild-eyed Bolsheviks—and promoted mass deportations, persecution, and speech restrictions to fight them. Russia's atomic bomb lent the current struggle an epic dimension. Many Americans welcomed a champion who could keep the country safe.

Joseph McCarthy, a self-styled war hero and first-term senator from Wisconsin, decided to be that fearless warrior—or at least to take a shot at playing the role. That January, after former State Department official Alger Hiss was sentenced to prison for lying about his connection to a Communist-affiliated spy ring, McCarthy let America know that Hiss was just the tip of the Soviet spear. The next month in a speech in Wheeling, West Virginia, McCarthy accused the State Department of harboring hundreds of Communists. And he promised to force President Harry Truman to "clean [the State Department] out."

Two days after that speech, McCarthy released a letter accusing the State Department of harboring fifty-seven Communists and demanded Truman provide information that would allow Congress to expose them. State Department spokesman Lincoln White called the allegations absurd: "We know of no Communist members in the Department and if we find any they will be summarily dismissed."

Deputy Undersecretary of State John Peurifoy demanded that McCarthy substantiate his claims. Instead, as columnist Drew Pearson pointed out, "when the Senator from Wisconsin finally was pinned down, he could produce not 57, but only 4 names of State Department officials whom he claimed were Communists." Of those four, one had never worked for the State Department, two had resigned years ago, and the fourth had been exonerated.

In a Senate speech that February, McCarthy claimed the spy ring in the State Department was directed by a "big three"—two men and one woman—but refused to identify them. "To broadcast vague charges about the State Department without supporting names or facts is merely to feed the atmosphere of suspicion and apprehension," argued columnist Marquis Childs, but McCarthy's Republican colleagues backed him. In early March, Truman grudgingly agreed to allow Senate investigators access to the State Department "loyalty files" only "because of the serious national issue raised by Senator Joseph McCarthy . . . in charging that 81 Communists now hold or have held State Department positions," reported the *Philadelphia Inquirer*.

During a Senate hearing that March, McCarthy accused former judge and ACLU board member Dorothy Kenyon of involvement with some twenty-eight Communist-linked entities. Kenyon fired back, calling McCarthy an "unmitigated liar" who was "taking cowardly refuge in his Congressional immunity." As for the organizations he accused her of being involved in, "most of them I never heard of and a few I remember vaguely as some I made speeches before."

McCarthy also leveled charges of Communist affiliation against the State Department's roving ambassador-at-large and against the wife of Secretary of State Dean Acheson.

As the State Department disputed McCarthy's claims, the executive branch redoubled its efforts to keep sensitive information out of Soviet hands. Agents from the Atomic Energy Commission (AEC) forced *Scientific American* magazine to burn all three thousand copies of its April 1950 issue and to destroy all plates used in printing an article on moral issues raised by the hydrogen bomb.

Scientific American publisher Gerard Piel pointed out that any technical information in the article was already known in scientific circles. The AEC action, he said, amounted to a "gag on atomic scientists."

That May, the ACLU wrote a letter to the AEC expressing concern "over this censorship of persons who do not discuss classified material" but whose knowledge makes them "the best qualified to speak" on "perhaps the most important issue confronting the nation today." Gorden Dean, acting chairman of the AEC, replied that he was not "muzzling" scientists but merely restricting information of possible use to enemies "undertaking an H-bomb project."

Meanwhile, anxiety over vulnerability to espionage and aggression grew. That June 25, after soldiers from the North Korean People's Army marched across the 38th parallel, former Army Undersecretary Tracy S. Voorhees told a House committee that an atomic attack on America was "more than a possibility." Congressman Lloyd Bentsen demanded that the United States give North Korea an "atomic ultimatum."

Demands for cracking down on Communists grew more insistent. Only by breaking relations with all countries under Soviet domination could America prevent agents from controlling the "Communist fifth column," argued Nevada Senator Patrick McCarran. He proposed requiring Communists to register as well as barring them and other presumed insurgents from governmental positions, residency, or naturalization.

As McCarran's bill moved through Congress, some legislators warned that it would trample the Bill of Rights. "All of us may become victims of the gallows we erect for the enemies of freedom," argued Senator Herbert Lehman of New York.

West Virginia senator Harley Kilgore put forth what he viewed as a milder and less intrusive substitute. His proposal would empower the FBI—in the event of war, invasion, or a radical uprising—to incarcerate Communists until America, in Kilgore's words, "could weed out the sheep from the goats."

House and Senate conferees agreed to a version of the bill combining "the toughest features of legislation passed by both Houses," reported the *Washington Post*. Truman vetoed the bill on September 22, calling it "ineffective and unworkable" and "the greatest danger to freedom of speech, press and assembly since the Alien and Sedition Laws of 1798."

The House immediately overrode Truman's veto by vote of 286 to 48, and the Senate passed it 57 to 10. The bill created the Subversive Activities

Control Board and gave all Communist organizations thirty days to register with the Justice Department.

In the ACLU's annual report, ACLU Executive Director Patrick Murphy fretted about the emergent "pervasive social atmosphere of fear and intolerance" infusing America. He criticized McCarthy's attack on Dorothy Kenyon as "unworthy of a member of the Senate."

The growing national anxiety only fueled McCarthy's penchant for wild accusations. In September 1951, the *New York Post* launched a seventeen-part series titled "SMEAR Inc.—The One-Man Mob of Joe McCarthy." In introducing the feature, *Post* editor James Wechsler wrote, "many men know the scope of the McCarthy fraud, but too few men—especially in Washington DC—have dared to risk a public argument with him."

The exposé by reporters Oliver Pilat and William Shannon revealed that despite McCarthy's bluster and headline-making accusations, he had not uncovered one Communist spy in the government. They also tore into his shaky finances, his ethics, and what they considered to be his inflated war-record.

McCarthy labeled *Post* editor Weschler a Communist and continued to malign anyone who, in his opinion, harbored even a hint of Communist taint.

In September 1951, in response to what they saw as a "calculated assault" on McCarthy, twenty-five Republican senators released a statement supporting the senator and his aggressive tactics without mentioning his name. Instead, they denounced "smear tactics and propaganda techniques now being used to silence any critics." They promised to "vigorously resist any attempt to conceal the facts from the American people."

By 1952, intellectuals and journalists were increasingly pushing back. That January, a sociology professor at Duke University analyzed fifty specific charges McCarthy had made and concluded they were "radically at variance with the facts." Sociologist Hornell Hart's study was part of a larger project dedicated to finding "a practical way of reaching dispassionate and reasonably enlightened conclusions." Of McCarthy's assertion that 205 Communists worked in the U.S. government, Hart pointed out that not only was the statement untrue but that McCarthy, under oath, subsequently denied making it. He deemed all fifty McCarthy allegations to be false.

"Senator McCarthy's activities have contributed little or nothing to discovering or weeding out Communists from our government," concluded Hart.

When caught lying, McCarthy typically responded in one of four ways, said Hart. He would (1) continue to repeat the statement; (2) deny having made it or substitute a "less extreme form" of what he previously had said; (3) repeat it with embellishments; or (4) denounce those who challenged him.

McCarthy threatened Hart and Duke University with a lawsuit. He tried similar intimidation tactics on other critics, including *Time* magazine. After the magazine published a critical article, McCarthy threatened, in a letter to publisher Henry Luce, to make advertisers "fully aware of the type of publication they are supporting." Democratic Senator Estes Kefauver called it "a blow aimed at freedom of the press." "The whole thing reeks of totalitarianism" charged *Editor & Publisher.*

The ACLU responded with an open letter reminding Republican senators that they had promised to defend "any person against whom reprisals are directed as the result of the exercise of his constitutional right of free speech."

In fall 1952, Northwestern University journalism professor Dozier Cade published an article in *Journalism Quarterly* faulting the press for McCarthy's rise. "The American press is mainly acting as a 'stooge' for the hunter, by being his mouth-piece," wrote Cade. "It tries the victim by printing accusations by the prosecution in the headlines and lead paragraphs, and any rebuttals by the defendant toward the end of the stories or . . . maybe not until the next day or later," resulting in McCarthy's victims being "tarnished . . . for life."

Journalists of conscience were increasingly taking that critique to heart. In February 1953, Palmer Hoyt, editor and publisher of the *Denver Post* and a recent addition to the ACLU national committee, addressed the problem in a memo to his staff.

The *Post,* he wrote, was "alert to the problem of McCarthyism" and "anxious to take every possible step to protect the innocent" and give those attacked "every possible chance to defend themselves." Therefore, he wrote, the *Post* "will not consider any story complete and covered until rebuttal and answering statements are printed."

In explaining the new policy at an industry dinner in Lawrence, Kansas, Hoyt called McCarthyism "a synonym for irresponsible charges" and pledged that anyone accused of disloyalty by him would be allowed to respond in the *Post*. It was a turning point for the *Post* and for Hoyt—a staunch anti-Communist who had been initially inclined to support McCarthy.

When McCarthy criticized the policy, the *Post* responded with an editorial declaring, "we cannot agree with the senator that the way to fight Communism is to tear down the American concept of fair play and the protection of the innocent from outrageous accusations."

Over the next several months, Hoyt crusaded nationally against McCarthy's tactics. In July at the Harvard Conference on Public Unrest in Education, he declared, "far too many of our national leaders are afraid of Joseph R. McCarthy," including "newspaper editors."

The ACLU did not join Hoyt's crusade. Although Malin loathed McCarthyism, he wasn't enthusiastic about some of Hoyt's ideas for exposing McCarthy's chronic lies. He was uncomfortable with Hoyt's suggestion that reporters "apply the principle of 'reasonable doubt'" to stories they knew to be false. And he fretted that Hoyt's suggestion of consciously downplaying (or calling out) McCarthy's accusations might slant the news or suggest that McCarthy was lying. In fact, McCarthy almost always was lying, but Malin's reluctance to denounce the senator's statements reflected a broader resistance within the ACLU to confronting the senator head on.

Meanwhile, McCarthy took aim at *New York Post* editor and ACLU board member James Wechsler, whom he had never forgiven for the "One Man Mob of Joe McCarthy" series. In 1953, he hauled Wechsler before his Permanent Subcommittee on Investigations for closed-door sessions exploring Wechsler's supposed Communist leanings and his books.

While a student at Columbia University, Wechsler had become a member of the Young Communist League. After a visit to Russia while in his early twenties, Wechsler had rejected communism. Currently thirty-seven, he described himself as "vigorously anti-Communist." Fearful of the backlash he might engender by attacking the *Post*, McCarthy summoned Wechsler "not as a newspaperman but as an author" of four books. Because some of Wechsler's books had been acquired by the State Department and put into libraries overseas, McCarthy considered himself entitled to Wechsler's testimony so as to assess whether he was a Communist operative.

After examining a transcript, the *Christian Science Monitor* concluded that only about five minutes of Wechsler's five hours of testimony dealt with his books. Instead, questioning focused on the *New York Post* and on Wechsler's supposed Communist activities.

McCarthy denied he was "investigating the press" and justified the line of questioning by arguing that Wechsler was "leading the fight against everyone who is exposing communists in the government."

Wechsler ardently disagreed, accusing McCarthy of instituting "the whole proceeding as a reprisal against a newspaper and its editor." Wechsler predicted that he was merely "the first of a long line of editors who are going to be called because they refused to equate McCarthyism with patriotism."

Wechsler insisted the *Post* had "nothing to hide" and told reporters he had submitted "a long list of anti-Communist writings" to McCarthy proving his current anti-Communist bent.

Five days after Wechsler testified, McCarthy released the text of a telegram he had sent to "Arthur Lawson," which apparently was the name Wechsler had gone by as a member of the Young Communist League: "Received your wire in which you still take the position that your Communist activities are immune from investigation because you are an editor. You are advised that there is no privileged profession in so far as our investigation is concerned."

Wechsler accused McCarthy of "deliberately" falsifying his position and of having no interest in his "youthful Communist activities which ended more than fifteen years ago and which I have never concealed." He challenged McCarthy to release a transcript of the hearing: "You have previously asserted that the transcript could not be made public until I submitted certain additional material. I am preparing that material and am trying to reach [Committee Chief Counsel] Mr. [Roy] Cohn to arrange for submission of it and prompt checking of the final record."

The additional material included a list of people that Wechsler had known to be Communist during his days as a Young Communist League member. After some soul searching and a conversation with *New York Post* publisher Dorothy Schiff, Wechsler offered up sixty names.

Later that year, Wechsler published *The Age of Suspicion*. The book was both a political biography and a reflection on his time with McCarthy. Daniel Seligman, who reviewed the book for the *New Leader*, wrote that it was "bad enough to have to re-read McCarthy's" accusations, but it was "even more dispiriting . . . to watch Mr. Wechsler trying to reason with this madman logic."

As Wechsler was an ACLU board member, Malin felt duty-bound to weigh in on the McCarthy-Wechsler encounter. The ACLU commented that although McCarthy was "fully entitled to investigate possible illegal acts," the committee was "not entitled to question [an author] about something which is both perfectly legal and utterly unrelated to the proper subject matter of the committee's investigation." The statement concluded: "that Mr. Wechsler is an editor makes even worse the threat to civil liberties which is implicit in Senator McCarthy's questioning."

The American Society of Newspaper Editors examined the transcript of Wechsler's grilling but could not decide on a unified response. The ASNE released a report explaining that some members believed "McCarthy, as committee chairman, infringed freedom of the press with his questions of the *Post*," while others felt the inquiry "did no damage" to that freedom. "Since the committee is not in agreement on this crucial issue, it is the responsibility of every editor to read the transcript and decide for himself, and, if he likes, to try to convince the public his view is the correct one," said the ASNE.

The ASNE's timorous response underscored how powerful McCarthy was in those days and how potent his self-assumed role as champion Communist fighter had become. Few critics had the appetite to aggressively take him on. Indeed, an admiring profile of McCarthy by William Nolan in the *Irish Monthly* claimed that even the ACLU's Washington representative approved of McCarthy: "Irving Ferman . . . has told the writer that he rates the conduct of Senator McCarthy's committee as among the best in Congress. And that, moreover, he regards the method of the Congressional investigations as being the least undemocratic way of dealing with problems of national security, precisely because Congressional investigations are subject to vigilant public scrutiny, whereas even the most objective FBI investigation must remain confidential."

It would come out more than two decades later that, during the McCarthy era, the ACLU's Ferman "regularly provided the FBI with information on ACLU members suspected of left-wing activity." (See Chapter 10.)

In September 1953, ACLU board member Corliss Lamont attracted McCarthy's attention. Like Wechsler, Lamont (a philosopher and former chairman of the National Council of American-Soviet Friendship) had authored books apparently purchased by the State Department for libraries abroad. At a closed hearing presided over by McCarthy, Lamont refused to answer questions concerning his alleged Communist affiliations. McCarthy threatened him with contempt.

Afterward, Lamont declared himself "a loyal American and I am not now and never have been a member of the Communist Party." He also challenged McCarthy's authority to question him: "Under the rules of the Senate . . . this committee has no authority to examine into the personal and private actions of private citizens." A few days after testifying, Lamont released a statement citing some fifty times when he had disagreed with Communist thinkers in various fields.

The ACLU backed Lamont's refusal to answer certain questions. "All the questions Mr. Lamont refused to answer were either irrelevant to the scope of the Committee's inquiry or infringed upon his rights as under the First Amendment," noted the ACLU in its annual report.

The ACLU's cautious pushback in the face of McCarthy's blatant provocations likely stemmed from its own vulnerabilities and painfully conflicted feelings about Communists. As Lamont was testifying before McCarthy's subcommittee, the ACLU was embroiled in an internal Communist controversy—ignited by longtime board member Norman Thomas's proposal that the organization formally adopt a strong anti-Communist position.

Thomas's advocacy for a statement calling the American Communist Party "an organization operating conspiratorially in the service of a foreign government" and a "danger to civil liberties" led to a referendum on three competing propositions of varying levels of hostility to the Communist Party. It was the first resolution on which local affiliates were allowed to vote. And to the national office's surprise, all three proposed statements were rejected because of the affiliates' opposition. The ACLU eventually agreed on softer language that nonetheless made clear its distaste for American communism.

A statement issued by the ACLU board in March 1954 stated, "the American Communist movement, in sharp contradistinction to other American political parties, is subject to the dominance of the rulers of a foreign nation. In theory it rejects all the concepts of civil liberty which the ACLU exists to defend and in practice it crushes every assertion of individual dignity and freedom which may conflict with the party's commands."

The statement supported the government's right to "seek out and punish lawbreakers," but rejected punishing "any person, Communist or other, without due process of law and procedure."

The episode angered Lamont and left him convinced that his energies were better spent fighting McCarthyism rather than working with the ACLU.[1]

In an article written years later, Lamont, who left the board in 1954, reflected on the ACLU's decision to purge Elizabeth Gurley Flynn. In those days, recalled Lamont, "[board member] Morris Ernst was in secret contact with J. Edgar Hoover, Director of the Federal Bureau of Investigation, revealing to him the names of supposed Communists in the ACLU. . . . During this difficult period I remained a Director of the Civil Liberties Union and fought against its various compromises. . . . Looking back now to the onset of the Cold War in 1940, I find that the behavior of the ACLU was the most shameful thing in my entire experience with non- governmental organizations."[2]

Malin saw things in a significantly less polarizing light. "Some people say, 'You must choose either Communism or McCarthyism.' The ACLU chooses neither," he wrote. "We will continue to oppose tyrannical Soviet Communism as the chief threat to our civil liberties from the outside, and 'McCarthyism' as the chief threat to our civil liberties on the inside."

By late 1953, the country was becoming fed up with McCarthy. A Gallup Poll of prominent Americans released in July 1953 found 66 percent agreeing that Congress was "abusing its powers to investigate" and 63 percent held an unfavorable opinion of McCarthy. A Gallup Poll of the general population released that August found that, in a one-month period, the percentage of people who viewed McCarthy unfavorably had risen from 30 to 42 percent and those with an "extreme dislike" of him rose from 16 to 23 percent.

Writing in *Commentary* magazine in early 1953, Harold Lavine, associate editor of *Newsweek*, noted that President Eisenhower, although hugely popular, had a McCarthy problem: "The aspect of the Eisenhower administration that creates the most heat in Washington is the President's failure to isolate and destroy Senator Joseph R. McCarthy. . . . The New Dealers seem to consider him the secret ruler of the United States government, bent on driving the nation to fascism; and the liberal Republicans are convinced that he plans to wreck the Eisenhower administration so that he can grab the Republican Presidential nomination for himself in 1956."

Eisenhower attempted to change the conversation, but McCarthy kept bringing it back to his favorite subject. In November 1953, he said the Eisenhower administration had "struck out" in exposing Communist infiltration. If voters thought he was "wrong to dig out and expose traitors," McCarthy told reporters, they could give Democrats control of the Senate.

In his January 1954 State of the Union address, Eisenhower congratulated the "new employee security program" for having separated "more than 2,200 employees . . . from the Federal government." He presented no evidence that such separations had occurred, nor did he mention McCarthy's name; but he presumably hoped the remark would play well with McCarthy's base.

Ultimately, it did not much matter, as events were conspiring to end McCarthy's era. One key event was McCarthy's spat with broadcaster Edward R. Murrow, host of CBS's *See It Now.* On his March 9 broadcast, Murrow had observed, "the line between investigating and persecuting is a very fine one and the junior senator has stepped over it repeatedly." Given time to rebut the critique in a subsequent broadcast, McCarthy instead used the time to accuse Murrow of engaging "in propaganda for communist causes."

On his April 13 broadcast, Murrow hit back. Since McCarthy "made no reference to any statements of fact that we made, we must conclude that he found no errors of fact," said Murrow. "He proved again that anyone who exposes him, anyone who does not share his hysterical disregard for decency and human dignity and the rights guaranteed by the Constitution, must be either a Communist or a fellow traveler."

Murrow forcefully refuted McCarthy's personal attacks on him, including claims that Murrow had been a member of the IWW and supported a group that had worked with the Russian secret police. "Having watched the aggressive forces at work in Western Europe, having had friends in

Eastern Europe butchered and driven into exile . . . having been denounced by the Russian radio for these reports, I cannot feel that I require instruction from the Senator on the evils of Communism," said Murrow.

The following week, McCarthy's antics were again on public display as the Army-McCarthy hearings convened. Those hearings centered around a previously obscure young man who had briefly worked for McCarthy's subcommittee.

Gerard David Schine was a six-foot, three-inch, twenty-seven-year-old Harvard graduate born into a wealthy family of hotel owners. He had forged a close friendship with Roy Cohn—also twenty-seven and chief counsel to McCarthy's subcommittee—and eventually become an unpaid member of the staff. Rumors of a sexual relationship between Cohn and Schine were never proved, but it was clear Cohn had spent countless hours seeking favors from the army on his friend's behalf. Before and after Schine was drafted into the army as a private in 1953, Cohn and McCarthy insisted that officials make Schine's service as pleasant and perk-filled as possible.

Among the favors sought for Schine, according to Army Secretary Robert Stevens, were an officer's commission (to which he was not entitled), weekends off (which he had not earned), jobs (for which he was not qualified), and either a waiver from or a shortened period in basic training. Cohn and McCarthy also wanted Schine stationed in the New York City area.

McCarthy claimed Steven's allegations were concocted and charged his critics with trying to cover up their own misbehavior—and of attempting, by "blackmail," to prevent him from investigating Communist infiltration of the army.

The Senate asked McCarthy's subcommittee to sort out the truth. Senator Karl Mundt, a Republican from South Dakota, temporarily assumed McCarthy's chairmanship because of McCarthy's obvious conflict of interest. The nationally televised hearings began on April 22, 1954, and culminated on June 17. Much of the story was difficult to follow and even more difficult to fathom. But the nation watched enthralled as it finally got to watch, close up, the most famed Communist hunter in America.

The tone was set the first day by a pugnacious McCarthy, who interrupted the proceeding to assert that his dispute was not with the army but with "a few Pentagon politicians attempting to disrupt our investigations." The bulk of the time that day, however, went to McCarthy's accusers.

Army Secretary Stevens and Major General Miles Reber testified that McCarthy, Cohn, and staff director Frank Carr incessantly approached army officials on Schine's behalf. After Schine learned that he was scheduled to report for induction on November 3, 1953, Cohn called Stevens and asked that Schine begin his service with a two-week furlough. He also asked that Schine be exempted from basic training. And he floated the idea of Schine serving in the CIA rather than in the army. McCarthy and Cohn repeatedly made the case that Schine deserved officer status.

Major General Reber testified he was summoned to McCarthy's office, where the senator told him that Schine should get a "direct reserve commission." The army processed the paperwork but discovered that Schine— apparently having misrepresented his experience—was not qualified for it.

Meanwhile, claimed Stevens and Reber, Cohn called repeatedly, and McCarthy called occasionally, to lobby on Schine's behalf. The officers did what they could, within reason, to accommodate. They inquired into a CIA job, but CIA director Allen Dulles squelched the idea.

McCarthy charged that Miles Reber's brother, Sam, was forced to leave a government post in Germany after McCarthy outed him as a security risk and that Miles was now fabricating the charges in revenge. Reber replied he knew nothing about McCarthy forcing his brother to retire but assumed the brother had left because he had reached retirement age.

The hearings took bizarre detours. The sides wrangled over a photo that appeared to show Schine and Stevens alone. The photo was presumably supposed to demonstrate an unseemly familiarity between the private and the Army Secretary. The army responded with its own copy, showing three additional individuals present along with, as one newspaper reported, "the hat and arm of a fourth."

Army officials testified that during a seventy-five-day assignment at Fort Dix, Schine had logged a record forty-three absences. Schine's former commander, Captain Joseph Miller, testified the private had left his post to take a New Year's holiday and had improperly offered Miller a trip to Florida. McCarthy walked out on that testimony, declaring, "we should be investigating Communists. . . . There are one hundred and thirty in the defense plants right now."

Cohn charged the army with trying to "blackmail" the subcommittee by threatening to ship Private Schine overseas unless McCarthy stopped an investigation of Fort Monmouth. Stevens had proposed instead, said Cohn, that the subcommittee investigate the air force and navy and "give the Army a rest." Army Counselor John Adams, said Cohn, had even offered information about "sexual deviates" in the air force. Staff director Francis Carr also accused the army of "trying to use Schine as a hostage to pressure us to stop hearings on the army."

Army Counsel John Welch forced staff director Francis Carr to acknowledge that "if the hearings got called off," it wasn't because of threats or blackmail against Schine. He also pressed Carr on what exactly the army was threatening to do to Schine "besides letting him wear the uniform of the United States Army."

"Well, I don't know that they were threatening to take him out and shoot him or anything like that, sir," replied Carr.

"The worst we have heard is KP on Sunday, isn't it. . . . That is the worse we have heard," said Welch.

"Right," Carr grudgingly responded.

Eisenhower barred his cabinet officials from testifying about conversations within the executive branch. "Any man who testifies as to the advice he gave me won't be working for me that night," said Eisenhower. It was an early form of executive privilege, to which the legislators were uncertain how to respond.

The most memorable moment of the hearings occurred on June 9, 1954, during Chief Army Counsel Welch's questioning of Cohn. Cohn acknowledged that his committee had been slow to alert army officials to possible subversives working at the Army Signal Corps radar laboratories at Fort Monmouth, New Jersey. In the future, countered Welch, the committee should alert authorities to the threat immediately.

McCarthy could not resist the opening. In light of Welch's request to be informed of Communist infiltrators, said McCarthy, "I think we should tell him that he has in his law firm a young man named Fisher whom he recommended, initially, to work on this committee who has been for a number of years a member of an organization" that served as "the legal bulwark of the Communist Party."

McCarthy prattled on about the young traitor at Welch's law firm, accusing Welch of "unknowingly aiding" the Communist Party. The more McCarthy talked, the more agitated Welch grew. Finally, Welch turned to chairman Mundt and asked for a moment of "personal privilege."

Welch demanded McCarthy's attention. Preoccupied with getting a news article to bolster his point, McCarthy replied, "I can listen with one ear."

"This time I want you to listen with both," replied Welch. He told McCarthy that he had no need of the documents the senator was trying to find because he would tell the senator everything.

"Until this moment, senator, I think I never really gauged your cruelty or your recklessness," he said, and proceeded to tell McCarthy about the young man he had just accused—a recent Harvard Law School graduate named Fred Fisher, who seemed poised for a brilliant career, and whom an associate had originally picked to work on the case with McCarthy's committee. Over dinner, Welch had asked the two young men chosen for the case whether there was anything "funny" in their backgrounds. Fisher had confided that, for a short time while in law school, he had belonged to the Lawyers Guild. Welch had responded by gently warning the youth against working on the McCarthy project because of its potential to damage his reputation.

"So, Senator, I asked him to go back to Boston. Little did I dream you could be so reckless and so cruel as to do an injury to this lad. It is true he is still with Hale and Dorr. It is true that he will continue to be with Hale and Dorr. It is, I regret to say, equally true that I fear he shall always bear a scar needlessly inflicted by you. . . . I like to think I am a gentle man, but your forgiveness will have to come from someone other than me."

McCarthy spoke up in his own defense, accusing Welch of baiting Cohn.

Welch exploded: "Senator, may we now drop this. . . . Let us not assassinate this lad further. Senator, you have done enough. Have you no sense of decency, sir? At long last, have you left no sense of decency?"

McCarthy spoke, provoking Welch into a final retort. "Mr. McCarthy, I will not discuss this with your further. You have sat within six feet of me, and could have asked me about Fred Fisher. . . . If there is a God in heaven, it will do neither you nor your cause any good. I will not discuss it any further. I will not ask Mr. Cohn any more questions. You, Mr. Chairman, may, if you will, call the next witness."

The exchange riveted the audience, which sat attentively silent before thunderously clapping—"the biggest burst of sympathetic applause since the hearings began," reported the *Baltimore Sun*.

Mundt called a recess, during which a visibly agitated Welch told reporters, "I'm close to tears. Here's a young kid with one mistake—just one mistake—and he tries to crucify him. I don't see how in the name of God you can fight anybody like that. I never saw such cruelty—such arrogance."

The hearing went on another eight days, but the damage to McCarthy was done. On June 15, former President Truman weighed in: "I'm ashamed of the Senate. The Senate shouldn't allow that to happen," he said.

The editorial reviews were even more devastating. "Mr. McCarthy has condemned himself by his own words and his own actions. . . . In the larger sense, it is the case of Sen. McCarthy . . . vs. the constitutional government of the United States," opined the *New York Times*.

The *Washington Post* commented, "Sen. McCarthy's absurd concoction of an administration plot to thwart his investigation of communism in the Army was supported by nothing save his own redundant recital of it."

In late July, a group of twenty-three prominent Americans—including publishers, university leaders, movie producers, and former government officials—telegrammed all sitting senators urging them to support a motion authored by Ralph Flanders, a Republican from Vermont, to censure McCarthy.

On December 2, the Senate considered a revised censure resolution and voted 67 to 22 (forty-four Democrats, one Independent, and twenty-two Republicans voted for the measure) to condemn McCarthy on two counts out of three: that he refused to cooperate with a subcommittee investigating his finances and other matters and repeatedly abused members trying to carry out their assigned duties; and that he "acted contrary to senatorial ethics and tended to bring the Senate into dishonor and disrepute, to obstruct the constitutional processes of the Senate, and to impair its dignity." The Senate tossed out a third charge, having to do with "intemperately" abusing General Ralph Zwicker, who appeared before the committee, by calling Zwicker unfit to wear the uniform.

The vote did not expel McCarthy from the Senate, nor strip him of his powers as a senator, but it essentially ended his political career.

The saga of McCarthy's hearings and the senator's eventual comeuppance was not the biggest domestic story of 1954. That distinction went to the *Brown v. Board of Education of Topeka* Supreme Court decision, which was announced Monday, May 17—the day the McCarthy hearings began a one-week recess.

"Segregation of white and colored children in public schools has a detrimental effect upon the colored children," declared Chief Justice Earl Warren as he rejected the "separate but equal" precedent (*Plessy v. Ferguson*, 1896) and kindled a raging hope in the hearts of those who had fought to break Jim Crow's back. "The impact is greater when it has the sanction of the law; for the policy of separating the races is usually interpreted as denoting the inferiority of the negro group. . . . We conclude that, in the field of public education, the doctrine of 'separate but equal' has no place. Separate educational facilities are inherently unequal."

There were actually two decisions, involving five separate cases—in South Carolina, Virginia, Delaware, Kansas, and Washington, DC—all of which came collectively to be known as *"Brown."* Instead of abolishing segregation straightaway, the justices sought advice on how—and when—desegregation was to come about. *Brown* spawned what came to be known as *Brown II*—a decision in May 1955 that provided neither a timetable nor a plan. Instead, it ordered the South—a region filled with the most obstructionist politicians imaginable—to proceed with "all deliberate speed."

The justices advised the lower courts, which would oversee compliance, to show "a practical flexibility in shaping remedies." Meanwhile, "all deliberate speed" gave opportunistic politicians a chance to mobilize against integration.

The lead attorneys for *Brown v. Board of Education of Topeka* were not ACLU lawyers. They came from the NAACP and were led by Thurgood Marshall. But the ACLU helped the NAACP's lawyers prep for oral arguments, shared briefs and ideas with them, and filed a friend of the court brief (along with numerous other organizations, including the American Jewish Committee and the Japanese American Citizens League).

In an argument adopted by the court, the ACLU highlighted social science documenting the damage done by segregation, citing an array of journal articles and books with such titles as *Some Psychogenic Hazards of Segregated Education of Negroes, The Intelligence of Colored Elementary Pupils in Washington, D.C.,* and *A Study of Prejudice in Children.*

The ACLU also cited a prior judicial finding that had embraced the social science: "The lower court found as a fact that the segregation of white and Negro children in the public schools 'has a detrimental effect upon the colored children'; that such segregation creates in Negro children a 'sense of inferiority' which 'affects the motivation of a child to learn."

The ACLU pointed out, "the United States is now engaged in an ideological world conflict in which the practices of our democracy are the subject of close scrutiny abroad. . . . Legally imposed segregation in our country, in any shape, manner or form, weakens our program to build and strengthen world democracy and combat totalitarianism."

The ACLU released a statement by Vice Chairman Edward J. Ennis that celebrated the Supreme Court victory while also taking a swipe at Communists: "The Supreme Court's decision . . . is an historic landmark in the effort to achieve what is guaranteed to everybody under our democratic system, equality for all. Its effect will be felt not only by the thousands of school children who will now, for the first time, enjoy their education on a truly equal basis. It will be felt in the far corners of the world, wherever America's faith in its democratic concepts is challenged falsely by Communist propagandists."

NAACP lawyer Thurgood Marshall was ecstatic. School segregation would perish within five years, he predicted. By 1963, he conjectured, all forms of segregation in America would be nothing but a memory. "Free by 63" was the popular slogan that summer at gatherings of the NAACP.

That dream was not to be realized. But *Brown v. Board of Education* nonetheless jump-started the modern civil rights movement and forced a reluctant America to wrestle with the then-improbable idea that all God's children are fully human.

A year and a half after *Brown*, Martin Luther King Jr., then twenty-six, came to prominence as the leader and voice of the Montgomery Bus Boycott.

"We are not wrong in what we are doing. If we are wrong, the Supreme Court of this nation is wrong. If we are wrong, the Constitution of the United States is wrong. If we are wrong, God Almighty is wrong," declared King at his first Montgomery Improvement Association meeting in Holt Street Baptist Church. The boycott would last more than a year. Shortly before the boycott ended, the Supreme Court ruled (*Browder v. Gayle*, November 13, 1956) that that Alabama's law requiring segregation on intrastate buses violated the due process clause of the Fourteenth Amendment. The two events, though not directly linked, reflected the rising urgency of black demands for equality. Looking forward to 1957, Malin saw the South as fertile territory. "We seek to broaden our organization in the South in order to provide new support for the national campaign against discrimination," he wrote.

That year saw passage of the first federal civil rights bill since the Reconstruction era. Attorney General Herbert Brownell, a Nebraska native, Yale Law School graduate, and school desegregation advocate, proposed the legislation in his annual report to Congress. Over the past year, he said, the Justice Department had been under "a great amount of pressure" to investigate various civil rights incidents—including the kidnapping and murder of a black teenager, Emmett Till, in Mississippi—over which the feds lacked jurisdiction. The federal government, he argued, required additional authority to ensure "the free exercise by all citizens of the civil rights guaranteed by the Constitution."

The new proposed law would create a civil rights division within the Justice Department, establish a bipartisan civil rights commission, protect voting rights, and provide clearer remedies when civil rights were denied.

In late August, the bill passed the House but immediately encountered opposition from Southern Democrats, who felt the bill would disrupt what Senator Richard Russell of Georgia called "the social order of the South."

In a speech that July, Russell said the bill "could be utilized to force the white people of the South at the point of a federal bayonet to conform to almost any conceivable edict directed at the destruction of any local custom, law, or practice separating the races and enforce a commingling of the races."

The Senate passed a version of the bill that removed the provision allowing federal prosecutors to obtain injunctions to allow black students to attend segregated schools. The Senate version also made juries—which, in the South, typically barred blacks—the final arbiter of voting rights violations.

In a letter to senators, the ACLU declared that "to accept the Civil Rights Bill in its present Senate form would not be in keeping with our obligation to millions of fellow Americans to accord them at long last as citizens equal status under the law." Wayne Morse, a Republican senator from Wisconsin, also blasted the bill: "It was a source of great disappointment to me to see the Congress, in the midst of its mad rush to adjournment, push through the amended, hobbled and watered-down civil rights bill."

President Eisenhower signed the measure on September 9 without bothering to issue a signing statement. He was aware of the widespread disappointment with the bill and also didn't want to aggravate a crisis then unfolding in Little Rock, Arkansas.

Arkansas Governor Orval Faubus had rejected a federal judge's order that the previously all-white Central High School accept nine handpicked black students. In early September, Faubus had ordered the national guard to physically bar the students from entering the school. When the students arrived, snarling white mobs pummeled them with threats and racist insults and beat several black newsmen.

The *Chicago Daily Defender* caustically observed, "the section of the new civil rights law which would have applied to the present school situation in Little Rock was eliminated while the bill was under consideration in the Senate."

On September 24, 1957, at the mayor of Little Rock's request, President Eisenhower sent 1,200 soldiers from the 101st Airborne Division to Little Rock. In a televised address, Eisenhower explained, "It was my hope that this localized situation would be brought under control by city and state authorities . . . but when large gatherings of obstructionists made it impossible for the decrees of the court to be carried out, both the law and the national interest demanded that the President take action."

On September 25, as the troops engaged the mob, one white man was clubbed and another stabbed with a bayonet. The paratroopers moved the crowd back and escorted the black students into school roughly a half hour after classes had begun. Black airborne division members, in a bow to Southern sensibilities, were kept away from the front line. On the second day of the troop intervention, a white man was arrested with a hunting rifle in his car and a revolver in his shoulder holster.

In February 1958, the Little Rock school board asked U.S. District Judge Harry Lemley for a reprieve from integration until midsemester 1961. The board cited various incidents (including "slugging, pushing, tripping, catcalls, abusive language, destruction of lockers, and urinating on radiators," numerous bomb threats and small fires, "bedlam and turmoil in and upon the school premises," and tensions arising from the presence of the black students). On June 21, 1958, Judge Lemley granted the thirty-month delay and barred the seven blacks currently enrolled from returning to

Central High. Of the nine who had originally enrolled, one had graduated and another—after being suspended for dropping a bowl of chili on boys who assaulted and taunted her—had transferred to a private high school in New York City.

In his decision, Judge Lemley explained that "while the Negro students at Little Rock have a personal interest in being admitted to the public schools on a non-discriminatory basis as soon as practicable, that interest is only one factor of the equation. . . . There is also another public interest involved, namely, that of eliminating, or at least ameliorating, the unfortunate racial strife and tension which existed in Little Rock during the past year and still exists there."

Governor Faubus advised blacks they "would do well to accept today's ruling, which will do much to reestablish the normal and friendly relations which prevailed here before."

That July, at the urging of the NAACP, Malin sent a letter to Attorney General William P. Rogers asking the Justice Department to intervene. "We believe that the recent decision by Judge Harry J. Lemley . . . will have serious adverse consequences for the decision announced by the U.S. Supreme Court," wrote Malin, adding, "if the concept of 'all deliberate speed' includes waiting for the abatement of hostility to desegregation, then the conceit is a chimera."

That August, the Eight Circuit Court of Appeals overruled Lemley in a 6 to 1 decision. The court pointedly noted that "at no time did the board seek injunctive relief against those who opposed by unlawful acts the lawful integration plan."

The school board appealed the decision to the Supreme Court, which on September 12 unanimously upheld the appellate court's order, effective immediately, because of the "imminent commencement of the new school year."

Malin applauded the decision. "The Supreme Court properly has refused to abdicate its responsibility to guarantee that its 1954 and 1955 decisions must be obeyed," he declared.

Malin also praised Attorney General William Rogers for assembling a team to assist in implementing the order. "The school board should follow the government's lead," he said.

Instead of obeying the order, Faubus invoked a new law enabling him to close schools integrated by federal order. He closed Little Rock's four public high schools—to "avoid the impending violence and disorder which would occur and to preserve the peace of the community."

By nearly a three to one margin, voters opted to keep the schools closed. In campaigning for the shutdown, Faubus told voters the choice was between "whether we are to completely integrate the Little Rock school system with all the troubles this is likely to bring, or whether we operate our senior high schools on a private, segregated basis."

The school board handed the schools over to a private group that planned to operate them as private segregation academies. On March 9, 1959, a federal district ordered an end to state funds paying tuition at those segregated private schools. On June 18, in response to a filing by the NAACP, federal judges declared unconstitutional the newly enacted laws Faubus had used to shut down the schools.

On August 12, after two years of turmoil stirred up by the governor and his supporters, after re-election of an anti-Faubus school board, and after most high school students in Little Rock had missed a year of school, the city's high schools formally reopened. The date, a month earlier than school normally would have started, was chosen "in an apparent move to head off interference by Gov. Orval E. Faubus," reported the *Baltimore Sun*.

A few days later, the single remaining segregation academy announced that it was closing due to lack of public support. The other segregated private schools had already announced plans to close.

Although the ACLU had long been involved in issues of race, it had rarely been on the front lines. It had functioned, instead, as a strong supporting player, principally assisting the NAACP. As America's emergent civil rights movement caught fire, that did not fundamentally change; but, as Malin acknowledged, the fight for racial justice had entered a new phase, one that, as he put it in the 1961 annual report, would require "more than Freedom Rides."

By Malin's reckoning, it would require a renewed focus on voting participation in the South and on anti-discrimination efforts by local and state government in the North—even as the ACLU continued to work on issues as wide-ranging, and potentially polarizing, as Hollywood blacklisting, Communist persecution, inappropriate surveillance, censorship, and assorted threats to free expression.

Malin left the ACLU at the end of 1961 to head Robert College of Istanbul. He had won a reputation as a competent manager who had impressively grown the ACLU without particularly shining as an advocate. Perhaps his biggest contribution was instituting a highly successful membership program of the sort the ACLU board previously had rejected. The program essentially sextupled membership during his tenure. Membership, which stood at 9,355 in 1950 had risen to 54,719 by 1961, according to the ACLU annual report.

"Had Baldwin remained, or had the board rejected Malin's membership plan, the subsequent history of the ACLU would undoubtedly have been very different," Samuel Walker conjectured. "It might well have drifted off into amiable respectability, filing briefs in occasional cases, while other organizations tapped the rising tide of political activism. . . . Malin's program inaugurated a twenty-four-year period of almost uninterrupted growth that brought the ACLU up to 275,000 members by 1974."[3]

8

A Moral Crusade, an Immoral War, and a Forbidden Romance

The sixties were like no decade America had ever experienced. Everything seemed to be changing. Gender and racial roles were being challenged, along with assumptions the country had fostered for centuries.

Race was very much on America's collective mind in 1961. That January, two African American students enrolled at the previously all-white University of Georgia. They were spirited through the back door only to be met by a mob hurling epithets, rocks, and other projectiles. After a day, the school kicked both students out "for their own safety." Some three hundred faculty members signed a resolution demanding their return with "all measures necessary" taken to protect them. A federal judge ordered the students reinstated. They returned later that month, under police protection, without significant incident.

Harper Lee's *To Kill a Mockingbird*, which won the Pulitzer Prize that year, told the story of a black man wrongfully convicted in Alabama of raping a white woman during the Depression. The story of racism and injustice in a small Southern town spoke eloquently to the racial confusion sweeping the South as blacks pushed for fair treatment and inclusion.

Competition with Russia was a national obsession. That April, twenty-seven-year-old Soviet cosmonaut Yuri Alekseyevich Gagarin zoomed into space: "The first man in history to fly out of this world and return safe and sound to tell about it," reported the *New York Times*. "Let the capitalist countries try to catch up," crowed Soviet leader Nikita Khrushchev.

President John Kennedy responded May 25 with what he called a "second" State of the Union message to address "urgent national needs." The United States was "anxious to live in harmony with the Russian people," said Kennedy, but the Soviet Union, he suggested, was still a rival at a moment when the "great battleground for the defense and expansion of freedom . . . is the whole southern half of the globe—Asia, Latin America, African and the Middle East—the lands of the rising peoples."

He implicitly included outer space to the contested territories when he proposed sending a man to the moon and back "before this decade is out" at a projected cost of up to 9 billion dollars.

His speech—grounded in what Kennedy called the "freedom doctrine"—also evoked the threat of nuclear war. He called for "a nationwide long-range program of identifying present fallout shelter capacity and providing shelter in new and existing structures," evoked "subversives and saboteurs and insurrectionists" in Vietnam, and urged Americans "to practice democracy at home, in all States, with all races, to respect each other and to protect the constitutional rights of all citizens."

For John "Jack" Dejarnette Pemberton Jr., comfortably ensconced in a private law practice in Minnesota, the time seemed right for taking on the challenges of the changing world. "The struggle for freedom is a struggle for individual rights. I think that maintaining the ideals of liberty is central to the whole contest between the Western way of life and the Eastern challenge to it," Pemberton, a Quaker and a Republican, told a reporter for the *Christian Science Monitor.*

A native of Rochester, Minnesota, where his father had been a surgeon at the Mayo Clinic, Pemberton, forty-two, was a graduate of Swarthmore College and Harvard Law School. At Swarthmore, he had studied under Patrick Murphy Malin, who had recommended Pemberton as his successor as ACLU executive director.

A slender man with dark thinning hair, Pemberton had five children and a wife who was a graduate of Oberlin College. He had served as chairman of the Minnesota ACLU, during which he had successfully represented a white man and an Indian woman who were prohibited from buying a joint cemetery lot in a whites-only cemetery.

The ACLU announced his appointment as executive director in December 1961, with a start date of April 1, 1962. In an interview shortly after starting his new job, Pemberton confided, "I'm shaking in the big shoes I have to fill."

Pemberton spoke excitedly of the challenges before him. He was intent on fighting proposals to expand wiretapping authority in national security and major criminal cases. And he was eager to help officials of the Congress of Racial Equality (CORE), who had been charged in Louisiana with "criminal anarchy."

The Louisiana trouble had been brewing for a while. Some sixteen Southern University students had been arrested in 1960 after being refused service at three lunch counters in Baton Rouge stores. They had been convicted under a state law that defined breach of peace as acting "in such a manner as to unreasonably disturb or alarm the public." The students were fined $100 apiece and sentenced to thirty days in jail.

In December 1961, the U.S. Supreme Court threw out those convictions, unanimously finding no evidence the students "disturbed the peace, either by outwardly boisterous conduct or by passive conduct." The arresting officers had "nothing to support their actions except their own opinions," declared the court.

In Jackson, Mississippi, "over 300 freedom riders have been arrested under a statute word-for-word identical with that in Louisiana," pointed out James Farmer, national director of CORE. The decision "gives hope . . . that the Freedom Rider cases which Mississippi chose to fight . . . will result in victory," said the NAACP's Roy Wilkens, whose legal counsel, Jack Greenberg, had argued the case before the Supreme Court.

Louisiana officials insisted that the decision had not outlawed discrimination in lunch service but had simply found insufficient evidence to convict the students. As stores continued refusing service to blacks, students at Southern University refused to let the matter drop.

Three days after the Supreme Court decision, twenty-three demonstrators were arrested, including CORE Field Secretary Dave Dennis. CORE responded by organizing more than two thousand marchers. As they paraded down the street singing patriotic songs and wielding protest signs, police dispersed them with tear gas and German shepherds.

University president Felton Clark suspended seven supposed student ringleaders along with another student he deemed to be a sympathizer. He also temporarily shut down the school. Some 142 faculty members sided with the students, dispatching a letter to President Clark criticizing his decision to put "himself in opposition to the currents of history."

Prosecutors charged four of the protestors with "criminal anarchy"— which carried a potential ten-year sentence.

That May, protestors testified in Washington before a "Committee of Inquiry into the Administration of Justice in the Freedom Struggle" convened by Eleanor Roosevelt. Roger Baldwin and Norman Thomas were among the ACLU members on the commission.

During the hearing in a community room of the *Washington Post*, two black youths arrested in Baton Rouge told of being housed for seventy-eight days in a seven-by-seven cell because they were unable to post bail of nearly $20,000 apiece. Eventually CORE put up the money. "We ask that the judicial machinery be no longer used as a weapon to crush the civil rights movement," CORE's James Farmer told the committee.

Members also heard from Eric Weinberger, a young white resident of Norwich, Connecticut, who moved to Brownsville, Tennessee, to help black sharecroppers who had been evicted for attempting to register to vote. Weinberger hoped to teach the women to make leather tote bags, whose sale would replace their lost income. Shortly after he arrived, police arrested and held him for days without cause and brutally beat him. Demonstrators imprisoned in Mississippi told similar stories.

Eventually—after pickets seeking federal intervention descended on the Justice Department and the White House—Louisiana dropped the charges against the students.

Pemberton wrote Attorney General Robert Kennedy asking that the Justice Department consider prosecuting local officials in the Weinberger case. He noted that Weinberger, a pacifist, didn't want to press charges against his persecutors because he felt "hate and fear led them to attack me."

Burke Marshall, the assistant attorney general for civil rights, replied that Weinberger's refusal to file a complaint left the department "no choice but to close its file in this matter." Little more than a year later, Weinberger, threatened with a four-year prison sentence, left Brownsville in defeat— although the *Tri-State Defender* reported that the project he helped establish "provides an income for more than 70 women."

Harassment and persecution of civil rights activists was only one of many outrages drawing the ACLU's gaze southward. Bombings of black churches became epidemic. In August 1962, arsonists reduced Shady Grove Baptist Church, three miles east of Leesburg, Georgia, "to a few black embers, a twisted tin roof and smashed concrete block walls," reported the *Norfolk Journal and Guide*. The church had been the center for a local voter registration drive.

That September, two black churches in Terrell County, Georgia, involved in voter registration campaigns were torched. Months earlier, white men led by the Terrell County sheriff had burst into one of the churches, Mount Olive Baptist, and advised those inside that "not a nigger in Terrell County needed northerners to help them vote." Sheriff Zeke Matthews warned that it wouldn't be in their "best interest" to continue their voter registration efforts. Two days after the church burnings, Sheriff Matthews announced that after a "thorough investigation," his office could find no evidence the fires were intentionally set.

Pemberton sent a telegram to Attorney General Kennedy calling for "a large scale" investigative effort to track down the persons responsible for the arson. He reminded Kennedy that "a sizeable corps of FBI agents" had tracked down the "bigots responsible for the bombing of a Jewish synagogue in Atlanta several years ago. Certainly Sunday's outrageous attack on Negro citizens . . . deserves similar investigational attention."

Two days later, President Kennedy denounced the attacks during a press conference. "I don't know of any more outrageous action which I have seen occur in this country in a good many months or years than the burning of a church, two churches, because of the effort made by the Negroes to be registered to vote," said Kennedy.

Shortly after Pemberton sent his letter, arsonists, under cover of pre-dawn darkness, destroyed the High Hope Baptist Church near Dawson, Georgia. The FBI quickly arrested four white men, who confessed to burning down the church after drinking beer. Dawson's mayor immediately promised that white residents of the community would rebuild the church. "We feel that since this particular church was burned by people who live in Dawson and Terrell County, it is our job to do this," he said.

That October, much of America's attention shifted to Oxford, Mississippi, where a twenty-nine-year-old former air force staff sergeant was intent on integrating the University of Mississippi. James Meredith, who had a wife and a two-year-old son, was one of ten children born on a corn and cotton farm in north central Mississippi. A quiet man of five feet six and 135 pounds, Meredith said his hope was to "get into the school and . . . become as nearly as possible just another student."

Ole Miss wanted nothing to do with him, but lawyers for the NAACP Legal Defense Fund got Supreme Court Justice Hugo Black to vacate a local judge's order denying Meredith admission.

That September 20, Meredith arrived with an escort of federal marshals. Twenty-seven minutes later Meredith reemerged, followed by Governor Ross Barnett, who announced Meredith's application had been rejected. Students cheered.

On September 25, in defiance of a federal restraining order, Barnett rejected Meredith a second time. The next day, Mississippi officials blocked Meredith yet again. Lieutenant Governor Paul Johnson told federal marshals, "I'm going to have to refuse on the same grounds the governor did." That Friday, Meredith was turned away yet a fourth time, by what the *Baltimore Sun* described as "a small army of 500 peace officers."

The president and the attorney general both spoke with Barnett by telephone several times that weekend, urging him to stand down. Sunday night, September 30, a five-truck convoy of U.S. marshals attired in riot gear escorted Meredith onto the campus and secured him in a room. Barnett and peace officers did nothing to block his entry. That evening, President Kennedy, in a national televised speech, made it clear his administration had not encouraged Meredith's actions. Meredith, Kennedy pointed out, had "brought a private suit in federal court against those who were excluding him from the university." Nonetheless, suggested Kennedy, Mississippians were obliged to obey the law. "You have a new opportunity to show that you are men of patriotism and integrity. . . . It lies in your courage to accept those laws with which you disagree."

The speech and phone calls proved futile. Ole Miss erupted with a five-hour riot that pitted U.S. marshals against students and angry residents. When it was over, at least seventy-five were injured and more than 150 were arrested. Paul Guihard, a correspondent for *Agence France Presse*, was shot in the back. Walter Ray Gunter, a local jukebox repairman, was shot in the forehead. Both died. Finally, Meredith was registered.

The next day, despite the drizzle, the scent of tear gas hung in the air, and the resistance seemed to be broken. Robert Kennedy blamed Barnett for the violence, claiming his people had withdrawn some two hundred Mississippi patrolmen from the scene just when they were most needed. Barnett blamed the trouble on "trigger-happy" U.S. marshals and on federal officials who refused to grant the university a "cooling-off" period before bringing Meredith on campus.

By late October, Ole Miss had settled into a semblance of normalcy.

The *Chicago Defender* published an article by poet Langston Hughes in which Simple, one of his most popular fictional characters, commented on Meredith and his plight: "Only once, did I see his lip tremble on the TV screen. He is one brave colored boy! . . . To walk through the gates of Ole Miss was like Daniel walking into the lion's den."

A report of Meredith's first year prepared by an uncredited ACLU volunteer estimated that, at the height of the crisis, some 23,600 peacekeepers were stationed in the area at a cost of roughly $3 million.

On October 9, reported the ACLU, some five hundred jeering students tossed rocks and cursed Meredith while he ate. One rock, tossed through the cafeteria window, "narrowly missed a U.S. Marshall, another hit a photographer outside." On Halloween night, students bombarded Meredith's door with firecrackers. When the chancellor threatened to expel disruptive students, much of the harassment ceased, although, according to the ACLU, Meredith continued to be threatened and psychologically abused. Meredith's elderly father, still working the family farm, was also harassed.

Faculty members, for the most part, were intimidated into silence. Senator James Eastland "sent U.S. Senate Judiciary Committee investigators to the campus to gather dossiers on teachers who defended Meredith's right to be there," reported the ACLU.

The ACLU disseminated what ACLU Associate Director Alan Reitman called "the facts about harassment and intimidation" on the campus to the relevant accrediting associations and other educational monitors. The ACLU's Academic Freedom Committee wrote the Southern Association of Colleges and Secondary Schools charging that "academic freedom at the University of Mississippi does not now exist" and urging the association to consider revoking the university's accreditation.

At the end of November, the Southern Association found Ole Miss guilty of bowing to political interference but stopped short of rescinding its accreditation. Instead, it warned that if signs of such interference resurfaced, or if riots again broke out, its accreditation would be revoked. Senator Eastland denounced the association's action, accusing it of covering up "blackmail" and "Marxism."

Under the unrelenting pressure, Meredith's grades slipped. In an interview with the *New York Times* that December, he sounded almost defeated. "Not one problem has been solved, not one issue has been settled," he said.

In a last-ditch effort to sabotage Meredith, Barnett tried to block his graduation, claiming that anti-segregation remarks by Meredith violated a university rule against students making statements about the racial crisis. Unwilling to risk loss of accreditation, the State College Board voted 6 to 5 to let Meredith graduate. The final contingent of troops was removed weeks before graduation, leaving a small force of marshals to ensure Meredith's safety.

He accepted his diploma, without comment or applause, in an outdoor ceremony on Sunday, August 18, 1963. "Except for reporters, on hand to watch the end of a chapter in the boiling civil rights controversy, it was like any other college campus at commencement time, and Mr. Meredith was just another student marching up for his degree," reported the *Globe and Mail*. Meredith's parents, his wife, and his three-year-old young son attended. Governor Barnett did not.

In an odd twist, the ACLU soon found itself allied with Ross Barnett and his lieutenant governor, Paul Johnson. Because of their efforts to block Meredith's registration, the U.S. Court of Appeals in New Orleans had charged them with criminal contempt. Barnett was demanding a trial by jury. He assumed a jury comprised of white Mississippians was unlikely to find him guilty of any offense committed in the name of segregation. At issue was whether "petty offenses" such as contempt required a trial by jury—as opposed to a panel of the circuit court. The court of appeals had split 4 to 4 on that question and asked the Supreme Court to resolve it.

Even though the ACLU knew a Mississippi jury was likely to side with Barnett and Lieutenant Governor Johnson, it submitted an amicus brief supporting his position. In a letter explaining the ACLU position, Pemberton pointed out that the ACLU considered "the guarantee of a jury trial . . . an integral element of our entire civil liberties structure."

In other words, the ACLU felt the denial of a jury trial to Barnett would set a precedent that could harm such organizations as CORE, the NAACP, and the Student Nonviolent Coordinating Committee, all of which had been enjoined for anti-segregation efforts.

The ACLU argued in its brief that a jury trial was "an indispensable component of a fair trial"; the "power of a judge to inflict punishment for criminal contempt by means of a summary proceeding," it said, was "an anomaly in the law" and "an unwarranted breach of the Bill of Rights." The ACLU also objected to the notion of a judge, who in a contempt proceeding was the "aggrieved party," to "act as prosecutor, witness, jury, and judge."

William White of the *Philadelphia Inquirer* applauded the ACLU's position, noting that "the only 'liberal' voice thus far raised—not in behalf of Barnett but in behalf of an indispensable constitutional right—has been that of the American Civil Liberties Union." If Barnett could be "hustled" out of his rights today, argued White, "a far better man, in a far better cause, can be hustled out of his rights tomorrow."

The only other friend of the court brief filed on Barnett's behalf was a notably cantankerous screed from the state of Mississippi. It declared that if "the U.S. may punish the state by unlawfully Impeaching, pauperizing and Imprisoning the governor, with deference, we need not wait for communism to destroy our great constitution."

The Supreme Court announced its 5 to 4 decision on April 6, 1964, rejecting Barnett's appeal.

In January 1965, the Justice Department announced that it was dropping two of the four contempt counts facing Barnett. "There is no likelihood, assuming conviction on the remaining counts, that any greater penalty could be imposed," said Attorney General Nicholas Katzenbach. That May, the circuit court dropped the remaining charges. "No sufficient reasons exist for further prosecution of the proceedings," said the court.

Given all the action in the South, the opening of an ACLU southern-region office was virtually a foregone conclusion. And Charles Morgan Jr., a thirty-three-year-old rising star of the Alabama bar, seemed destined to head it.

On Sunday morning, September 15, 1963, four black girls (three were fourteen, one was eleven) died instantly when a bomb planted by Ku Klux

Klansmen exploded in their Birmingham, Alabama, church. At least seventeen others were injured in the attack. Later that Sunday, a disturbance broke out, leading police to shoot a black teenager in the back of the head, killing him. Another black youth was shot and killed that same day by white teenagers who happened upon him in a Birmingham suburb. The murders provoked national outrage, although no one was brought to justice in the bombing case until years later. The following Monday, Morgan spoke before the Young Men's Business Club in Birmingham.

Morgan focused on the city "where four little girls can be born into a second-class school system, live a segregated life, ghettoed into their own little neighborhoods, restricted to Negro churches, destined to ride in Negro ambulances to Negro wards of hospitals or a Negro cemetery. . . . And who is really guilty?" "Each of us," he concluded. "Each citizen who has not consciously attempted to bring about peaceful compliance with the decisions of the Supreme Court . . . each citizen who has ever said, 'they ought to kill that nigger,' every citizen who votes for the candidate with the bloody flag." Everyone in the community who had in any way contributed to hatred was "at least as guilty, or more so, than the demented fool who threw that bomb."[1]

For Morgan, the speech was a personal and professional turning point. He suddenly became a pariah in the city he had called home since the age of fifteen. As the *New York Times* observed years later, "the speech destroyed his budding law practice, which he had already damaged by taking on unpopular civil rights cases, and it led to death threats against his family."

Morgan's speech, covered by the *New York Times*, brought him admirers far from Montgomery, including Aryeh Neier, who was then the ACLU's national field director. At the time, the ACLU had affiliates in Louisiana, Florida, Kentucky, and Texas, but no office charged with overseeing the proliferating array of initiatives attacking racial oppression in the South.

In May 1964, Neier pulled together a meeting in Atlanta of roughly a dozen lawyers to kick around the idea for a southern strategy. Morgan's "we are all guilty speech," as Neier described it, made inviting him an easy decision. The group recommended creating a southern regional office, an idea Neier carried to the ACLU biennial conference in June 1964 in Boulder, Colorado.

The meeting occurred during Freedom Summer—a ten-week-long voter registration effort carried out in Mississippi by an array of civil rights groups in alliance with hundreds of volunteers. Among them were Andrew Goodman, Michael Schwerner, and James Chaney, who all vanished that June near Philadelphia, Mississippi. They were later found to have been murdered.

A cousin of Goodman's who was among the ACLU delegates heard about the disappearances while in Boulder, recalled Neier. "That created an overwhelming civil rights conscientiousness at that meeting. And there was a sort of endorsement by acclamation of creating this southern regional office."

The board officially approved the office on September 14, a year after Morgan's controversial speech. During that year, Morgan had served brief stints at the American Association of University Professors and the NAACP's Legal Defense and Educational Fund. For Morgan, Birmingham had become toxic. He was a natural choice to head the new regional office in Atlanta.

In announcing the appointment, Pemberton explained that Morgan would "facilitate and coordinate legal work in local communities" and also "directly participate in civil liberties litigation" himself.

Morgan selected an office building at 5 Forsyth Street NW that already housed several liberal organizations, including the Southern Regional Council and the National Sharecroppers Fund. "I was told they would allow me to have an office in their building if I brought a statement from J. Edgar Hoover to the effect that the American Civil Liberties Union was not a Communist organization," he later told the *New Yorker* magazine. "And, of course, I told them that I wouldn't bring them a statement from J. Edgar Hoover on anything, but that I would provide them with statements from Presidents Johnson, Kennedy, Eisenhower, and Truman and Douglas MacArthur endorsing the ACLU. I think MacArthur was the one that sold them."

At the height of the civil rights revolution, Morgan's skills were in high demand—in part because civil rights lawyers were extremely unpopular (and therefore rare) in the South. Over the next several months, Morgan and his associates took on a broad array of cases and causes—some primarily symbolic, others deadly serious. They got black students reinstated at

Alabama State College after they were suspended for demonstrating on campus. They also got a white student at Tulane reinstated after he was suspended for bringing black guests to the student union. They defended a Black Muslim in Georgia denied visits from clergymen of his religion. They sought relief for a factory worker in Georgia denied promotion because of his race. And they defended scores of demonstrators charged with parading without a permit in Mississippi.

Morgan also took on the case of a man who had been convicted of murder in Georgia sixteen years earlier (as a barely literate fifteen-year-old). He got the conviction set aside and a new trial ordered. He argued the case of a black man accused of killing a man and woman in Alabama who was neither advised he had a right to counsel nor to remain silent. He handled the appeal of two black death row inmates in Louisiana convicted of raping a white woman, as well as the appeal of two blacks convicted of murdering a white man in Georgia. He criticized white Protestant churches for not welcoming black worshipers; and he made ending the Southern all-white jury system into a crusade.

His ultimate aim, Morgan told the *New Yorker*, was to transform the political structure of the South "so that there'll be a Negro in the clerk's office, a Negro down at the police department, or many Negroes, and there'll be a cross-sectional jury system . . . that truly represents the people."

The ACLU was not in the forefront of the legendary voting rights campaign organized by the Southern Christian Leadership Conference (SCLC) in Selma, but it kept close tabs, documenting official misconduct and sending lawyers when needed.

The police killing of Jimmie Lee Jackson was the catalyzing event that turned the Selma campaign into a crusade. Jackson, a twenty-six-year-old farmhand and Baptist deacon from nearby Marion, Alabama, worked on the Selma voter registration effort. On the evening of February 18, 1965, Jackson, along with some five hundred fellow civil rights workers, marched to the jail where a colleague was being held. State troopers and police, who later claimed they thought the peaceful march was an attempted jailbreak, waded into the marchers swinging billy clubs.

Jackson and several others, including his mother, fled to a nearby café. The police and troopers followed. At some point—Jackson claimed while he was trying to shield his mother—officers manhandled and beat him. One shot him twice in the stomach. Jackson stumbled out of the café, walked some 150 feet, and collapsed, moaning, "I'm shot." Authorities took him to a white hospital in Marion, which transferred him to a black hospital (hospital officials said they did so because they had no blood bank; others suspected it was because of his race). He died the morning of February 26.

His death competed for coverage with the death of Black Muslim leader Malcolm X, who was assassinated in New York on February 21 and whose funeral was held on February 27. A thousand mourners filled the Faith Temple of God in Christ in Harlem. Hundreds also came out for Jackson, who, on March 3, was honored with two funerals—one in his hometown of Marion and the other in Selma. The Reverend Martin Luther King Jr. delivered both eulogies. He proclaimed Jackson a "martyred hero in the holy crusade for human dignity."

Jackson's death deeply affected his SCLC colleagues and inspired the idea of a fifty-mile march from Selma to Montgomery.

The march was set for Sunday, March 7. It was to begin with a walk across Selma's Edmund Pettus Bridge, which spans the Alabama River. John Lewis, chairman of the Student Nonviolent Coordinating Committee, recreated that afternoon in his memoir.

Some six hundred protestors dressed in their Sunday best had assembled on a ballfield. Led by Lewis and SCLC organizer Hosea Williams, they headed for the bridge. "We walked two abreast in a pair of lines that stretched for several blocks," Lewis wrote. "When we reached the crest of the bridge, I stopped dead still. . . . There, facing us at the bottom of the other side, stood a sea of blue-helmeted, blue-uniformed Alabama state troopers, line and line of them." When the group did not immediately turn around, the troopers charged the crowd with tear gas and billy clubs. Lewis recalled a "human wave, a blur of blue shirts and billy clubs and bullwhips."

The future congressman was savagely beaten and "bleeding badly. My head was now exploding with pain." He struggled to his feet: "'Please, no,' I could hear one woman scream. 'God, we're being killed!' cried another."[2]

As United Press International reported, "The troopers and possemen, under Gov. George C. Wallace's orders to stop the Negroes' 'Walk For

Freedom' to Montgomery, chased the screaming, bleeding marchers nearly a mile back to their church, clubbing them as they ran."

Alabama Governor George Wallace remained defiant. "We can't give in an inch," he declared.

The nationally televised orgy of police violence enraged citizens around the world and extracted a condemnation and a pledge from President Lyndon Johnson. Johnson deplored "the brutality with which a number of Negro citizens of Alabama were treated" for trying to attain "the precious right to vote." The government's "best legal talent," he said, was "preparing legislation which will secure that right for every American."

Two days after Bloody Sunday, a carefully choreographed re-do—secretly orchestrated by Martin Luther King and the Johnson administration—took place. Despite a federal court order prohibiting the demonstration, some two thousand marchers assembled behind Dr. King and marched toward the bridge. Once again, troopers awaited them on the other side. King directed the marchers to kneel in prayer and then led them in singing "We Shall Overcome."

They approached the troopers, who parted to let them pass. King directed everyone to turn around and they walked back to the church. Pestered by the press for an explanation, King said, "We could not in good conscience ask the thousands of religious persons who expressed their indignation over the beating of our people last Sunday to return home without making their witness known."

For those not in the know, the scene made no sense. As John Lewis put it, the marchers "had no idea what was going on. They had come to put their bodies on the line and now they were backing down."

Early that morning, after consulting with federal and local officials, King had decided that, injunction or no injunction, the march must go on; but to avoid a repeat of Sunday's violence, the marchers would only proceed so far. Everyone would save face, and the protestors would make their point.

But though the march ended peacefully, the evening did not. A group of whites shouting racial insults attacked three white Unitarian ministers who had come to march with King. One of them, James Reeb of Boston, suffered skull fractures. He died two days later.

Reeb's memorial service was held in Baltimore the following Monday. Irving Murray, a Unitarian minister and chair of the Maryland ACLU affiliate, praised Reeb as "a quiet young man . . . utterly devoted to human brotherhood." That night, King led a nighttime memorial vigil of four thousand mourners in Selma, during which he urged the assemblage "to rededicate our lives to the position that all men should have the right to vote."

The same night, President Johnson addressed Congress and asked members to work nights and weekends to pass a bill that would "eliminate barriers to the right to vote." The proposed bill would "strike down restrictions to voting in all elections" that had been used to deny Negroes the vote; and it would allow citizens to be registered by federal officials if local officials refused to do so. He called upon all Americans to make the Negro cause "our cause too." There was "no Negro problem. . . . There is only an American problem. . . . And we shall overcome," he pledged to thunderous applause.

King and his associates set the Selma to Montgomery march for March 21. But they did not leave the fate of their people to Governor Wallace and his goons. They coordinated with the Johnson administration, which protected the marchers (estimates of participants ran from four thousand to ten thousand) with some three thousand federal troops and national guardsmen.

The campaign ended on March 25 with a huge rally at the state capitol. A crowd of thirty thousand listened as King promised that segregation was "on its deathbed." The only question was "how long and how costly Governor Wallace and the legislature will make the funeral." That evening, Wallace refused to see demonstrators who carried a petition demanding voting rights.

On March 25, Viola Liuzzo, a white, thirty-nine-year-old mother of five from Detroit, was shot in the head and killed as she chauffeured marchers between Montgomery and Selma. The shooters pursued the car as it veered off the road and onto the shoulder. Trapped in the car was Leroy Moton, a black teenager returning to Montgomery who, drenched in blood, pretended to be dead when the assailants flashed a light on him. That same night, the FBI arrested four Ku Klux Klansmen (one of whom, it was later revealed, was FBI informant Gary Thomas Jr., later suspected in the Sixteenth Street bombing case).

Following Liuzzo's murder, she became the victim of a smear campaign aided by the FBI, which leaked erroneous information implying she was a drug user, and by the Detroit police department, which prepared a dossier detailing her membership in the NAACP and her support of other radical causes.[3] The *Detroit Free Press* attacked the dossier as "inaccurate," and the ACLU denounced the Detroit police for compiling and circulating it.

That May saw the murder trial of Ku Klux Klansman Collie Leroy Wilkins Jr., one of Liuzzo's three accused assailants. FBI informant Rowe described the hundred-mile-per-hour chase that ended with her death. The defense attorney accused Leroy Moton, who survived, of being Liuzzo's lover and of killing her himself. The all-male, all-white jury deadlocked— with two former members of the White Citizens Council adamantly refusing to consider Wilkins's guilt. "I would have struck with an acquittal 'till hell froze over," one of the jurors told the press. The state attorney general promised a retrial.

Later that month, the three accused killers were feted at a Klan rally attended by hundreds in Anniston, Alabama. Their defense attorney attended two Klan rallies in North Carolina, where he promised the three would be exonerated.

The ACLU filed suit asking that juries be mandated to be representative of the county's population (which was 81 percent black). The ACLU also asked that the trial of the remaining two defendants be postponed until jury composition could be changed. The suit was part of a larger ACLU effort dubbed "Operation Southern Justice," aimed at eliminating the segregated justice system.

In October 1965, the ACLU and the Southern Regional Council published "Southern Justice: An Indictment." The Liuzzo case, argued the paper, "was not an isolated incident. From the sit-in demonstrations of 1960 through the spring of 1965, at least 26 Negroes and white civil rights workers died at the hands of racists in the South. Only one of the assailants was sentenced to prison and that was 10 years."

The paper documented one case after another in which blacks were severely punished for acts that whites committed with impunity. It concluded, "white people sometimes complain that they are weary of being constantly reminded of the Negro revolution. Their weariness is nothing compared to the Negro's."

That December Liuzzo's three alleged assailants—Klansmen Eugene Thomas, William Eaton and Collie Leroy Wilkins—were tried on the federal charge of violating her civil rights. After eight hours of deliberations, the jury (again, all male and all white) pronounced itself deadlocked. Judge Frank Johnson ordered them to keep deliberating. "This case must at some time be decided," he said. A few hours later, the jury convicted all three. Johnson sentenced them to the maximum of ten years provided by the 1870 Reconstruction-era vintage statute. Attorney General Nicholas Katzenbach pronounced the convictions a "victory for equal justice in the South."

In February 1966, a three-judge panel embraced the ACLU's arguments, outlawing racial discrimination in one Alabama county and ordering that women be allowed to serve on juries beginning the following year. The panel's decision, said Pemberton, "brings one step closer the realization of the promise of a fair trial to every citizen which the United States Constitution guarantees."

After graduating from Ole Miss, James Meredith had gone to Lagos, Nigeria, to study political science at Ibadan University. He soon grew unhappy and accused university officials of not delivering a promised fellowship. Meredith announced he would be returning to America, and in September 1965 enrolled in Columbia Law School. Shortly thereafter, he launched an insurgent candidacy for a seat as a delegate to New York State's constitutional convention but did not make it onto the ballot. At the end of May 1966, after completing final exams at Columbia, he announced he would lead a 220-mile march from Memphis to Jackson, Mississippi, to encourage blacks to register to vote.

Women and children would not be allowed to accompany him: "I am sick and tired of Negro men hiding behind their women and children." No major civil rights organization backed his effort, but the media covered his "homecoming march" as a major event.

Meredith set off on Sunday, June 5, wearing hiking boots and accompanied by a few companions. "There are a million Negroes in Mississippi. I think they will take care of me," he told reporters.

Meredith cut quite the figure: "An elfin black Don Quixote with a Bible in his pack, a pith helmet shading his misty eyes, an ivory-headed African cane clicking off his steps," observed *Newsweek*.

That Monday evening, reported *Newsweek*, a voice called out from "the thicket of water oak and honeysuckle edging the highway—an ice-cool

voice that said, "James . . . I just want James Meredith.'" James Aubrey Nor-
vell, a forty-year-old unemployed hardware clerk, leveled "a 16-gauge automatic shotgun at the pilgrims. . . . A first blast sent birdshot skittering
harmlessly over the pavement. But the second struck home, and so did the
third," reported *Newsweek*. The next day's *Atlanta Constitution* ran a picture of a terrified Meredith crawling on the ground.

NBC Newsman Chet Huntley reported him dead. The next day, after
meeting with Meredith in the hospital, Floyd McKissick, national director of CORE, announced that he, Martin Luther King, and Stokely Car-
michael of SNCC would continue Meredith's "homecoming walk."
Volunteers from all walks of life, said McKissick, were "welcome to unite
in this pilgrimage to encourage Negro voting in Mississippi."

For three weeks they marched, after detailing their grievances in a manifesto protesting the "failure of American society, the government of the
United States and the state of Mississippi" to allow equal access to the ballot.

Meredith joined the marchers for their triumphal entrance into Jackson,
Mississippi, where, at a rally attended by some fifteen thousand, King pronounced the march the "greatest demonstration for freedom in the history
of Mississippi." More than four thousand blacks registered during the
march, according to the Department of Justice.

One unexpected offshoot of Meredith's march was a flag-burning case fea-
turing a Bronze Star recipient employed by the New York Transit Authority. When Meredith was shot, Brooklyn resident and World War II veteran
Sidney Street became livid. He pulled out an old forty-eight-star flag that
had draped the coffin of his stepfather, also a veteran, walked to an intersection roughly a block from his home, deposited the flag on a piece of
paper (so it would not touch the ground), and set it aflame with a match.

A nearby policeman approached in time to hear Street lament, "we don't
need no damn flag . . . if they let that happen to Meredith."

The cop charged Street with disorderly conduct and violating a state statute prohibiting flag desecration. Street was convicted, and the state Court
of Appeals affirmed the conviction. He appealed to the Supreme Court,
which had ruled in 1967 that burning a draft card did not qualify as "symbolic speech" but had yet to pass judgement on the flag desecration statute.

In October 1967, the ACLU filed a brief backing Street. The same day, it also filed a brief defending a white supremacist group called the National States Rights Party of Virginia.

In April 1969, the Supreme Court decided, 5 to 4, in Street's favor. Given the wording of the New York statute—which made it a crime to deface, "publicly defy . . . or cast contempt" on the flag—the court could not determine whether Street was prosecuted for his words or for his act. His words were protected speech. So Street was in the clear. The court left open the question of whether future flag burners also would be.

In the early 1960s, the Vietnam War had not yet become an American obsession. The battle for racial justice and civil rights was center stage, and Morgan threw himself into that battle with a vengeance.

He fought for Johnnie Coleman, a black man convicted by an all-white jury of murdering a white man in Alabama. The ACLU twice took the case to the Alabama Supreme Court, and ultimately to the U.S. Supreme Court, which reversed the conviction on grounds that blacks had been excluded from the jury. Coleman was retried on the same evidence before an all-black jury and exonerated after seven years on death row.

Morgan had also successfully fought—in *Hadnott v. Amos*—to return black candidates to the ballot in Alabama after white state officials had kicked them off. He championed cases aimed at integrating prisons. And he signed on to represent boxer Muhammad Ali, when the boxer appealed his conviction for refusing induction into the U.S. military.

The Howard Levy case was an entirely different—and more complicated—matter. It was not about a simple question of law or a narrow focus on government error; it went to the heart of the Vietnam War's legitimacy.

The anti-Vietnam movement was tiny in 1962 when, after finishing at SUNY Downstate College of Medicine, Howard Levy got a deferment while doing a three-year residency at NYU Medical Center's Skin Cancer Clinic. The so-called Berry plan—named for former Defense Department official Frank B. Berry—allowed physicians to defer military service until after they had completed their residency. At the time Levy signed up, Vietnam was "barely on the horizon," he said. Three years later, "the horizon had changed."

The year 1965 was the first year of Operation Rolling Thunder, Lyndon Johnson's bombing assault on targets in North Vietnam. It was also the year of the Battle of la Drang, three days of the most intense fighting American troops had yet experienced in the war. The engagement brought home to many Americans how deeply the United States was now involved.

Between starting his dermatology residency and finishing it, the idealistic Brooklyn native had found his political voice. As he rotated through the Veterans Administration Hospital, Bellevue Hospital, and an NYU hospital, Levy saw how bad treatment was for the poor. "If you're a doctor working with poor people, you're always struggling somewhere along the line with somebody who's trying to minimize [costs]," he discovered. He found himself fighting on behalf of his poor patients for access to drugs and equipment. He also began attending civil rights meeting and gatherings of radical groups—including the War Resisters League.

Levy considered, but rejected, claiming conscientious objector status. He was not sure he qualified. Instead, he decided to try to get sent south and become involved in civil rights work while in the military.

Levy ended up at Fort Jackson, South Carolina. Instead of living on base, he found an apartment in nearby Columbia. Although his rank as a captain entitled him to membership in the officers' club, he had no interest in hanging out there. He wanted to spend his free time fighting racism.

After reading an article about blacks registering to vote in Newberry County, he took the half-hour drive there and went searching for the black community. "It wasn't hard . . . because that's all there was in Newberry County," he discovered.

Levy asked a bartender for directions to the voter registration project. Within hours, "I was trudging down dusty roads registering people or trying to register people to vote. . . . It felt good. I wasn't accomplishing much but it did feel like I was doing something other than being in the army."

The voter registration project consumed most of his evenings and weekends. At some point, an army official spotted his car (and its New York license plates and Fort Jackson sticker) in Newberry and reported him to army intelligence. Levy's civil rights work "did not endear him to the white, career, southern superior officers," observed Ira Glasser, an ACLU staffer who eventually got involved in the case.

Levy's civil rights work was only one of several things that set him apart. Levy typically did not salute: "I sort of waved to people." And he "could never get the damn insignias on right." Then there was his outspokenness. During lulls in his work at the clinic, he often made provocative remarks to other soldiers. He suggested blacks should not be in Vietnam, since they were discriminated against in America. And he helped soldiers avoid service in Vietnam: "I got . . . literally hundreds of guys out of the army on medical grounds. . . . It was part of my job to know [the exemptions]."

It was also his job to teach special forces soldiers rudimentary medical skills. "The appeal of dermatology for them was that [with] just a little bit of knowledge, you could treat people . . . and have a visibly dramatic effect." But the main goal, Levy concluded, "wasn't to help some poor kid who had impetigo." It was to "win the hearts and minds," to "encourage people to join your side of a war that is . . . destroying them."

Levy refused to train the Green Berets. Colonel Henry Fancy, Levy's commanding officer, advised him to reconsider. Levy did not. A month or so later, Fancy called him in again. He gave a direct order to train the Green Berets. If Levy refused, he faced a court-martial.

Levy turned for advice to Richard Miles, an ex-Marine who directed the voter education project in Columbia. Miles told him to call Charles Morgan, who, after kidding Levy about being just "another Jewish troublemaker," agreed to take his case. Aware that the case might have media potential, Morgan invited a few reporters to meet with Levy.

Levy protested that he had never previously spoken to the press. Morgan assured him that he would do fine.

Eventually Jack Nelson of the *Los Angeles Times* and syndicated columnist Nicholas von Hoffman showed up. "They came to my little apartment and we put out some beer and pretzels," recalled Levy.

On May 10, 1967, the court-martial began at Fort Jackson. Levy was charged with willfully disobeying "a lawful command of his superior officer," engaging in "conduct unbecoming an officer and a gentleman," and publicly uttering statements calculated "to promote disloyalty and disaffection among the troops . . . to the prejudice of good order and discipline in the armed forces." He faced a maximum of eleven years.

In his opening statement, Morgan called the trial a "witch hunt" motivated by animosity toward Levy's political beliefs. Under Morgan's

questioning, each of the ten members of the trial panel promised to uphold the First Amendment and not to prejudge Levy because of his voter
registration work.

Over the next week, army prosecutors documented Levy's refusal to conform or obey orders and his propensity for making provocative comments.
A wounded black GI said Levy had persuaded him that "there wasn't anything in the Army for me." A Special Forces medic recalled Levy comparing Lyndon Johnson to Adolf Hitler. Another witness testified that Levy
had asked whether communism was "worse than the United States-oriented
government."

Even though Levy had challenged white soldiers and their motives for
fighting in Vietnam, government prosecutors focused largely on his interactions with blacks.

Wednesday, May 16, as Morgan began presenting his defense, the judge,
Colonel Earl Brown, opened an unexpected door. He sustained a prosecution objection, ruling irrelevant Morgan's question to a Green Beret about
the damage howitzers could do. Even if Levy's statements describing Green
Berets' violent acts were true, Brown said, that would not justify Levy disobeying orders. But if he could prove they were directed to commit atrocities, he might have a defense. The Nuremberg trials and various post-war
treaties, Brown pointed out, "have evolved a rule that a soldier must disobey an order demanding that he commit war crimes, or genocide."

Morgan grabbed the bait and suggested that, given a bit of time, he might
be able to prove war crimes. He would show "that those they don't cure,
they kill, because they have to."

Colonel Brown granted Morgan permission to use the so-called Nuremberg defense.

The trial's "wildly improbable turn," noted *Newsweek* magazine, left Morgan "obviously flabbergasted."

Brown granted Morgan a week's recess to come up with appropriate witnesses and evidence. Morgan immediately issued a public appeal asking
anyone with knowledge of such crimes to come forth.

The news media perked up.

The *Irish Times* noted that Levy's trial was the first time "in the United
States that the commission of atrocities" was being used as a defense for
refusing a military order.

"A small, incredulous audience of newspapermen had sensed Colonel Brown was moving in this direction, but nobody believed he would actually put the war on trial before this court martial composed of 10 officers, four of whom have served in Vietnam," wrote Nicholas Von Hoffman.

"Acquittal in the Levy case could conceivably promote disobedience of orders by thousands of enlisted personnel who don't want to go to Vietnam," predicted Homer Bigart of the *New York Times*.

The national office of the ACLU was stunned. Ira Glasser, who had just joined as associate director of the New York affiliate, recalls: "The ACLU board goes nuts and says, 'Why is the ACLU in this? . . . Suddenly the ACLU had to prove war crimes . . . with two lawyers that are down there in Columbia South Carolina [with] no sources and all the evidence is in Vietnam?"

Aryeh Neier, then the executive director of the New York Civil Liberties Union (NYCLU), "sends some of us down to Columbia to help out on the case," said Glasser. Others also were dispatched. ACLU general counsel and board member Edward Ennis, Assistant Legal Director Eleanor Holmes Norton, and Ramona Ripston, then the ACLU communications director, also showed up.

Ennis's job, assumed Glasser, was to "rein Chuck in."

Glasser witnessed an intense exchange between the two men during which the reserved, dignified Ennis pointed out that the ACLU would be publicly pilloried if Morgan persisted with his war crimes argument. "Chuck says, 'Well I'm sorry. . . . I don't work for you . . . I work for Levy. He's my client." Legal ethics required him to use "the only argument that has a chance" to exonerate Levy, even if it caused embarrassment to the ACLU, said Morgan.

"Chuck stayed firm and Ed spoke his piece and left and the board never did anything about it," observed Glasser.

During the recess, Morgan reached out to Supreme Court Chief Justice Earl Warren and asked him to halt the trial so a federal court could hear Levy's challenge to the military code of justice. The Supreme Court refused to intervene. Shortly after the trial resumed, Brown ruled that Morgan had not proved the Green Berets had committed war crimes. Brown also rejected Morgan's argument that Levy could disobey the orders simply because they violated medical ethics.

On June 2, after six hours of deliberation, the panel convicted Levy. The next day he was sentenced to three years confinement in a military prison.

Levy was led off in handcuffs. "This is a disgrace! My client has a right to be accompanied by counsel," cried Morgan, as Levy's girlfriend, Trina, wept and his parents gently held each other, reported von Hoffman.

The United States Court of Military Appeals upheld the verdict. In a brief prepared for the U.S. District Court, Morgan argued, "under the Bill of Rights, the Uniform Code of Military Justice is a non sequitur. For justice in the military is, at best, an anomaly." The district court rejected Morgan's argument that the Uniform Code of Military Justice violated Levy's right to free speech and that he had been prosecuted for ideological and racially prejudiced reasons.

Initially, Levy was confined in an abandoned barracks at Fort Jackson. After several months, he was transferred to Fort Leavenworth, Kansas, with his last six months spent at Lewisburg Penitentiary in Pennsylvania.

The Supreme Court, in June 1974, upheld Levy's conviction 5 to 3.

Writing for the majority, Justice William Rehnquist declared, "while military personnel are not excluded from First Amendment protection, the fundamental necessity for obedience, and the consequent necessity for discipline, may render permissible within the military that which would be constitutionally impermissible outside it."

In a dissent read from the bench, joined by Justices William Douglas and William Brennan, Justice Potter Stewart delivered a withering critique of the Uniform Code of Military Justice. "I find it hard to imagine criminal statutes more patently unconstitutional than these vague and uncertain general articles," he wrote.

The ACLU also took an interest in child care expert Dr. Benjamin Spock's anti-Vietnam War exploits. In January 1968, the Department of Justice announced that it was charging Spock and four others with "a continuing conspiracy to aid, abet and counsel violations of Selective Service law." The crimes—which consisted of advising men to avoid the draft and discard their draft cards—carried a maximum penalty of five years' incarceration and a $10,000 fine.

The indictments stemmed from an anti-war demonstration in Washington in October 1967, during which Spock, Yale University chaplain

William Sloane Coffin Jr., Harvard graduate student Michael Ferber, author Mitchell Goodman, and Institute for Policy Studies co-founder Marcus Raskin presented 992 abandoned draft cards to the Department of Justice.

ACLU legal director Melvin Wulf called the indictments a "major escalation in the Administration's war against dissent" and promised that the ACLU would challenge them.

Spock and Coffin already had lawyers. Two of the other three had reached out to the ACLU. The ACLU agreed the case was important and were willing to help with an amicus brief. But board members worried that offering direct legal assistance might again lead them down the politically fraught Nuremberg war crimes path.

Leonard Boudin, Spock's attorney, had already indicated he intended to employ the so-called Nuremberg Defense. Government attorneys had made it clear in pre-trial motions they would oppose that tactic. The court, they argued, had no authority to rule on "political" issues.

At its board meeting on January 12, the ACLU debated and ultimately rejected a motion offered by general counsel Osmond Fraenkel that the ACLU offer to defend the anti–Vietnam War protestors. In advocating a yes vote, legal director Melvin Wulf argued that the "current case and its central free speech issue present one of the most profound challenges to civil liberties in many years . . . and the Union should not allow them to pass without its most aggressive action."

"The question of direct representation vs. amicus briefs is one which the Union has faced increasingly," said Wulf, who pointed out that the ACLU had gradually moved toward direct representation. To abandon that now, he said, "would be a dangerous reversal and would be heralded as such by those who pay close attention to the Union's work."

A lengthy article in *Harper's* magazine explored the ACLU's dilemma. Joseph W. Bishop Jr., the author and a Yale law professor, opined that the "warring factions" within the ACLU highlighted "the differences between the national position and the affiliates"—with the affiliates strongly in favor of directly defending the anti-war dissidents.

On February 2, the *New York Times* reported the ACLU's announcement that it "would not defend individuals who refuse to register for military service as a protest against war or the draft," since the ACLU assumed the draft laws were constitutional "regardless of how unwise or unjust they may be from the viewpoint of the individual who violates them."

The *Times* pointed out that the position put the national ACLU in conflict with affiliates in New York, New Jersey, Massachusetts, and Southern California. The *Times* noted that the board had voted not to become involved directly in the Spock case.

After the story broke, and under pressure from affiliates, the board reconsidered. On March 2 it decided, by a vote of 26 to 20, that the ACLU would "provide direct representation to any defendant in this indictment who wishes it." The motion made clear the ACLU was not judging the draft to be unconstitutional or professing belief that the United States "is or is not committing a pattern of war crimes in Viet Nam or is or is not violating international law."

The board turnabout provoked another round of press coverage, with the AP reporting that the previous decision had provoked "anguished cries" from various affiliates.

On April 17, ruling on pre-trial motions, a federal judge shut down plans for a Nuremberg defense in the Spock-Coffin case. "Legality of the war is not a relevant issue in this case," declared Judge Francis J.W. Ford. The decision rendered irrelevant the work attorneys had done in soliciting evidence from twenty-five nations of supposed criminal acts committed by American troops in Vietnam.

Marcus Raskin was acquitted of all charges on June 14, 1968. The remaining four were convicted. Spock and his three co-defendants were sentenced to two years in prison, with fines ranging from $1,000 to $5,000.

On July 11, 1969, Spock and Ferber won a directed acquittal from the First Circuit Court of Appeals. The majority concluded there was insufficient evidence to prove the two had participated in a conspiracy. The next month, the Nixon administration filed papers in the Supreme Court indicating the government would not appeal that ruling. Nine months later, the U.S. government quietly dropped the charges against Coffin and Goodman, saying that retrial was unwarranted.

For the ACLU, the case marked acceptance of an evolution forced upon it by the civil rights struggle and the Vietnam war. Increasingly, the ACLU would represent actual clients—as opposed to ideals—and, in doing so, it would risk getting its hands dirtier than some traditionalists considered appropriate.

Perhaps the ACLU's most controversial sally into the thicket of the Vietnam War was with William A. Calley Jr., a second lieutenant in the U.S. Army charged in connection with the My Lai Massacre. During that siege, in March 1968, American soldiers murdered several hundred Vietnamese.

The tragedy was exposed in November 1969 by investigative journalist Seymour Hersh, who had received a tip that the army would be taking legal action against a platoon leader accused of killing Vietnamese civilians. "They just marched through shooting everybody," one soldier told Hersh. The revelations stunned America and dominated news coverage for weeks.

Shortly after Hersh's revelations, the army announced that Calley would be court-martialed for the premeditated murder of 109 Vietnamese civilians.

That December, Pemberton and ACLU legal director Wulf wrote Defense Secretary Melvin Laird a letter suggesting that it might be impossible for Calley to receive a fair trial. The extensive publicity, the publication of shocking photographs from the scene, and the resulting "national self-examination" had effectively "eliminate[d] the possibility" of finding officers who could objectively sit in judgment, they wrote. They recommended "a public commission . . . independent of both the armed services and the Administration" be appointed so "all the facts surrounding the events of Songmy can be ferreted out and placed on the public record."

In an interview with *Newsweek* magazine, Charles Morgan made the same point: "There are some kinds of cases . . . where it may be impossible to get an unbiased jury . . . cases involving deeds so national in scope and so political in nature that there's no way to avoid having the First Amendment conflict with the Fifth and Sixth Amendment guarantees of due process and a fair trial."

In such cases, argued Morgan, "it is better for the American people to know what it is doing overseas than to cover that up in the interests of a fair trial and an unprejudiced jury. This may mean it will be impossible to bring Calley . . . to trial."

The ACLU position gained no public traction. Even inside the ACLU, some thought the position ridiculous. George Soll, secretary to the Roger

Baldwin Foundation, wrote, "If wide publicity about a case means that charges must be dropped again the accused, then the accused involved in almost every widely discussed crime in the U.S. would be able to avoid trial."

The Department of Defense was equally dismissive. Robert Jordan, general counsel, responded to Pemberton's letter: "After noting certain excesses and possible errors of judgment on the part of the press, you conclude that the Government has no choice but to drop its prosecution of Lieutenant Calley." Under this "novel doctrine," noted Jordan, "the Government must sit helplessly by, while persons over whom it has no control" make it impossible for Government to "discharge its important public functions. . . . This is hardly an acceptable answer to the admittedly complex problems raised by the conflicting rights of the press and of an accused."

The court-martial began in November 1970. On March 29, 1971, the court found Calley guilty of murdering "not less than 22 Vietnamese noncombatant civilians." He was sentenced to hard labor for life. The day after his sentencing, President Nixon ordered Calley transferred from Leavenworth prison to house arrest at Fort Benning to wait out his appeal. Nixon gave no concrete reason for his action, which the *Christian Science Monitor* speculated "was to avoid a further depressing of morale at home and in the armed forces in Vietnam." Captain Aubrey Daniel, the prosecutor in the case, accused Nixon of having "damaged the system of military justice."

After Calley spent three and a half years under house arrest, a federal judge set aside the conviction, ruling his trial had been tainted by publicity. That judge was subsequently overruled by the Fifth Circuit Court of Appeals, but Calley was paroled by the secretary of the army in November 1974. He settled in Columbus, Georgia, where many considered him a hero, and endorsed the presidential campaign of Alabama Governor George Wallace.

The ACLU also had a history of supporting Governor Wallace—or, at least, supporting his right to speak. In September 1968, presidential candidate Wallace and the Courage Party (which nominated him in New York) applied for a permit for Wallace to speak at Shea Stadium that October 9. Negotiations were going well enough that Wallace's people put down a deposit of $10,000. Suddenly, New York Parks Commissioner August Heckscher declared the venue unavailable for a "partisan" rally.

Mayor John Lindsay's office had decided that the moment did not favor a rally for an openly racist political candidate. A few months earlier, Martin Luther King's murder had ignited riots across America. That June, Robert F. Kennedy had been assassinated. The Democratic National Convention in Chicago that summer had been disrupted by anti-war riots and police violence. Hosting Wallace during such a fraught period struck some as a fundamentally bad idea.

Aryeh Neier, director of the NYCLU, sent a telegram to Commissioner Heckscher pointing out that "government officials must not interfere with freedom of speech." Refusing Wallace a forum, he said, was just as wrong as Chicago's refusal to allow anti-Vietnam activists to demonstrate in Soldier Field during the Democratic Convention.

Neier asked Eleanor Holmes Norton, the ACLU's young, black assistant legal director, how she felt about working on the Wallace case. "I would love to," she replied.

From a legal viewpoint, "I thought . . . it was an easy case," she recalled during an interview. And although—having worked with SNCC—she was devoted to civil rights, she also was a strong advocate of free speech.

Norton wrote an amicus brief supporting Wallace's right to rent the stadium. Ira Glasser drove her to Queens to meet the Wallace team. No one informed them she was black. "I just appeared on the scene. I remember when I introduced myself, saying, 'I am Eleanor Holmes Norton, here to represent Governor Wallace.' [Wallace's] communications director was surprised. But not his lawyers. I think Wallace's lawyers [went to] the same kind of law school I went to," said the Yale Law School graduate.

On October 1, Queens Supreme Court Justice Harold Tessler ruled for Wallace. He called the city's restriction "arbitrary and capricious," "patently unreasonable," and in violation of both the state and federal constitutions.

The city said it would appeal. That became moot when the Wallace team announced it had retained Madison Square Garden for his speech, which had been moved to October 24.

On the appointed evening, an estimated two thousand protestors surrounded Madison Square Garden. A force of three thousand police watched over them. Bottles, soda cans, eggs, and stones were tossed. At one point the police, nightsticks flailing, charged into the crowd. At another point policemen on horseback dispersed the throng. Some twenty-seven protestors were arrested, and several complained of being beaten by police.

Inside Madison Square Garden, Wallace wallowed in the crowd's acclaim, which welcomed him with a fifteen-minute ovation. "I've been waiting to fight the main event in the Garden for a long time," screamed Wallace, who had once been a Golden Gloves boxer. As supporters waved confederate flags, Wallace called for law and order, promised to return government "back to the people," and pledged "not one penny of federal money would be used to bus anybody you don't want bused."

As Wallace became the "main event" at Madison Square Garden, Norton appeared before the Supreme Court to argue on behalf of another group of racists. The National States Rights Party had held a rally in Somerset County, Maryland, in 1966, during which members used anti-Semitic and anti-black language. Local officials, worried about violence, got an injunction preventing the white supremacists from holding a rally the following day. That injunction was later extended for ten months.

While acknowledging its commitment to white supremacy, the group claimed it was nonviolent and asked the ACLU to fight the injunction—which ultimately ended up before the Supreme Court. The week before Norton's high court debut, the ACLU alerted the press that a "young black lawyer" would be arguing the white supremacists' case.

Norton won. In a unanimous decision, authored by Justice Abe Fortas (handed down in November 1968), the Supreme Court found that Somerset County officials had committed unconstitutional prior restraint, which "suppresses the precise freedom which the First Amendment sought to protect against abridgement."

When I asked Norton, years later, about that Supreme Court presentation, she pointed out that she had only been a member of the bar for three years, the minimum experience required to argue before the court: "I just made it in." It was the only case she ever argued before the Supreme Court, she said, and she took pleasure in winning it unanimously. As for whether cases like those of Wallace and other racists were worth the bother, she recalled a sentiment attributed to Roger Baldwin: "If you don't defend the free speech of these sons of bitches, we won't have any ourselves."

Of all the cases the ACLU was involved in during the 1960s, the most poignant had a love story at its heart. Richard Perry Loving and Mildred Loving were a photogenic interracial couple with a simple wish: to legally raise a family as husband and wife in the state of Virginia.

Virginia had no intention of letting that happen, as interracial marriage was outlawed there, as it was in fifteen other southern states.

The Lovings got their wish on June 12, 1967, when the Supreme Court struck down the law—but not before they endured years of hell. Their ordeal began on July 11, 1958, when a Virginia county sheriff got a warrant charging them with "cohabiting as man and wife against the dignity of the Commonwealth of Virginia." That warrant set in motion a series of events that culminated with a pre-dawn raid on the home the Lovings shared with Mildred's parents. The sheriff and his deputies, shining flashlights in their faces, demanded to know why they were together. The reply that they were husband and wife got them arrested.

Historians trace the intermarriage prohibition in Virginia to 1691, when the House of Burgesses concluded interracial marriage was a threat to slave-owning society.[4] "Apparently social pressure was insufficient to prevent such marriages," noted an ACLU brief. So the assembly passed "An Act for Suppressing Outlying Slaves," which eventually morphed into the Racial Integrity Act of 1924, which the Lovings were charged with violating.

On January 6, 1959, a pregnant Mildred and her bricklayer husband pled guilty. Caroline County Circuit Court Judge Leon Bazile passed along his thoughts: "Almighty God created the races white, black, yellow, malay, and red, and he placed them on separate continents. . . . The fact that he separated the races shows that he did not intend for the races to mix."

Bazile accepted their plea and sentenced both to a year in jail but suspended the sentence for twenty-five years provided they left the state immediately and did not return as a couple.

They moved to the District of Columbia, where they had gotten married in June of 1958. Four and a half years later, they had three children—Sidney, Donald, Peggy—but were unhappy. They missed their friends and family. And Washington was distressingly expensive. Mildred wondered whether it might be possible to return home—if only for a visit.

A lot had changed in America since their sentencing. Governor George Wallace, who had promised "segregation forever" in his inauguration, had obeyed when troops ordered him to permit black students to integrate the University of Alabama.

All it took was President Kennedy mobilizing the National Guard under the command of Brigadier General Henry Graham, who saluted the governor and told him, "It is my sad duty to have to ask you to step aside, sir.

Race "has no place in American life or law," President John Kennedy had declared. "When Americans are sent to Viet Nam or West Berlin, we do not ask for whites only. It ought to be possible, therefore, for American students of any color to attend any public institution they select without having to be backed up by troops."

This was not the America that had driven the Lovings from their home. Mildred Loving wrote Attorney General Robert Kennedy to explain her situation; his office directed her to the ACLU, which impelled her to write another letter, in which she explained that she was "part negro, and part Indian" and her husband was white. When they had married five years ago in Washington, DC, they "did not know there was a law in Va. against mixed marriages. Therefore, we were jailed and tried in a little town of Bowling Green. We were [forced] to leave the state to make our home."

The judge had threatened to send them to jail for a year if they returned to the state: "We know we can't live there, but we would like to go back once and awhile to visit our families and friends." She added that they could not afford a lawyer, but the attorney general had "suggested that we get in touch with you for advice. Please help us if you can. Hope to hear from you real soon."

The ACLU directed the letter to Bernard Cohen, then twenty-nine and based in Alexandria, Virginia. His primary legal focus was "horses and divorces," he later confided to the press. Cohen recruited Philip Hirschkop, another young attorney and a former Green Beret. In a *Washington Post* interview years after the Loving case, Hirschkop imagined what might have happened had Richard Loving been a black man: "It would have been much harder as a black man and a white woman. They might have been hanged for that."

That the ACLU took the case said something about its own evolution. In 1944, Baldwin wrote a memo noting an organizational decision to avoid such cases. "It was agreed that it would not be useful to attack the many state laws barring intermarriage because they are commonly circumvented and do not constitute a practical issue."

On November 6, 1963, Cohen filed a motion before Judge Bazile to set aside the Lovings' sentence on the grounds that it violated due process and the Fourteenth Amendment. In October 1964, with that motion undecided, the lawyers filed a class action in the U.S. District Court of Virginia requesting that a three-judge federal court panel declare the prohibition on intermarriage unconstitutional and therefore the law unenforceable. On January 22, 1965, the state court denied the Loving's motion to set aside the sentence. That February the federal panel continued the case so the lawyers could submit their arguments to the Supreme Court of Appeals of Virginia. That court upheld the statutes, at which point the ACLU lawyers appealed to the U.S. Supreme Court.

Virginia Attorney General Robert Button argued against the Supreme Court accepting jurisdiction. "The Virginia statutes here under attack reflect a policy which . . . still obtains in almost half of the 50 states of the Union. . . . [It] is clear that the challenged enactments infringe no constitutional right."

The ACLU brief argued that the case "gives this Court an appropriate opportunity to strike down the last remnants of legalized slavery in our country" and observed, "no other civilized country in the world has such laws except the Union of South Africa."

Whatever rationale may have made such laws acceptable in the past, that time was gone, argued the ACLU.

Chief Justice Earl Warren delivered the court's unanimous opinion: "This case presents a constitutional question never addressed by this Court: whether a statutory scheme adopted by the State of Virginia to prevent marriages between persons solely on the basis of racial classifications violates the Equal Protection and Due Process Clauses of the Fourteenth Amendment. For reasons which seem to us to reflect the central meaning of those constitutional commands, we conclude that these statutes cannot stand consistently with the Fourteenth Amendment. . . .

"Marriage is one of the 'basic civil rights of man,' fundamental to our very existence and survival," he observed. "Under our Constitution, the freedom to marry, or not marry, a person of another race resides with the individual, and cannot be infringed by the State."

"I feel free now," said Mrs. Loving after the decision.

The *Christian Science Monitor*, while hailing the ruling as "inevitable," wrote an editorial apparently aimed at reassuring those frightened by the implications. "There is ample evidence that the overwhelming majority of marriages will continue to be along racial lines. There is little proof that even the freer attitudes of the 1960's have brought any major increase in miscegenation," claimed the *Monitor*.

A year later, the *New York Times* took note of several high-profile interracial marriages and commented, "clearly interracial marriage is in a kind of vogue, though it is hardly the racial amalgamation that Arnold Toynbee once saw as one of the two routes to world peace."

In 2017, fifty years after the Loving decision, the Pew Research Center issued a report based on 2015 data noting that "17% of all U.S. newlyweds had a spouse of a different race or ethnicity, marking more than a fivefold increase since 1967."

Michael Meyers, former ACLU board member and frequent critic of the
ACLU's staff leadership. *Photograph by Jonathan Lenglain.*

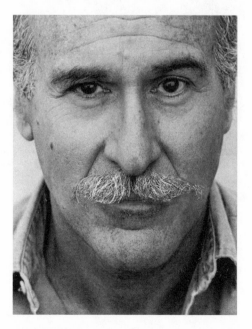

Ira Glasser, former ACLU executive director. *Photograph by Bob Adelman.*

Ira Glasser in Jackson, Mississippi with Al Bronstein, head of the ACLU's National Prison Project, and NYCLU board member Faith Seidenberg.

Ira Glasser on *Firing Line* with host Bill Buckley.

ACLU executive director Anthony Romero. *Photograph by Quinn Russell Brown.*

ACLU team on the steps of the Supreme Court in March 2013, following oral arguments in the case of *United States v. Windsor*. Edie Windsor, second from left, contested the refusal of the federal government to recognize her marriage to another woman. On the far left is Roberta Kaplan, an attorney in the Windsor case. James Esseks, director of the ACLU's LGBT project, is in the center next to Windsor's friend and advisor Karen Sauvigne. Anthony Romero is on the right. The Supreme Court found in Windsor's favor. *Photograph courtesy Molly Kaplan of the ACLU.*

Aryeh Neier, former ACLU executive director. *Photograph courtesy Open Society Foundations.*

Aryeh Neier. *Photograph courtesy Open Society Foundations.*

Eleanor Holmes Norton, former assistant legal director of the ACLU.

Ben Wizner, right, and Ed Snowden in Moscow. *Photo courtesy ACLU.*

Anthony Romero and Laura Poitras, who worked on the Ed Snowden
expose. *Photograph courtesy ACLU.*

Deputy ACLU executive director Dorothy Ehrlich. *Photograph by Jock
McDonald.*

Crystal Eastman. Cropped version of the photograph published in *The Suffragist* 3, no. 19 (May 8, 1915). *From the Records of the National Woman's Party, Manuscript Division, Library of Congress.*

Communist Party member and ACLU board member Elizabeth Gurley Flynn. *Photograph courtesy Library of Congress Prints and Photographs Division.*

Howard Levy, anti–Vietnam War physician defended by the ACLU.

Ruth Bader Ginsburg, former director of ACLU's Women's Rights Project and Associate Supreme Court Justice.

Laura Murphy, former head of ACLU Washington office. Attorney General Eric Holder seated. *Photograph by Donnamaria R. Jones.*

Laura Murphy with Senate majority leader Mitch McConnell at her ACLU retirement reception. *Photograph by Don Baker.*

Former ACLU executive director Roger Baldwin, actor Paul Muni, and ACLU executive director Patrick Murphy Malin. *Photograph courtesy of the Department of Special Collections, Princeton University Library.*

Former ACLU executive director John Pemberton. *Photograph courtesy of the Department of Special Collections, Princeton University Library.*

Crystal Eastman of the American Union Against Militarism. *Photograph courtesy Library of Congress Prints and Photographs division.*

9

Resurrecting a Communist
as the Nixon Era Ends

During the early 1960s, society's pent-up demand for justice, recognition, and equality exploded. Battles were fought in the streets and in the courts, where the ACLU was becoming increasingly potent.

It was the era not just of Martin Luther King and Malcolm X, but of John F. Kennedy, a politician who seemed tailormade for a time of transformation. In July 1960, accepting the Democratic nomination for president, Kennedy acknowledged his status as a trailblazer when he declared, "I hope that no American, considering the really critical issues facing this country, will waste his franchise and throw away his vote by voting either for me or against me because of my religious affiliation."

The vision Kennedy laid out was in keeping with the unbounded idealism he embodied. His opponent Richard Nixon, said Kennedy, is "a young man" but his "party is the party of the past." Kennedy's party, in contrast, was the party of the "new frontier." That new frontier, Kennedy insisted, "is here, whether we seek it or not. Beyond that frontier are unchartered areas of science and space, unsolved problems of peace and war, unconquered pockets of ignorance and prejudice." America, he said, stands "on this frontier at a turning point in history."

The sense that America could no longer accept the status quo, that it had to question virtually every aspect of existence, created an opportunity to reconsider policies that had not previously been seriously challenged. And the ACLU, along with other reform-minded organizations, deftly stepped into the opening. That was a godsend for Clarence Earl Gideon.

In 1961, Gideon, an impoverished, unemployed drifter and sometime gambler, was charged with breaking into and burgling a pool hall in Panama City, Florida. The Florida trial court refused to provide Gideon an attorney because his alleged crime was not a capital offense, meaning the court had no obligation to ensure his defense. Gideon defended himself, incompetently, and was convicted.

Prompted by Gideon's handwritten request, the Supreme Court decided to review his case. Represented by future Supreme Court Justice Abraham "Abe" Fortas, Gideon prevailed. Indigent defendants were entitled to legal representation at the public's expense, ruled the court (*Gideon v. Wainwright*, 1963). The "noble ideal" of "fair trials . . . cannot be realized if the poor man . . . has to face his accusers without a lawyer to assist him," declared Hugo Black in a unanimous opinion.

Eight months after the Gideon decision, President Kennedy was assassinated. On November 27, 1963, less than a week after Kennedy's death, Johnson addressed a joint session of Congress and outlined Kennedy's dreams: to conquer the "vastness of space, to educate "all of our children," to provide jobs "for all who seek . . . and need them," to care for the elderly, attack mental illness, and, above all, to provide "equal rights for all Americans." Those "ideas and the ideals," said Johnson, "must and will be translated into effective action."

Johnson had plenty of company in his quest to remake the American compact. Of fundamental importance was the U.S. Supreme Court, over which Chief Justice Earl Warren presided. As constitutional law scholar Lucas A. Powe Jr. has observed: "The Warren Court created the image of the Supreme Court as a revolutionary body."[1]

One of that court's most consequential decisions was *New York Times v. Sullivan*. The case began with a full-page ad in the March 26, 1960, edition of the *New York Times*. The ad, headlined "Heed Their Rising Voices," quoted from a *Times* editorial of the previous week: "The growing movement of peaceful mass demonstrations by Negroes is something new in the South, something understandable. . . . Let Congress heed their rising voices, for they will be heard."

Placed by a group calling itself the "Committee to Defend Martin Luther King and the Struggle for Freedom in the South," the fund-raising ad told the story of the heroic students at the forefront of the southern civil rights struggle.

Included among them were four hundred students in Orangeburg, South Carolina, "forcibly ejected, tear-gassed, soaked to the skin in freezing weather with fire hoses, arrested en masse and herded into an open barbed-wire stockade" for seeking, peacefully, to buy doughnuts and coffee. Featured also were students in Montgomery, Alabama, who, for the sin of protesting, were padlocked in a dining hall as authorities "attempted to starve them into submission." The ad slammed "Southern violators of the Constitution" for persecuting Dr. King. "They have bombed his home almost killing his wife and child. They have assaulted his person" and "arrested him seven times." The ad bore signatures of eighty-four supporters, including several prominent black ministers.

Although the ad mentioned no "Southern violators" by name, Alabama officials took offense. Several sued for libel, citing errors in the ad—including the facts (as summed up by *Newsweek* magazine) that "the dining hall was not padlocked, the police did not ring the campus, the students were expelled for another demonstration, and King had been arrested only four times."

The first case to be decided (in November 1960) was that of L.B. Sullivan, a Montgomery city commissioner who oversaw the police and fire departments. The Circuit Court awarded Sullivan $500,000 in damages (to be paid by four black ministers and the *New York Times*). Sullivan seized upon the verdict as proof the ad was a "pack of lies." Press reports called the $500,000 judgement the largest award ever granted by a jury in Alabama. In August 1962, the verdict and damage award were upheld by the Supreme Court of Alabama.

That September, Clarence B. Jones, an advisor and speech writer for Martin Luther King, wrote to the ACLU's Mel Wulf, reminding him: "About a year ago, Dr. Martin Luther King, Jr., Rev. Joseph Lowery and myself met with Mr. Patrick Malin and [ACLU Associate Director] Mr. Alan Reitman and discussed possible support and assistance the American Civil Liberties Union could render to the defendants. The position of the Union then was that while it recognized the basic constitutional issues involved, it was more appropriate when some or any one of the cases reached the United States Supreme Court."

The ACLU signed on for the appeal to the Supreme Court. In its amicus brief, the ACLU argued that the case was not merely about freedom
of expression. Sullivan's suit, charged the ACLU, was designed to "punish
the Negro clergymen" and the newspaper that printed their ad. The ACLU
also criticized the trial, "conducted in a segregated courtroom placing
Negroes in an inferior position."

Alabama had sued not only on Sullivan's behalf, but had brought "ten
suits by other public officials seeking damages aggregating $6,100,000,"
noted the ACLU. The state had also charged *New York Times* reporter Harrison Salisbury with forty-two counts of criminal libel. Salisbury's sin was
publishing a *Times* article ("Fear and Hatred Grip Birmingham") that portrayed Alabama as a bastion of racism, terror, and hate.

In his article, Salisbury reported, "In Birmingham neither blacks nor
whites talk freely. . . . Dynamite attempts have been made against the two
principal Jewish temples in the last eighteen months. In eleven years there
have been twenty-two reported bombings of Negro churches and homes."

Addressing the Supreme Court, Herbert Wechsler, lead lawyer for the
New York Times, argued that the Alabama libel law was unconstitutional
and "offensive on its face to the First Amendment." That law, he pointed,
out, allowed a public official to recover "punitive damages subject to no legal
limit . . . for the publication of a statement critical of his official action or
even of the official action of an agency under his general supervision."

The Constitution, he added, did not prefer "protection of official reputation" to the right to criticize official conduct. There was also "no evidence
of an injury to justify the magnitude of the award," which would be "a death
penalty for any newspaper if multiplied."

The unanimous decision delivered March 9, 1964, by Justice William J.
Brennan Jr. rejected the Alabama libel verdict. "A State cannot, under the
First and Fourteenth Amendments, award damages to a public official for
defamatory falsehood relating to his official conduct unless he proves 'actual
malice'—that the statement was made with knowledge of its falsity or with
reckless disregard of whether it was true or false," declared Brennan.

Even stronger than the Warren Court's commitment to a free press was its
passion for criminal justice, and the addition of Arthur Goldberg, after
Felix Frankfurter retired following his deliberating stroke in 1962, created

a solid 5–4 majority for radical reform. *Gideon v. Wainwright* was the first step in the Warren Court's overhaul of the American justice system. *Escobedo v. Illinois* (1964) was the second.

Although the ACLU had not played a major role in Earl Gideon's case, it was deeply involved in *Escobedo*.

Danny Escobedo was suspected of shooting and killing his brother-in-law. Police arrested and questioned him without informing him of his right to remain silent or allowing him access to a lawyer. Escobedo's self-incriminating statements led to his conviction for murder. Bernard Weisberg of the Illinois ACLU argued and won his case before the Supreme Court.

The 5 to 4 decision, authored by Arthur Goldberg, ruled that once accused of a crime—"when the process shifts from investigatory to accusatory"—a suspect must be allowed a lawyer.

Escobedo was the prelude to the much more famous *Miranda* case.

Ernesto Miranda was accused of robbery and of abducting, driving into the desert, and raping an eighteen-year-old woman. He was arrested and interrogated, and confessed, but at no point told that he had a right to remain silent. He was convicted of both crimes. The convictions were upheld on appeal. Robert Corcoran, an ACLU lawyer in Phoenix, took the case to the Supreme Court after recruiting a crack team of lawyers, including John Flynn, a professor at the University of Utah School of Law who authored the ACLU Supreme Court brief.

Flynn argued that Miranda's treatment violated his Fifth Amendment right against self-incrimination. A confession obtained under such conditions was inadmissible barring a showing "that adequate safeguards were present to protect the privilege," asserted Flynn.

Chief Justice Earl Warren agreed. The Fifth Amendment privilege "serves to protect persons in all settings in which their freedom of action is curtailed in any significant way from being compelled to incriminate themselves," wrote Warren for the 5 to 4 majority. Consequently, a suspect "must be warned prior to any questioning that he has the right to remain silent, that anything he says can be used against him in a court of law, that he has the right to the presence of an attorney, and that, if he cannot afford an attorney one will be appointed for him prior to any questioning if he so desires."

In the decades since *Miranda v. Arizona* (1966) was decided, legal experts have continued to debate its impact.

In marking the decision's fiftieth anniversary, Pennsylvania Supreme Court Justice David Wecht argued that *Miranda* "did not create new rights" but it "imposed on law enforcement a uniform, blanket rule that would put steel in these rights and create a consequence of suppression in the event the rights were violated."[2]

In 1967, the Supreme Court handed down another landmark decision (*In re Gault*). Gerald Gault, of Globe, Arizona, had been arrested at the age of fifteen for allegedly making an obscene phone call to a neighbor. At the time, judicial proceedings for juveniles were governed by the doctrine of *parens patriae*, a concept rooted in English chancery law that put the state in charge of children when parental rule was deemed inadequate. As a result, Gault ended up in court with no attorney and no opportunity to question his supposed accuser, his fate entirely up to the whims of a judge. Gault was sentenced to up to six years (until he became an adult) in a juvenile facility. An adult convicted of the same offense would have served a maximum of two months. The ACLU took Gault's case to the Supreme Court.

Justice Abe Fortas, who wrote the 8 to 1 majority decision, thought it absurd that policies supposedly designed to protect children stripped them of important rights. *Parens patriae*, he declared, was "a great help to those who sought to rationalize the exclusion of juveniles from the constitutional scheme; but its meaning is murky, and its historic credentials are of dubious relevance."

The decision marked a revolutionary turn in the evolution of juvenile justice and in the rise of the movement to guarantee even the most vulnerable children a shot at a decent life. It also, in some sense, completed a circle, as Roger Baldwin had started his professional life as a social worker and co-authored a book on juvenile courts and probation.

Change was not just being demanded of the judicial system, but of society through and through. But the revolutionary change that had seemed inevitable in the aftermath of Kennedy's election was giving way to apprehension. Frustration was taking hold as the nation floundered in an apparently impossible-to-win war. Johnson, the torchbearer of Kennedy's optimism, became the focus of disenchantment.

In a speech broadcast on the evening of March 31, 1968, President Johnson announced he would not run for re-election. He would not permit the presidency, he said, "to become involved in partisan divisions."

The speech dominated front pages on April Fool's Day, but it was no one's idea of a joke. It threw the presidential race into chaos. The two most prominent Democratic candidates welcomed the news. Senator Robert Kennedy of New York called the decision "magnanimous." Senator Eugene McCarthy of Minnesota declared, "with this generous judgment, President Johnson has cleared the way for the reconciliation of our people . . . and for a redefinition of the purpose of the American nation."

Four days after Johnson's announcement, James Earl Ray murdered Martin Luther King Jr. Riots broke out across America—and "reconciliation of our people" seemed a distant dream. Two months later, Robert Kennedy was murdered.

In the wake of Robert Kennedy's death, many Americans called for gun legislation. The *Christian Science Monitor* reported, "[Some] congressmen are daily getting up to 1,000 letters, cards and telegrams on the subject—all but a few support stricter laws." National Rifle Association president Harold Glassen bemoaned the "hysteria" Kennedy's death had engendered and warned, "the right of sportsmen in the United States to obtain, own and use firearms for proper lawful purposes is in the greatest jeopardy in the history of our country."

With Kennedy dead, Democrats turned to Vice President Hubert Humphrey, who accepted the nomination that August in Chicago. He lamented the rioting that accompanied the convention: "Surely we have learned the lesson that violence breeds more violence and that it cannot be condoned—whatever the source. . . . And may we, for just one moment, in sober reflection, in serious purpose, may we just quietly and silently—each in our own way—pray for our country."

Where Hubert Humphrey saw reason for sadness and prayer, Richard Nixon saw opportunity. With race riots riveting America's attention and George Wallace openly appealing to racists, Nixon saw victory in racially charged oratory. So a Republican Party that had seen value in wooing black voters as recently as the Eisenhower administration placed a bet on bigotry.

"Among Atlanta Negro voters Dwight Eisenhower was the choice over Adlai Stevenson in 1952 and 1955, and Richard Nixon split their votes about evenly with John F. Kennedy in 1960," but more than 90 percent of the black vote went Democratic in 1964, reported the *Atlanta Constitution*. At a time when black outrage roiled America, winning black votes back might mean alienating whites. Nixon doubled down on white anxiety, and polls suggested he might hold a winning hand: "Among that part of the electorate which views Negroes in traditional stereotyped terms, Richard Nixon holds a lopsided 43-26 per cent lead," reported pollster Louis Harris.

Harris also noted that over the past five years, "the softening in white attitudes toward blacks has been minimal at best. In fact, the number who feel that Negroes 'want to live off handouts' 'have less native intelligence than whites' and 'care less for their families than white' has actually increased."

Nixon won the election, splitting the South with Wallace (who won five states). Humphrey held the New Deal coalition together—but that was not enough. "Nixon won with almost no votes from Negroes and low totals in the big industrial cities of the North," reported the *Philadelphia Inquirer.*

In 2016, *Harper's* magazine made news with an interview that confirmed what had long been clear. "The Nixon campaign in 1968, and the Nixon White House after that, had two enemies: the antiwar left and black people. . . . [By] getting the public to associate the hippies with marijuana and blacks with heroin . . . [we] could arrest their leaders, raid their homes, break up their meetings, and vilify them night after night on the evening news," John Ehrlichman, Nixon's former domestic policy adviser, told *Harper's.*

The war on blacks and progressives that Ehrlichman acknowledged nearly fifty years after the fact was widely assumed in liberal circles all along. Whereas the ACLU had been willing to grant some presidents the benefit of the doubt, it viewed Nixon with suspicion from the beginning. In summer 1968, the New Jersey affiliate of the ACLU slammed him for "participating actively in discrimination against Negroes and Jews" by belonging to Baltusrol Golf Course and Club in Springfield, New Jersey.

Nixon responded, "I believe in working for change from the inside." The ACLU dismissed Nixon's statement as a "mockery of the fight against discrimination in public facilities." A Baltusrol spokesman denied that his club discriminated against anyone—although he admitted it had no black or Jewish members "to my knowledge."

The month after Nixon's inauguration, the ACLU of Pennsylvania attacked Attorney General John Mitchell's wiretapping and electronic surveillance plan. The "wiretap provisions of the 1968 Act and Mr. Mitchell's stated intention to broaden use of them are dangerous, heavy-handed intrusions by government into the private lives of individuals," charged Pennsylvania affiliate president Thomas M. Kerr.

The ACLU and its affiliates aggressively criticized various other aspects of the Nixon administration, from its welfare proposals (deemed hostile to the privacy rights of welfare recipients), to its "provocative and even punitive" harassment of the Black Panther Party, to its claims of "unrestricted authority to snoop on dissident individuals and organizations in the interest of national security."

The ACLU notably did not oppose Nixon's first two Supreme Court nominations. On May 23, 1969, Nixon nominated Warren Burger, then on the U.S. Court of Appeals for the District of Columbia, to replace retiring Chief Justice Earl Warren. There was grumbling about the more conservative direction in which Burger presumably would take the court, but the appointment generally drew praise. He was confirmed on June 9, by a vote of 74 to 3, over the objections of some liberal critics.

People were not as accepting of Nixon's next Supreme Court nominee: Clement Furman Haynsworth, a U.S. Court of Appeals judge originally from Greenville, South Carolina. Haynsworth was proposed in August 1969 to succeed Abe Fortas, who resigned over ethical questions involving payments received for speaking engagements. Many considered Haynsworth an unlettered segregationist who would be out of his depth on the high court—an "obscure judge with little reputation for . . . depth, social sensitivity and philosophic insight," as the *Atlanta Constitution* put it.

George Meany, president of the AFL-CIO, said Haynsworth's nomination was "clearly part of a pattern of placating Southern segregationists and other conservatives." The AFL-CIO, he announced, would oppose the nominee who lacked an "understanding of the aspirations of workers and minorities." Haynsworth also turned out to own stock in a vending company that he had supported in a labor decision.

On November 21, Haynsworth was rejected 55 to 45. The *Chicago Sun-Times* advised Nixon to avoid "using the court's vacancy to build his political support in the South."

Nonetheless, in January 1970, Nixon nominated another Southerner. George Harrold Carswell, originally from Irwinton, Georgia, served as a

U.S. District Judge in Florida. His appointment was "expected to breeze through the Senate," reported the *Atlanta Constitution*. Almost immediately, however, reports surfaced of a speech Carswell had made before the American Legion in 1948 swearing allegiance to the "principles of white supremacy." Carswell responded by saying he no longer believed in white supremacy.

The Reverend Ralph David Abernathy, Martin Luther King Jr.'s successor as head of the Southern Christian Leadership Conference, sent an indignant telegram to the Senate leadership saying Carswell's "presence on the court would be against the blacks and other poor people and ultimately true justice to all Americans." Coretta Scott King called the nomination an affront "to black people, to the Supreme Court, and to the vast majority of American citizens—white and black."

The Senate rejected Carswell 51 to 45 on April 8, with thirteen Republicans joining the opposition. Such a thing had not happened since 1894, "when Grover Cleveland, stouter than ever, saw his two candidates turned down," reported the *Christian Science Monitor*.

A week after Carswell's defeat, Nixon nominated U.S. Court of Appeals Judge Harry Blackmun, who was confirmed without incident by a unanimous 94 to 0 vote.

Through the debate over the two controversial jurists, the ACLU had remained largely silent. The ACLU would soon reconsider that policy; but first, it was faced with choosing a new leader.

On January 21, 1970, the ACLU celebrated its fiftieth anniversary. It was also Roger Baldwin's eighty-sixth birthday.

The celebrations began with a grand party at New York's Americana Hotel, presided over by former Supreme Court Justice Arthur Goldberg, who praised Baldwin and the ACLU for their dedication to keeping America "free and equal."

The *New York Times* noted that in "recent years the ACLU and its city branches have been busier than ever because of Vietnam war dissent, confrontations in the ghettos and unrest on campuses. In protecting minority or unorthodox viewpoints, its attorneys in the last six years have won 40 of 46 cases carried to the United States Supreme Court—which speaks well for the Supreme Court as well as the ACLU."

An ACLU press release touted 1970 as an occasion for a year-long cele-bration focusing on "special litigation in pressure points on civil liberties" and "an expanded program of public information and education." The ef-fort, as envisioned by Pemberton, would amount to a relaunch of the ACLU. Through books, a TV documentary, investigative reports on civil liberties, and various other activities, Pemberton anticipated the emergence of a stronger and more visible ACLU poised to "move America, even amidst today's divisive, anti-libertarian forces, toward a new degree of security in her democratic institutions."

In his biennial report, issued early in 1970, Pemberton struck a hopeful yet wary tone. He acknowledged that Attorney General John Mitchell's tenure evoked similar anxieties to that of A. Mitchell Palmer but concluded "the indifference of great numbers within the electorate" was the bigger problem. "The challenge of the Union," he concluded, was to "direct the attention of the nation" to democracy. Pemberton was not a graceful or lu-cid writer, so it's impossible to know precisely what he meant. But he clearly was urging the ACLU to take on a larger public role.

Whatever his vision might have been, unbeknownst to Pemberton, his days with the ACLU were ending. Although he had planned to stay for another two years, in April 1970 he was forced out.

In taking over an organization overshadowed by its founder—who con-tinued to sit on its National Advisory Council—Pemberton had never had an easy job. Nor did his personality seem particularly suited to maneuver-ing within the ACLU's congenitally contentious culture.

"Pemberton was not a gladiator. . . . He was a quiet, soft-spoken guy from the middle of the country and his bias was toward thought rather than con-fronting people. He tried to avoid the bruising fights within the ACLU as much as he could," recalled Martin Garbus, who served as director-counsel of the Roger Baldwin Foundation during part of Pemberton's tenure.

"He was not a manipulator of people, which I think was then [an] es-sential quality to keep the Board moving," added Garbus. "He really wanted to practice law."

He loved practicing law so much, observed author Samuel Walker, that in the late 1960s Pemberton temporarily abandoned his administrative du-ties to go to Clovis, New Mexico, to join the ACLU legal team defending Air Force Captain Dale Noyd. A decorated officer who deemed the war in

Vietnam immoral, Noyd was court-martialed for refusing to fly a training mission. Despite the ACLU's vigorous efforts, Noyd was convicted and forced to serve a one-year sentence before being dishonorably discharged.

"I thought it was a mistake for Jack to go [to New Mexico] for weeks at a time . . . rather than attending to the day-to-day business of directing the ACLU," observed Aryeh Neier, then head of the New York Civil Liberties Union.

Pemberton's personal life was also a mess. His marriage was collapsing, and he had embarked on an indiscreet affair with a secretary on the ACLU staff.

Garbus rejects the notion that his personal life did Pemberton in: "He was ineffectual because [managing people] is not what he should have been doing."

It was also an extremely frenzied time. Operation Southern Justice was going gangbusters, the Lawyers Constitutional Defense Committee (which had worked closely with 1964's Freedom Summer protestors) was being absorbed into the Roger Baldwin Foundation, the Howard Levy case was working its way through the courts, and the ACLU was essentially declaring war on the Nixon administration. It was no time for a distracted executive to be heading the ACLU.

Aryeh Neier was among those pushing to get Pemberton out. "The national office was functioning very poorly," he said during an interview. "All the significant work in that period . . . was being done by the affiliate." Valuable staffers were leaving, and the people Pemberton appointed were "third rate," said Neier.

Disenchantment ran so deep that a group of affiliate directors met with Board Chair Edward Ennis to discuss their problems with Pemberton. "He said he would act on it, and he did," said Neier. Pemberton resigned, with no successor in sight.

Neier, who turned thirty-three in April of 1970, was a refugee. His parents, Jews born in Poland, had fled Nazi Germany in August 1939 and ended up in England. For nearly a year he had lived in a hostel, separated from his parents, which he dimly recalls as an awful time.

The family eventually reunited in London, and Neier spent much of his childhood in Northampton, where his father (a linguist) and sister taught in a group home for Jewish boys who had survived Nazi death camps. In

1947, the family made its way to New York City. Neier attended Stuyvesant, a very competitive public high school then on East Fifteenth Street, "precisely in the four-year period in which Senator Joseph McCarthy was at his height." Neier became "committed to civil liberties," in part because some of his teachers were investigation targets.

At Stuyvesant, Neier became an activist—at one point inviting Raphael Lemkin, architect of the United Nations' anti-genocide convention, to the school. His activism continued at Cornell University, which he attended on a state scholarship.

He wrote for the *Cornell Daily Sun*, where he chronicled the Montgomery Bus Boycott ("To me it was a revolutionary moment") and eventually became president of the Student League for Industrial Democracy, which spawned Students for a Democratic Society. After a post-college stint at the League for Industrial Democracy, Neier became an editor at *Current* magazine. In 1963, he became the ACLU's director of field operations, charged with strengthening and organizing affiliates. He became head of its New York affiliate in 1965.

He was an obvious contender for Pemberton's job. But the timing was less than ideal. The NYCLU was just emerging from the carnage of the community school battles in New York, where it had maneuvered through a series of strikes and racially charged controversies—starting with the removal of nineteen white teachers and supervisors deemed "out of tune with the political atmosphere" in Brooklyn's Ocean Hill–Brownsville area.

As Neier put it, "I had become very controversial in New York during the Ocean Hill-Brownsville dispute." Also, since he had actively tried to push Pemberton out, he felt it awkward to consider Pemberton's job. Ennis reassured Neier, "You're young. Your turn will come."

But as the search process proceeded, Neier became alarmed when an activist lawyer for whom he had little respect told Neier that he was interviewing for the job. After confirming the news with ACLU general council Marvin Karpatkin, Neier called Ennis and said, "Ed, you and I had agreed that I wouldn't be a candidate for the post, but in light of the selection of this guy . . . I'm going to put my name forward so as to try to obstruct his selection."

The five-person nominating committee reconvened. They dropped the lawyer from consideration and narrowed candidates down to Neier and Lawrence Speiser, who had been director of the Washington office since 1959.

A former Northern Californian ACLU legal director and World War II veteran born in Toronto, Speiser was a strong critic of government surveillance and an outspoken advocate of civil rights. While in California, he had successfully challenged (on his own behalf, all the way to the U.S. Supreme Court) a requirement that veterans applying for a state property-tax exemption sign a loyalty oath. During the Selma protests in 1965, Speiser had lambasted the federal government for not protecting demonstrators and had consistently accused the Justice Department's civil rights division of shirking its duty.

The five-person nominating committee split two to two on the candidates. Harriet Pilpel, general counsel of Planned Parenthood and the fifth member of the committee, was unreachable in Europe; so the committee presented both candidates to the board.

The board voted 35 to 31 for Neier. The appointment was announced in the *New York Times* on September 28, 1970.

The transition process rankled Roger Baldwin, who wrote chairman Edward Ennis the day the *Times* article appeared. "I tell you directly that I think the procedure was bungled both by the Nominating Committee and the Board in accepting, instead of a report, the views of four of its members equally divided," wrote Baldwin.

"We owed it to ourselves to get the best qualified man available," added Baldwin, who observed that no search was needed to find candidates already employed by the ACLU. "I hope you share in the uneasiness which recent events have created," he concluded.

In a three-page response, Ennis empathized with Baldwin's frustration. He also noted the board was under tremendous pressure because it had no desire "to continue at least for another two months the administrative drift which led us to decide not to continue with Jack [Pemberton] in the hope that some superior candidate outside the Union might appear."

Over the last twenty years, Ennis pointed out, the ACLU had expanded to forty-eight affiliates in forty-five states and the District of Columbia. The growth of those increasingly independent affiliates, he suggested, had contributed to the chaos.

Given the organizational turmoil, and Neier's distress at the nominating committee coming up with a candidate whom Neier considered incompetent, "It's entirely understandable that . . . [the] Executive Director of the largest affiliate should reconsider and decide to become a candidate."

"I think we made the right choice," concluded Ennis.

Although Baldwin begrudgingly accepted Neier's selection, he had reservations about his suitability. In Baldwin's view—which he outlined in a confidential memo—Neier was a lone ranger and a martinet: "His temperament . . . does not encourage group consultation because of his shyness. . . . His decisions are reached by himself, with great self-confidence and a toughness in defending them without argument. . . . His letters are curt, often brusque. . . . His speech tends also to abruptness." Nonetheless, he thought "Aryeh will make . . . an excellent executive manager, mainly behind the public scene."

When I asked about Baldwin's assessment, Neier told a story about meeting Baldwin at the age of twenty-three in Venezuela. During the democracy conference both were attending, Neier found himself physically protecting a Venezuelan delegate whose comments had so angered other attendees that one punched him in the face. Neier sprang to the man's defense even though—because the argument was in Spanish—he had no idea what was going on. Baldwin observed it all: "So I thought he would've thought I was hotheaded for jumping up and putting my arms around the Venezuelan."

"It was true," Neier added, "that in that period, I didn't like staff meetings. Pemberton held weekly staff meetings that lasted for hours. That seemed to me a complete waste of time. So that sort of turned me off on staff meetings. I was in certain respects, quite shy, so Roger wasn't wrong in his description of me."

Whatever his faults as a leader, Pemberton had presided over a period of spectacular growth. When he had come on board in 1962, the ACLU counted twenty-eight affiliates and some 61,000 members. When he left, membership had more than doubled—to 144,000—and the number of affiliates had grown to forty-eight. There were some 325 local chapters. At the same time, income had nearly quadrupled, from $535,000 annually to roughly $2 million.

The 1970 annual report noted, "more than 5,000 attorneys and about another 1,500 persons are more or less regularly engaged in ACLU volunteer work. At present about 2,200 ACLU cases are in litigation. . . . [During] the year, the ACLU litigated about 4,000 cases. About one per cent of all ACLU court cases were in the U.S. Supreme Court during 1970–71. However, cases in which the ACLU participated accounted for about 20 per cent of the Supreme Court's docket."

The ACLU had waged one historic court battle after another—expanding the rights of criminal suspects in *Gideon v. Wainwright* and *Miranda v. Arizona*, opening access to birth control in *Griswold v. Connecticut*, striking down miscegenation statutes in *Loving v. Virginia*, even as the ACLU became a leader in America's battle for racial justice and evolved from an organization largely weighing in with amicus briefs to one that actually tried cases.

Neier was not content to coast on the strength of the ACLU's past successes. Despite the messiness of the transition, he immediately took on the mission of taking the ACLU to new heights. "There had been an explosion in thinking about rights. . . . We had gotten involved in women's rights, in prisoner's rights, in mental patient's rights, in juvenile rights—a whole series of things. So, I drew up, in effect, a wish list of the things I wanted to create."

In all, he proposed eleven different projects, budgeted at nearly $2.5 million. He approached foundations he had cultivated and presented his wish list: "Over a period of time, I essentially got those things funded and launched the various projects that I had intended to create."

For help with the Women's Rights Project, Neier recruited Ruth Bader Ginsburg, a young law professor who had been on the fringes of the ACLU for some time. Neier invited her to lunch early in his tenure. But her real link to the ACLU was Melvin Wulf, whom she had originally met as a pre-teen at Che-Na-Wah summer camp. "He was a waiter and all of the girls were in love with him," recalled Bader Ginsburg during an interview.

In the years since that encounter at camp, Wulf had become legal director of the ACLU and Bader Ginsburg had studied at Harvard Law School, transferring after two years to Columbia Law School because of her husband's job in New York. Bader Ginsburg had shared the number one spot at the top of her May 1959 law school graduating class but no law firm was interested in her: "Only two asked me to come to an interview. And neither of those offered me a job."

With the road to a major law firm blocked, Bader Ginsburg clerked in a U.S. District Court in New York and then worked as a research associate with Columbia Law School's Project on International Procedures. She was researching the judicial system in Sweden when an article in a Stockholm newspaper caught her eye. "Why should the woman have two jobs and the man only one?" was her recollection of the question raised by the author. "In the sixties in Sweden, it was not at all unusual to have a two-worker family," she explained, but the wife was also expected "to have dinner on the table at 7."

At the time, America had very few female judges, but Sweden had many. The more Bader Ginsburg learned about women's roles in Sweden, the more she questioned their status in the United States.

In 1963, she became Rutgers University's second full-time female law professor. Betty Friedan's *The Feminine Mystique*, published that year, "didn't have any impact on me," Bader Ginsburg recalled. "She was talking about the discontent of suburban housewives. . . . The book that turned me on was . . . Simone de Beauvoir's *The Second Sex*," a dive into psychology, biology, literature, philosophy, and history in consideration of women's place in the world. "That was an eye-opener," she said.

Bader Ginsburg renewed her friendship with Wulf when he visited Rutgers to see constitutional law professor Frank Askin. He stopped by her office and they discussed the possibility of her working on some cases for the New Jersey affiliate. She was particularly intrigued by those involving gender discrimination: female teachers who could not get insurance coverage for family members although male teachers could; female middle-schoolers barred from a prestigious Princeton summer engineering program that only accepted boys.

Such cases fueled the passion for public service she had discovered as an undergraduate at Cornell, where she had worked as a researcher for constitutional law professor Robert Cushman. Cushman "wanted me to be aware . . . of what [Joseph] McCarthy was doing," recalled Bader Ginsburg.

The McCarthy hearings reminded her of the central role lawyers played in determining people's rights. It was they "who reminded Congress that we have a First Amendment and a Fifth Amendment." The ACLU offered her a chance to put her idealism to work.

One memorable case revolved around Charles Moritz, a never-married Denver resident who cared for his eighty-nine-year-old mother. Bader Ginsberg's involvement in his case began with her husband, Martin, whose legal specialty was taxation.

One evening Martin asked her to read some documents on a case.

"I said, Marty, you know I don't read tax cases," Bader Ginsburg recalled.

"Read this one," he said.

She found Moritz's story irresistible.

Moritz was a publishing firm employee who worked at home but was often called upon to travel. During such times, he hired a caretaker for his elderly mother, and he had deducted those expenses on his 1968 taxes. The IRS disallowed the deduction. The tax court concurred, ruling that a single man (unlike a woman, widower, or divorcee) was not entitled to the "dependent care" deduction.

Bader Ginsburg suggested to her husband that they "brief it," but—to emphasize the case's seriousness to the court—she wanted the ACLU involved. She wrote Wulf suggesting the ACLU take it on, arguing, "if the Tax Court ruled correctly, the equal rights amendment is surely needed." But if they could prove the tax court wrong, an "important foothold will be secured for women's rights cases."

Bader Ginsburg's co-counsels included her husband and Wulf. Her brief argued that it was "arbitrary and unequal treatment" to deny Moritz the benefit "solely because of his status as a never married man." Both federal and states courts, she observed, had looked with increasing skepticism on "lines drawn or sanctioned by governmental authority on the basis of sex" in the absence of "strong affirmative justification."

She sent the brief to Norman Dorsen—a New York University law professor and future president of the ACLU. "I have no comment on your brief in the Moritz case except to say it is one of the very best presentations I have seen in a long time," he replied.

As Moritz's case awaited a decision from the Tenth Circuit Court of Appeals in Denver, Bader Ginsburg took on another ACLU sex discrimination case.

Sally Reed's sixteen-year-old son, Skip, had been found dead in 1967 after apparently shooting himself with a rifle. Reed was divorced from Skip's father, and she suspected the father, Cecil, of having caused his death. Skip possessed virtually nothing of value, but his mother wanted to administer his estate.

Idaho did not permit it. Probate court, by law, "preferred" the male. After Sally Reed sued, the district court reversed the probate court, but was itself reversed by the Idaho's Supreme Court.

Allen Derr, a Boise, Idaho, attorney, had argued Sally Reed's case in those early battles. But he welcomed the ACLU's assistance as the case headed to the U.S. Supreme Court. Ginsburg happily took on the case, which she saw as intimately connected to Moritz. Indeed, she called the brief she had drafted for Moritz the "grandparent" brief. The brief for Reed leaned heavily on the analysis she had done for Mortitz. She hoped the cases would arrive before the Supreme Court simultaneously—and the justices would make the obvious connection: "My dream was that . . . the [Supreme Court] could see Moritz, discrimination against a man, and Reed, against a woman—both irrational." But the Tenth Circuit moved too slowly for that.

Meanwhile, a battle broke out between Derr, the Idaho attorney, and Wulf at the ACLU over who would make the oral arguments for *Reed* before the Supreme Court.

Having taken the case when no other Idaho attorney would have it and having done all the preliminary work, Derr thought that he was entitled to appear before the court. But Wulf judged him monumentally unfit for the task. He also thought a woman should be presenting the case.

In a letter to Derr that September, Wulf floated the name of Eleanor Holmes Norton, who was then head of the New York City Commission on Human Rights. "She is a national figure," argued Wulf, "and is one of the most persuasive lawyers I know."

Derr was not having it. Reed was his client, and he should argue her case. A week and a half before oral arguments, Wulf wrote Derr a letter, bluntly telling him he was "not competent to do the job."

Wulf explained his "fears were based on the brief" filed for Reed in the Idaho Supreme Court, which he called "an awful piece of work which demonstrates total ignorance of the equal protection clause and of the cases involving sexual discrimination."

He reminded Derr that the Supreme Court was the big leagues, "and I have no reason to believe that you are any more prepared to handle the case competently now than in . . . Idaho, and Wulf was "not looking forward to the case being incompetently argued before the Supreme Court."

In his appearance before the court, Derr was visibly nervous, struggling to answer certain questions, but he strongly made the point that *Reed v. Reed* was "at least [as] significant for women" as *Brown v. Board of Education* had been for racial minorities.

Two days after that appearance, Wulf offered Derr a harsh review: "The argument may have been one of the worst in the history of the Supreme Court. . . . I sorely resent the fact that your vanity prevented your recognizing your own limitations."

On November 22, 1971, the Supreme Court unanimously decided in favor of Sally Reed. "Arbitrary" discrimination against women was unconstitutional, declared Chief Justice Warren Burger. "To give a mandatory preference to members of either sex over members of the other, merely to accomplish the elimination of hearings on the merits, is to make the very kind of arbitrary legislative choice forbidden by the Equal Protection Clause of the Fourteenth Amendment."

The victory, through sweet, was not total. As the *Baltimore Sun* pointed out, the ACLU "had urged the court to go further and declare sex a 'suspect classification' [which] would have made sexual discrimination almost automatically unconstitutional." Nonetheless, Sally Reed, reached by the AP, pronounced herself "very happy for all women and myself." That same day, coincidentally, the U.S. Senate subcommittee rejected consideration of a constitutional amendment barring sexual discrimination.

The Tenth Circuit finally decided the Moritz case on November 22, 1972. As Bader Ginsburg put it, "they waited for Reed." Citing the new Supreme Court precedent, the Tenth Circuit concluded that Moritz was entitled to his deduction. A "special discrimination premised on sex alone . . . cannot stand," declared the court.

In a letter to Sally Reed that December, Derr thanked his client. "I am proud to have in some small way justified your faith in staying with me in spite of the efforts of Mr. Wulf," he wrote. He acknowledged their debt to the ACLU: "They paid your $100 U.S. Supreme Court filing fee. They actually wrote the jurisdictional statement and the briefs and paid for the printing of the briefs."

Wulf continued to steam. He wrote Allen Derr another letter, taking issue with Derr's comment to Reed that he could "only guess" what had set Wulf off. His only motive, said Wulf, was "to assure that the case was argued . . . in a competent and persuasive manner. . . . In my opinion, the bland and very narrow opinion of the Supreme Court reflects the quality of the argument made on behalf of Mrs. Reed."

The day after Christmas, 1971, Derr responded via telegram expressing regret for allowing Wulf to "help in the case. . . . Your correspondence is about to be released to the national press. We will duel by pen."

Bader Ginsburg took the success as a sign that the court finally "was ready to move." She contrasted that flexibility with a decade earlier, when the court had considered *Hoyt v. Florida*.

Gwendolyn Hoyt, an abused woman from Hillsborough County, Florida, was sentenced by an all-male jury to thirty years for killing her husband. In her appeal, Hoyt argued that female jurors would been more understanding of her situation as an abused woman. The Supreme Court unanimously dismissed her argument against excusing women from the jury pool.

Justice John Harlan's opinion rejected the notion that she was owed female jurors. "Despite the enlightened emancipation of women from the restrictions and protections of bygone years . . . woman is still regarded as the center of home and family life," he wrote. It was therefore fine for states to exempt women from jury duty unless they themselves decided jury duty was consistent with their "own special responsibilities."

In 1972, shortly before the *Moritz* decision was announced, Bader Ginsburg moved from Rutgers to Columbia Law School, becoming its first female tenured professor. Her agreement with Columbia allowed her to spend half of her time as a volunteer general counsel for the ACLU, where she would head the Women's Rights Project.

The *New York Times* announced her appointment on January 26. "In a new accelerating competition among the nation's law schools," the paper wrote, "Columbia University has just scored a major coup: its law school, to its undisguised glee, has just bid for and won a woman for the job of full professor—the first in its 114-year history."

In an interview with the *Times*, Ginsburg said she didn't expect to have "any problems" at Columbia: "People will be pleasant on the outside. Some of them may have reservations about what I'm doing, but I don't think they'll be expressed."

Bader Ginsburg found some resistance to her work at the ACLU, but Neier was supportive, and any misgivings soon faded away. At the time, the ACLU had two women-focused projects: the Reproductive Freedom Project and the Women's Rights Project. "The Ford Foundation was ready to support the Women's Rights Project but wanted nothing to do with abortion. But the Rockefeller Foundation was very much interested in reproductive rights, mainly because they were [interested in] population control," recalled Bader Ginsburg. So the ACLU kept the projects separate.

Among Bader Ginsburg's supporters were *Playboy* publisher Hugh Hefner and his Playboy Foundation: "They offered to send out all our mailings. They arrived at people's homes with a big bunny stamp."

As the Women's Rights Project picked up steam, so did Neier's initiatives on numerous other fronts, including within what he called "closed institutions": prisons, mental hospitals, juvenile institutions, and schools.

The ACLU also continued to focus on voting rights, litigating *Dunn v. Blumstein*, which challenged a Tennessee law requiring a year-long residency in the state in order to vote.

The case was initiated by James F. Blumstein, an assistant professor of law at Vanderbilt University who had moved to Tennessee in summer of 1970 and was rejected when he attempted to register. He litigated the case himself but took on the ACLU's Charles Morgan and Norman Siegel as "of council." The men argued that the state requirements violated the Fourteenth Amendment. The Supreme Court agreed, handing down a 6 to 1 decision in March 1972, authored by Justice Thurgood Marshall, that invalidated the waiting period.

Some twenty-four states had one-year qualifying laws, and twenty-three had six-month requirements. All would have to change their policies. The *Christian Science Monitor* estimated the ruling would add somewhere between three and five million voters.

The ACLU continued to expand its efforts in the area of "homosexual rights," taking on some thirty such cases between mid-1971 and mid-1972—dealing, among other things, with local sodomy statutes, denial of government security clearances, and job discrimination. The ACLU was also rethinking its approach to Supreme Court nominees.

Justice Hugo Black, who was eighty-five and ailing, retired from the bench on September 17, 1971. The Alabama native and former member of the Ku Klux Klan had evolved into one of the court's more liberal members. Six days later, conservative Justice John Marshall Harlan, seventy-two, suffering from "a cancerous process in one of the bones of the lower spine," announced he was also retiring.

"If just-retired Associate Justice Hugo L Black was the evangelist of the Constitution and its Bill of Rights, then retiring Associate Justice John M. Harlan was the Supreme Court's apostle of consistency," editorialized the *Christian Science Monitor.*

Black died September 25, and Harlan died on December 29.

In a meeting in Chicago in late September, a group of civil rights leaders demanded that at least one of the seats be filled by an African American. But most bets were on a white Southerner, and the name of Richard H. Poff, a conservative Virginia congressman and signatory to the segregationist "Southern Manifesto," quickly floated to the top. President Richard Nixon fueled the speculation by commenting that he might appoint "a legislator with experience in the Judiciary Committee of the House or Senate."

Leon Shull of Americans for Democratic Action said that, if confirmed, Poff would be "the first justice in more than twenty years to have declared that segregation is constitutional." Senate Democratic whip Robert Byrd warned Poff's nomination might evoke a filibuster.

The floating of Poff's name set off panic within the ACLU board, which was meeting the weekend of October 2. Vice Chairman George Slaff suggested revising current policy, which prohibited the ACLU from endorsing or opposing "candidates for elective or appointive office." Slaff proposed striking "appointive." His proposal was referred to the executive committee. Meanwhile, the board empowered the executive committee to stake out a public position "regarding particular vacancies," while the review of the 1936 policy took place.

That weekend, Poff suddenly withdrew from consideration. He said he wished to spare his family the "agonies" of a likely "protracted and controversial" confirmation process.

Upon hearing of Slaff's proposal, Roger Baldwin was furious. Though not a member of the board, Baldwin (who remained on the National Advisory Committee) took personal offense at not being consulted before the board acted on Slaff's suggestion.

He sent a letter to the board pointing out that going down the endorsement road "would inject the Union into politics" and force the ACLU to make judgments about individual men as opposed to policy. Such judgments, he noted, were "far more subjective and divisive" than policy judgements. Working with public officials would also become agonizingly difficult if those officials were divided "into friends we supported and opponents we had tried to defeat." Moreover, "[any] Supreme Court nominee we would oppose on civil liberties grounds would surely be opposed by so many others that our choice would add little."

He closed with a hope "that the board will in future avoid considering a proposal not on the agenda."

Slaff responded by pointing out that his proposal had been offered in a moment of extreme anxiety. When he arrived in New York that Thursday night, Poff's nomination seemed imminent. He therefore felt it imperative that "the foremost and purest" civil liberties organization express its "horrified concern."

During a nationally television address that October 21, Nixon revealed two nominees: Lewis F. Powell, sixty-four, a World War II veteran and former president of the American Bar Association from Virginia, and William Rehnquist, forty-seven, an assistant attorney general who had never served as a judge.

With two new names in play, and the press reporting that both nominees supported wiretapping without warrants, Slaff again pressed the board for a policy change. In a letter to Neier, he asked that the ACLU "send an appropriate representative to the Senate Judiciary Committee" to ask that the Senate reject both Powell and Rehnquist because nothing in their records demonstrated a "strong understanding and commitment to the Bill Of Rights."

Several board members shared Slaff's discomfort. James Heller, chair of the Washington, DC, affiliate, was disturbed by Rehnquist's behavior during an anti–Vietnam War protest in Washington in May 1971. Tens of thousands had gathered to disrupt the government, more than eleven thousand of whom were arrested. Rehnquist argued that "qualified martial law" allowed for the suspension of normal police procedures and for arrests even in the absence of specific charges of wrongdoing. As a result, said Heller, thousands were arrested "solely on the basis of personal appearance."

"Rehnquist's casuistic attempt to justify all this is a very serious matter because it betrays a lack of any sense of proportion, a willingness to distort known facts, and a dishonest intellectual excursion—all in the service of justifying large-scale violations of personal liberty," wrote Heller to board chair Ennis.

Robert L. Carter, former general counsel of the NAACP (and a future federal judge), also argued for a policy change. Although he frowned on the ACLU endorsing specific candidates, he was all for opposing objectionable nominees. "I believe the Union has the duty and responsibility to oppose the appointment to high public office of persons whose past utterances and activities indicate a definite anti-civil libertarian bias," argued Carter. The ACLU could no longer "afford the luxury of indifference," he wrote, to nominees "who would suppress dissent or . . . undermine those civil liberties safeguards which the Union seeks to conserve, strengthen and expand."

Ralph Brown, a professor at Yale Law School, opposed Slaff's initiative. "Our duty is to advance the cause of civil liberties in the ways we think best. The Senate cannot require an expression from us, nor even expect one. If it ever harbored any expectations, they must have withered during a half-century of silence on our part," he argued in a letter to the ACLU's executive committee.

Initially, the ACLU attempted to steer a middle course. It neither stayed silent nor actively opposed Nixon's nominees. Instead, it had Neier send all senators a letter, dated November 9, quoting a newly adopted resolution by the ACLU's executive committee. The resolution deplored "the President's announced intention of making Supreme Court appointments for the purpose of tipping the balance of the Court away from civil liberties" and urged Senators to "carefully Investigate the records of Mr. Rehnquist and Mr. Powell . . . with a due regard to the candidates' views on the Bill of Rights."

The letter added, "We hope that the members of the Senate will consider devotion to the Bill of Rights to be an important part of the judicial philosophy of any Supreme Court Justice."

A month later, the board announced its opposition to Rehnquist. In a press release distributed December 5, the ACLU attempted to explain why, after fifty-one years, it was now changing course.

Although the ACLU prized its tradition of political nonpartisanship, it had taken "an extraordinary step because of extraordinary circumstances," read the statement attributed to Chairman Ennis. "We believe that it would be a betrayal of the principles of our Constitution to entrust their interpretation to a person who has devoted himself to undermining those principles," declared the ACLU, citing Rehnquist's record of advocating "dragnet arrests," opposing racial integration, championing electronic eavesdropping and political surveillance, and engineering "the Justice Department's programs to abrogate the rights of persons accused of crime."

"While the hour may be late, the ACLU plans to launch a campaign to bar the confirmation of William Rehnquist as a Justice of the Supreme Court," pledged the ACLU.

In addition to the factors cited in the press release, the ACLU was convinced that Rehnquist had misled the Supreme Court when arguing *Ehlert v. United States.* The Court had decided (on April 21, 1971) that a prospective inductee who became a conscientious objector after receiving his induction order could not demand that the local selective service board reconsider his classification. Instead, the inductee had to report for duty and request conscientious objector status. But that decision presumed that the military would hear the claim—a presumption based on Rehnquist's supposedly false assurance that the military would do so.

So argued a memo sent November 19 by ACLU general counsel Marvin Karpatkin to the editorial board of the *New York Times.* Karpatkin argued that the evidence "casts serious doubt on Mr. Rehnquist's veracity, legal ethics, and therefore, on his fitness to serve as Associate Justice."

In a column published November 22, *New York Times* editorial board member William Shannon opposed Rehnquist's confirmation: "His bleak record on racial equality, civil liberties and the overweening power of government to coerce private individuals in the name of order and security is wholly consistent with that of his political sponsor. . . . The Rehnquist record is not that of a true conservative. It is the record of an aggressive ideologue with combative impulses and strong commitment to a harsh, narrow doctrine concerning government and individual. It would be an ironic turn of events if this Goldwaterite doctrine so overwhelmingly rejected by the voters should be legitimized on the Supreme Court."

Lewis Powell was confirmed by the Senate on December 7 by a vote of 89 to 1. Only Fred Harris, the Democrat from Oklahoma, voted against him. "Mr. Powell does not have the kind of exemplary record in the fields of civil liberties and civil rights that I'd like to see in a man or woman appointed to the Supreme Court for life," explained Harris.

The day Powell was confirmed, Edward Brooke, a Republican and the nation's only black senator, urged his colleges to reject Rehnquist, whom he said "could be an influence for wrong." Given Rehnquist's relative youth, "he could be on the court . . . through the lifetime of our children and through the lifetime of our children's children," added Brooke.

That same week, *Newsweek* magazine disclosed a memorandum defending the segregationist concept of "separate but equal" that Rehnquist had written as a Supreme Court law clerk. In theory, minority rights might merit protection, argued the memo, but "in the long run it is the majority who will determine what the constitutional rights of the minority are."

The revelation only deepened concern in an activist community that already viewed Rehnquist as toxic. "If Mr. Rehnquist is approved, the bleakest chapter in what has been an unremittingly sorry Nixon Administration race relations record will have been written," wrote Bayard Rustin in the New York *Amsterdam News*, as he called out Rehnquist's "right wing zealotry."

Numerous news organizations reported that two Arizona men had signed affidavits accusing Rehnquist of harassing blacks waiting in line to vote in Phoenix, Arizona, in 1964. One of the men said Rehnquist had told a black woman that she had to recite the Constitution before she would be allowed to vote.

In testimony before the Senate Judiciary Committee, Clarence Mitchell of the NAACP said, "the Rehnquist nomination raises a grim warning. Through that nomination the foot of racism is placed in the door of the temple of justice." Joseph Rauh Jr. of the Leadership Conference on Civil Rights presented the committee with an affidavit from an Arizona state senator who claimed Rehnquist had told him, "I am opposed to all civil rights laws."

Meanwhile, a law clerk who had served with Rehnquist claimed that he, not Rehnquist, was the principal author of the memo defending the separate but equal doctrine; and a Rehnquist ally, Georgia Republican Congressman Ben Blackburn, asked the Internal Revenue Service to review the ACLU's tax status and determine whether the organization was "engaged in lobbying."

Despite the clamorous opposition, the Senate confirmed Rehnquist by a vote of 68 to 26 on December 10, 1971. The following June 26, Rehnquist joined the 5 to 4 majority in dismissing *Laird v. Tatum*, a suit brought by the ACLU to stop the Department of the Army's "surveillance of lawful and peaceful civilian political activity."

"The 5–4 decision sharply sets back ACLU legal efforts to dismantle the nation's political surveillance network," explained the ACLU in its annual reporting, noting, "ACLU petitioned for a rehearing on the ground that Rehnquist was biased because of his involvement in the case while he was Assistant Attorney General. On the opening day of the Supreme Court's 1972–73 term Rehnquist issued an opinion refusing to disqualify himself, claiming that his bias was no greater than that of other Supreme Court Justices in other cases, and that he had a duty to sit in the case to break a 4–4 tie."

In dissenting from the *Laird v. Tatum* decision, William Justice Douglas, joined by Thurgood Marshall, wrote, "The act of turning the military loose on civilians, even if sanctioned by an Act of Congress, which it has not been, would raise serious and profound constitutional questions. . . . Surveillance of civilians is none of the Army's constitutional business, and Congress has not undertaken to entrust it with any such function. . . . This case involves a cancer in our body politic. . . . Army surveillance, like Army regimentation, is at war with the principles of the First Amendment."

Nineteen-seventy-one was not just the year of Rehnquist, it was also the year of Daniel Ellsberg—or, to be more precise, of his dissemination of a secret Defense Department study of decision-making during the Vietnam War that came to be known as the Pentagon Papers.

Ellsberg, a former military analyst, had come to see the Vietnam conflict as an unjust war. He decided to release the study because "bombs were falling in Vietnam at that time, and I wanted to shorten that war as much as I could," he subsequently told National Public Radio.

He got a copy of the papers to the *New York Times*, which in April 1971 assigned a team of journalists under Neil Sheehan's direction to work on what the newspaper called Project X. An eleventh-floor suite at the New York Hilton became their headquarters.

Working virtually around the clock for the next six weeks, Sheehan and his team, in the words of the *Atlanta Constitution*, "began mining their historic lode, a massive 47-volume, 7,000-page 'Top Secret' Pentagon study of the decision-making that shaped the course of the Vietnam conflict."

On Sunday June 13, the *Times* published the first installment. "Vietnam Archive: Pentagon Study Traces 3 Decades of Growing U. S. Involvement," read the headline splashed across three columns of the front page. The story beneath promised details on "a massive study of how the United States went to war in Indochina, conducted by the Pentagon" that "demonstrates that four administrations progressively developed a sense of commitment to a non-Communist Vietnam, a readiness to fight the North to protect the South, and an ultimate frustration with this effort—to a much greater extent than their public statements acknowledged."

A headline beneath the main story read, "Vast Review of War Took a Year." The accompanying story described the frustration that led Secretary of Defense Robert S. McNamara to commission the study.

Sharing the front page, occupying two columns on the left, was a large photo of a beaming President Nixon and his daughter Tricia (enveloped in white) strolling arm in arm under a headline reporting, "Tricia Nixon Takes Vows in Garden at White House." The story reported, "after a tension-filled delay because of rain, Tricia Nixon was married today in the Rose Garden of the White House to Edward Finch Cox, the man she has described as 'my first and last love.'"

The next day, Attorney General John Mitchell asked the *Times* to halt publication. The *Times* refused, issuing a statement declaring "it is in the interest of the people of this country to be informed of the material contained in this series of articles." The following day the Justice Department obtained a temporary restraining order. The *Times* temporarily ceased publication.

That same day, the ACLU intervened in support of the *New York Times'* right to publish with a statement and a friend of the court filing.

Aryeh Neier argued the documents should not even be classified, as they "do not deal with any information that poses a real threat to national security," and he criticized the government's reliance on the Espionage Act. "The Attorney General is trying to use against the *New York Times* the same laws under which the Rosenbergs were prosecuted for revealing military secrets," he pointed out. "The purpose of those laws is grossly perverted when they are used to censor the kind of information the *Times* is disclosing." The other laws cited by the government, he said, were "unconstitutionally vague" and compared current government actions to the prosecution of Eugene Debs and other critics of America's role in War World I.

The ACLU brief, submitted on behalf of itself and twenty-seven members of Congress, was a powerful rejection of prior restraint and argued that the government lacked "inherent power to seek an injunction" to protect its supposed interest unless Congress precisely delineated "the range of the desired authority."

On June 18, the *Washington Post*, to whom Ellsberg had also leaked a copy of the study, published its first installment. The front-page article by Chalmers Roberts discussed American efforts to delay elections in the mid-1950s in North and South Vietnam out of fear voters would give the victory to Communist leader Ho Chi Minh. An article by David Broder documented efforts on Vice President Hubert Humphrey's part to "moderate the Vietnam policies of the Johnson Administration." And a column by Marquis Childs addressed "the extraordinary deception practiced by Lyndon Johnson and the men around him in plotting the bombing of the North and the escalation of the ground war."

The next day, the *Post* reported that "Johnson Administration strategists had almost no expectation that the many pauses in the bombing of North Vietnam between 1965 and 1968 would produce peace talks but believed they would help placate domestic and world opinion."

The *Post* suspended publication on June 20 after being ordered to do so by the U.S. Court of Appeals for the District of Columbia.

On June 30, the Supreme Court ruled 6 to 3 against prior restraint of the Pentagon Papers. Chief Justice Warren Burger read a short consensus opinion (from which he dissented): "Any system of prior restraints of expression comes to this court bearing a heavy presumption against its constitutional validity. The Government 'thus carries a heavy burden of showing justification for the enforcement of such a restraint.' The District Court for the Southern District of New York, in the *New York Times* case, and the District Court for the District of Columbia and the Court of Appeals for the District of Columbia Circuit, in the *Washington Post* case, held that the Government had not met that burden.

We agree."

Each of the nine justices filed his respective opinion. The three dissenters—Burger, John Marshall Harlan, and Harry Blackmun—all complained of the haste with which the decision had been forced upon them. As Blackmun put it, "Two Federal District Courts, two United States Courts of Appeals, and this Court—within a period of less than three weeks from inception until today—have been pressed into hurried decision of profound constitutional issues on inadequately developed and largely assumed facts without the careful deliberation that, hopefully, should characterize the American judicial process."

The four papers under various injunctions—the *New York Times*, *Washington Post*, *Boston Globe*, and *St. Louis Post-Dispatch*—all announced plans to resume publishing.

"We stand a little taller today, don't we?" said Benjamin Bradlee, executive editor of the *Washington Post*.

New York Times publisher Arthur Ochs Sulzberger said the decision "reaffirmed the fact . . . that the government can't just march in and stop us from publishing."

Ira Glasser, NYCLU executive director, was relieved but feared that the *Times'* attorneys had conceded too much ground. "The *New York Times* made a great contribution to freedom of the press," he said. "The same cannot be said of some of the arguments advanced in court, which we feel conceded too much to the government in allowing the use of prior restraint."

"For the first time in our history, the government succeeded in stopping the presses for over two weeks while more than two dozen judges examined the propriety of what they wanted to publish," pointed out ACLU Legal Director Mel Wulf. "We would have been more pleased if the Court had ruled that a prior restraint on the press was never justified. We think that's what the 1st Amendment requires."

While civil libertarians pondered the implications of the Pentagon Papers, an even more explosive situation was coming to a head. It began with what was to become the most famous (if puzzling) break-in in the history of America. In the early morning hours of June 17, 1972, Frank Wills, a security guard at the Watergate complex in Washington, DC, noticed some tape holding a door open leading to a garage. A bit of investigation turned up five men in the sixth-floor suite of the Democratic National Committee with surgical gloves and electronic equipment.

On September 15, a federal grand jury indicted the men found at the scene (apparently installing electronic bugs), along with former White House aides G. Gordon Liddy and E. Howard Hunt.

That November, Nixon won re-election in a landslide, getting over 60 percent of the popular vote and winning forty-nine states, leaving only Massachusetts and the District of Columbia to George McGovern.

In his victory speech from the Oval office, Nixon relished pulling off "one of the greatest victories of all time," but warned the victory would be complete "only if in these next four years we . . . can work together to achieve our common great goals."

Nixon was not to have another four years. May 17, 1973, was the first day of televised hearings for the Senate Select Committee on Presidential Campaign Activities. On June 3, former White House counsel John Dean directly implicated President Nixon in the Watergate cover-up. That July 13, Nixon's former deputy assistant exposed the White House taping system.

Throughout the drama, the ACLU debated how and whether to weigh in. The ACLU had never much cared for Nixon—with his animosity to free speech, fondness for surveillance, penchant for secrecy, coded appeals to racism, and overall disdain for civil liberties. As early as 1971, the Southern California affiliate had urged his impeachment for "initiating unconstitutional war actions in Cambodia and Laos and committing other abuses of power." As the Watergate scandal played out, the case against Nixon grew stronger by the day, setting off a contentious debate within the ACLU.

In August 1972, the ACLU came out in defense of a group calling itself the National Committee for Impeachment of President Nixon, when the Justice Department filed suit seeking to block the organization from spending money on Nixon impeachment ads. The Justice Department claimed the organization was not in compliance with the Federal Election Campaign Act of 1971.

The ACLU saw the Justice Department's "attempt at prior restraint" as "the most incredible violation of the First Amendment yet to come to our attention." It pledged support to "any organization or individual prosecuted under these regulations."

For all the loathing Nixon engendered, the ACLU hesitated jumping on the impeachment wagon. For many members, the prospect of being perceived as soldiers in a partisan battle was discomforting in the extreme. Nonetheless, when the Southern California affiliate put forth a draft impeachment resolution in July 1973, the board was ready to pay attention. The resolution, formally reviewed by the board on September 30, built on the affiliate's previous impeachment call. It charged Nixon with continuation of the "unconstitutional war actions" in Cambodia and Laos, "extensive and deliberate illegal conduct" in the executive branch of government, "admitted crimes and violations of civil liberties and civil rights," and threatening "our constitutional form of government."

Board members debated the merits of particular charges, and several expressed doubt over whether now was the time to act; but in the end, the board voted unanimously, 49 to 0, on a resolution urging the House to "initiate impeachment proceedings" against Nixon. The resolution cited various violations of civil liberties, including his approval of domestic political surveillance, his harassment of political enemies, his interference with a free press, his secret recording of conversations in the White House, his violations of citizens' right to peaceful protests, his usurpation of the war powers

of Congress, his persecution of dissenters, and his perversion of "the operation of various federal agencies."

In weeks to follow, there was debate over the exact meaning of "initiate
impeachment proceedings." Many ACLU associates sought reassurance the
ACLU was not calling for Nixon's removal or prejudging his guilt, but
merely saying things had reached a serious enough state that Congress
ought to take a close look.

A week and a half later, Spiro Agnew resigned as vice president. After
accepting a Justice Department plea deal, with the consent of Attorney
General Elliot Richardson, the former Maryland governor pled no contest
to a single felony of tax evasion in connection with a bribery kickback
scheme.

"After 65 days of fighting the government . . . with a blitzkrieg of bluff,
Spiro T. Agnew surrendered Wednesday and admitted that at least some
of those 'damned lies' were true," reported United Press International.

Four days after Agnew's resignation, on Sunday, October 14, the ACLU
published a full-page ad in the *New York Times*' Week in Review section
headlined: "Why it is necessary to impeach President Nixon. And how it
can be done."

The text did not much focus on Watergate, but on what the ACLU considered violations of civil liberties: covert surveillance, the burgling of Daniel Ellsberg's psychiatric records, spying on political opponents, etc. "The
country can withstand the resignation of the Vice President. The country
can withstand the impeachment of the President. The country cannot withstand a system of presidential power unlimited by the Bill of Rights," read
the ad, which urged readers to write their congressperson in support of impeachment and included an appeal for funds.

That Friday, Nixon refused, in violation of a federal court order, to hand
over the White House tapes to special Watergate prosecutor Archibald
Cox. His lawyer proposed instead that Nixon deliver a summary to be au-
thenticated by Senator John Stennis of Mississippi. Stennis had agreed "to
listen to every requested tape and verify that the statement I am preparing
is full and accurate." Nixon also directed Cox "to make no further attempts
by the judicial process to obtain tapes, notes or memoranda of presidential
conversations."

Cox emphatically rejected Nixon's offer. "A summary of the content of the tapes lacks the evidentiary value of the tapes themselves. No steps are being taken to turn over the important notes, memoranda and other documents that the court orders require. I shall bring these points to the attention of the court and abide by its decision," Cox said in a statement released to the press.

Cox bluntly dismissed Nixon's order that he stop demanding materials that Nixon didn't want him to have. "For me to comply to those instructions would violate my solemn pledge to the Senate and the country," replied Cox.

The so-called Saturday Night Massacre ensued. Nixon ordered Attorney General Elliot Richardson to fire Cox. Richardson resigned. When Deputy Attorney General William Ruckelshaus refused to carry out the order, Nixon fired him and promoted Robert Bork, the solicitor general, to acting attorney general. Bork carried out the order, and Nixon eliminated Cox's office.

Press Secretary Ronald Ziegler announced that Cox's functions would be transferred back to the Justice Department, which he promised would carry out the mission "with thoroughness and vigor." Cox responded with his own statement: "Whether ours shall continue to be a government of laws and not of men is now for Congress and ultimately the American people."

The Sunday following Saturday's massacre, columnist Tom Wicker, writing in the *New York Times*, reported that within four days of the ACLU's ad appearing, "the ACLU had received 873 pieces of mail, 810 of them favorable to impeachment, 751 volunteering services in the cause, and 410 containing contributions totaling $10,835.25."

Within the organization, however, uneasiness remained. Roger Baldwin was particularly troubled: 'I realize how emotional people have become over such shocking betrayals of trust by a president without principles or moral convictions. But I question whether such an emotion justifies so emotional a crusade as we have conducted. It isn't like our style; it looks a bit hysterical."

A group within the Cleveland Civil Liberties Union issued a minority report questioning the "propriety of the ACLU publicly endorsing what is essentially a political process. . . . Our integrity is very much at stake."

On August 8, 1974, Nixon announced he was resigning at noon the next day, which he did in a one-sentence letter to Secretary of State Henry Kissinger.

As the ACLU wrestled with Nixon's abuses, it also wrestled with a dark chapter from its past.

Board member George Slaff, chair of the Southern California affiliate, had campaigned for repudiation of the 1940 resolution barring Communists, Fascists, and members of the German American Bund that had, in practice, only affected Elizabeth Gurley Flynn.

In December 1967, Slaff had succeeded. The board superseded the 1940 resolution with a new resolution limiting leadership positions to those "unequivocally committed to the objectives" of the ACLU who rejected discrimination based on "race, religion, sex or opinion" and accepted "the principles of political democracy."

But Slaff was not yet done. Although he had never met Flynn, he greatly admired her and was set on restoring her good name, which greatly annoyed Roger Baldwin. The day after Christmas in 1973, Baldwin wrote Slaff to discourage his effort to revisit the issue. He argued that "[to] rescind Miss Flynn's expulsion would raise the question of rescinding the present policy," which barred from ACLU leadership persons not "committed to the objects of this Union . . . and to the concept of democratic government and civil liberties for all people."

"So we would have over again the divisive arguments that were finally put to rest in 1967 by general agreement," wrote Baldwin, who added, "I hope you will reconsider your proposal and withdraw it in the interest of the harmony on this issue you did so much to promote."

Slaff rejected Baldwin's advice. In 1974, he asked the board to formally reconsider Flynn's expulsion. He sent them all a copy of *The Trial of Elizabeth Gurley Flynn by the American Civil Liberties Union.*

The book, edited by former ACLU board member Corliss Lamont, consisted largely of a transcript of Flynn's "trial." It also included an introduction from Lamont, which alleged that ACLU co-counsels Morris Ernst and Arthur Garfield Hays had conspired with Martin Dies, chairman of the House Committee on Un-American Activities. After the three men met in Washington, wrote Lamont, "Representative Dies and his Committee stopped claiming that the Civil Liberties Union was a Communist front," which Lamont attributed to "off-the-record" assurances Dies had received that the ACLU "would take the necessary steps to 'cleanse' itself of Communists."

Baldwin and several influential board members objected to Slaff's initiative, but he continued to raise the issue. In April 1976, the board voted 32 to 18 to rescind the expulsion.

Even as the ACLU welcomed the ghost of Flynn into the fold, Charles Morgan was shown the door. Since 1972, when Morgan was named head of the Washington office, he had been a fixture in the nation's capital. As Washington had wrestled with Watergate, he had injected himself into its center, representing those targeted by the so-called White House Plumbers. Most notable was R. Spencer Oliver, executive director of the Association of State Democratic Chairmen, whose phone within the Democratic National Committee had been bugged. During the trial of the Watergate burglary defendants in January 1973, Alfred Baldwin, a former FBI agent who had monitored many of those conversations, was scheduled to testify.

Earl Silbert, principal assistant U.S. attorney and chief Watergate plumber prosecutor, conjectured that Oliver was the target of a blackmail attempt linking him to a local call girl ring. He hoped Albert's testimony would bolster that theory. Morgan thought the White House had manufactured the blackmail angle to deflect attention from Nixon and his inner circle. As Neier put it, "Chuck Morgan believed that Silbert and the other prosecutors came up with their ridiculous theory of the case because they were part of Nixon's attempt to cover-up the Watergate burglary." If Silbert pursued that theory in court, believed Morgan, the truth might never surface. Plus, Oliver's reputation—and perhaps his marriage—would be ruined.

So, when Alfred Baldwin was called to testify about the conversations on the tape, Morgan objected. Judge John Sirica rejected Morgan's motion but ordered that Baldwin be heard in closed session. Subsequently the District of Columbia Court of Appeals overruled Sirica, excluding the testimony altogether; and ultimately the truth about White House involvement came to light.

As Neier recalled, Morgan "came to believe that his interlocutory appeal on behalf of Spencer Oliver played a crucial role in Watergate. He thought he deserved as much or more credit than Woodward and Bernstein for exposing the conspiracy." It was a matter, said Neier, about which he and Morgan "had endless arguments."

In June 1973, the ACLU asked that the convictions of the seven Watergate defendants be set aside so they could be retried "under a properly drawn indictment which charges all of those responsible for the Watergate conspiracy regardless of their station in life."

In a 114-page review and critique of the trial released by the ACLU, Morgan essentially congratulated himself for steering the Watergate investigation away from the taped conversations and the conjectured call girl ring: "[Wrapped] into this struggle to protect privacy . . . there lay the essential truth about Watergate. Without evidence of the contents of the conversations, Mr. Silbert would be unable to convince anyone that the motive for the crime was blackmail. And without a believable non-political motive . . . the search for truth in the Watergate case would continue."

That October, the *Washington Post* honored Morgan with a fawning tribute: "Sincerely called 'the Clarence Darrow of his time' by one usually caustic newsman, he remains a widely unsung hero of the Civil Rights movement—probably the single most effective and influential trial lawyer in the South during the turbulent '60s. . . . Committed to a cause, he is not interested in sacrificing a client or case for the greater purpose. Morgan doesn't seem to be at war, though his career has been spent waging battles and winning them—one at a time."

In January 1974, President Nixon nominated Silbert for U.S. Attorney for the District of Columbia. In testimony before the Senate Judiciary Committee, Silbert responded point-by-point to Morgan's charges. He disputed Morgan's contention that introducing the intercepted conversation would have been illegal. "I continue to believe that Judge Sirica, the appellate dissent, and the prosecutors were correct."

He also disputed Morgan's argument that the White House had cooked up the blackmail scheme: "We never were able to determine the precise motivation for the burglary and wiretapping, particularly on the telephone of a comparative unknown—Spencer Oliver. . . . Therefore, one motive we thought possible was an attempt to compromise Oliver and others. . . . We never had any direct proof of this. . . . It was, therefore, only an inference based on the above facts."

Testifying before the same Senate Committee, Morgan contradicted Silbert's account. He concluded his testimony with an assault on Silbert's character: "Had he acted independently . . . had he refused to accept those limiting orders . . . then he would have been a lawyer of whom we could all be proud. But he did not."

The Judiciary Committee concluded Silbert's nomination was too hot to handle and tabled it pending resolution of Nixon's impeachment proceedings. "Any action now . . . could be viewed as Senate approval or disapproval of the handling of the Watergate investigation by President Nixon," Senator John Tunney told the *Washington Post* in July. That August, Nixon resigned. When Congress recessed in November, it allowed Silbert's nomination to die. That same month, President Ford resubmitted the nomination—but the Senate chose not to act during its lame-duck session.

When Congress reconvened next year, Ford nominated Silbert again—which Morgan considered outrageous. "Morgan believed that this was a continuing part of the cover-up—a payoff to Silbert," recalled Neier. "He was determined to block Silbert's confirmation. I told Morgan to lay off. It would violate the ACLU's policy of not taking sides on elections or appointments to public office." Morgan "was very upset with me for that."

Morgan ignored Neier's direction: "He used a couple of staff members in the DC office to collect as much dirt as possible on Earl Silbert. . . . Morgan thought that if he blocked Silbert, he would finally get the credit he deserved for Watergate," said Neier.

Despite Morgan's crusade, Silbert was confirmed by a vote of 84 to 12 in October 1975. The process had taken some twenty-one months and required four nominations by two presidents, but Silbert emerged essentially unscathed. The relationship between Morgan and Neier did not.

The following year, Morgan weighed in on Jimmy Carter's presidential campaign. In a *New York Times* story that March, Morgan slammed Carter's liberal opponents. "The real reason the Northern liberals don't like Mr. Carter is that 'they don't have their hooks in him,'" said Morgan. The *Times* noted that Morgan "favors Mr. [Fred] Harris for President. But he gives high marks to Mr. Carter for 'staying decent' as Governor of Georgia."

"I should have gotten on the phone with Morgan about this," said Neier. "But I didn't. I sent a note to him saying that he should make clear that he wasn't speaking for the ACLU."

On Monday, April 12, the *Washington Post* reported that Morgan had resigned the previous Friday "over what he sees as a far-reaching civil liberties issue—the right of an employee to publicly say things the bosses may not like."

The paper printed the text of Morgan's brief resignation letter: "You ask me what steps I am taking to correct the impression that when I am 'Identified' by my employment I 'appear to speak for the organization.' The step I am taking is to resign."

Neier was inclined to "let matters cool down a bit," he told the *Post*. "I'm entirely open to persuasion that he did indeed exercise the proper care."

In fact, the men's relationship was shattered beyond repair. Even the resignation, in Neier's opinion, was a veiled power play. "Morgan converted this [dispute] into my restraining him from denouncing the prejudice against a Southerner, Jimmy Carter. . . . And then Morgan basically resigned . . . with the thought that, at the next board meeting, the board would support him and not me."

Instead, the Board voted 66 to 10 to accept Morgan's resignation. By that point, said Neier, "many of the members of that board thought Morgan was a loose cannon. . . . So, they wouldn't back him at that moment."

In a sympathetic column in the *New York Times*, Tom Wicker wrote, "The A.C.L.U.'s Washington director since 1972, and its Southern regional director for eight years before that, Mr. Morgan became one of the few public figures of the time to resign an advantageous and useful position on a matter of principle.

"The public is the poorer for having lost a fearless, tireless, voluble and exceptionally able defender of the Bill of Rights and common human decency."

By 1983, Morgan had reinvented himself. The *Times* reported that he was heading a thirteen-member Washington law firm with big-money clients including the American Tobacco Institute, the New York Power Authority, and Sears, Roebuck & Company. Some of his former associates said he had sold out, but Morgan attributed his transformation to societal change. "There is no burning cause out there that goes unrepresented, or that I am particularly concerned about. Am I supposed to speak out against malaise?" The lawyer's role, he added, "is not to save society. . . . If liberty is dead among the people, no lawyer in the world can do anything about it."

10

Nazis, Jews, and the FBI

Even as the frenzied sixties gave way to the more quiescent seventies, controversial clients continued to pop up; so the ACLU did not find it particularly remarkable in 1977 when a group of self-styled Nazis came to the ACLU seeking assistance.

The Nazis planned to march on the Chicago suburb of Skokie, where an estimated seven thousand survivors of the Holocaust lived. The Nazi leader, Frank Collin, had been booted out of the American Nazi Party after his father was revealed to be a Jewish Holocaust survivor. He subsequently formed the National Socialist Party of America. Syndicated columnists Jack Germond and Jules Witcover described him as "a 32-year-old clown in a Stormtrooper's uniform."

It's not clear what planted the idea of the march in Collin's head, but Skokie wanted nothing to do with him. In May 1977, the Skokie Village board unanimously passed three ordinances aimed at stopping the demonstration. The laws prohibited demonstrations by political groups wearing "repugnant" military uniforms, banned distribution of materials meant to incite racial hatred and required the posting of a $350,000 liability bond for demonstrations with more than fifty spectators or participants.

Within the ACLU, defending Nazis was not uncontroversial. In its 1934 pamphlet entitled "Shall We Defend Free Speech for Nazis in America?" the ACLU had declared: "We do not choose our clients. Lawless authorities denying their rights choose them for us.

"To those who advocate suppressing propaganda they hate, we ask—where do you draw the line? They can answer only in the terms of revolutionists—at our political enemies. But experience shows that 'political enemies' is a broad term, and has covered the breaking up even of working class meetings by rival working class organizations. It illustrates the danger, and the impracticability of making any distinctions in defending rights sought by all."

"In 1977, when the Skokie case arose, the Illinois ACLU initially regarded it as so routine that they never informed the national office about it," recalled Neier.

David Hamlin, executive director of the Illinois ACLU, denounced Skokie's new law as "appallingly unconstitutional." Nonetheless, Skokie obtained a temporary injunction against Collin's demonstration. Upon appeal, the ACLU won a partial victory from the Illinois Appellate Court. The march could proceed, but the Nazis could not display Nazi regalia and had to post the $350,000 bond. The ACLU deemed those conditions unacceptable and appealed.

David Goldberger, a 1967 graduate of the University of Chicago Law School, was the ACLU lawyer who handed the case.

Collin's headquarters, recalled Goldberger, was in Marquette Park—a largely Eastern European working-class neighborhood on the Southwest Side of Chicago into which blacks were beginning to move. Collin had hoped to organize an anti-black protest in the park, but the city was not providing the access that he wanted. Skokie was the alternative.

As legal director of the affiliate, Goldberger was authorized to take Collin's case, which seemed "a no-brainer. This is what the ACLU is about. I had no inkling at the time that it was going to explode the way that it did."

Goldberger called his general counsel, Ed Rothschild, and told him, "I just wanted to let you know this is within policy and as legal director I have the authority to take the case as opposed to bringing it to the committee or anything like that."

Rothschild interrupted with, "David, you listen to me for a while. I think you're right and I order you to take it."

"Why are you ordering me to take it?" asked Goldberger.

"You have no idea what's coming," replied Rothschild. "If it blows up, I don't want you to be out there by yourself."

Despite the ACLU's long-standing position, some ACLU supporters were puzzled by its involvement. The "Skokie affair clearly represents a major turn for the worse in the organization's relations with the Jewish community," reported the *New York Jewish Week* that August, which quoted a Jewish lawyer saying, "American Jews are simply not going to accept the view that justice is somehow being served by helping Nazis parade through a Jewish neighborhood."

To counter such criticism, a group of prominent Jews signed a statement slamming Nazis but supporting "the rights of free expression. We recognize, as does the ACLU, that the rights of individuals are inextricably tied to the rights of all," read the statement, which was signed by sixty prominent Jews, including broadcaster Daniel Schorr and civil liberties lawyer Joseph L. Rauh Jr.

That December, representatives of several Jewish organizations met with Neier and Norman Dorsen, chair of the ACLU board. The organization leaders were told that the ACLU had so far lost some 2,100 members as a result of standing with the Nazis in Skokie.

Naomi Levine, executive director of the American Jewish Congress, countered, "when you march through Skokie with swastikas, you are doing it not to generate ideas but to spread fear and terror."

Goldberger felt conflicted: "There was never any doubt that I should take the case; but my thought was, 'Did I do something that's gonna hurt the ACLU? Is this a more hurtful case than I ever dreamt?' I felt some real strong pangs of guilt, I felt responsible for the pain that people in Skokie were having, that the ACLU was enduring and so forth."

"Of course, the board could've said no, we don't want the ACLU involved in this," acknowledged Goldberger. "David and I discussed that possibility," he said, although neither thought it would happen. "But we said, 'If the ACLU won't take it then the two of us are just gonna go off by ourselves and take it because it has to be done.'"

"We estimate that we'll lose 25 percent of our [Illinois] membership and our financial support because of this Nazi-Skokie case," the ACLU's David Hamlin told the *Jerusalem Post*. "We are stunned by the magnitude of the protests. . . . But no one in this office has even suggested dropping the case."

Hamlin wrote an op-ed in the *Chicago Tribune*, published on New Year's Day, 1978, that argued the merits of the case. He pointed out that the

Skokie ordinances were tantamount to a declaration that a Nazi march was not protected by the First Amendment.

"Village officials do not argue, remarkably enough, that the Nazis will engage in criminal conduct," noted Hamlin. "They say the village residents might engage in criminal conduct, and so Nazis should be stopped." All the arguments, he said, amounted to the same thing: "If the audience doesn't like the message . . . then the message should be censored," which was "the direct opposite of the 1st Amendment."

If all it took to stop a demonstration was an audience threatening violence, "then no idea is safe," he added. "Public officials in Selma, Alabama, could have used the Skokie theory to prevent the famous civil rights march in the sixties. . . . Selma could have stopped the march before it started. . . . We are no more energetic in our work on this case than on any of the 90 others we are currently handling. We are doing, simply, the best job we can for the 1st Amendment."

Later that January, the Illinois Supreme Court came down in favor of Collin and his Nazi group. "We do not doubt that the sight of this [swastika] symbol is abhorrent to the Jewish citizens of Skokie. . . . Yet it is entirely clear that this factor does not justify enjoining defendant's speech," declared the unsigned opinion. The next month, a federal court deemed the local ordinances targeting the march to be unconstitutional.

The march never took place. The Nazis rescheduled their demonstration for a later date in Marquette Park. On the appointed Sunday, June 25, 1978, a lot of people showed up in Skokie, but no one in a uniform or a brown shirt calling himself a Nazi.

Chicago Tribune columnist Anne Keegan described the atmosphere of Skokie at peace: "No storm trooper on the steps of the village known around the world. . . . No bricks. No stones. No riot at all. There were no sounds of ugly taunts or the smash of wooden bats on Sunday morning. Instead, it was quiet. . . . A Midwest storm crackled overhead and the rain poured down on empty streets, pattered on the roof of a peaceful village hall and turned all the lawns a brilliant green."

Even setting aside the Skokie tsunami, the ACLU in the late 1970s was a tumultuous place—and in the throes of a major transition. In January 1977, only months after Charles Morgan stormed off, legal director Melvin Wulf (who had joined the ACLU in 1958 and become legal director in 1962) stepped down. "We had different views about how the legal department should run," board chairman Norman Dorsen told the *Times*.

Dorsen, a New York University law professor, had been elected chairman in December 1976, replacing Edward Ennis. Upon taking office, Dorsen "immediately said to me that we should replace Mel Wulf," recalled Neier. "This took me by surprise. . . . I thought they were personal friends."

Wulf later blamed his ejection on unspecified "enemies." The *Times* quoted an unnamed lawyer saying that management "wanted a different legal director who gets along better with foundations and the established bar."

Ira Glasser, head of the New York affiliate, concluded the job had simply become too big for Wulf: "The ACLU had outgrown him. When I came into the organization in 1967, the whole ACLU legal staff was two people—Mel, as legal director, and the assistant legal director, who was Eleanor [Holmes Norton]. The legal staff began to expand when Aryeh got there in 1970. . . . People like Ruth [Bader Ginsburg] came in . . . people like Al Bronstein, who headed up the prison project. They were above Mel's level. . . . Mel's [skill] was filing amicus briefs. . . . Mel had never tried a case in his life. . . . When Aryeh hired Chuck [Morgan], it was an enormous leap forward in capacity. Chuck was a major, bigtime accomplished, trial lawyer. . . . Mel couldn't begin to supervise him."

Wulf was replaced by Bruce Innis. A University of Chicago Law School graduate and former director of the NYCLU's Mental Patients' Rights Project, Innis had filed a class-action suit in 1972 on behalf of children at the Willowbrook State School for the disabled in Staten Island. The case had drawn considerable public attention and resulted, in 1975, in a consent decree ordering Willowbrook to disperse its patients to more-congenial community facilities.

As the ACLU coped with its management challenges, a potential embarrassment emerged from its past. An ACLU Freedom of Information request to the FBI unearthed a trove of documents that, as Aryeh Neier puts it, "contained correspondence from ACLU officials to their contacts in the FBI naming those within the ACLU they suspected of communist associations." The information, Neier realized, could be a public relations disaster.

Neier and Dorsen agreed to go public, but in a relatively controlled fashion. They would share the files exclusively with *New York Times* reporter Anthony Marro. He "would go through all the files on his own and only publish when he completed the process. . . . At the same time, we would give copies of the files concerning them to Irving Ferman and [former ACLU staff counsel] Herbert Monte Levy and ask them for statements that would be furnished to Anthony Marro," said Neier.

That June, the *Washington Post* scooped the *Times* with a related story from the ACLU's past. The FBI had infiltrated the ACLU, it revealed, "when it was formed in 1920 and kept files on leading members, including Felix Frankfurter, Helen Keller, Jane Addams, Upton Sinclair, and Clarence Darrow." "Confidential operatives" had "infiltrated the ACLU at every level, providing detailed reports on closed meetings, membership lists and financial contributions and, in some cases, copies of private correspondence between ACLU officials and other private citizens."

On August 4, Marro's story came out. "For about seven years in the 1950's a number of officials of the American Civil Liberties Union gave the Federal Bureau of Investigation on a continuing basis information about the organization, its activities and some of its members," he reported.

In addition, revealed Marro, various ACLU officials apparently sought the FBI's help in identifying "Communist Party members who might be trying to gain seats on the boards of the ACLU's state affiliates." As a result, the FBI "opened files on scores of persons whose names they had received from the ACLU." The ACLU also provided reports on upcoming ACLU activities, copies of ACLU correspondence, and even gossip on internal feuds in order to "cultivate the good will of the bureau to help to offset charges in that Cold War era that the ACLU itself was subversive."

Dorsen and Neier issued a statement: "Whatever their motive, such contacts with the FBI were wrong, inexcusable and destructive of civil liberties principles. These incidents took place in a different era and are contrary to the way the ACLU operates today."

Former counsel Levy defended the collaboration, arguing that it was "thoroughly advantageous to the ACLU and to the cause of civil liberties to enlist the aid of the FBI whenever we could do so in support of civil liberties—then under severe attack by McCarthyism." The "good offices of the FBI" helped "to set the record straight when anyone mistakenly claimed ACLU was a Communist organization."

Ferman, now teaching law at Howard University, was equally unapologetic. The ACLU's policy of working with the FBI "reflected a recognition that particularly during the Cold War period of the 50's, there was need for some clear channels to those agencies operating in the political framework similar to that of the union," he said.

Ten days later, the *Times* ran a sympathetic editorial: "The present leaders of the ACLU, of course, are worried about the impact of the disclosures on their supporters. Some two thousand members have recently resigned over a very different issue—the union's defense of the right of Nazis to parade in Skokie, Ill. The actions taken two decades ago could cause thousands of others to turn away. . . . It is not easy in 1977 to recall the temper of the 1950's and the situation that confronted dedicated people. . . . Condemnation by hindsight is too simple a judgment."

"Though I had feared that the revelations would do a lot of damage to the ACLU," Neier confided, "that did not happen. . . . I like to think that our forthrightness in disclosing the skeleton in our closet helped prevent . . . significant harm."

Another public relations crisis broke out in Mississippi, where the ACLU had agreed to represent yet another hate group: Ku Klux Klan members planning a rally on public school grounds in Jackson. Black board members and some white colleagues opposed the ACLU's decision, which they found unfathomable at a time of cross burnings and other threatening KKK activities.

ACLU officials inflamed the situation further by comparing crossburnings—as symbolic speech—to burning draft cards. Several national board members flew in to defuse the situation. They failed.

The Mississippi dissidents issued a statement declaring, "we . . . will not submit to the pressures of the national ACLU representatives that have come here to sell us on acceptance of the Klan as a client" and affirming their commitment to fighting "racism, oppression and the denial of human rights in this country."

All six black board members of the affiliate resigned, as did three white members. Ultimately, the KKK held its rally on private property—making their defense moot. "At the year's end, the Mississippi ACLU was still in turmoil over the matter," observed Neier.

Overlapping with the Mississippi scandal was another KKK imbroglio. The San Diego ACLU had filed suit on behalf of KKK members serving as Marines at Camp Pendleton. Several of the Klan members, after being accused of harassing black enlisted men, were ordered transferred. The men engaged ACLU attorneys, who claimed violation of their rights. Meanwhile, black Marines were accused of attacking whites they believed to be participating in a KKK meeting. They also were represented by the ACLU. The squabbles attracted the attention of the *New York Times*, which reported, "the San Diego suit has generated an ideological and policy dispute among Southern California ACLU members, provoking emergency meetings marked by angry debate at almost all of the 28 chapters, and has led to a number of protest resignations."

Meanwhile, the national office was still dealing with the fallout from Skokie. Like virtually everyone at the ACLU, New York affiliate head Ira Glasser was stunned by the intensity of the blowback. "It surprised the hell out of us that this became so explosive. . . . I got so many of those letters that I begin to look them up on our membership records, and I discovered that fully 70 percent of the people who [wrote] telling me they're quitting were not members."

An internal February 1978 memo outlined the scope of the "financial crisis." Income from membership renewals, it noted, "declined from about $3,300,000 in 1976 to about $2,800,000 in 1977."

Consequently, the ACLU was cutting back: "All field services to ACLU state affiliates . . . from the ACLU's national office have been eliminated. One of the four litigating lawyers supported by the general funds of the ACLU and the ACLU Foundation has been dropped . . . The policy-making staff of the ACLU has been sharply cut. Many ACLU affiliates around the country have laid off lawyers and other key staff members. The ACLU national office has eliminated so many clerical posts that . . . investigative reports, litigation dockets and other important operating materials" were being delayed by as much as six weeks.

In early 1978, several outsiders were brought in for a fund-raising brainstorming session. Morris Dees was a lawyer and direct-mail marketing guru who had made millions with the sale of his marketing firm. He had re-invented himself as an advocate for death penalty defendants and was co-founder of the Southern Poverty Law Center. Tom Collins, a New York advertising man and direct-mail marketing expert, had worked for former presidential candidate George McGovern. Roger Craver was a successful direct-mail marketer and co-founder of Common Cause. The NYCLU's Glasser was summoned, he surmised, because "I had talked in synagogues all over New York . . . to Jewish audiences about this." Neier and Dorsen presided. But the floor belonged to the outsiders. As Glasser put it, "They were the direct-mail gurus . . . [and] we were weak enough and unsure of ourselves enough to listen to them."

Although the normal ACLU fund-raising letter was limited to a page, "Morris Dees was known for sending much lengthier fund-raising letters, and we agreed that his approach should be followed in this case," recalled Neier. The first issue they confronted was who would sign it. The initial impulse was to go with a Jewish luminary, recalled Dorsen. The considered Arthur Goldberg, the recently retired Supreme Court Justice, and Senator Jacob Javits. Neither was available. Someone suggested David Goldberger, the ACLU attorney who had tried the Nazi case.

Goldberger was "personally a little ambivalent. I said. 'I'm getting enough attention on this. Why don't one of you guys do it?'"

In the end, Goldberger crafted a draft letter, which was found lacking. "It just didn't have the impact that Aryeh and [incoming executive director of the ACLU of Illinois] Jay Miller wanted," Goldberger acknowledged.

Glasser took over the writing. Collins added a phrase that Craver found particularly compelling. "I'll never forget it," said Craver. "It was 'You,' meaning reader, are 'part of the saving remnant' of our society. I always thought that was a wonderful way to describe people who would stand up for the ACLU at a moment like that."

"I had to negotiate it line by line with David," recalled Glasser. Goldberger acknowledges pushing back against some of the wording and against capitalizing the word Nazi. "They wanted to capitalize 'Nazi' and I wouldn't let them. . . . I did a lot of editing. I think they weren't happy about it because my attitude was, 'If it's gonna be my words, it's gonna be me.' Finally, we worked out a text that I felt was dignified—not that what they were proposing was undignified; but I did not want it to be too sharp, and I was nervous about sounding shrill."

The final version was four single-spaced typewritten pages. The letter-head identified the writer simply as "David Goldberger, Attorney at Law." In the letter, addressed to "My Dear Friend," Goldberger introduces him-self as the lawyer who defended the "nazis," a case which affected him deeply and "gravely injured the ACLU financially."

He explains that he had defended other free speech defendants, includ-ing anti-war demonstrators and civil rights protestors. He acknowledges sharing the agony of those who thought that to "allow people calling them-selves nazis to parade" in Skokie was simply "too much to bear." He points out that Aryeh Neier, a Holocaust survivor, "has more reason than most to despise what people calling themselves nazis stand for."

Goldberger notes that Skokie had used the same law it aimed at Nazis against Jewish War Veterans: "Think of such power in the hands of a racist sheriff, or a local police department hostile to anti-war demonstrators." He points out that cases like Skokie's make up a tiny portion—"one-tenth of one percent"—of the ACLU's portfolio; but because of the controversy over Skokie, the ACLU's other clients "are in danger." The ACLU, he adds, "is now on the edge of a precipice. . . . As a citizen deeply concerned with human rights, you have identified yourself as a part of the 'saving remnant' of our time." He invites the reader "to join others like yourself all over the country not just to support ACLU but to save it."

Attached was a coupon urging donations of anything from $15 to $100 or more.

That July, as the Goldberger letter was circulating around the country, the *New York Times* magazine ran a story by J. Anthony Lukas titled, "The ACLU Against Itself."

"Booming in the 60's, the American Civil Liberties Union is now in disarray," reads the subhead of the article, which focused not just on the faltering ACLU but the crisis of liberalism in America. ACLU members had begun fleeing "long before David Goldberger got his first call from the Nazis in April 1977," reports Lukas, who notes that membership had fallen in three years from 270,000 to 185,000.

"Clearly, the organization's troubles stem from something much deeper than Skokie," concludes Lukas, who suggests there may no longer be a "public issue capable of generating sustained commitment from large numbers of civil libertarians." He also notes that the public interest field, "which the ACLU once had largely to itself, is now crowded with dozens of groups . . . scrambling for slices of the smaller pie."

Lukas reports that management consultants traced the ACLU's financial troubles "less to its involvement in controversial issues like Skokie than to what they call 'systemic weakness.' In particular, they blamed disastrous management of the membership department, inadequate record-keeping and poor communications with members."

In a letter published in the *New York Times*, Dorsen wrote, "The ACLU is not in 'disarray' or 'against itself.' Far from it. There always has been and always should be debate about the meaning of civil liberties, both within and outside the ACLU. But the ACLU board and staff are working with a common sense of purpose." He added, "our fund raising over the past few months has been successful, and there is little doubt about our long-term strength."

That statement was at least half true. Thanks in large part to the Goldberger letter, the most recent ACLU fund-raising effort had been spectacularly fruitful. Indeed, the Goldberger appeal went down in ACLU lore as the most successful ACLU direct-mail fund-raising effort ever. Craver puts the amount brought in at between $500,000 and $700,000. Such appeals to membership "normally would bring in between $150,000 and $250,000," he said.

The letter's life extended far beyond the Skokie crisis. As Craver recalled, "it brought in tens of thousands of people who gave millions and millions of dollars in the ensuing years."

But, as Lukas suggested, the roots of the ACLU's financial crisis went deeper than Skokie. The ACLU had experienced a spike in membership as a result of the Nixon impeachment campaign. Those new members were not renewing at the same rate as previous members. More importantly, the ACLU's budget projections were more optimistic than the situation merited. Skokie or no Skokie, a reckoning was inevitable.

The situation was complicated by the inconsistent treatment and reporting of contributions from foundation grants and bequests. Even though membership income dropped during the Skokie crisis, funds from foundation grants, individual bequests, and fund-raising events increased. Those funds, however, were not necessarily available for general purposes. According to the annual report, the combined income of the

ACLU and the ACLU Foundation was roughly $7.7 million in 1977. That was up from $7.4 million in 1976.

Even though total income went up, membership income went down. But it's impossible to assess the possible mitigating impact of the foundation income without knowing what restrictions applied to how that income could be spent. Unfortunately, the ACLU's financial documents do not clearly spell that out. What is clear is that foundation income was not negatively affected by the Skokie crisis. Meanwhile, membership income—the most flexible form of support—was affected by Skokie, but also by other things.

The ACLU's impeachment effort had generated a surge in members. As a memo prepared for the ACLU board in December 1977 put it, "in 1973 . . . the ACLU recruited the largest number of new members in its history, 50,545. In 1974, largely as a result of that success, the ACLU renewed and recruited 170,195 members. This represented the highest total membership figure in ACLU's history although we only recruited 38,000 new members that year."

Such growth proved to be unsustainable. In 1975, the ACLU recruited roughly thirty thousand new members and, as a result, the total membership fell. The next year was only slightly better. And by 1977, when the Skokie crisis hit, the Nixon impeachment boomlet was over. What that meant is that membership income dropped several years in a row, from $3,406,000 in 1974, to $3,368,000 in 1975, to $3,273,000 in 1976. Because the ACLU's method of reporting income was not consistent, it's difficult to know precisely what effect that had on the budget. For instance, the 1977 annual report claims that membership income in 1977 was $3.5 million, "a decline from close to $4 million the previous year." The report also claims that entire decrease was "a direct consequence of our defense of free speech for Nazis in Skokie."

Given the steady decrease in membership following the Nixon boomlet, that claim makes no sense—no matter which numbers are accurate in terms of membership revenue. But without doubt, there was a strong feeling both within and outside the ACLU that the Skokie controversy was devastating. As the *Jewish Week* put it in August 1977, the decision to represent Collin appeared to have resulted "in the most serious crisis in the ACLU's 57-year history."

The distress was deeply felt within the ACLU. In September 1977, Neier sent a memo to his board declaring, "the prospects for 1978 are gloomy. We are not doing well in 1977." He discussed possible cuts and added, "the only thing of which I am certain is that it will be a bad year. Barring some new windfall, or use of the extraordinary bequest we are getting this year, some cuts in operations are inevitable."

Donald Hackel, chairman of the ACLU's Budget, Audit, and Investment Committee, wrote a memo to the board noting that the ACLU had projected an increase in membership income. When Hackel's committee met in November, he revealed, "we discovered that October produced not a further increase but a decline in the renewal rate. . . . It was apparent that we faced nothing short of financial disaster." During the December board meeting, cuts were approved in clerical staff, executive salaries, and travel.

In an interview shortly before his death in 2017, Dorsen confided, "we used to exaggerate" the magnitude of the Skokie crisis. "It was good publicity for us. . . . But in fact, a lot of [members] left for other reasons, . . . [and] there was inefficiency in the membership department."

In addition, said Dorsen, the impact of the Skokie backlash was mitigated not only from the financial influx from the Goldberger letter but by a large, unexpected donation from "some guy from Rochester. I'd never heard of him. I still don't remember his name. . . . When this happened, he sent us a big check. . . . It was maybe 100,000 dollars."

I could find no record of a $100,000 donation from a mysterious man in Rochester. I did locate several references to various bequests, including a forthcoming $200,000 bequest from Idaho and $1,000,000 from Illinois.

Ira Glasser's explanation differs from Dorsen's. "It wasn't that [the income loss] was exaggerated. It *was* a shock. [Skokie] was not the principle underlying cause of the financial decline. . . . But it was a knockout blow." The ACLU's financial operation, he said, "was a house of cards that finally caved in. . . . It wasn't exactly a Ponzi scheme, because nothing nefarious was going on; but it was a kind of shell game."

In April 1978, Neier announced his resignation. In a two-page letter, Neier reviewed his main accomplishments: supporting the civil rights movement in the South, organizing the defense of anti-war protestors, working for "the right to obtain safe and legal abortions," and leading the fight to extend civil liberties protections to millions "confined in prisons, mental hospitals, training schools for children and other" such institutions.

His job, he wrote, enabled him "to try to define a right to privacy, to mobilize our energies to protect it, and to challenge the government's effort to function in secrecy." It also allowed him to "fight against Richard Nixon's abuses of civil liberties and in the effort to limit the powers of the government's intelligence agencies."

He congratulated the ACLU for its handling of the Skokie crisis and pointed out the great growth that had occurred during his tenure. He did not directly address the reasons for his departure, but wrote, "after fifteen years of ACLU employment, the last eight as Executive Director, it will be very refreshing both for the organization and for me personally for a change to take place."

The next day, April 18, the *New York Times* reported Neier's pending departure, pointing out it was not related to the Skokie crisis. In an interview for this book, Neier explained, "I was exhausted. . . . I was very tired of all the fund-raising in which I engaged to support the many special projects I had launched." He would have stepped down sooner, he added, if not for the Skokie crisis. "Once the case was underway, I felt I could not step down because my resignation would have been attributed to the dispute over ACLU representation of the Nazis. . . . Fairly soon after the Skokie case ended, with the ACLU victorious in all the court cases involving Skokie, I announced my resignation."

Neier declared "flatly wrong" author Samuel Walker's assertion that he was "battered" by Skokie: "I enjoyed dealing with the Skokie crisis. . . . It enabled me to spend my time speaking and writing about First Amendment issues that I cared about deeply. It was getting back to the day-to-day grind of raising large numbers of foundation grants that I wished to relinquish."

The ACLU launched a search for his successor. It quickly dawned on Ira Glasser that "if there was going to be a candidate from among the affiliate executive directors, I was going to be it."

For years, the ebullient, casual Glasser and the reserved, formal Neier had been inseparable, but they could not have been more different. Glasser, a third-generation American with family roots in Poland, grew up in East

Flatbush, Brooklyn. His father was a glass worker, or glazier: "That's where our name comes from. I was the first male member of the family going back as far as they could trace in Europe who didn't go into the glass business."

Although his dad had only a fifth-grade education, Glasser showed an early aptitude for math and science. Despite his personal preference for literature and sociology, he was steered toward math. "What can you do with [literature] except teach?" he recalls teachers telling him.

He graduated in 1959 with a mathematics degree from Queens College in New York and got married two weeks later. He ruled out an Ivy League graduate school, since he doubted he could afford to both go to an expensive school and raise a family. He headed to Ohio State University in Columbus, where he was awarded a teaching fellowship and a scholarship covering tuition.

After earning his master's degree, he took a teaching assignment at Queens College as he weighed pursuing a PhD. He loathed his alma mater's rigid approach to teaching and left to take a half-time faculty position at Sarah Lawrence College, known then as a "finishing school for rich young women," recalled Glasser. He enjoyed the work, but it did not pay enough, since his wife, a kindergarten teacher, was pregnant and not working at the time.

Curious about journalism, Glasser wrote letters to various publications. *Current*, a monthly magazine of news and commentary founded in 1959 by activist journalist Sidney Hertzberg, responded. Hertzberg was sufficiently intrigued to grant him an interview.

"He agrees to hire me as associate editor and to let me continue to teach math half-time," said Glasser, who began in fall 1962. Glasser could do much of his *Current* work at home—as it "was all reading and editing extracts."

Aryeh Neier had already been at *Current* for about two years. The two men bonded. As Glasser put it, "He, like I, was married to a woman who was not Jewish and a year-and-a-half, two-years, older than he was; and we both had young sons named David."

Both Neier and Glasser left *Current* in early 1963, during one of *Current*'s periodic financial crises. To supplement his income, Glasser returned to Queens College as a part-time math professor. Shortly thereafter, he was rehired at *Current* and left the Sarah Lawrence job.

During his vacation from *Current* in summer 1964, Glasser worked at the University of Illinois. Shortly thereafter, his boss left *Current* and Glasser found himself de facto editor of the magazine.

By 1966, Glasser had become restless. America was afire with talk of revolution. Glasser craved a deeper level of political engagement and thought Robert Kennedy might offer it.

Despite Senator Kennedy's repeated assertions of support for President Johnson, speculation was rampant he might run. Glasser wrote Kennedy a letter which argued, as he recalls, that "this country needs a person who is not a traditional liberal, not a traditional conservative, who crosses that line and who can speak to white working-class people."

Having grown up with such people, Glasser was convinced that Kennedy could reach them. Getting no response, Glasser reached out to Richard Salinger, whom he had met at Ohio State, and whose older brother, Pierre, had served as John F. Kennedy's press secretary.

Richard Salinger put Glasser in touch with Robert Kennedy's press aide Frank Mankiewicz, who, after much pestering, squeezed Glasser in to talk to Kennedy while the senator got a haircut. Kennedy told Glasser he was not yet ready to run for president but advised him to stay in touch. When he asked Glasser what else he had in mind, Glasser mentioned that his friend Aryeh had recently talked to him about becoming associate director of the NYCLU.

"He says to me, 'You should take that job. . . . The ACLU is a unique organization in American life. . . . It's the only organization that is based on the founding principles of the country, and it's radically so. . . . Yet it operates within the mainstream of American political institutions.'" Glasser got back in touch with Neier, and "he offers me the job subject to the confirmation of the NYCLU executive committee."

In May 1967, Glasser joined the NYCLU and succeeded Neier as its director in 1970. Still, he wasn't sure he wanted to follow Neier into the organization's top job. He had little managerial experience and four children. "And I knew this was going to be a job that makes you travel all over the country."

Ambivalent as he was, Glasser was also ambitious. "I came to understand that if I didn't go for that job, I was making a decision to leave the organization." Glasser became a candidate.

The search committee toyed with the notion of enticing a big name, such as former U.S. Attorney General Ramsey Clark; but in the end the committee nominated Glasser and two members of the national board: Marvin Schachter, an economist and former board president of the Southern California ACLU affiliate, and Monroe Freedman, a Hofstra University law professor and former chair of the National Capital Area Civil Liberties Union. Final selection was set for the September 1978 board meeting.

Campaigning for the job was straightforward. "I knew how to run that campaign because I had run it for Aryeh . . . years earlier," recalled Glasser. His mission was to garner as many votes as possible before the meeting. "By the time the meeting approached, I was pretty confident I was going to win easily."

The board meeting took place at New York's Barbizon Plaza Hotel the weekend of September 23–24. Dorsen reported the ACLU had "almost wholly recouped its financial losses" from the Skokie crisis. Neier pronounced the Goldberger solicitation a success, projecting an additional 42,000 members by the end of the year.

Freedman was no longer in contention. The choice was between Schachter and Glasser. Two board members spoke on behalf of either candidate. Glasser and Schachter were given fifteen minutes each to address the board. Schachter pledged to strengthen the management structure and see that the ACLU maintained a strong, unified national presence. Glasser pledged to fight to end racial discrimination and to deal decisively with various managerial issues. Glasser won by a vote of 60 to 13.

Glasser felt exhilaration as he walked to the lectern. Board members, seated at their tables, rose to congratulate him as he passed. Neier, who was standing near the front of the room, walked over and shook his hand. Despite Neier's choice to resign, "I remember his face looked almost grotesquely bitter," said Glasser. As the two parted, Glasser recalls Neier saying, "My condolences." Reflecting on that moment, Glasser observed, "he and I were the closest associates in the whole organization for many years, but now I was replacing him; and I had been one of these affiliates who criticized the way the place was managed. So there had begun to be some tension between us. It was overwhelmingly sad."

11

Mourning a Founder, Defeating Bork, and Atoning for Internment

At the New York Civil Liberties Union, Glasser had developed an economic model for predicting income based on membership renewal rate. His projections had told him that 1977 and 1978 were going to be rough, and he planned accordingly. The national office had "projected too optimistically based on seat of the pants kind of stuff," said Glasser. "And . . . they got confronted with year-end deficits. And that's what partly plunged the national office into financial crisis."

When he became national executive director in October 1978, said Glasser, he found the membership system "a mess" and the record keeping "anachronistic."

Neier had presided over a period of rapid growth, which had rendered the ACLU's small-time system obsolete: "Everything was in-house. Everything was done by hand. If a reporter asked me, 'How much money does the ACLU . . . raise and spend each year?'" said Glasser, he would have been unable to answer the question.

"There was no fund-raising staff. There was no bequest program." Because so much was structurally lacking, Glasser's immediate priority became administration—not programs. "You think you're a concert violinist [or] a pianist. [Instead] you are an orchestra conductor, and you don't get to play. You deal with program staff, fund-raising," said Glasser.

In his first annual report, Glasser spelled out a vision for the ACLU that focused primarily on expansion and reorganization: "The ACLU for all its growth is today a very uneven organization. Over three-quarters of our total expenditures of $8 million nationally are accounted for by the national office and a literal handful of our larger state affiliates. The remainder is divided among many state affiliates, which struggle along in heroic isolation and under incredibly trying circumstances." Over the next five years, wrote Glasser, "our task is to build a truly national organization, and to develop our resources in as many states as we can."

Little more than a year after taking over, Glasser announced that the ACLU had made up its losses and was on the verge of announcing a major fund-raising campaign.

During the final year of the Carter administration, the ACLU's biggest dispute with the federal government was over Carter's decision to reinstitute the draft in response to Soviet military action in Afghanistan. That proposal prompted, on March 22, 1980, the biggest anti-draft protest in years. Between 22,000 and 30,000 protestors descended on the Ellipse shouting "No war, no way."

The administration planned to register only men, which the ACLU deemed unconstitutional. The ACLU prevailed in federal court. "Complete exclusion of women from the pool of registrants does not serve important governmental objectives," ruled the U.S. Court of Appeals for the Third Circuit.

In June 1981, the Supreme Court overruled that decision 6 to 3. Justice William Rehnquist, writing for the majority, declared, "This is not a case of Congress arbitrarily choosing to burden one of two similarly situated groups. . . . Men and women, because of the combat restrictions on women, are simply not similarly situated for purposes of a draft or registration for a draft."

The ruling was moot. Carter was gone and Ronald Reagan, although pleased with the decision according to his spokesman, was not interested in drafting anyone. The ACLU's focus shifted to the newly emergent religious right.

In August 1979, the *Washington Post* reported on two new Christian organizations: The Moral Majority and Christian Voice. Both, reported the *Post*, aimed "to organize the nation's Christian population into a new and potent political force."

"The churches have been so passive politically for so long that we're losing the nation by default simply by not doing anything," said the Reverend

Richard Zone, chief spokesman for Christian Voice. The new organization's primary goal was to build a juggernaut for conservative policies.

The Moral Majority, organized in June 1979 by televangelist Jerry Falwell, had essentially the same goal. In January 1980, in Lynchburg, Virginia (where he was based), Falwell told a crowd of more than three thousand worshippers, "we're fighting a holy war."

On April 29, a coalition of evangelical leaders drew a crowd of 200,000 to the National Mall for a "Washington for Jesus" rally.

In a "time of crisis in our land," the group had come together to say, "God of our fathers, you will save us," said the Reverend Pat Robertson, founder of the Christian Broadcasting Network. Representatives of twenty mainstream religious organizations criticized the group for trying to "christianize the government." Organizers acknowledged they were for school prayer and against abortion and homosexuality but said they had come to Washington simply to praise God and revive America. "The scream of the great American eagle has become but the twitter of a frightened sparrow," preached the Reverend Adrian Rogers, president of the Southern Baptist Convention.

In December, the ACLU took out a full-page ad in the *New York Times* warning: "If the Moral Majority has its way, You'd Better Start Praying." The ACLU argued that the Moral Majority wanted to force children to pray in school, believed birth control was sinful, thought abortion was wrong and that homosexuality should be punished, and wanted the law to "keep women in their place."

For Glasser, the battle against the Moral Majority was a fight the ACLU could not avoid. "The Moral Majority was formed explicitly to oppose and reverse the advances civil liberties had made in the sixties and seventies," he said. Whereas previously "evangelicals had basically stayed out of politics in any organized way," they were now "seeking to establish what amounted to a theocracy."

Ronald Reagan had courted the religious right. "When I hear the First Amendment used as a reason to keep traditional moral values away from policymaking, I am shocked. The First Amendment was written not to protect the people and their laws from religious values, but to protect those values from government tyranny," he declared in Dallas in August 1980.

Two days after Reagan's inauguration, fifty thousand protesters converged on Washington for a "March for Life," a demonstration in support of a constitutional amendment to protect the unborn. Several of the group's leaders met in the Oval Office with the newly sworn-in president. Richard Schweiker, Reagan's designated Secretary of Health and Human Services, addressed the rally and promised to "work to implement a pro-life policy in the Department of Health and Human Services."

Leery of what appeared to be burgeoning cooperation between the Christian right and the Reagan administration, the ACLU, in fall 1981, announced a series of conferences on threats to civil liberties.

At a news conference to explain the new initiative, John Shattuck, director of the Washington office, criticized pending legislation that would curtail federal judges' authority over school prayer, busing, and abortion. "We don't think the Bill of Rights has been under such severe attack in the political arena in the last three or four decades," he said.

On August 26, 1981, Roger Baldwin died of heart failure at the age of ninety-seven. Many obituaries remembered Baldwin as a recipient of the Presidential Medal of Freedom (awarded the previous year) and as a penny-pinching patrician who paid himself peanuts and expected his staff to settle for the same. "Worthy-cause organizations are always lousy employers, but of all the do-gooders I've worked for, Roger Baldwin was by far the worst," a former employee told the *Boston Globe*. Dorsen and Glasser praised him as "in a way one of our country's founding fathers. They wrote the Constitution and he invented a way to enforce it."

The *New York Times* recalled the impact that listening to Emma Goldman lecture had on a young Baldwin in 1909. "What I heard in that crowded working-class hall," he said, was a "passion and intelligence, a challenge to society I had never heard before." In the years since, said Baldwin, "I have never departed far from the general philosophy" that it should be society's goal "with a minimum of compulsion, [and] a maximum of individual freedom and of voluntary association" to promote "the abolition of exploitation and poverty."

The *New Republic* highlighted the latter part of his life, after he retired as executive director of the ACLU: "He spent the next 30-odd years working . . . indefatigably for human rights throughout the world. He did not hesitate to respond to Douglas MacArthur's invitation to institutionalize civil liberties in occupied Japan. Nor did his vigorous support for

Indian independence and for Nehru's democratic India give him the slightest hesitation in condemning the autocratic excesses of Nehru's daughter. In civil liberties his taste was catholic, his energy limitless."

In October 1982, ACLU published a sixty-four-page report, *Civil Liberties in Reagan's America*, that warned of the danger the Reagan administration posed to civil liberties.

"Never in its 62-year history has the American Civil Liberties Union grappled with a wider range of critical civil liberties issues," asserted Norman Dorsen.

"[The] record of the last two years shows that the most dangerous threats to civil liberties have come and will continue to come not primarily from the religious right, but from the Reagan Administration itself and its allies in Congress," wrote Glasser. He accused the administration of attacking the very constitutional system on which the United States was founded. For the Reagan administration, he concluded, "the erosion of the Bill of Rights seems to be a primary goal, not a side effect."

The report slammed the administration's hostility to the Freedom of Information Act, the Legal Services Corporation, and the Voting Rights Act, and accused it of plotting "to unleash the police and the intelligence agencies from legal limits on their discretion that protect us from their abuses."

Suddenly, it felt "like we're in a twelve-front war," recalled Glasser. "And it was coming at us from all directions."

One of the more important battles in that unexpected war was over renewal of the Voting Rights Act. The law was originally passed in 1965 in the wake of "Black Sunday." In a moving speech, following the brutal assault of Alabama troopers on peaceful voting rights protesters, President Johnson had described the barriers erected to keep blacks from voting in the South: "The Negro citizen may go to register only to be told that the day is wrong, or the hour is late, or the official in charge is absent. And if he persists . . . he may be disqualified because he did not spell out his middle name or because he abbreviated a word on the application. . . . And even a college degree cannot be used to prove that he can read and write."

The Voting Rights Act, signed by President Johnson in August 1965, prohibited racial discrimination in voting practices. It outlawed so-called literacy tests and other measures that unfairly targeted blacks. Section 5, the so-called preclearance provision, mandated that states with a documented history of voter discrimination get approval from the U.S. attorney general before changing voting procedures or districts. That provision was scheduled to expire in August 1982, and the Reagan administration had joined Strom Thurmond, head of the Senate Judiciary Committee, in claiming the act was obsolete since the South no longer discriminated against black voters. The ACLU felt that was nonsense.

In 1981, the Reverend Jesse Jackson's Operation PUSH (People United to Save Humanity) scheduled a rally in Edgefield, South Carolina, Thurmond's home district, to protest his opposition to the Voting Rights Act. Edgefield officials banned the march, calling it a "disgrace to the senator's name."

The ACLU charged prior restraint. A federal judge agreed. The march took place in July 1981. Some two-thousand-plus marchers, escorted by highway patrol cars, walked the route from Strom Thurmond High School to the Edgefield courthouse.

The ACLU was litigating against the voting scheme in Edgefield County. The suit, filed in 1974, focused on the county's failure to seek the required Justice Department approval when it had adopted an "at large" voting system. That system made it impossible, in racially polarized South Carolina, for blacks to get elected to the Edgefield County Council. A federal court had refused to order the county to change its election rules; the Supreme Court was yet to rule.

No black person since the Reconstruction Era had served on the Edgefield County Council. Thurmond insisted racism had nothing to do with that: "There is no discrimination of any kind that exists throughout South Carolina."

The ACLU was concerned not just about events in Edgefield County, but about the Voting Rights Act and the controversial preclearance provision. That battle pitted the nation's civil rights establishment against the leadership of the still-segregated South.

In October 1981, the House voted 389 to 24 to extend the law. House Speaker Thomas P. "Tip" O'Neill called it the "greatest congressional achievement of this century." But the bill's fate in the Senate was uncertain.

For Laura Murphy, who had joined the Washington office of the ACLU in 1979, getting the measure passed was a priority. A member of a prominent Baltimore family whose great-grandfather had founded the *Baltimore Afro-American* newspaper, Murphy had previously worked for two black congressional powerhouses: Parren Mitchell, the first black congressman from Maryland; and Shirley Chisholm, who had run for president in 1972.

"A lot of the coalition did not want to work with the Republicans; but I befriended [Senators] Henry Hyde and James Sensenbrenner. And they ended up voting for the extension," recalled Murphy.

With Murphy's encouragement, the senators came to agree that supporting the measure was good politics. "I think . . . they needed something to counterbalance Reagan's reputation as being against civil rights." They also apparently realized that "majority-minority" districts might geographically limit the impact of the black vote. "So I think there was enlightened self-interest" in their decision to support the law, Murphy said: "Reagan looked like an outlier; so he changed his position."

In June 1982, the bill passed the Senate 85 to 8. In signing the measure, Reagan called the right to vote "the crown jewel of American liberties." The legislation's passage, he said, "proves that differences can be settled in the spirit of good will and good faith."

In February 1984, the Supreme Court found (in *McCain v. Lybrand*) that the Edgefield County voting scheme violated the law. The unanimous decision authored by John Paul Stevens declared, "the purposes of the Act would plainly be subverted if the Attorney General could ever be deemed to have approved a voting change when the proposal was neither properly submitted nor in fact evaluated by him."

That November, the Edgefield Council elected three black members, including Thomas McCain, a named plaintiff in the ACLU's case.

Despite Reagan's grudging acceptance of the Voting Rights Act, three years into his presidency the ACLU remained concerned about his approach to civil liberties and human rights. In a report issued in January 1984, Washington office director John Shattuck charged Reagan with "operating far outside of any national consensus on issues of fundamental justice." He criticized Reagan's "use of raw executive power to pack the Civil Rights Commission" and pronounced the president "at war with the First Amendment."

Shortly after the report's release, Harvard University announced Shattuck's appointment as its new vice president for government and community affairs.

As the ACLU contemplated replacing Shattuck, attention focused on Morton Halperin. With a PhD in international relations from Yale, Halperin had become the founding director of the Center for National Security Studies—an ACLU affiliate—in 1975. He was vaguely famous, as the former National Security Council staffer wiretapped by the Nixon administration who subsequently sued Nixon and Henry Kissinger for approving the surveillance; and he had worked on Daniel Ellsberg's defense team after Ellsberg was charged with violating the Espionage Act by leaking the Pentagon Papers.

At the time, Halperin—not the ACLU's Washington office—was primarily responsible for the ACLU's national security portfolio. "Aryeh said he thought that it was more important for me to focus on that work, which I knew about, than to take on civil rights and all kinds of other issues," said Halperin.

Glasser had considered merging the Center and the ACLU's Washington office. But the ACLU's affirmative action policy meant he could not simply name a white guy to the job. There had to be a search that included candidates of color.

In June 1984, the board appointed an advisory committee to assist in "the affirmative action search." The committee had difficulty finding suitable candidates and, in December, Glasser appointed Halperin acting director. Georgia State Senator Julian Bond was approached about the job but eventually withdrew his candidacy. Shortly thereafter, Roger Wilkins, a black member of the National Advisory Council, resigned from the search committee. Halperin's appointment, said Wilkins, was discouraging minority candidates from applying. Hannah Atkins, a black board member, observed that combining the two Washington jobs had fueled public perception that the search was a sham.

The *New York Times* ran an article in which board member Michael Meyers accused the ACLU of ignoring its own affirmative action policies. The

Times also quoted from Roger Wilkins's letter of resignation from the search committee, in which he accused Glasser of having made "a true affirmative action search impossible."

At the June 1985 board meeting, a motion was made and defeated, 55 to 3, to "instruct the Executive Director to discharge the Director of the Washington Office."

Halperin was concerned about the controversy swirling around him: "I told Ira that if we found a minority candidate or a woman who was qualified to do the job I'd leave quietly. . . . I'd stay as their deputy for a couple years and help them and then leave if that's what they wanted; or I'd stay indefinitely and work with them if that's what they wanted."

At the June board meeting, after the resolution seeking his ouster failed, Halperin was granted permission to speak. He said he had been committed from the beginning to working with a minority candidate if one were appointed, and that he thought the search process had been conducted with integrity. He pledged to follow whatever policies the board set, and to do all within his power to maintain the ACLU's status as the nation's paramount organization fighting for equality and justice.

The ideal "affirmative action" candidate never materialized. Less than a week after the contentious board meeting, the John D. and Catherine T. MacArthur Foundation announced its "MacArthur Fellows." The honor came with tax-free cash grants ranging from $155,000 to $300,000. Halperin was among the winners.

"It meant that I could stop worrying about how I was going to pay off the debt that I was about to incur to put my three sons through college. . . . I was divorced and paying a lot of alimony and living on my salary," Halperin recalled.

Halperin settled in and "acting" was quietly dropped from his title. In July 1987, when Reagan nominated an arch-conservative, former Yale law professor Robert Bork, to replace Justice Lewis F. Powell on the Supreme Court, he became the point man of the opposition.

Despite the ACLU's general policy against opposing high court nominees, Halperin felt an exception had to be made: "Bork's view of the role of the Supreme Court in defending civil liberties and civil rights was so narrow that I thought it was a threat to everything the ACLU stood for. . . . It was clear to me he didn't believe women had any rights in the Constitution." Halperin found his views on privacy and the First Amendment to be equally problematic.

Bork—as the *New York Times* dutifully reminded its readers—had famously argued in an *Indiana Law Journal* article: "Constitutional protection should be accorded only to speech that is explicitly political. There is no basis for judicial intervention to protect any other form of expression, be it scientific, literary or that variety of expression we call obscene or pornographic."

In announcing his nomination, Reagan called Bork "the most prominent and intellectually powerful advocate of judicial restraint." To many others, however, Bork seemed like a wrecking ball aimed at the Constitution. At a special two-day board meeting the weekend of August 29 and 30, the ACLU debated what to do. That necessarily became a debate over Policy 519, which prohibited endorsing or opposing candidates for elective or appointive office.

The policy had been temporarily suspended in 1971 to oppose William Rehnquist. Wasn't Bork just as dangerous?

Halperin believed that the ACLU should weigh in. It had the largest Washington lobbying staff of any public interest organization, he argued, along with a robust roster of affiliates. Many senators, he said, looked to the ACLU for guidance on civil liberties issues. Plus, the ACLU's many press contacts would enable it to launch a major publicity campaign. "There is no doubt that we would make a difference in the fight," he insisted.

Others worried that opposing a nominee—even one as worrisome as Bork—could put the ACLU on a slippery slope toward partisanship.

The board ultimately decided to revise its policy. It also agreed to require a 60 percent supermajority vote to put the organization in opposition, not to get into the business of supporting specific nominees, and only to act if a nominee would "fundamentally jeopardize the Supreme Court's critical and unique role in protecting civil liberties."

The board voted 47 to 16 to amend Policy 519, and the following day it voted, 61 to 3, to oppose Bork.

At a press conference, Dorsen called the Reagan administration description of Bork as a mainstream conservative "absolutely false." Bork "is, in fact, more radical than conservative," said Dorsen, adding, "if Bork's views were to prevail . . . the protection of individual rights would atrophy, and the system of checks and balances that protects such rights would be upset."

The ACLU had prepared a forty-seven-page report documenting Bork's record and views. "We intend to let Judge Bork speak for himself. . . . We intend to ring an alarm bell. There is a grave threat here to the Constitution," Halperin told reporters.

The ACLU position drew fire from the White House. "I think the ACLU has made a serious mistake," said presidential spokesman Marlin Fitzwater.

The hearings began September 15. Former president Gerald Ford defended Bork's firing of special Watergate prosecutor Archibald Cox: "I think in retrospect that history has shown that his performance was in the nation's interest," said Ford. Senate minority leader Bob Dole vouched for Bork as a "man of unquestionable ability and integrity."

Senator Edward Kennedy tossed niceties aside. Bork, he said, "falls short of what Americans demand of a man or woman as a Justice on the Supreme Court. Time and again, in his public record over more than a quarter of a century, Robert Bork has shown that he is hostile to the rule of law and the role of the courts in protecting individual liberty."

Kennedy was just getting warmed up: "It is easy to conclude from the public record of Mr. Bork's published views that he believes women and blacks are second-class citizens under the Constitution. . . . In Robert Bork's America, there is no room at the inn for blacks and no place in the Constitution for women, and in our America there should be no seat on the Supreme Court for Robert Bork."

Kennedy asserted that Bork "has been equally extreme in his opposition to the right to privacy," citing a 1971 article in which "he said, in effect, that a husband and wife have no greater right to privacy . . . than a smokestack has to pollute the air."

Wall Street Journal editorialist Paul Gigot condemned the ferocity of Bork's critics, but also glimpsed a silver lining: "Judge Bork's supporters in the White House believe that all of this helped his cause, that it proved he wasn't, as one put it, 'a neanderthal.'"

Meanwhile, Halperin was conspiring with Senate Judiciary Committee Chief Counsel Mark Gitenstein, with whom he had worked briefly at the ACLU. "We had an idea about how to beat Bork which was different than

Kennedy's and different than the liberals',” said Gitenstein during an interview. The strategy essentially required many normally outspoken members of the progressive coalition to keep their mouths shut.

Normally in such hearings, the views of assorted stakeholders, including those in the public interest community, would be solicited. As Halperin recalls, Gitenstein “came to me and said, 'I don't know how to choose among all these groups. Everybody wants to testify.' . . . I said to him, 'It's simple . . . none of them should testify.'”

Halperin explained, “If these people come to testify, [Senator Alan] Simpson is ready for them. And what he's going to do is show that they have an extreme view of every constitutional principle.” If the progressives were not present, Halperin pointed out, Simpson would have no target.

Norman Dorsen got a call from the committee telling him his testimony was not needed.

He immediately called Halperin and asked, “Is there anything we can do about this?”

Halperin replied, “Norman, I recommended it.”

Dorsen was flabbergasted. “How can you do that? I wanted to testify,” he said.

“No,” responded Halperin—and proceeded to explain how Senator Simpson would twist his views into something embarrassing, objectionable, and misleading beyond recognition: “Let me tell you what your testimony's going to be like. You come in, talk about the Constitution, how wonderful it is, and then Simpson's going to say to you, 'Mr. Dorsen, you believe that a nine-month pregnant woman with a healthy baby is entitled to an abortion and a dead fetus—even over the objection of her husband. Is that correct?' Answer, 'Yes.' 'You believe that there can be no limit on the sale of child pornography even if it is actual video of a child being molested?' 'Yes.'”

“I said, 'That's what your testimony's going to be about. You're going to be asked only yes or no about the most extreme ACLU positions.'

“He said, 'Okay, I get it.'

“A lot of people were very angry at me, but it was clearly the right thing to do,” said Halperin.

The ACLU also compiled a collection of Bork's writings. "We gave one to the . . . staffer for every senator, and we said, 'We only ask one thing, you read this book and call to the attention of your senator the things . . . which we think he ought to understand about what Bork's positions are,'" said Halperin.

In *Matters of Principle*, Gitenstein recalls the tension Halperin's strategy generated: "Molly Yard of the National Organization for Women and Ralph Nader simply would have nothing of the argument. They were certain they could have handled the committee." Gitenstein worried that "with their prickly personalities, it was likely they, not Bork, would become the issue."[1]

Eventually all but NOW and Ralph Nader were on board with the strategy. Gitenstein bluntly told their representatives, "Joe Biden does not think your testimony is necessary because we have carefully structured these hearings so that independent public figures are making all the points you would make in your testimony."

Although the ACLU didn't testify, it submitted a fifty-eight-page statement and analysis of Bork's record and testimony, which was included in the hearing record.

The document argued that Bork was hostile to prevailing legal sentiment regarding privacy rights, limits of executive power, and the "the equal protection clause in race and sex discrimination cases." And it criticized his philosophy of "original intent," which undergirded his view that rights "not specifically enumerated in the Constitution" did not exist.

"Judge Bork, despite obfuscation and apparent recantation, remains a radical jurist with an extreme philosophy which would seriously alter the role of the Supreme Court in protecting civil rights and liberties," argued the ACLU.

The ACLU also produced a list of landmark Supreme Court decision Bork had rejected, including decisions that struck down a statute making it a crime for married couples to use contraceptives, barred enforcement of racially restrictive covenants, protected illegitimate children against arbitrary discrimination, protected the use of obscene language for political purposes, struck down state abortion laws, forbade sterilization of habitual criminals, struck down poll taxes and literacy tests, and prohibited mandated prayer in public schools.

"As Judge Bork interprets the Constitution few rights are shielded from the majority's judgments," argued the ACLU, concluding, "Judge Bork may well have strong intellectual credentials, but that is not enough."

In late October, Bork told Alan Simpson that he had enough of the battle and thought it was time to call the vote. "He has no desire to protract or prolong this," Simpson declared. By that time, Bork's allies had realized they were in a losing fight. Fifty-five senators were on record against Bork. The result was "a foregone conclusion, and much of the second day of debate consisted of warnings from the administration's supporters about the battle over the nominee who would follow," reported *Newsday*.

Shortly before the vote on October 23, Senator Pete Domenici of New Mexico addressed his colleagues from the floor. He lauded Bork as a "brilliant and provocative legal scholar." Yet, he observed, "Robert Bork is about to become a footnote in history. . . . This Senator is convinced that the Senate has just participated in a process that has added a new verb to our language: 'to Bork,' which means to destroy by innuendo or distortion. Judge Bork got borked."

Senator Howell Heflin explained why he had gone from undecided to opposed: "Judge Bork testified for four and a half days. . . . I read many of his opinions as well as his speeches and other writings. . . . I do not question Judge Bork's strong belief in the Constitution. I question his rigid adherence to a judicial philosophy that seems to ignore compassion for the individual embodied in the Constitution."

The vote was 58 to 42 against: "the largest margin ever of the 27 times, over 200 years, that the Senate has rejected Supreme Court nominations," reported the *New York Times*.

Reagan responded defiantly. "My next nominee for the court will share Judge Bork's belief in judicial restraint," he declared. "If we receive a nominee who thinks like Judge Bork, who acts like Judge Bork, who opposes civil rights and civil liberties like Judge Bork, he will be rejected like Judge Bork," responded Kennedy.

In describing the Bork fight in the ACLU's annual report, Glasser called it "perhaps the most significant civil liberties battle of the past two years."

In an interview years after the vote, Glasser endeavored to explain what made the Bork battle unique: "Bork was different than any other person nominated for the Supreme Court . . . because he took the position that the Bill of Rights could be overcome by legislation."

On October 29, Reagan nominated Douglas H. Ginsburg. A Washington, DC, appeals court judge and a former Harvard Law School professor, Ginsburg, 41, had virtually no paper trail and less than a year of experience on the bench. He received the lowest acceptable rating ("qualified") from the American Bar Association. After information surfaced about his use of marijuana while a professor at Harvard, Ginsburg withdrew.

Reagan's next pick was Anthony Kennedy, 51, a Harvard Law School graduate and U.S. Court of Appeals judge from Sacramento. In announcing his nomination, Reagan asked for "cooperation and bipartisanship" during the confirmation process. "The experience of the last several months has made all of us a bit wiser," he added. Kennedy was confirmed unanimously in February 1988.

The 1980s saw a reckoning, of sorts, for the agony imposed on Japanese Americans during World War II. That was due largely to the efforts of Peter Irons. While doing archival research, Irons—a lawyer, historian, and former ACLU board member—discovered that the U.S. government had buried information that refuted allegations Japanese Americans comprised an internal security threat. That unethical behavior, concluded Irons, might offer a legal path to justice (via the so-called *coram nobis* petition process) for Japanese Americans convicted of violating the wartime rules.

Irons persuaded Gordon Hirabayashi, Minoru Yasui, and Fred Korematsu to press for exoneration. Working with Irons and other lawyers, the men filed petitions in February 1983 to vacate their convictions. "The . . . evidence for reversing these convictions comes from the government's own files. Records show that the efforts of government lawyers who objected to the suppression of evidence were rejected," observed Irons.

Dale Minami, another attorney on the case, acknowledged the role of "wartime hysteria" in the internment decisions. "But this case reveals that the internment was also a product of calculated and cynical decisions on the part of high officials to uphold the evacuation almost at any cost—even if it meant lying to the Supreme Court."

In October 1983, government lawyers moved to vacate the men's convictions for violating military orders (because "we believe that it is time to put behind us the controversy which led to the mass evacuation"). The government refused, however, to admit wrongdoing.

Korematsu was underwhelmed. "I still remember 40 years ago when I was shackled and put in prison . . . being an American citizen didn't mean a thing. It's about time they came around," he told reporters.

Writing in the *UCLA Law Review*, Jerry Kang observed, "the reality is that, regarding the Judiciary, we do not have acceptance of responsibility; we have supreme denial."[2]

The three plaintiffs, intent on forcing the government to admit fault, pressed ahead with their cases. In November 1983, federal district Judge Marilyn Hall Patel in San Francisco ruled in Korematsu's favor. She pronounced the internment illegal and asserted that the policy had been based on racism, distortions, fabricated intelligence, false perceptions, and lies.

"What happened 40 years ago involved my family and my personal life, and I had to do some real deep thinking in order to reopen this case again. I am very happy I did," said Korematsu.

Gordon Hirabayashi's vindication came in 1987. That September, a three-judge panel of the Ninth Circuit Court of Appeals in Seattle ruled that he had been wrongly convicted. Hirabayashi, then sixty-nine, hailed the decision as "very good news" but lamented the failure of the U.S. Supreme Court to condemn internment.

In November 1986, following surgery for cancer, Minoru Yasui died in Denver at the age of seventy. The Justice Department asked the U.S. Court of Appeals to declare his case legally moot. At a memorial service for him that December, friends and relatives called for its continuation. Neither the court of appeals nor the U.S. Supreme Court opted to rule on the merits of Yasui's petition.

The high court similarly avoided ruling in another high-profile internment case. This 1987 case (*United States v. Hohri*) revolved around nineteen Japanese Americans interned during the war. Plaintiffs charged the government with some twenty-two counts of taking property without just compensation and sought $10,000 per detainee per count.

An ACLU friend of the court brief argued that (because of the "acts of concealment by the War Department" uncovered by Peter Irons), the

Supreme Court should have paused the statute of limitations on the claims. That June, the Supreme Court "sidestepped a ruling" (as the *Los Angeles Times* put it) on whether the Japanese Americans were deserving of compensation. Instead it handed the case back to the U.S. Circuit Court of Appeals to rule on whether the six-year statute of limitations had run out. In May 1988, the appeals court dismissed the suit because the statute of limitations had run out. In November 1988, the U.S. Supreme Court agreed.

"I'm severely disappointed. The decision is very much like death," admitted William Hohri, the named plaintiff. Nonetheless, the case became, in the words of one activist, "the hammer over the heads of Congress" driving consideration of a reparations bill.

Hohri, president of the National Council for Japanese American Redress, had testified on behalf of the bill the previous June. During those hearings, Wade Henderson of the ACLU's Washington office noted Congress had awarded millions to demonstrators detained during anti–Vietnam War protests: "Can we do less for victims of so massive an injustice as the wartime internment?"

Reagan signed the Civil Liberties Act of 1988 on August 10. The bill apologized for the policies that had forced some 120,000 Japanese Americans from their homes and set up a $1.25 billion trust fund to provide $20,000 tax-deductible payments to those deemed eligible. Those accepting the money were required to drop all legal claims against the government.

Rep. Norman Mineta, a camp survivor and prime sponsor of the bill, said the government's apology would erase "the unwarranted stigma of disloyalty which clings to us to this day."

As Reagan gave his blessing to victims of wartime internment, George H.W. Bush, his vice president and designated successor, was preparing to be nominated as the 1988 Republican presidential candidate. In his acceptance speech on August 17, Bush defined the election as a battle for "the beliefs we share, the values we honor, the principles we hold dear."

Bush came out for the Pledge of Allegiance, prayer in school, the death penalty, and gun ownership and against abortion. Many of his positions—though popular with the Republican base—conflicted with those of the

ACLU, which presumably contributed to Bush's decision to highlight his opponent's connection to an organization many Americans considered radical.

At an event in Milwaukee, after noting that Massachusetts governor Michael Dukakis belonged to the ACLU, Bush added, "Most of the time, I
disagree with them."

ACLU officials were ambivalent about Bush's attacks. Glasser saw them
as a form of "McCarthyite" slander. But they also significantly raised the
ACLU's visibility, which led Glasser to roll out new fund-raising letters
and ad campaigns to capitalize on the Bush-driven controversy. The intent
was to clarify the ACLU's positions—not simply defend a handful of positions easily attacked by Bush.

Leading up to the first presidential debate in September 1988, most polls
showed Bush to be slightly ahead of Dukakis. But his lead "was not only
small, it was also shaky," explained the *Chicago Tribune* (citing a poll by Peter D. Hart Research Associates). Bush hoped attacking the ACLU would
change that.

In his opening statement, Bush bemoaned the "deterioration" of American values. For the next half hour or so, the candidates wrangled over the
drug problem, the federal deficit, tax policy, health insurance, and who was
the better leader. Finally, an interviewer gave Bush the hoped-for opening
by asking: "What is so wrong with the governor being a member of an
organization which has come to the defense of, among other people, Colonel Oliver North?" North, a hero of the far right, had been indicted for
his involvement in the Iran-Contra scandal.

Bush was prepared: "Nothing's wrong with it," he said, "but . . . I don't
agree with a lot of . . . the positions of the ACLU. I don't want my ten-
year-old grandchild to go into an X-rated movie. . . . I don't think they're
right to try to take the tax exemption away from the Catholic Church. I
don't want to see . . . kiddie pornographic laws repealed. I don't want to see
'under God' come out from our currency. Now, these are all positions of
the ACLU. And I don't agree with them."

Pollsters for ABC News found a plurality of watchers (44 percent to
36 percent) judged Dukakis the debate winner. CBS News polls ranked
Bush the victor (42 percent to 39 percent), and Gallup found them essentially tied. The ACLU, however, emerged as an unambiguous beneficiary.

"We've been getting hundreds of calls from people who want to be members. A lot of them are asking for membership cards so they can also be card-carrying members," Dorsen told the *New York Times*.

Bush won decisively on November 8.

At the December ACLU board meeting, Glasser reported that Bush's attacks had been a godsend. Roughly $400,000 had been raised through a special appeal to members; and new members were joining at an accelerated pace. But outside its circle of supporters, he warned, the ACLU's reputation may have suffered. Many Americans had first heard of the ACLU through Bush; the ACLU planned to execute a public relations campaign aimed at correcting any lingering misperceptions.

The first test of Bush's Supreme Court inclinations came with the retirement, in July 1990, of William Brennan, appointed by Dwight Eisenhower in 1956. Brennan, eighty-four, had recently suffered a small stroke. The "strenuous demands of court work and its related duties required or expected of a justice appear at this time to be incompatible with my advancing age and medical condition," wrote Brennan.

Upon learning of the retirement, Senator Edward Kennedy released a statement: "Justice Brennan's America is the kinder, gentler nation of which President Bush has eloquently spoken," he said. "I urge the president to nominate a successor worthy of that vision."

On July 25, Bush nominated U.S. Court of Appeals Judge David Souter. The predominant reaction was "David who?"

Justice Thurgood Marshall told TV journalist Sam Donaldson that neither he nor Brennan had "ever heard of this man." He added, "I just don't understand what [Bush] is doing." *Washington Post* columnist Richard Cohen commented that Souter, "at age 50, seems to have burst from a cocoon. His views on just about anything are not known." *Wall Street Journal* writer Paul Gigot called Souter "a stealth candidate." Bush acknowledged Souter was "not the most well-known figure in the country" but predicted he easily would win confirmation.

When Souter appeared before the Senate Judiciary Committee, Kennedy noted that Souter had taken some "troubling positions." He had called abortion the "killing of unborn children" and ordered flags on state buildings lowered to half-mast on Good Friday. But those positions, acknowledged

Kennedy, "were taken by Judge Souter while serving in the New Hampshire Attorney General's Office . . . and the views that he expressed as the State's lawyer are not necessarily his own."

The coalition that had fervently opposed Bork took a wait-and-see position toward Souter. Although most liberal groups ended up opposing him, they didn't turn that opposition into a major campaign. The ACLU never officially took a position.

The ACLU worked up an extensive report on his record, but the executive committee found no basis for opposing him.

On October 2, Souter was confirmed by a vote of 90 to 9. After the vote, Kennedy, who was one of the nine who had voted against him, observed, "The Senate is still in the dark about this nomination. The lesson of the past decade . . . is that we must vote our fears, not our hopes."

The second vacancy Bush would fill was created June 27, 1991, when Thurgood Marshall, at eighty-two, announced he would leave once his replacement was confirmed. The court's demands were incompatible with his "advancing age and medical condition," wrote Marshall, in a letter virtually identical to the one penned by his friend William Brennan.

At a press conference the day after his announcement, Marshall echoed a reporter's question: "What's wrong with me?" He responded, "I'm getting old and falling apart." Asked whether Bush should name someone black as his successor, he replied, "[There's] no difference between a white snake and a black snake. They'll both bite."

Marshall had become the court's first black justice when appointed by Lyndon Johnson in 1967. The White House acknowledged that Bush felt obliged to choose someone black. Speculation focused early on Clarence Thomas, forty-three, a Yale Law graduate and former head of the U.S. Equal Employment Opportunity Commission (EEOC) who had been named to the U.S. Circuit Court of Appeals in Washington, DC, the previous year.

In announcing Thomas as his choice on July 1, Bush insisted that his race was not a factor: "He is the best qualified at this time, the best man for the job on the merits."

Paul Weyrich, head of a conservative group calling itself Coalitions for America, pronounced Thomas a "brilliant jurist." But others had doubts.

Arthur Kropp, president of the People for the American Way Action Fund, criticized Thomas's "dismal record on civil rights" and added, "I can hardly imagine a more troubling choice." The press noted that in more than fifty decisions on criminal matters, Judge Thomas had always sided with prosecutors.

The NAACP deferred taking a position until after its forthcoming annual convention. Executive Director Benjamin Hooks suggested that perhaps Thomas's climb up from poverty in Pinpoint, Georgia, had sensitized him to the discrimination faced by poor minorities. The NAACP met in Houston shortly after Thomas's nomination. Delegates, unable to decide whether to support him, asked for a meeting. The meeting never took place.

At the end of July, both the NAACP and the AFL-CIO announced they would oppose the nominee. "While we appreciate the fact that Judge Thomas . . . pulled himself up by his own bootstraps . . . we are concerned about his insensitivity to giving those who may not have any bootstraps the [same] opportunity," said NAACP chairman William F. Gibson. The Congressional Black Caucus criticized Thomas's "blind commitment to an ideology which has caused him to misinterpret, misconstrue or ignore statutory laws with which he disagrees." The National Urban League, People for the American Way, and the National Organization of Women also opposed him.

The ACLU was quiet. Ramona Ripston, head of the Southern California affiliate, joined the American Jewish Congress, Planned Parenthood, and several other public interest groups in denouncing the Thomas nomination. Meanwhile, the national office debated whether his record was troubling enough to meet the standard required by the revised Policy 509.

The ACLU commissioned a group of Washington lawyers to pore through Thomas's rulings and writings. ACLU staffers and board members contributed their own analyses and opinions. "While our research is far from complete, there appears to be growing evidence that Judge Thomas has not previously exhibited much concern for civil liberties and civil rights," wrote Nadine Strossen, an outspoken Harvard Law graduate and New York Law School professor who had been elected ACLU board president earlier that year.

In a July 31 memo, board members James Ferguson, Meg Gale, and Gara LaMarche made their case against Thomas. They cited his views on abortion, affirmative action, criminal justice, separation of power, separation of church and state, and his adherence to a "natural law" philosophy that seemed rooted in religious beliefs. They also noted that, during his tenure, the proportion of discrimination lawsuits the EEOC found lacking in merit doubled.

The ninety-two-page analysis produced by the Washington lawyers engaged by the ACLU noted that Thomas had attacked the landmark *Brown v. Board of Education* desegregation decision for having been decided on "sentiment" rather than "reason." The lawyers also noted that his belief in individual rather than group rights led him to reject claims of group discrimination. They tried to make sense of his embrace of "natural law" and suggested the doctrine might lead him to believe in the right of a fetus to be born.

With memos and arguments flying back and forth, and amidst growing concern about Thomas, the ACLU moved up the date of its fall board meeting, from October to August 17. Before that meeting, Glasser sent out a memo arguing that, bad as Thomas might be, he was no Robert Bork. Glasser pointed out that even though Thomas rejected many ACLU positions, his views were not inherently hostile to the Constitution. It was likely, conceded Glasser, that his appointment would "further solidify the [conservative] majority. . . . But if such were sufficient to justify our opposition to Thomas, then almost certainly we would be compelled to oppose most, if not all candidates that President Bush would likely nominate in his stead."

The ACLU agreed that Thomas threatened many ACLU ideals and puzzled over the meaning of his allegiance to natural rights but struggled with whether they could condemn him without violating Policy 519.

A majority voted to oppose Thomas. But the 36 to 25 tally left them one vote (and less than 1 percent) short of the 60 percent supermajority required for official opposition. The board thereupon accepted unanimously a resolution offered by Michael Meyers to "remain neutral in this battle." The resolution noted that Thomas's record "raises important questions about his commitment to civil liberties and civil rights that the Senate must examine thoroughly."

Nearly two months later, on October 11, Yale Law School graduate and University of Oklahoma law professor Anita Hill appeared before the

Senate Judiciary Committee. The youngest of thirteen children raised on a farm in Okmulgee County, Oklahoma, Hill had worked as an assistant to Thomas at the EEOC.

Acutely aware of the incendiary subject matter before the committee, Chairman Joe Biden warned those in attendance, "if there is not absolute order and decorum in here, we will recess the hearing and those who engage in any outburst at all will be asked to leave the committee room."

Biden acknowledged an awkward reality. "I know there are many people watching today who suspect we never will understand, but fairness means doing our best to understand, no matter what we do or do not believe about the specific charges."

Thomas, the first witness, explained that his mission was "to clear my name today." He "categorically" denied all allegations against him and specifically denied "that I ever attempted to date Anita Hill."

Later they heard from Hill, who testified that after being hired as Thomas's assistant at the Department of Education, he persisted in asking her out despite her repeated refusal of his overtures. She said he also insisted on talking about penises, bestiality, and his sexual prowess. In time, the offensive behavior stopped, and "I began both to believe and hope that our working relationship could be a proper, cordial, and professional one."

When he was appointed EEOC chairman, he offered her a job. She accepted and eventually the sexual overtures resumed, she testified. Finally, she quit. During her last day on the job, said Hill, Thomas told her that if she ever exposed him "it would ruin his career. This was not an apology."

When Thomas returned to the hearing room, he denied Hill's allegations "unequivocally" and "uncategorically." He denounced the hearing as a "travesty" and asked how committee members would feel if they were assailed with such "sleaze" and "dirt." He called the proceeding "a national disgrace," and then pronounced the words that drew gasps around the nation: "From my standpoint, as a black American [this] is a high-tech lynching for uppity blacks who in any way deign to think for themselves, to do for themselves, to have different ideas; and it is a message that, unless you kowtow to an old order, this is what will happen to you. You will be lynched, destroyed, caricatured by a committee of the U.S. Senate rather than hung from a tree."

On Sunday, the committee heard from perhaps the most curious panel of the proceedings, made up of current and former EEOC staffers: J.C. Alvarez, a Chicago businesswoman and single parent; Nancy Fitch, a historian trained at the University of Michigan; Diane Holt, an EEOC management analyst, and Phyllis Berry-Myers, Thomas's former assistant.

Their role was to destroy Hill's credibility, with Senator Orrin Hatch playing straight man. Hatch led the panel through the following exchange:

"If you had a young daughter in her early twenties, would you want her to work with Judge Thomas?"

Alvarez: "Absolutely. Absolutely."

"From your experience of working with Professor Hill and Judge Thomas at the EEOC, did Professor Hill think that she had some sort of a special relationship with Judge Thomas?"

Alvarez: "Yes, she used to give that impression . . . that was something she always sort of held out in front of everyone at the staff, that she had this sort of inside track to him."

"How could she have testified the way she did here?"

Fitch: "Senator, to me it was incredible . . . I was dumbstruck. I have no idea."

Holt: "I have no idea, senator."

"Do any of you believe her testimony here?"

Holt: "I do not believe a word."

Fitch: "Senator, I don't believe it, either."

"How about you, Ms. Myers?"

Myers: ". . . I can imagine she probably would say anything."

"What do you think of those comments made by her attributed to him and his comments back about those comments?"

Fitch: "As a historian, I know those comments to be stereotypical."

"Why would you think she would say that?"

Fitch: "Senator, I have no idea . . . but they are certainly kind of pat formulaic statements that people have historically made about black men in this country."

"Don't they play on white prejudices about black men?"

Fitch: "Of course they do, senator."

Riveted as much of the nation was by the drama, the ACLU's position on Thomas remained unchanged. Years later, Strossen recalled that although Hill's testimony was discussed by the ACLU leadership, "the ACLU criteria for potentially opposing a Supreme Court nominee . . . would not have been affected by Hill's testimony."

On October 15, Thomas was confirmed by a 52 to 48 vote. He appeared before reporters waiting in the rain outside his suburban home and said, "This is more a time for healing, not a time for anger or for animus or animosity."

The next Supreme Court nominee came with none of the drama that accompanied Thomas or Bork. After working his way through an initial list of fifty candidates reviewed by some seventy-five volunteer lawyers, President Bill Clinton settled on Ruth Bader Ginsburg, sixty, as his choice to fill the seat vacated by the retiring Byron White. He introduced her to the public on Monday, June 14, 1993, at a Rose Garden press briefing.

"Throughout her life, she has repeatedly stood for the individual, the person less well-off, the outsider in society, and has given those people greater hope by telling [them] that they have a place in our legal system, by giving them a sense that the Constitution and the laws protect all the American people, not simply the powerful," said Clinton.

He said she was neither liberal nor conservative: "She's proved herself too thoughtful for such labels."

In her remarks, Bader Ginsburg recalled that her law school class of over five hundred students had fewer than ten women. She spoke of her daughter who, in her high school yearbook, had written that her ambition "was to see her mother appointed to the Supreme Court." She also paid tribute to her own mother, who had died years ago: "I pray that I may be all that she would have been had she lived in an age when women could aspire and achieve, and daughters are cherished as much as sons."

Although Bader Ginsburg was well known to the ACLU, she had spent her last thirteen years on the U.S. Court of Appeals for the DC Circuit. She was no longer the ACLU crusader she had once been. She was widely seen as a moderate—a "healer," in Clinton's words.

In keeping with its custom, the ACLU commissioned a lengthy analysis of Bader Ginsburg's civil rights and civil liberties record. The outside experts described her as a cautious judge, respectful of precedent who continued to show "sensitivity to discrimination issues involving gender." They found her record "more ambiguous" on gay rights than on other rights issues but concluded she "reflects a thoughtful and sympathetic consideration of many issues of concern to the civil liberties community. . . . Her record reflects her unwillingness to be labelled or to adhere to an agenda."

During her first day of hearings, Judiciary Committee Chairman Biden observed that they had not made the front page of the *New York Times,* "which was the most wonderful thing that has happened to me since I have been chairman of this committee."

In fact, the article was on page A15, under the headline "High Court Nominee Faces Easy Road Through Senate." The *Times* noted that if confirmed, "as widely expected," Bader Ginsburg would become the second woman on the court, joining Sandra Day O'Connor, and the first Jewish member since Abe Fortas.

The front page that day happened to be devoted to Clinton's "Gay Troop Plan," which became known as "Don't ask, don't tell." The new guidelines, reported the *Times*, were supposedly "strict enough to force homosexuals to remain discreet but loose enough to allow a discreet homosexual to live his or her life without harassment."

On July 29, the Senate Judiciary Committee endorsed Bader Ginsburg unanimously. The following Tuesday, the Senate voted 96 to 3 to confirm her—making her the first Democratic appointment since Thurgood Marshall's confirmation in 1968.

While Bader Ginsburg's elevation was close to a non-event for the ACLU, it marked the end of what the ACLU had seen as an unrelenting war on civil liberties. Reagan's election had ushered in, it said, "the most dangerous times for civil liberties since the founding of the ACLU." And the Bush years had brought home the fact that "the Supreme Court and other federal courts are no longer our allies in the fight for civil liberties." With Clinton in office, the ACLU view was not so bleak. Nonetheless, the ACLU still saw a multitude of threats to civil liberties and democracy and much to criticize in the Clinton administration, including its approach to criminal justice.

Retribution-based policies fueled by race-based fears defined, in large measure, the Clinton approach to crime. The so-called Violent Crime

Control and Law Enforcement Act, signed by Clinton in September 1994, provided billions for new prisons and police officers, expanded the reach of the federal death penalty, eliminated college education grants for inmates, stiffened penalties for repeat offenders, and generally sought to make life tougher for those committing (or presumed likely to commit) crimes.

At the signing ceremony for the crime bill at the White House, Clinton was accompanied by police officials, patriotic music, and assorted politicians as he declared, "Let us roll up our sleeves to roll back this awful tide of violence and reduce crime in this country. We have the tools now. Let us get about the business of using them."

But Republicans wanted even tougher policies. Led by House Minority Whip Newt Gingrich, the 1994 mid-term elections became a referendum on the Republican Party's "Contract with America." That contract promised to toughen criminal penalties, cut welfare, and eviscerate product liability laws.

The election gave the Republican Party control of both houses of Congress. Egged on by so-called experts peddling fear, Republicans moved to toughen already toughened laws. In testimony before the Senate Judiciary Committee in February 1995, John J. Dilulio Jr., a professor at Princeton University, claimed the "murder rate for black males between the ages of 14 and 22" had tripled in six years and predicted a crime wave: "Between now and the year 2000 . . . we are going to have another 500,000 males in the population between the ages of 14 and 17."

James Q. Wilson, a professor of management at UCLA, also warned of the impending crime wave. "There are going to be a lot more robbers and muggers on the streets."

The projections proved wildly off the mark. Instead of rising, violent crime dropped over the next several years. The Bureau of Justice Statistics' National Crime Victimization Survey for 2000 concluded that America was experiencing "the lowest rates of violent crime recorded since the inception of the NCVS in 1973." Although the academicians making scary predictions lacked a functioning crystal ball, their view that a black youth crime wave was imminent was still driving policy.

One element of the Republicans' Contract with America, the so-called "Taking Back Our Streets Act," aimed to toughen sentencing provisions and make it more difficult for prisoners to sue.

In hearings on the Taking Back Our Streets bill in 1995, congressmen heard from Philadelphia police detective Patrick Boyle. A twenty-eight-year veteran of the department, Boyle talked about his son, Daniel Boyle, who became a cop after a childhood spent idolizing his father. In 1991, "Danny stopped this vehicle in north Philadelphia. Before he could stop his car, the operator of the vehicle jumped out and began firing a nine-millimeter semiautomatic weapon at Danny. One of the 13 or 14 shots went through the right passenger window and struck him in the right temple. . . . Danny died of his wounds on February 6, 1991. He was 21 years old."

The killer was sentenced to death. The presiding judge stated "this senseless murder should never have happened. Danny should never have been a victim of this homicide because the individual who committed this" act was a beneficiary of the "prison cap," which mandated releasing prisoners to reduce overcrowding. "I attribute Danny's death as a direct result of this prison cap," said Boyle.

Alvin Bronstein, executive director of the ACLU's National Prison Project, addressed the committee after Boyle.

"I am the father of five children and have three grandchildren. Two of my daughters have been the victims of rather nasty muggings, one in the city of Philadelphia, one in the city of Boston. I felt anger and pain, not anywhere near what you felt given the loss of Danny," said Bronstein. "I just want you to know I really feel for you."

Bronstein then confessed confusion concerning the relevance of the preceding testimony, "because I thought we were here to talk about" another bill altogether, "which has nothing to do with prison caps" but with "so-called frivolous prisoner lawsuits." He argued that the proposal to curtail such lawsuits was not just unnecessary but would trap prisoners in hellish conditions. And he proceeded to tell a story about his client, Keith Hudson, who "had been in prison illegally for five years."

During the period of Hudson's illegal imprisonment in Louisiana, he was forced to wash his clothes in his toilet because he was not permitted to use the prison laundry. His complaints about his treatment resulted in a dispute with two burly sergeants who shackled him with a waist chain and handcuffs at 2 a.m. and took him to an isolated corridor. "Then, in the sight of a lieutenant who stood by, they beat him up."

Hudson filed a lawsuit about that incident himself. "[He] could have been prevented from having a day in court by this legislation," Bronstein said. "The prisoner is a citizen, has certain rights. . . . Let us not march back. That is what this legislation does. . . . It marches us back to the 19th century."

Nineteen-ninety-five was the year of the Oklahoma City bombing. On April 19, just after 9 a.m., a truck packed with explosives destroyed the Alfred P. Murray Federal Building in downtown Oklahoma City, killing some 168 persons and injuring nearly 700 more. Army veteran and security guard Timothy McVeigh was convicted of the murders, along with fellow army veteran Terry Nichols, who was accused of helping to make the bomb.

Days after the attack, House Judiciary Committee Chairman Henry Hyde promised to move legislation that was "adequate, effective and within the parameters of the Constitution." The Clinton administration got behind a proposal by Congressman Charles Schumer that would prohibit fundraising for groups considered dangerous and ease deportation of residents "certified" as having terrorist links. "I think this bill will move like lightning through Congress," said Schumer.

Gregory Nojeim, legislative counsel for the ACLU, pointed out that the bill was constitutionally problematic, as it essentially eliminated the right to "confront and respond to the evidence the government has." He cautioned against rushing legislation through in the heat of anger.

At a hearing that spring, Senator Arlen Specter worried about "the incursion on First Amendment freedoms of association of having someone on a terrorism list without having an adjudication and . . . the right of confrontation." The ACLU and other groups, he added, had raised such concerns "which we will explore in greater detail before coming to judgment."

Donald M. Haines, testifying for the ACLU, strongly opposed "virtually every one of the electronic surveillance and intelligence gathering proposals presented by the administration." They had nothing to do with the events of Oklahoma City, nor would they make anyone safer, he said: "We hope that no one, in the administration or in the Congress, will use the trauma and grief of Oklahoma City to advance legislative interests unrelated to that incident."

Even as it battled to avoid a repeat of the fear-driven legislative sins of an earlier age, the ACLU continued its fight in the voting rights arena. It bemoaned two 1996 Supreme Court decisions—*Shaw v. Hunt* and *Bush v. Vera*—that struck down so-called majority-minority voting districts (drawn to give black voters a better shot at electing black representatives). As a result of the decisions, Congress would become whiter "at a time that the nation is becoming increasingly diverse," argued Loughlin McDonald, director of the ACLU's Southern Regional Office,

The ACLU also took on the Communications Decency Act, legislation born out of anxiety about young people viewing internet porn.

In 1995, Senator Charles Grassley had presided over what he called "the first congressional hearing on the topic of pornography in cyberspace." In his opening statement, Grassley talked of playgrounds becoming "hunting grounds for child molesters" as the incidence of teenage pregnancy rose. A cause of both, in his view, was internet pornography.

To combat it, he introduced the "Protecting Children from Computer Pornography Act." The law, he said, would "punish those in the computer communications industry who knowingly transmit indecent pornography to children or who willfully aid and abet such activity."

Some of the research Grassley cited was fraudulent and deeply flawed. His proposal fizzled. But the Communications Decency Act, championed by Senators James Exon of Nebraska and Slade Gorton of Washington, moved ahead. The bill, approved 84 to 16 by the Senate in June 1995, prohibited knowingly using computer technology to show minors "any comment, request, suggestion, proposal, image, or other communication that, in context, depicts or describes, in terms patently offensive as measured by contemporary community standards, sexual or excretory activities or organs."

The measure did not follow the usual route through the House. Instead, as Congresswoman Anna Eshoo, a California democrat, later complained, it was "slipped in," or incorporated into, the Telecommunications Act of 1996 during the House-Senate conference committee. Also slipped in was a provision by Congressman Henry Hyde that banned using computers "to provide information about how to obtain an abortion," reported the AP.

The Telecommunications Act, which deregulated the telecommunications industry (clearing the way for the so-called Baby Bells to merge with each other and with AT&T and other long-distance carriers), cleared Congress on February 1, 1986. Clinton signed it a week later.

Federal Communications Commission chairman Reed Hundt compared the new legislation to the removal of the Berlin Wall. "The gloves are off and we are now free to take on the monopolies head-on," said MCI executive Nate Davis.

But many techies did not join the celebration. "All across cyberspace, Internet users were voicing strong objections to a law they believe will destroy their most prized possession, the freedom of uncensored information," reported the *Chicago Tribune*.

Stefan Presser, legal director of the Pennsylvania ACLU, accused Congress of having criminalized "indecent speech sent by the Internet" without even bothering "to define what indecent speech is." Christopher Hansen, ACLU senior staff counsel, added that the law would block all "socially useful, nonpornographic speech that happens to be about sex."

The day Clinton signed the measure, the ACLU, joined by some twenty organizations, filed suit in federal district court in Philadelphia requesting an order temporarily prohibiting enforcement of the Decency Act provisions. A week later, Judge Buckwalter granted the order and a three-judge panel was convened to hear the case,

The trial before the panel began March 21, and closing arguments were heard May 10. On June 12, the judges ruled unanimously for the ACLU.

"As the most participatory form of mass speech yet developed, the Internet deserves the highest protection from government intrusion," declared the panel. "Just as the strength of the Internet is chaos, so the strength of our liberty depends upon the chaos and cacophony of the unfettered speech the First Amendment protects. . . . The government may not, through the [Communications Decency Act], interrupt that conversation."

"This is as historic a case as we have had in our history on the First Amendment," declared Glasser. Microsoft founder Bill Gates, a plaintiff in the suit, called the ruling "a victory for anyone who cares about freedom of expression or the future of the Internet. Technology can provide a much more effective safeguard without restricting the free flow of ideas and opinions on the Internet."

That December, the Supreme Court agreed to take the case, setting oral arguments for March 1997. In its brief, the ACLU argued that the measure was unconstitutional "as a flat ban on protected speech" and that it was overbroad, unconstitutionally vague, and ineffective. The brief also noted that since there was no easy way on the Internet to distinguish children from adults, "the CDA is the most restrictive censorship scheme imposed on any medium."

On June 26, 1997, the Supreme Court ruled 7 to 2 on behalf of the ACLU, striking down the CDA as unconstitutional. The decision, written by Justice John Paul Stevens, observed, "The Government apparently assumes that the unregulated availability of 'indecent' and 'patently offensive' material on the Internet is driving countless citizens away from the medium because of the risk of exposing themselves or their children to harmful material. We find this argument singularly unpersuasive."

"Everyone knew the CDA was unconstitutional, but Congress passed the law and the President signed it. Today's historic decision affirms what we knew all along: cyberspace must be free," said Glasser.

In 1998, for the first time in 130 years, an American president was impeached by the House and tried by the Senate.

Whereas the charges against Andrew Johnson arose from his firing of the secretary of war, Clinton's alleged transgressions had nothing to do with presidential powers but with lying about a sexual dalliance.

The House voted to impeach on December 19, less than a week before Christmas. The vote climaxed a surreal week during which Congressman Robert Livingston, scheduled to take over as House Speaker, acknowledged extramarital affairs and announced he would resign.

Because no civil liberties issues were involved, the ACLU did not take a position on Clinton's impeachment. Instead, it argued for fairness. It specifically criticized the perjury charge, the first of the two articles of impeachment. The impeachment article, argued the ACLU, needed to be supplemented with "a bill of particulars" that specifically identified the perjurious statements Clinton was accused of making. The "first Article," pointed out the ACLU statement, "does not currently specify any single statement as false."

The ACLU also asked that Clinton be allowed to see Independent Counsel Kenneth Starr's investigative files—"especially in light of the prosecutorial misconduct that has been alleged against the Independent Counsel and in light of the possibility that a perjury trap was set."

"Fundamental American principles of fairness allow defendants in our nation's criminal and civil courts to know what offenses they are charged with. We took that position in 1974 with respect to President Nixon and we take it now," said Glasser.

The ACLU had previously criticized Starr for jailing Susan McDougal indefinitely after she refused to answer questions about Clinton during her Whitewater trial. Mark Rosenbaum, legal director of the Southern California affiliate, had called McDougal's treatment "the most barbaric conduct by a federal prosecutor toward a resistant grand jury witness in the history of the Republic."

The ACLU had also asked a federal judge to end Starr's investigation into the bookstore purchases of Monica Lewinsky. "In his investigatory zeal, Ken Starr seems to give little heed to the basic right of all Americans to read what they want free from government surveillance," commented ACLU Legal Director Steven Shapiro.

Against the backdrop of the impeachment, and partially in response to what the ACLU saw as Starr's morality crusade, the ACLU announced a year-long advertising campaign to provoke "discussion over what constitutes public 'morality' in America."

"Right now, a battle is being fought for the hearts and minds of the American people by those who would judge whether we are a moral nation by scrutinizing what is essentially private, personal behavior," said Glasser. "The ACLU believes that the morality of a nation is measured not by what occurs in the privacy of our bedrooms or doctor's offices or telephone conversations, but by how the government treats its people. Through these ads, we hope to offer a vision of a world where it's safe to be different, easier to be free."

On February 12, 1999, the impeachment drama ended. Voting largely along party lines (55 to 45 on perjury and 50 to 50 on obstruction of justice, with 67 votes required for conviction), the Senate acquitted the president.

Later that day, Clinton briefly addressed the nation from the Rose Garden. He apologized "for what I said and did to trigger these events" and expressed hope that "all Americans here in Washington and throughout our land, will rededicate ourselves to the work of serving our nation and building our future together."

In Philadelphia, U.S. District Judge Lowell Reed had just issued a preliminary injunction against the "Child Online Protection Act," yet another measure aimed at protecting youngsters from pornography online. The law required commercial websites to attempt to verify—using credit cards or other means—that only adults viewed certain content.

The ACLU had argued that the law violated the First Amendment and could be used against news providers whose stories featured sexually explicit but non-pornographic content. "If Congress wins this, the Internet would go from being the most revolutionary, creative technology in history to a pretty tame, often meaningless means of communicating only about things that are fit for a 6-year-old," said Stefan Presser, of the Pennsylvania ACLU.

"Perhaps we do the minors of this country harm if First Amendment protections, which they will with age inherit fully, are chipped away in the name of their protection," wrote Judge Reed in prohibiting the law's enforcement.

12

Terrorism, Torture, and the Pursuit of Justice

The nation's capital celebrated New Year's Eve 2000 with a lavish party. Some 300,000 gathered at the Lincoln Memorial for the extravaganza. Singers Tom Jones and Bebe Winans, poets Rita Dove and Maya Angelou, and basketballers Bill Russell and Nikki McCray all graced the stage. President Clinton extolled "America's remarkable achievements" and invited everyone to imagine "an even more remarkable 21st century."

The year that began with such high expectations ended on a note of disconcerting confusion, as the most technologically sophisticated nation on earth couldn't figure out whom it had elected president. The Supreme Court took that task onto itself; and on December 12, for the first time in history, the court selected America's president. Florida's rules demanded a hand recount of some 45,000 disputed ballots. The Supreme Court decided there was no time for such foolishness and stopped the count, awarding Bush the presidency by a vote of 5 to 4.

Justice John Paul Stevens observed, "Although we may never know with complete certainty the identity of the winner of this year's Presidential election, the identity of the loser is perfectly clear. It is the Nation's confidence in the judge as an impartial guardian of the rule of law."

Ira Glasser criticized the court for finding discrimination in the wrong place. The inequality, he argued, was not so much in the aborted recount as in the "differential use of punch-card machines in some counties but not in others." Nearly two-thirds of Florida's black voters, he pointed out, were in counties that used the punch-card systems, compared to 56 percent of whites. "Sixty-three percent of Gore's vote, which included heavy majorities among black voters, were counted on punch-card machines while only 55 percent of Bush's vote was," he noted. Consequently, "black voters disproportionately were rejected."

Minority voters were also purged based on alleged felony records that were never verified. A data-service firm hired by the Republican Party had provided a list of eight thousand largely minority "possible felons," but no one bothered to investigate the names on the list. Instead, authorities simply disqualified them all. Such actions, suggested Glasser, may have depressed Gore's vote by significantly more than the 537 votes that ended up being the new president's margin of victory in Florida—whose electoral votes delivered him the presidency.

A consortium of news organizations (including the Associated Press, the *New York Times*, the *Wall Street Journal*, and the *Washington Post*) that reviewed the Florida ballots could not conclusively determine who won. But the Associated Press reported some nineteen thousand "overvotes"—ballots that recorded votes for more than one presidential candidate.

The *Washington Post* surmised that Bush likely "still would have won Florida and the presidency last year if either of two limited recounts—one requested by Al Gore, the other ordered by the Florida Supreme Court— had been completed." But "if Gore had found a way to trigger a statewide recount of all disputed ballots . . . the result likely would have been different. An examination of uncounted ballots throughout Florida found enough where voter intent was clear to give Gore the narrowest of margins." The news organizations did not consider the impact of knocking thousands of suspected felons off the voter rolls.

In the months after the contested election, the ACLU filed suits in several states—including Georgia, Illinois, California, and Florida— confronting some of the problems highlighted by the Florida debacle and what seemed to be systematic discrimination against minority voters. In Illinois, California, and Georgia, as in Florida, voters in certain parts of the state used punch cards and in others used more reliable technologies, such as optical scanners. The worst systems generally were in poorer, largely non-white areas. Some states were also extremely aggressive in purging voters or had policies that eliminated felons. Florida alone had disqualified some 400,000 felons and had instituted a "reform" law that essentially created a literacy test. The ACLU filed suit against those practices.

"Florida exposed some systemic national voting problems that have been going on a long time but didn't get a lot of attention," said the ACLU's Laura Murphy.

The Florida-inspired voter rights campaign was one of Glasser's closing acts. On June 28, 2000, he formally submitted his letter of resignation—setting his retirement date for July 1, 2001, "a few months past my 63rd birthday."

In more than thirty-four years at the ACLU, wrote Glasser, he had essentially done what he was going to do: "What I could accomplish in another couple of years, compared to what has been accomplished, would be incremental." He was leaving when he was still young enough to go the gym, spend hours at the beach, play softball with his son, and "sit with my honey in the Luxembourg Gardens in April in Paris."

The ACLU, he wrote, was stronger than ever. He would leave "loving this organization . . . and what it has provided" him: an opportunity to fulfill his teenage dream of a life immersed in issues he cared about.

In September, the ACLU announced Glasser's retirement. The press release noted that Glasser had dramatically increased annual income—from "$4 million in 1978 to $45 million in 1999" and that he fought for adequate funding for small affiliates. He "brought to the ACLU a genuinely rare combination of intellectual leadership and managerial skill," along with vision and organizational expertise that "will allow the ACLU to continue its work into the next century," read a statement attributed to ACLU President Nadine Strossen.

To find his replacement, the board hired Isaacson Miller, an executive search firm recommended by Glasser that claimed expertise in "affirmative action recruitment." With the executive committee serving as a screening committee, the ACLU hoped to wrap up the search by the following April.

In the meantime, Glasser would prepare for the transition and finish some major projects, which included negotiating a $7 million grant from the Ford Foundation, a major gift from the MacArthur Foundation, and garnering new financial support for various portfolios—among them voting rights, gay and lesbian issues, and prisoners' rights.

Over the next few months, the search firm and the ACLU screened more than one hundred candidates. By early 2001, only two remained: Theodore "Ted" Shaw and Anthony Romero.

Shaw, forty-six and raised in Harlem, was a 1979 graduate of Columbia Law School. He had worked for the Civil Rights Division of the Justice Department before joining the NAACP Legal Defense Fund and Educational Fund. He had left the Legal Defense Fund in 1990 to teach at the University of Michigan Law School before returning as associate director counsel in 1992.

Romero, thirty-five, was also a native New Yorker. He had spent part of his childhood in a housing project in the Bronx before the family moved to a largely white, working-class community in Passaic County, New Jersey. The son of Puerto Rican parents, Romero had earned a BA from Princeton in 1987 and then went on to Stanford Law School. Romero had worked for the Rockefeller Foundation before joining the Ford Foundation in 1992, where he became the organization's director of human rights and international cooperation. He was openly gay.

ACLU president Nadine Strossen oversaw the search. A New York Law School constitutional law professor and graduate of Harvard and Harvard Law, Strossen (forty when elected president in 1991) had become the first woman and youngest person to head the ACLU.

Strossen, who was born in Jersey City and raised largely in Hopkins, Minnesota, had become involved with the ACLU while clerking for a judge in Minnesota. She eventually was recruited for the local ACLU board. When she moved to New York, her Minnesota contacts put her in touch with the national office.

Romero dazzled her. "He is like one of the most phenomenal people that I've ever met in my life," she said during an interview. He had an impressive command of "history, current events, politics, civil liberties issues" and also impressive managerial experience, which persuaded her he "would be best positioned to take [the ACLU] to the next level."

A troubling racial split, however, had developed within the screening committee. The only two black members, Michael Meyers and James Ferguson, were strongly in favor of Shaw. Neither was willing to quietly go along with Romero.

Meyers and Ferguson both had grown up fighting for racial justice. A native of Asheville, North Carolina, Ferguson, as a teenager during the 1960s, had been a leader of the student movement for integrated schools and public facilities. After graduating from Columbia Law School in 1967, he moved to Charlotte, North Carolina, where he co-founded the first integrated law firm in the state.

Ferguson saw Shaw not only as a distinguished constitutional scholar but as someone who "came out of the civil rights movement." Shaw's race was also a plus: "I thought anytime you had, particularly at that time, a qualified African American to take on a position of national leadership like that . . . we ought to take advantage. . . . I came to the ultimate view that Ted was the stronger candidate of the two."

Meyers, the first in his family to graduate from high school, went to Antioch College, interned at the ACLU, and ended up at Rutgers Law School. He chose Rutgers in part because of Arthur Kinoy, a constitutional scholar and celebrated civil libertarian who taught there. Years later, Meyers co-founded and became executive director of the New York Civil Rights Coalition, formed in the wake of a racially motivated attack on three black men in Howard Beach, Queens, in 1986.

As a member of the ACLU screening community, Meyers was sworn to secrecy about the identities of unsuccessful candidates. Instead of referring to Shaw by name during our interviews, Meyers insisted on calling him "the candidate of opportunity." As Meyers it, "the candidate of opportunity was well known to the civil rights contingent" and seemed perfect for the job. Ferguson said he "was hoping that we could persuade the executive committee to put forth Ted as the nominee."

At some point during the screening committee's deliberations, Meyers and Ferguson caucused in a bathroom. As Meyers recalls, "Fergie says to me, 'Well, do you think we can persuade them to change their votes?' I say, 'No.' He says, 'Give me reasons.' I say, 'I can give you seven million reasons,'" in an allusion to the $7 million contribution the Ford Foundation had recently promised toward the ACLU endowment. Ford Foundation President Susan Berresford said it was among the largest grants in the foundation's history. "So, as far as I was concerned, he had, in fact, laid the groundwork to buy the job."

When they returned to the deliberations, someone suggested the group consider Meyers and Ferguson's reservations, but someone else objected to delaying the decision. "Fergie got quiet," recalled Meyers. "I didn't say anything more because there was nothing else to say. They voted to give the appointment to Anthony. We made it clear that we were dissenting."

Meyers and Ferguson nonetheless agreed to join in with the board's final vote. "That kind of relieved everybody," recalled Meyer, "when they heard that Michael and Fergie won't dissent publicly."

At the board meeting on Saturday, April 28, Meyers made a motion, accepted by acclamation, to appoint Romero. The next morning, Strossen introduced Romero to his new employers. That Tuesday, the *New York Times* announced the appointment.

Shaw went on to become the fifth director-counsel and president of the NAACP Legal Defense and Educational Fund and a law professor at Columbia University. Subsequently, he was awarded an endowed chair at the University of North Carolina School of Law.

Years later, Shaw recalled being conflicted about the ACLU's overture: "I was really focused [on] and dedicated to the work that I was doing at the Legal Defense Fund, which was all about . . . racial justice." While the ACLU did some such work, that "wasn't a primary focus. . . . The more I found out about it, the more I realized that that would be challenging. . . . Here's the other thing . . . I was conscious of the phenomenon of black folks rounding out searches," of black candidates asked to apply to organizations that had no intention of hiring them. "I had a range of mixed feelings and uncertainties about this." In the end, when someone else was picked, he said, "I wasn't terribly disappointed. "

Romero took roughly four months to wrap up things at Ford, during which he pondered what his "flagship initiative" at the ACLU might be. In the aftermath of the *Bush v. Gore* fiasco, he was thinking about voting rights and felony disenfranchisement: "I thought it would be good for us to lean in quick on those sets of issues."

Then the world changed.

On the morning of September 11, exactly a week after Romero reported for work, two commercial planes slammed into the twin towers of the

World Trade Center and another into the Pentagon, leaving heaps of rubble and glass and nearly three thousand dead. Another plane crashed near Pittsburgh. Shortly before the crash, a man had called an emergency operator claiming, "We are being hijacked." The ACLU headquarters, blocks away from the crumbling Twin Towers, was evacuated.

President George Bush ordered investigators to "hunt down the folks who committed this act." For the first time, the United States shut down its commercial air space as its citizens stumbled through an isolated fog of grief.

That morning, much of the ACLU brass was in Washington, DC, for a meeting of major donors and supporters.

As Romero remembers it, "We were going around the room introducing ourselves when someone came in and slipped me a note asking me to step outside. And then I saw on the TV that the planes were going into the World Trade Center."

"I'll never forget Anthony coming in and making this announcement that the World Trade Center had been hit," said board president Strossen.

The group adjourned in shock. "I remember getting scared," recalled Romero, as a sense of the hugeness of his new job suddenly struck him. "I remember worrying about the safety of the staff, which I had just met the week before, being worried about how [to] respond."

Romero went to his hotel room, called his mother, and assured her that he was okay; then he knelt and prayed. "I prayed for my partner. I prayed for my staff. And I prayed for strength. I remember thinking, 'Help me with this.'"

Of all the issues that could have erupted, this was one of the farthest from his comfort zone. He knew "racial justice issues, I understood immigration issues, I understood voting issues, I understood the death penalty. National security is not anything I had ever thought about in the civil liberties context."

Romero asked the board and staff to resist any impulse to make political points. "Grieve the loss of life, talk about this tragedy. Do not talk about the erosion of civil liberties." A stunned, angry, grieving America, he assumed, was in no mood to hear arguments about the rights of terrorists or to hear history lessons on Japanese internment. Such talk was only "going to reinforce the stereotype that this is a knee-jerk organization that doesn't deal with the moment."

Meanwhile, everyone was dealing with the personal consequences of the attack. It was a time, recalled board member Susan Herman, when "a lot of the people on the staff were traumatized. You know, they were afraid to be in downtown Manhattan . . . personally fearful. . . . So Anthony arranged psychiatric counseling just, you know, to have somebody who the staff could talk to. Really just dealing with the human aspect."

"We were all discovering issues that we never . . . had to handle before," recalled Washington director Laura Murphy. "We would have conversations confessing our bewilderment to each other. . . . We'd have to go back the next day and shore up our staff and give them a pep talk."

With the ACLU's public advocacy operation essentially shut down under Romero's orders, there was uncertainty about how to move forward. "I said, 'I mean, if we don't speak up now, when are we going to speak up? This is the civil liberties crisis of our time," said Murphy. "This is when, you know, civil liberties are the hardest when people are scared. And everybody was scared."

"We didn't have to wait too long," said Romero. "I remember we weren't [yet back] in the office when the first series of proposals that would become the Patriot Act were being bandied about in Washington."

That legislation moved at a lightning pace—thanks in part to ideas that had been circulating since the Oklahoma City bombing of 1995. Following that tragedy, Congress passed the 1996 Anti-Terrorism and Effective Death Penalty Act. The new law gave the government greater latitude in deporting or excluding suspected terrorists, prohibited fund-raising for terrorist activities, and made it harder for death row inmates to get death sentences reviewed.

Within months of passing the anti-terrorism law, Congress passed two other laws—the Illegal Immigration Reform and Immigrant Responsibility Act and the Prison Litigation Reform Act—that cracked down on criminal immigrants and litigious prisoners. Now Congress was eager to make the laws tougher.

The USA Patriot Act (formally called the Uniting and Strengthening America by Providing Appropriate Tools Required to Intercept and Obstruct Terrorism Act) was the ultimate result of two bills introduced in Congress in early October. On October 2, James Sensenbrenner introduced a bill in the House, and on October 4, Thomas Daschle introduced his version in the Senate.

Bush urged legislators to "quickly get the bill to my desk." Patrick Leahy, a co-sponsor, also stressed the need for haste: "I believe the American people and my fellow Senators, both Republican and Democratic, deserve faster final action."

Legislators' obligatory talk of protecting civil liberties brought little comfort to Murphy and other civil libertarians, who saw a bill take shape conceived largely in fear. Murphy recounted: "One congressman put his finger in the chest of one of my female lobbyists and said, 'You don't understand. We could have been dead. That plane was headed for the U.S. capital. So, no, 'I'm not going to vote against the Patriot Act.' . . . We lost a lot of Democrats who did not want the finger pointed at them for not voting for or weakening the Patriot Act."

Romero felt the pressure as well. "I remember having a conversation with Senator [Paul] Wellstone before he died . . . and he said, 'Look, Anthony, this is not the time to be concerned with civil liberties. We'll come back and fix it at some later point . . . I said, 'Senator, with all due respect, that's a huge mistake. We've been down this road before.'"

In late October, after the bill cleared Congress, Murphy told the press, "most Americans do not recognize that Congress has just passed a bill that would give the government expanded power to invade our privacy, imprison people without due process and punish dissent."

The legislation enhanced law enforcement powers in several ways. It gave federal officers greater access to voicemails and more authority to share evidence from wiretaps and electronic surveillance. It made warrants for electronic evidence easier to get, toughened money laundering laws, and gave the president greater authority to seize foreign-owned property.

President Bush signed the bill on October 26. He pledged to enforce it "with all the urgency of a nation at war."

Murphy told reporters: "This bill goes light-years beyond what is necessary to combat terrorism. While we are ourselves concerned for the country's safety, we are also concerned by the attorney general's apparent gusto to implement certain provisions in the bill that threaten liberty."

The ACLU promised to monitor the law closely and set up a meeting with FBI director Robert Mueller to discuss it.

A few weeks later, in an interview published in the *New Crisis*, Murphy complained, "This law removes the power of the federal courts to limit wiretapping by the FBI or CIA. It makes the role of the federal court virtually meaningless. . . . The police can now come into your home, download information off of your computer, go through your personal possessions, and you'll never know that they were there."

That November, the ACLU released a seventy-two-page report, "Upsetting Checks and Balances: Congressional Hostility Toward the Courts in Times of Crisis," that critiqued the anti-terrorism legislation of 1995 and 2001, focusing largely on the weakening of the judicial review process.

Amidst the blizzard of disturbing news on the surveillance front, civil libertarians got an encouraging nod from the Foreign Intelligence Surveillance Court. In a decision handed down in May 2002 and made public in August, the court ruled that new Justice Department rules were "not reasonably designed" to protect Americans privacy. As a result of the Patriot Act, counterintelligence investigators could more easily get wiretaps. The Justice Department had extended the more relaxed rules into the realm of criminal investigations. In its first public opinion, the Foreign Intelligence Surveillance Court pushed back, to the dismay of Attorney General John Ashcroft.

That August the ACLU won another victory. In a case brought by the ACLU on behalf of several newspapers, a three-judge panel of the U.S. Sixth Circuit Court of Appeals in Cincinnati rejected the government's decision to hold secret deportation hearings for suspects thought to have links to terrorism. "A government operating in the shadow of secrecy stands in complete opposition to the society envisioned by the framers of our Constitution," declared the unanimous opinion. That decision upheld a ruling in April by U.S. District Court Judge Nancy Edmond.

In October 2002, the ACLU announced what it called the "Campaign to Defend the Constitution" with rallies and televised ads. "We perceive a real need to reach out to the American public and inspire discussion and debate on these issues," said Romero.

That same month, a 2 to 1 decision by the Third Circuit Court of Appeals in Philadelphia contradicted the closed courtroom opinion of the appeals court in Cincinnati. In an ACLU case brought on behalf of several New Jersey newspapers, the court agreed with the government that open hearings, which would make detainees' names public, might thwart anti-terrorism efforts. The Supreme Court declined to resolve the conflict between the courts, effectively leaving closed hearings for so-called "special interest aliens" constitutional in some jurisdictions and unconstitutional in others.

Meanwhile, Ashcroft appealed the surveillance court decision, and in November 2002 a three-judge panel appointed by Chief Justice Rehnquist agreed with him. The panel pronounced itself reluctant "to jettison Fourth Amendment requirements in the interest of national security" but concluded that circumstances justified such drastic action: "After the events of Sept. 11, 2001 . . . it is hard to imagine greater emergencies facing Americans than those experienced on that date."

The "appetite for these new spying powers seems to be insatiable," observed Ann Beeson, ACLU associate legal director, who vowed, "we'll continue to fight to curb the abuse of government surveillance power."

As the ACLU fiercely fought battles over governmental abuse and overreach, Romero was also coping with fire from within. The rumbling of discontent began with a 2002 incident precipitated by a contractor's mistake. The contractor, who was managing an ACLU website, carelessly exposed some contributors' personal information. An inquiry by New York's attorney general resulted in a fine and a promise by ACLU to fix the problem.

Romero and his staff negotiated the $100,000 fine down to $10,000, which the contractor paid. The settlement required Romero to disclose the situation to his board within thirty days, which he neglected to do. Instead, he waited several months. Although he apologized for not informing board members earlier, some nonetheless were annoyed.

In an interview with *The Nation*, Romero confided, "I probably was a bit cavalier about it. But $10,000 is not a huge sum of money, and it was fully reimbursed to the ACLU."

Board members were even more troubled with Romero's response to restrictions—instigated by the Patriot Act—imposed by donors on grant recipients. Seeking to prevent terrorists from benefitting from their donations, some charities toughed their monitoring requirements. The Combined Federal Campaign, a program though which federal employees donate to qualified charities, adopted a rule requiring beneficiaries to certify they were not "knowingly employing" individuals on various government watchlists.

In order to receive a $500,000 grant, Romero signed the agreement. He had no intention of hiring terrorists, but neither did he intend to check names against a likely flawed list and saw signing the certification as a meaningless concession. When informed of what he had done, some board members objected. One wondered whether signing the agreement might force the ACLU to "ask questions of its Board members and staff that ACLU policy clearly did not permit."

On July 31, 2004, the *New York Times* took the conflict public. Adam Liptak reported the ACLU was "in turmoil over a promise it made to the government that it would not knowingly hire people whose names appear on watch lists of suspected supporters of terrorism" of "the very type it has strongly opposed in other contexts."

"We oppose 'no fly' lists. Now we have a 'no hire' list that we've signed onto," Michael Meyer told the *Times*.

The director of the Combined Federal Campaign (CFC) was also annoyed to learn that Romero had made a commitment he did not intend to keep. "To just sign a certification without corroboration would be a false certification," which could endanger an organization's funding, CFC director Mara T. Patermaster told Liptak.

The article sent tremors through the ACLU community. After the article appeared, Romero wrote to Patermaster spelling out the ACLU's objections. The ACLU, he pointed out, had found government watchlists to be "notoriously riddled with errors." They also left falsely smeared individuals helpless to correct the record. The ACLU therefore was withdrawing from the CFC charity drive and forgoing the $500,000 already committed.

Romero told Liptak that his lawyers had approved signing the agreement since it only prohibited *knowingly* employing people on a blacklist. They agreed with his strategy of not checking the lists.

"[We] wake up this morning and . . . read" that the head of the CFC wants "us to check those lists. What do we do . . . when an employee is falsely matched up? . . . That puts us in a fundamentally untenable situation," he told National Public Radio.

NPR also interviewed board member Wendy Kaminer, who said, "I'm very pleased that the ACLU is rescinding this agreement, but I am very dismayed that it took a front-page story in the *New York Times* to get the ACLU to [do so]."

As the CFC crisis simmered, an even more significant controversy arose involving some of the ACLU's biggest financial backers, including Romero's former employers.

Both the Ford and Rockefeller Foundations had inserted terrorist-avoidance language in their funding agreements. In May 2004, Romero had raised the issue of Ford Foundation money with terrorist restrictions, and the ACLU leadership had directed him to accept the funds. The grant amount was $136,000, and the ACLU was required to agree not to "promote or engage in violence, terrorism, bigotry or the destruction of any state, nor" to make "subgrants to any entity that engages in these activities."

The question came up again at the July 9 board meeting. The total amount at risk was roughly $4 million—from Ford, Rockefeller, and five other donors and foundations. Romero wanted to know where the board stood.

Legal Director Steven Shapiro agreed with Romero that, although the Ford language was regrettable, accepting it would not impair the ACLU's ability to do its work. Refusing the money would substantially diminish the ACLU's ability "to defend civil liberties at a time where civil liberties were under attack," he pointed out. On the other hand, he did not want to fuel the perception the ACLU was abandoning its principles for money.

The board essentially opted not to choose. It approved a resolution that expressed the ACLU's concern about the proliferation of chilling language in grant agreements, vowed that no ACLU activities would be curbed as the result of accepting money, and directed Romero to urge grantors to soften their restrictive language. As for whether to accept the money in question, the board opted to address that issue later.

At its mid-October board meeting, the ACLU again wrestled with the issue. Romero said he now realized he never should have signed the Combined Federal Campaign agreement and apologized for the grief that doing so had brought the ACLU. As for Ford and Rockefeller, he would make arguments on both sides on the issue and accept the board's decision.

Since the ACLU was not supporting terrorism, signing the agreement, he argued, would provide resources allowing the ACLU to strengthen its civil liberties programs without compromising its principles or programs. On the other hand, rejecting vague and ambiguous language that might infringe on the speech of others would demonstrate bold leadership and refute criticism that the ACLU had compromised itself.

On October 19, the *Times* reported that the ACLU was rejecting $1.15 million from the Ford and Rockefeller foundations because the foundations' efforts "to ensure that none of their money inadvertently underwrites terrorism or other unacceptable activities is a threat to civil liberties."

The story by Stephanie Strom discussed the decision by foundations to add anti-terrorism language to their grant agreements and reported that "angry donors and members descended on the ACLU" after the *Times* revealed the ACLU board battle over the decision to sign the CFC agreement. She then dropped a bombshell, reporting that the board had recently learned that Romero, a Ford Foundation alum, had been among those advising the Ford Foundation on the language it ultimately adopted.

She noted Michael Meyers's astonishment that Romero had advised the foundation "to mirror and parrot the language in the USA Patriot Act, aspects of which we have been fighting against. My jaw dropped at that."

The *Times* was not done investigating newsworthy activity at the ACLU. In late December 2004, Strom reported the ACLU was "using sophisticated technology to collect a wide variety of information about its members and donors in a fund-raising effort that has ignited a bitter debate over its leaders' commitment to privacy rights."

The revelation set off yet another wave of indignation from Kaminer and Meyers. "It goes against ACLU values to engage in data-mining on people without informing them. It's not illegal, but it is . . . hypocrisy," argued Kaminer.

Meyers accused management of implementing the policy with neither the board's approval nor knowledge and of having "sanctified their procedure while still keeping it secret."

New York attorney general Eliot Spitzer, reported Strom, was "conducting an inquiry into whether the group had violated its promises to protect the privacy of donors and members."

At its January 2005 meeting, the ACLU board took stock of how much the stand against Patriot Act–inspired language had cost. ACLU staff reported that some $3 million in funding had been rejected but seemed confident that the ACLU could weather the hit—especially since it had received several new grants, including an anonymous bequest of $1 million to support the Death Penalty Project and two new grants that exceeded $2 million.

The split within the ACLU continued to get attention. In the April/ May 2005 issue of *Free Inquiry*, Nat Hentoff wrote about attempts to silence critical board members and praised Meyers and Kaminer for rejecting a proposed "gag rule."

Two years later, recriminations were still flying. In January 2007, *The Nation* magazine ruminated about the ACLU's "tumultuous family feud." Critics had even launched a website. Ira Glasser, Romero's predecessor and former champion, had become one of his most fierce critics. He had joined the opposition "with sadness, but in the firm belief that the core mission of the ACLU is at stake," he told *The Nation*. Meanwhile, a counter-website was launched by Romero's supporters, which included Aryeh Neier and former chairman Norman Dorsen.

Romero's harshest critics—Meyers and Kaminer—no longer served on the board, noted *The Nation*, which observed that in the ACLU power struggle, Romero had ended on top. It was time, advised *The Nation*, for detractors to move on. The critics had "performed a useful service by confronting Romero and bringing his transgressions to light," editorialized *The Nation*. But the board "has spoken in favor of Romero."

New York Magazine weighed in on the ACLU that February with an article titled "The ACLU's Uncivil War: Freedom to Backstab." The magazine reported that since Romero had taken over, ACLU membership had nearly doubled (from 300,000 to 573,000), national staff had more than doubled (from 186 to 379), and total revenue had more than doubled as well (from $13.6 million to $28 million). The article credited Romero with strengthening the affiliates. . . . It also praised ACLU efforts opposing civil liberties transgressions—kidnapping, torture, and indefinite detention— in the aftermath of 9/11.

The magazine noted the disappearance of several long-serving directors. Kaminer and law professor Muriel Morisey had "resigned in disgust, and others have been voted out." Meanwhile, it continued, "Meyers, who joined the board in 1981 and served as the corporation's vice-president, lost his reelection bid as a write-in candidate in 2005 after taking his beef to Bill O'Reilly's show. In the fall, after two decades, [James] Ferguson walked away."

The article concluded with an interview with Romero. Asked to respond to his critics, the magazine noted, "his eyes darken, but for the most part he declines to reply for the record." He made a point about picadors, the mounted assistants who wound a bull before it is killed by the matador. "That's what they mostly feel like."

When I asked Romero his assessment of that period, he pointed out that his most ferocious critics had always been against him. He admitted the experience had been painful and that he had showed too much anger: "I was working my ass off, working seven days a week . . . building programs, fighting the Bush administration, winning over the likes of Aryeh." And he felt that instead of focusing on his accomplishments—the people he was hiring, the programs he was building—they were nitpicking him to death.

What he didn't fully comprehend, acknowledged Romero, "was that the kernel of the concern was well placed." A civil liberties champion should not sign letters such as those drafted by the Ford Foundation and the Combined Federal Campaign. But at the time, he was "too young and too immature" to admit that his critics had a legitimate point. "And I fucked up. And I knew I was fucking up when I did it."

Ford Foundation president Susan Berresford was both his former boss and a friend; his impulse was to cooperate with her. He also "needed the money to fight the 9/11 moment. . . . When I signed it, I was kind of like, 'I don't really like this, but she's not going to give any further.'"

Once he stopped "trying to manage my relationship" with Berresford, things became easier. He accepted that his job was not pleasing Berresford; his job was "to be the executive director of the ACLU. . . . And once I turned that corner . . . once I said, 'You have one institution you are responsible for—not the place you spent ten years—but the place you have been for two or three,'" his mission became infinitely clearer.

In August 2002, a federal district judge—at the ACLU's request—ordered the release of the names of hundreds of Muslim men held after the September 11 attack. The August 2 ruling by Judge Gladys Kessler swatted away Justice Department arguments that disclosure would thwart antiterrorism efforts. The "public's interest in learning the identity of those arrested and detained is essential to verifying whether the government is operating within the bounds of law," she wrote.

At the administration's request, Judge Kessler stayed her order. It was overruled June 2003 by a U.S. Court of Appeals panel. "If such a list [of detainees] fell into the hands of al Qaeda, the consequences could be disastrous," wrote Judge David Sentelle for the majority.

In December 2004, with the nation reeling from the abuses of prisoners revealed at the Abu Ghraib prison facility in Iraq earlier in the year, the ACLU won another major victory for governmental transparency, forcing the release of a trove of documents that refuted the Bush administration's contention that the Abu Ghraib nightmare was an aberration.

"The documents . . . reveal that senior U.S. officials, who claimed they were unaware of the abuse, were repeatedly informed of accusations of abuse through official channels. They also suggest that . . . reports of abuse failed to trigger investigations into what increasingly appears to have been a widespread pattern of prisoner abuse in Afghanistan, Iraq and at the Guantanamo Bay naval base in Cuba," reported the Knight-Ridder Tribune News Service.

In one case, a woman nursing a six-month-old child was held for two days as bait to lure her husband into custody. Other documents told of officials who physically abused or tortured detainees as they were questioned, and of threats made against military intelligence officials to cover up the abuse.

"These documents tell a damning story of sanctioned government abuse—a story that the government has tried to hide," commented Romero.

As it battled and obsessed over the administration's anti-terrorism tactics, the ACLU debated whether to oppose another nominee to the Supreme Court.

In early October 2005, Bush nominated White House counsel Harriet Miers to succeed the retiring Sandra Day O'Connor. Mier's nomination was torpedoed by her lack of relevant experience, modest educational credentials, poor performance during Senate interviews, weak political support, and a dispute over access to confidential White House documents to vet her candidacy.

On October 31, Bush nominated Samuel Alito, a Princeton University and Yale Law School graduate who was serving on the U.S. Court of Appeals. At a White House press briefing with Alito, Bush praised Alito's fifteen years of experience on the bench and his prior work as a Justice Department lawyer and U.S. attorney. The new nominee, he said, "has more prior judicial experience than any Supreme Court nominee in more than 70 years." Bush also introduced the nominee's wife, Martha, a former law librarian. "You can't go wrong marrying a librarian," joked Bush.

Senator Edward Kennedy criticized Bush's choice. "Rather than selecting a nominee for the good of the nation and the court, President Bush has picked a nominee whom he hopes will stop the massive hemorrhaging of support on his right wing."

Political progressives immediately coalesced in opposition to the nominee. Kate Michelman, the past president of NARAL-Pro Choice America, called Alito's nomination "the greatest threat to women's fundamental rights and liberties in more than three decades." A coalition of liberal groups announced a national television campaign to oppose him.

As usual, the ACLU commissioned an expert study of the new nominee. The resulting seventy-two-page document quoted from the nominee's 1985 letter to the White House seeking a job with the Justice Department. Then in his mid-thirties, Alito wrote, "I am and always have been a conservative and an adherent to the same philosophical views that I believe are central to this Administration."

He explained that his disagreements with the Warren Court—over criminal procedure, the Establishment Clause, and reapportionment—had moved him to attend law school. Alito expressed pride in his work for the solicitor general helping to craft briefs opposing abortion and racial and ethnic quotas.

Alito's letter, noted the ACLU report, was consistent with positions he had taken on the U.S. Court of Appeals for the Third Circuit. That was "particularly worrisome" given that those positions revolved around "a series of issues—race, religion, and reproductive rights—in which Justice O'Connor has played a critical role on the Supreme Court as an often-decisive swing vote."

The report acknowledged Alito's "stellar academic record" and the "important government positions" he had held, and it pronounced his opinions "thoughtful and, on the whole, cautious." But it noted that Alito had ruled "against civil rights and civil liberties claims," including arguing in a Planned Parenthood case "that a state's spousal notification requirement did not unduly burden a woman's right to privacy," a position later rejected by the Supreme Court." In another dissent, Alito had argued that a student-led prayer at a graduation ceremony was constitutional; and he had supported strip searches, the exclusion of black prospective jurors on a death penalty case, and the denial of newspapers and magazines to prisoners.

"By and large, Judge Alito's opinions make it more difficult for plaintiffs alleging discrimination to prevail, easier for the government to lend its support to religion, and harder to challenge questionable tactics by the police and prosecution," concluded the report.

At the ACLU's January 7, 2006, board meeting, Romero suggested that the ACLU take no position. After a spirited debate, the majority (43 to 25, with one abstention) voted to oppose Alito.

In a press release that January 9, the ACLU announced its position, slamming Alito for condoning spying on Americans and indefinite incarceration of terrorism suspects. In testimony submitted to the Senate Judiciary Committee, Romero criticized Alito's "proven record of undue deference to executive power." He cited a speech to the Federalist Society during which Alito claimed, "the president has not just some executive powers, but *the* executive power—the whole thing." He also challenged Alito's record on civil liberties and civil rights.

On January 30, as the Senate prepared to vote on Alito's confirmation, the ACLU sent out a letter advising senators that "confirming Alito, someone with a proven record of undue deference to executive powers, could dangerously upset" the constitutional balance.

The following day, the Senate confirmed Alito by a vote of 58 to 42, largely along party lines. He was sworn in by chief Justice John Roberts just in time to attend President Bush's State of the Union address. In that address, Bush acknowledged Dr. Martin Luther King's widow, who had died the previous day, and gave a shout-out to the new associate justice: "The Supreme Court now has two superb new members, Chief Justice John Roberts and Justice Sam Alito. I thank the Senate for confirming both."

Bush spoke of American resilience, purpose, and renewal, and of the ongoing war against terrorism. The terrorists hope their atrocities "will break our will, allowing the violent to inherit the Earth. But they have miscalculated," said Bush.

In a press release, the ACLU faulted Bush for "failing to address civil liberties concerns about his administration's actions since 9/11" or answer questions raised by the "overly intrusive" use of the Patriot Act.

That same week, the ACLU announced it was filing Freedom of Information requests to get information on government surveillance of anti-war protestors at college campuses. "Students should be able to express themselves freely on campus without fear of ending up in a military database," the ACLU's Mark Schlosberg told reporters.

As a child, Ben Wizner had no idea he would spend much of his adulthood fretting over the repercussions of America's so-called war on terror. Slight, soft-spoken, precise, and unfailingly polite, Wizner grew up in New Haven, Connecticut. His father was a clinical law professor at Yale and his mother was a Holocaust survivor. She gave up her ACLU membership because of its representation of Nazis in Skokie.

Wizner first visited the Supreme Court when he was ten: "I watched my father argue his first and only Supreme Court case." That case (*Pardons v. Dumschat*), focused on an inmate serving a life sentence for killing his wife. He had sued the Connecticut's State Board of Pardons after being rejected several times without explanation.

In a 7 to 2 decision delivered by Chief Justice Warren Burger in June 1981, the court said the pardon board was within its rights. The felon's expectation of a pardon, wrote Burger, was unjustified: "It is simply a unilateral hope."

Although he was not expected to follow in his father's footsteps, Wizner knew his family expected him to do something "meaningful" with his life.

Midway through his studies in history and literature at Harvard, Wizner took a year off to work with B'Tselem, a Jerusalem-based human rights organization that documented abuses in the Occupied Territories. After graduating in 1994, he moved to New York and worked with the Legal Action Center for the Homeless. That work convinced him to apply to law school.

He won New York University's Root-Tilden-Kern Public Interest Scholarship, a full-tuition grant for future public service attorneys. Wizner worked with the Juvenile Justice Project of Louisiana and the NAACP Legal Defense Fund before clerking for federal appeals court judge Stephen Reinhardt. Ramona Ripston, Reinhardt's wife, was executive director of the ACLU affiliate in Los Angeles.

Wizner went to work for the Los Angeles affiliate some five weeks after September 11. His first memorable case involved the Aviation and

Transportation Security Act of 2001. That law, passed in the wake of the Twin Towers attack, created the Transportation Security Administration. Unlike previous baggage screeners, those hired by the newly created TSA were required to be American citizens. The new law threatened to put roughly one-fourth of screeners (including military veterans with green cards) nationally, and between 40 and 50 percent in Los Angeles, Sacramento, and San Francisco, out of work.

Working with the Service Employees International Union, the ACLU challenged the constitutionality of the law. Mark Rosenbaum, legal director of the ACLU of Southern California, argued that it would eliminate "thousands of skilled . . . experienced screeners" and replace them with neophytes, "opening the door to unnecessary security risks."

U.S. District Court Judge Robert Takasugi, an internment camp survivor, agreed. In November 2001, Takasugi issued a temporary injunction on behalf of the ACLU's plaintiffs—eight permanent resident aliens and one man from American Samoa. The appeals court ordered Takasugi to reconsider the case, which the ACLU ultimately lost.

The baggage screener case was only one of many Wizner handled having to do with discrimination against foreigners. "There was kind of an epidemic of brown people being kicked off commercial flights," he said. "We saw this in enough places on enough airlines that we decided that we should litigate this in a coordinated and strategic way."

In 2002, the ACLU filed five lawsuits against four airlines in five states on behalf of passengers removed from flights. The airlines were American, Continental, Northwest, and United.

Two of the men represented by the ACLU were of Arab descent. The others were of Asian, Filipino, and Guyanese heritage. Four were American citizens and the fifth was a permanent legal resident. The airlines argued they had ejected the men for security reasons, but no grounds were apparent for any of the ejections other than ethnic bias.

"Those cases mostly ended in positive settlements that required the airlines to train staff on civil rights laws," recalled Wizner. The United case was different because the airline went bankrupt during litigation, which resulted in an automatic stay of the litigation. Wizner and fellow ACLU attorney Reginald Shuford flew to Chicago and appeared before the bankruptcy judge. If United was still flying planes, they argued, it should be forced to obey the law. "That was all United needed to hear, and they settled right away," said Wizner.

Wizner also handled a case, filed in August 2002, on behalf of two twenty-one-year-old students from California State University. They were escorted out of an AMC movie theater in Orange County for speaking Pashto, a language of their native Afghanistan. The two were chatting while awaiting the beginning of "Deuces Wild." Their "foreign tongue" was enough to arouse a guard's suspicions. "When they walked us out, everybody was laughing at us. I was ashamed; I didn't even want my mother to know," recalled Omar Zazia, one of the students.

The students dropped their suit in 2003 after the AMC theater chain apologized. "The students are extremely gratified and vindicated. From the very beginning they made it clear that they weren't in this for the money; what they wanted was an apology. That's often harder to get than money," said Wizner.

After Wizner transferred to national headquarters in 2004 to work with what eventually became the ACLU's National Security Project, more serious cases landed on his desk. Among those was the case of Khalid El-Masri, a German citizen born in Kuwait of Lebanese parents who—mistaken for a terrorist—was tortured and tossed into a CIA prison in Afghanistan.

El-Masri's ordeal began in 2003. According to a statement he gave to the ACLU, he boarded a bus in Germany on December 31 bound for a short vacation in Skopje, Macedonia. After crossing into Macedonia, officials confiscated his passport and took him to a hotel. "The curtains were always drawn. I was never permitted to leave the room," said El-Masri.

People brandishing guns interrogated him about his mosque and activities in Germany. They asked about people he had never met and meetings that never occurred. "After thirteen days I went on a hunger strike to protest my confinement."

On January 23, 2004, El-Masri was forced to record a video saying he had been treated well and would soon return to Germany. Instead, "I was handcuffed, blindfolded, and placed in a car." He was taken to a building where people pounded him with fists and "what felt like a thick stick." Someone sliced off his clothes and beat him again until he allowed them to remove his underwear. "I was thrown on the floor, my hands were pulled behind me, and someone's boot was placed on my back. Then I felt something firm being forced inside my anus."

From Macedonia, he was taken to the CIA's "Salt Pit" prison in Afghanistan, where he was held for five months before being dropped in Albania at night and ordered to walk a deserted road "and not to look back." When he finally got back to Germany, forty pounds lighter than when he had left, he discovered his family had fled their house in Ulm, thinking he had abandoned them.

In 2005, with the ACLU's assistance, El-Masri filed suit against former CIA director George Tenet, three private aviation companies, and others, seeking compensation and damages. "The CIA successfully invoked the state secrets privilege to have the case terminated," said Wizner. "That went all the way up through the Fourth Circuit Court of Appeals. We filed a . . . cert petition to the Supreme Court, in which we said, 'How can it be that there's a privilege that allows a torture victim's claims to be dismissed on the affidavit of the torturers themselves?'" The CIA argued that litigating the case could harm national security.

That case "offers a rare study of how pressure on the CIA to apprehend al Qaeda members after the Sept. 11, 2001, attacks has led in some instances to detention based on thin or speculative evidence. The case also shows how complicated it can be to correct errors in a system built and operated in secret," reported the *Washington Post* in December 2005.

In October 2007, the Supreme Court refused to review El-Masri's case. Meanwhile, Wizner was grappling with yet another rendition case. Having had no success in going after the CIA directly, the ACLU filed suit in May 2007 against Jeppesen DataPlan, a San Jose–based subsidiary of the Boeing Corporation that specialized in "extraordinary renditions." The suit alleged that Jeppesen was knowingly complicit in "unlawful abduction, arbitrary detention, and torture."

"This is the first time we are accusing a blue-chip American company of profiting from torture," said Wizner at a press conference. Flight logs revealed that, over a four-year period, the company had provided support for some fifteen aircraft "used by the CIA in its program of extraordinary rendition," ACLU lawyer Steven Watt told the *International Herald Tribune*.

The ACLU suit cited an October 2006 article by the *New Yorker's* Jane Mayer in which she described the write-up of Jeppesen on the Boeing website, boasting that the division "offers everything needed for efficient, hassle-free, international flight operations." The website does not mention "that Jeppesen's clients include the C.I.A., and that among the international trips that the company plans for the agency are secret 'extraordinary rendition' flights for terrorism suspects," wrote Mayer.

The five plaintiffs, said the ACLU, were all "forcibly disappeared and transported to arbitrary detention and torture on flights organized by Jeppesen DataPlan at the direction of the Central Intelligence Agency (CIA)." Two of the plaintiffs—an Ethiopian citizen and an Iraqi—were legal residents of the United Kingdom. The others were an Egyptian seeking asylum in Sweden, an Italian citizen originally from Morocco, and a Yemeni who was visiting Jordan. All, according to the ACLU, were forcefully abducted, beaten, stripped, blindfolded, and dragged into waiting airplanes.

During an early February 2008 hearing, U.S. District Judge James Ware appeared sympathetic to the ACLU's arguments and promised to rule promptly but indicated that the government's invocation of the so-called state secret privilege could derail the ACLU's case. The next week, Ware dismissed the case, noting that at the core of the case was "a subject matter which is a state secret." The ACLU announced plans to appeal.

In an op-ed article in the *Los Angeles Times* published the day after Ware's ruling, Wizner shared his frustration: "So as the law stands, the U.S. can engage in torture, declare it a state secret and, by virtue of that designation alone, avoid any accountability for conduct that violates the Constitution and universal human rights guarantees."

Judge Ware was not alone in wrestling over how to balance competing interests. Romero always had been acutely sensitive to perceptions that the ACLU was undermining America's security. Respect for civil liberties, he was determined to make clear, was the friend, not the foe, of national security and patriotism.

Romero put the stars and blue background of the American flag on the cover of the ACLU's 2004 annual report. Six years later, he adorned the cover with the Statute of Liberty: "Some of the old timers . . . found it problematic that the ACLU wrapped itself in such nationalistic symbols. I didn't really have a problem with it. We're a patriotic organization. . . . We will fight conventional wisdom, but we're not going to allow ourselves to be easily cornered as part of the fringe. We're going to claim the values of patriotism, of America, of due process."

The transition to the Obama administration presented the ACLU with yet another set of challenges. Obama had promised to close the Guantánamo Bay detention camp in Cuba, but days before his inauguration in January 2009, he seemed to be rethinking that. "It is more difficult than I think a lot of people realize," he told ABC news and suggested that closing the camp during his first one hundred days would be "a challenge."

At his inauguration, Obama promised "fidelity to our founding principles" and celebrated America's limitless possibilities. He did not address how he would balance the promise of those founding principles against the ugly impulses of a society fearful of terrorism.

Two days after taking office, Obama signed executive orders shuttering the CIA's secret overseas prisons and mandating the closing of the Guantánamo Bay detention facility within a year. The signing ceremony was attended by an array of military officers. "The individuals who are standing behind me represent flag officers who . . . made a passionate plea that we restore the standards of due process and the core constitutional values that have made this country great, even in the midst of war, even in dealing with terrorism," said Obama.

As he signed Executive Order 13492, Obama promised "to close the detention facility at Guantanamo, consistent with the national security and foreign policy interests of the United States and the interest of justice."

A second executive order, 13491, would "promote the safe, lawful and humane treatment of individuals in United States custody" by ensuring that "any interrogations taking place . . . abide by the Army Field Manual," which prohibits torture.

A third order set up an interagency task force to advise the president on how best to deal with detainees in Guantanamo who could not be transferred to other countries but posed "a serious danger to the United States."

The fourth document Obama signed during that ceremony was a so-called memorandum of review that dealt with one individual, Ali Saleh Kahlah al-Marri, whose case was currently before the Supreme Court. Al-Marri, a Qatar citizen and U.S. resident, was considered an agent for Al Qaeda and had been classified as an "enemy combatant." The document asked the Supreme Court to delay his case until the new administration could review it. (The following year, al-Marri's case was transferred to the federal court system, where he agreed to a plea, making Supreme Court action moot.)

The executive orders, said Obama, signaled that although the United States would vigorously prosecute "the ongoing struggle against violence and terrorism," it would do so "in a manner that is consistent with our values and our ideals."

Romero praised the president's actions but pointed out what he called "ambiguities" in the orders: "We are hopeful that as the process unfolds and gets clarified, there will be no doubt that detainees must either be charged, prosecuted and convicted or . . . released."

On February 4, 2009, the ACLU sent a letter to Secretary of State Hillary Rodham Clinton asking her to clarify the administration's renditions policy. It was becoming clear that the presidential transition would not usher in change quite as dramatic as the ACLU had expected. It was nothing like the transition from Herbert Hoover to Franklin Roosevelt in 1933, which was so striking the ACLU commented in its annual report on the "changed and far more liberal attitude . . . on the part of several departments of the government and of the President."

Nor was it comparable to the transition from George H.W. Bush to Bill Clinton, from someone who had actively campaigned against the ACLU to someone whose first series of executive orders lifted hearts in civil libertarian and progressive circles. Those orders ended the so-called gag order blocking federally funded clinics from advising women on abortion, ended the ban on fetal research, promised to end the ban on gays in the military, revoked an order prohibiting contractors with union agreements from bidding on federal projects, and restored the right of women serving overseas to have abortions in military hospitals.

Disappointment with Clinton eventually took hold in progressive quarters, but the initial reaction was largely one of relief. Obama received no such grace period.

As Obama hedged on his commitment to shut down Guantánamo, adopted the Bush administration position on the state secrets privilege, and hesitated to reverse surveillance policies, civil libertarians began to doubt the sincerity of his campaign commitments.

Nonetheless, they held onto a cautious optimism, which was reflected in Romero's February 4 letter to Secretary Clinton. The letter informed her that the ACLU would be presenting arguments in the Jeppesen DataPlan case the following week and expressed hope the new administration would not press forward with the Bush administration's "state secrets" argument.

That Monday, Obama Justice Department lawyers showed up before the three-judge panel of the U.S. Circuit Court of Appeals in San Francisco and delivered their answer. The Obama administration was taking "exactly" the same position as the Bush White House, attorney Douglas Letter told the court. The case, he explained, had been "thoroughly vetted" with the new administration.

Letter's statement moved a clearly skeptical Judge Michael Daly Hawkins to ask, "So any time the executive branch of the government says the fact is classified, it means it cannot be examined?"

National security was at stake, responded Letter, adding that the court should "not play with fire."

"Nor should the government," responded Hawkins.

"The only place in the world where these claims can't be discussed is in this courtroom," said Wizner, and asked that the case be allowed to go forward.

On February 28, 2009, the three-judge panel handed down a decision in a related case that favored the ACLU position. The court rejected the Justice Department's attempt to dismiss a case by a then-defunct Islamic charity that had charged the Bush administration with warrantless wiretapping. The Obama administration had adopted the Bush administration's position that such counter-terrorism actions were shielded from lawsuits.

A few weeks later, the judges ruled that the ACLU's case against Jeppesen could move forward. The government could not invoke a sweeping state secret privilege, said the court, but could only invoke the privilege with respect to specific evidence. People had "freedom from arbitrary and unlawful restraint," concluded the court.

Wizner declared that the "historic" decision demolished "once and for all the legal fiction, advanced by the Bush administration and continued by the Obama administration, that facts known throughout the world could be deemed 'secrets' in a court of law."

On May 15, the White House announced it would try some of the Guantánamo detainees under the military commission system but would expand their legal rights (by limiting hearsay evidence, banning evidence obtained through torture and allowing detainees more say in choosing a lawyer). "This is the best way to protect our country, while upholding our deeply held values," said Obama, to the dismay of Romero, who had taken to calling Obama's approach "the Bush-Obama doctrine."

The *New York Times* seemed equally perplexed by the shift, reminding readers that "during the campaign, Mr. Obama criticized the military commission system as a failure."

On May 21, 2009, Barack Obama was to deliver a major speech at the National Archives on national security. It was to be, in some sense, a reboot: a chance to clear the air and dispel confusion, to explain how his approach fundamentally differed from what had come before.

The day prior to his speech, Obama convened a meeting of civil libertarians and progressives in the White House cabinet room. Obama "wanted to escape the White House policy bubble. He was eager to speak to experts who were deeply immersed in these issues. He also knew that there were some things in the speech that would not please the left. The meeting was a chance to assuage a key pressure group and, perhaps, preemptively take the edge off their inevitable criticism," wrote journalist Daniel Klaidman, who recreates the meeting in *Kill or Capture*.[1]

During that seventy-five-minute session, Obama made an argument for restraints on presidential power in the fight against terrorism and solicited the group's thoughts on a range of issues, including preventive detention and the classification of suspects as enemy combatants. "Obama betrayed his irritation only twice, and both times he directed it at the ACLU's Romero," writes Klaidman.

Early in the meeting, reports Klaidman, Romero confessed that as a gay Puerto Rican kid growing up in the Bronx, he had been leery of politicians. Obama, he suggested, had won him over, "but now I'm troubled by what I'm seeing."

Obama, "visibly annoyed," responded, "I profoundly respect your role and you need to respect mine." The president reminded Romero he had "a broader set of responsibilities" and chided him for equating his policies with Bush's, which erased "all nuance."[2]

At another point in the meeting, reports Klaidman, Romero asked that the administration identify one case of torture under Bush to investigate as a statement of intolerance for such behavior. "The president waved Romero off in midsentence, conveying that he was utterly uninterested in, even contemptuous of, the idea. 'Well, that's one man's view,' Obama said coldly. Abruptly rising from his chair, he curtly thanked the group for coming and walked out of the room. 'He looked pissed,' recalled one participant."[3]

In an interview with the *Washington Post* following the meeting, Romero said, "President Obama's decision to continue George Bush's policies essentially means that they become his own. And if he continues down this path, these policies will certainly become known in the history books as the Bush-Obama doctrine."

The next day, Obama delivered his National Archives speech, in which he attacked the Bush administration and defended his approach to terrorism. It was, said the *Washington Post*, a day of "dueling speeches." That same day, as the *Post* put it, an "unrepentant and newly unbridled former vice president Richard Cheney" spoke at the American Enterprise Institute and accused Obama of "recklessness cloaked in righteousness" that would likely lead to American deaths.

Obama confirmed that he planned to hold some detainees indefinitely without trial. "We're going to exhaust every avenue that we have to prosecute those at Guantanamo who pose a danger to our country." But certain dangerous detainees might never be prosecuted because of tainted evidence or other impediments; they nonetheless would remain incarcerated— "within a system that involves judicial and congressional oversight"— because of the ongoing threat they posed to the United States.

In reviewing Obama's speech, Sheryl Gay Stolberg of the *New York Times* asked, "at what point is President Thinker in danger of being perceived as President Flip-Flop? . . . [With] his embrace of military commissions and his decision on the detainee photos—as well as a fresh proposal . . . for 'prolonged detention' of terrorism suspects who cannot be tried—Mr. Obama is drawing comparisons to Mr. Bush by critics, who say he has backtracked, in subtle yet important ways, from the positions he staked out as a candidate."

Months later, the debate continued over Obama's deference to Bush's policies. "No matter which way he turns, President Obama can't seem to shake the legacy of George W. Bush's presidency," observed *Washington Post* political columnist Dan Balz in August 2009. Balz noted Attorney General Eric Holder's decision to investigate allegations of detainee abuse by the CIA and its contractors, which "keeps the controversy alive indefinitely at a time when Obama has more than enough controversies to keep him busy." He also pointed to Romero's insistence that there was already enough evidence to warrant prosecutions, but Holder was just "appeasing the political interests in Washington."

In early March 2010, rumors circulated in Washington that the Obama administration was gearing up to break a key campaign promise. Khalid Shaikh Mohammed, the self-declared mastermind behind the September 11 attacks, and four others accused of involvement were being held at Guantánamo, and the government was rethinking Eric Holder's pledge to try them in a civilian court.

Although Holder had vowed that the men would "answer for their alleged crimes in a courthouse just blocks from where the twin towers once stood," public sentiment had turned against the plan—in part because of projected costs and likely traffic gridlock.

On March 4, White House press secretary Robert Gibbs conceded that the administration was under pressure to change its decision. "Congress and states have actively moved to foreclose venue options, so we're obviously reviewing the possibilities," said Gibbs.

Romero responded to the speculation with an email to reporters: "If this stunning reversal comes to pass, President Obama will deal a death blow to his own Justice Department, not to mention American values."

On March 7, the ACLU ran a full-page ad in the *New York Times* pleading with President Obama to keep his commitment to prosecute the 9/11 suspects in civilian courts.

The ad, in a panel of four photographs, shows a smiling President Obama morphing into a smiling former President Bush. "What will it be Mr. President?" asks a headline above the photos. "Change or more of the same?" asks a caption below.

The text reads, "Candidate Barack Obama vowed to change the Bush-Cheney policies and restore America's values of justice and due process. Many of us are shocked and concerned that right now President Obama is considering reversing his attorney general's decision to try the 9/11 defendants in criminal court. Our criminal justice system has successfully handled over 300 terrorism cases compared to only 3 in the military commissions. Our criminal justice system will resolve these cases more quickly and more credibly than the military commissions."

The ad goes on to argue that terrorists can be vigorously prosecuted without "violating our Constitution" and urges Obama "not to back down on his commitment to our justice system, and to try the 9/11 defendants in criminal court."

It closes with a warning: "The military commissions are seriously flawed and unprepared to handle these complex cases. If President Obama reverses his attorney general's principled decision under political pressure, it will strike a devastating blow to American values and do serious damage to our nation's credibility."

Romero also sent a letter to President Obama. "I believe that you will face few, if any, greater challenges to who we are as a nation and to our commitment to the rule of law than this question of sustaining the Attorney General's principled decision to use federal criminal courts for these trials. The trials of the defendants alleged to have had roles in the September 11 attacks are . . . arguably the most important criminal trials" in America's history. "It would be a colossal mistake to reverse the administration's decision to try these defendants in federal criminal court and again relegate these landmark trials to irretrievably defective military commissions," argued Romero.

That June, at the somber annual meeting of the Campaign for America's Future, the progressive community's disenchantment was on display. "Progressives have grown ever more dissatisfied, and for good reason. Our hopes or illusions were shattered," Robert Borosage, the organizer and co-founder, said from the stage of Washington's Omni Shoreham Hotel.

At a Wednesday morning breakout session during that meeting, Romero delivered off-the-cuff remarks. "I'm going to start provocatively . . . I'm disgusted with this president," he said. Romero made clear, in an interview with Politico, that he was not disgusted with Obama personally but with his "policies on civil liberties. . . . It's eighteen months and, if not now, when? . . . Guantanamo is still not closed. Military commissions are still a mess. The administration still uses state secrets to shield themselves from litigation. There's no prosecution for criminal acts of the Bush administration. Surveillance powers put in place under the Patriot Act have been renewed. If there has been change in the civil liberties context, I frankly don't see it."

Shortly after Romero shared those views, senior presidential advisor Valerie Jarrett advised ACLU Washington director Laura Murphy, via email, that she believed "Anthony's comments have made it impossible for us to have the kind of working partnership with the ACLU that I had hoped we would have."

Murphy, whose work with the Obama administration encompassed anti-crime legislation, voting rights, civil rights, education, police abuse and an array of other issues, dreaded losing White House support on policy issues where they were natural allies. She asked Jarrett to allow Romero to apologize to the president and urged Romero to do so.

Romero, who had never meant his remarks to come across as a personal attack on the president, realized he had verbally overstepped. He followed up Murphy's efforts with an email to Jarrett in which he apologized "unconditionally for my comments about the President that I made during the break-out session at the Campaign for America's Future."

Romero went on to explain that he respected "the office of President and I deeply admire President Obama personally. So I can appreciate how offensive it would be to him and to you that I had used the word 'disgusted' in my poorly chosen, off-the-cuff remarks about a particular set of issues." He went on to praise Obama's work in the areas of criminal justice reform, LGBT rights, and voting and other civil rights. But Romero acknowledged his "deep reservations—which we have tried to express honorably and openly—about the policies that he has continued from the previous administration on national security and civil liberties matters that [seem] to us inconsistent with our constitutional principles and our highest ideals."

Romero also complained that the ACLU found itself "in the untenable position of being subject to a public, criminal investigation for the first time in our 90-year history in connection with U.S. Attorney Fitzgerald's look at the activities of our lawyers at Guantanamo. And this has left our staff, members, and lay leaders troubled, frustrated, and concerned."

Jarrett accepted the apology. She informed Romero that she and Murphy had "a very frank and candid conversation. . . . Perhaps because I have known Laura and her family for my entire life, it was easier for me to explain my thoughts to her. Although she passionately defended both you and the ACLU, I still feel that great harm was done. I assured Laura that we will continue to work with the ACLU as we do all organizations. However, personal trust develops out of life experiences and right now there has been a material breach of that trust. My hope is that in time that will change."

On September 8, 2010, more than a year after the three-judge appeals court panel awarded the ACLU a victory in the Jeppesen rendition case, the full court—an "en banc" panel of eleven judges—reversed the panel by a 6 to 5 vote.

"Because the facts underlying plaintiffs' claims are so infused with [national security] secrets, any plausible effort by Jeppesen to defend against them would create an unjustifiable risk of revealing state secrets," ruled the majority.

Judge Michael Daly Hawkins, writing for the dissenters, emphatically disagreed. The case, he argued, should have been sent back to the district court, which then could have determined "whether Plaintiffs can establish the prima facie elements of their claims or whether Jeppesen could defend against those claims without resort to state secrets evidence."

The doctrine of state secrets "is so dangerous as a means of hiding governmental misbehavior under the guise of national security, and so violative of common rights to due process, that courts should confine its application to the narrowest circumstances that still protect the government's essential secrets," he wrote.

On May 16, 2011, the Supreme Court refused, without comment, to review the case, letting the Ninth Circuit's decision stand. "With today's decision, the Supreme Court has refused once again to give justice to torture victims and to restore our nation's reputation as a guardian of human rights and the rule of law. To date, every victim of the Bush administration's torture regime has been denied his day in court. But while the torture architects and their enablers have escaped the judgment of the courts, they will not escape the judgment of history," said Wizner.

European judicial bodies were more sympathetic to human rights arguments. In November 2010, the British government announced it was prepared to compensate some sixteen British nationals for anti-terrorism efforts gone awry. Though details of the settlements were not publicly disclosed, Great Britain said it would pay millions to settle claims by former Guantánamo detainees who said the British government was complicit in their torture by U.S. officials.

The ACLU's deputy legal director Jameel Jaffer found it "deeply troubling" that while Great Britain was accepting responsibility, "here in the United States the Obama administration continues to shield the architects of the torture program from civil liability."

In December 2012, the European Court of Human Rights unanimously announced it was awarding El-Masri 60,000 euros (roughly $78,500) for his ordeal at the hands of his American captors. The European Court said the decision was important "not only for the applicant and his family, but also for other victims of similar crimes and the general public, who had the right to know what had happened."

Jamil Dakwar, director of the ACLU human rights program, welcomed the "landmark" decision as "a stark reminder of America's utter failure to hold its own officials accountable for serious violations of both U.S. and international law."

Wizner acknowledges that his expectations were always limited. "We knew at the outset that it would be almost impossible, given the law and given the environment, for us to litigate the cases to judgment. We knew that we were going to crash onto one of these procedural hurdles. Therefore, the case was about something else, and the audience was broader than the judge. We needed to find a way to change the conversation around torture in the United States, which was a distressing conversation. The conversation was too often, 'What rights should terrorists have?' and not, 'What happens when you suspend the rule of law?'

"We very deliberately led with the El-Masri case because of his unquestioned innocence. . . . It was pretty important to change the face of the torture debate from Khalid Shaikh Mohammed [the so-called brains behind the 9/11 attack] to Khalid El-Masri, which I think we did fairly successfully."

In March 2011, the Obama administration reversed the ban imposed at the beginning of his presidency on military trials for suspects detained at Guantánamo. Military trials would be allowed, although with new guidelines, including due process rights, via executive order. "Providing more process to Guantanamo detainees is just window dressing for the reality that today's executive order institutionalized indefinite detention, which is unlawful, unwise and un-American," said Romero.

Tom Parker, speaking for Amnesty International, was just as harsh: "With the stroke of a pen, President Obama extinguished any lingering hope that his administration would return the United States to the rule of law by referring detainee cases from Guantanamo Bay to federal courts rather than the widely discredited military commissions."

That April, Holder announced that Khalid Shaikh Mohammed and four alleged fellow conspirators would be tried at Guantánamo. Although Holder said he still believed a federal court was the best place for the trial, "members of Congress have intervened and imposed restrictions blocking the administration from bringing any Guantanamo detainees to trial in the United States, regardless of the venue. We will continue to seek to repeal those restrictions. But we must face a simple truth: those restrictions are unlikely to be repealed in the immediate future. And we simply cannot allow a trial to be delayed any longer for the victims of the 9/11 attacks or for their family members who have waited for nearly a decade for justice."

13

Edward Snowden Joins the ACLU

Prior to June 6, 2013, few Americans were aware that Verizon, an American-based telecommunications giant, was working in league with the National Security Agency and collecting information on its customers. But that Thursday, the story made front pages across America thanks to reporters at the *Guardian*, a Britain-based newspaper, and the *Washington Post*.

"The National Security Agency is currently collecting the telephone records of millions of US customers of Verizon," reported Glenn Greenwald in the *Guardian*. The surveillance was approved by a top-secret order that mandated Verizon to report daily "on all telephone calls in its systems, both within the US and between the US and other countries," revealed Greenwald. The order prohibited Verizon from publicly disclosing the information was being collected.

Verizon was not targeting suspected wrongdoers but was collecting information "indiscriminately and in bulk," reported Greenwald. And although no one was recording the specific content of the calls, Verizon was providing "location data, call duration, unique identifiers, and the time and duration of all calls."

The Bush administration previously had acknowledged that the NSA was collecting call-records data, noted Greenwald, "but this is the first time significant and top-secret documents have revealed the continuation of the practice on a massive scale under President Barack Obama." The next day the *Guardian* came out with another astounding story, this one bylined by Greenwald and Ewen MacAskill. It described a program called PRISM, which gave the NSA access to information held by Google, Facebook, and other internet giants.

PRISM, they reported, "allows them to collect material including search history, the content of emails, file transfers and live chats." The revelations were contained in a forty-one-slide top-secret PowerPoint presentation "apparently used to train intelligence operatives on the capabilities of the programme. The document claims 'collection directly from the servers' of major US service providers."

Google admitted that it "disclosed user data . . . in accordance with the law" but denied it had a "back door" through which the government could access private data.

The *Washington Post* was reporting the same shocking information (albeit a bit more cautiously) about Verizon and crediting the *Guardian* as a source. The order "could represent the broadest surveillance order known to have been issued," observed the *Post*. "It also would confirm long-standing suspicions of civil liberties advocates about the sweeping nature of U.S. surveillance through commercial carriers under laws passed after the Sept. 11, 2001, terrorist attacks."

The *Post* quoted an "expert" who speculated that the order uncovered by the *Guardian* might be a "routine renewal" of an order first issued in 2006.

"The legitimate values of liberty and safety often compete. But for the public to be able to make a reasonable assessment of whether these programs are worth the security benefits, it needs more explanation," editorialized the *Post*.

The *Post* matched the *Guardian* story on the PRISM program with an article bylined by Barton Gellman and Laura Poitras. The government was "tapping directly into the central servers of nine leading U.S. Internet companies, extracting audio and video chats, photographs, emails, documents, and connection logs," reported the *Post*, which speculated that the program "may be the first of its kind."

Both newspapers reported that Government Communications Headquarters (GCHQ), Britain's version of the NSA, had secretly tapped into the same internet companies, courtesy of the NSA. "PRISM would appear to allow GCHQ to circumvent the formal legal process required in Britain" to seek such personal information, reported the *Post*, which added, "PRISM was launched from the ashes of President George W. Bush's secret program of warrantless domestic surveillance in 2007, after news media disclosures, lawsuits and the Foreign Intelligence Surveillance Court forced the president to look for new authority."

Jameel Jaffer of the ACLU called the PRISM program, "very disturbing. . . . These companies have an obligation to their subscribers and their customers to protect sensitive information."

The story that shocked America had been germinating for half a year before it finally leapt into print. An American civil rights lawyer turned political blogger and *Guardian* columnist (then living in Rio de Janeiro), Glenn Greenwald was an essential element.

Someone calling himself Cincinnatus—a pseudonym apparently meant to invoke the reputation of a legendary Roman statesman—had contacted Greenwald by email in December 2012. He urged him to get an encryption program so they could communicate about something Greenwald was sure to find interesting.[1] Greenwald brushed off the message. He also ignored Cincinnatus's subsequent messages. The matter vanished from his mind until that April, when, during a visit to New York, Greenwald met with Laura Poitras, an independent filmmaker he admired.

Poitras had also received mysterious, anonymous emails alluding to secrets. The emailer apparently planned to leak sensitive documents and thought Poitras should work with Greenwald in disseminating the information they contained. Poitras thought the source was on the level and showed Greenwald documents that convinced him as well.

Shortly thereafter, Greenwald agreed to meet the mysterious source in Hong Kong. He also learned that Poitras had reached out to *Washington Post* reporter Barton Gellman. Cincinnatus was annoyed the *Post* had involved a team of lawyers—who he felt were "driven by fear rather than conviction and determination."[2]

Before heading to Hong Kong, Greenwald received a tantalizing sample of documents, including a "manifesto." It seemed that Cincinnatus was not simply sharing information; he was interested in sparking "a worldwide debate about privacy, Internet freedom, and the dangers of state surveillance."

Greenwald called up Janine Gibson, the New York–based editor of the U.S. edition of the *Guardian*, to share the news about his impending blockbuster. She greenlighted the trip to Hong Kong with Poitras on the condition that Ewan MacAskill, a veteran *Guardian* reporter, accompany them. Poitras and Greenwald objected but eventually relented, with the understanding that MacAskill would not meet the source until Poitras and Greenwald agreed he should. They also learned that the *Post*'s Gellman would not be coming. The *Post*'s lawyers apparently thought traveling to a foreign country to receive stolen secret government documents would be crossing a line.

Reading through the stash of documents on the plane, Greenwald learned that Cincinnatus was Edward Snowden, whom he assumed to be a middle-aged bureaucrat. Poitras and Greenwald arrived in Hong Kong on Sunday night, June 2. The next morning, they headed to the five-star Mira Hotel, where Snowden apparently was staying.

After some cloak-and-dagger skulking about, they met the source. They were stunned to discover that Snowden was a young man who looked even younger than his twenty-nine years. Snowden took the journalists to his room and, to evade surveillance, placed Greenwald's cellphone in a refrigerator.

During a five-hour-long interview, Greenwald interrogated Snowden about his childhood, his education, his work history, and his motivation. Snowden told Greenwald that he had become increasingly disenchanted as he grasped the dimensions of government spying on Americans and other governmental abuses: "I began to understand what my government really does in the world is very different from what I've always been taught. . . . The stuff I saw really began to disturb me. I could watch drones in real time as they surveilled the people they might kill. . . . I watched NSA tracking people's Internet activities as they typed. I became aware of just how invasive U.S. surveillance capabilities had become. . . . And almost nobody knew what was happening."[3]

Greenwald decided to focus on four separate stories: the first on the government compelling Verizon to turn over records; the second on the Bush administration's warrantless eavesdropping program; the third on the PRISM program; and the fourth on BOUNDLESS INFORMANT, a program that quantified the NSA surveillance.

In contrast to Greenwald, Ewen MacAskill's involvement in the story began almost by happenstance. At the time, he recalled during an interview, he was working out of the New York office of the *Guardian*. One day, "U.S. editor Janine Gibson called me across the newsroom and said, 'I want to have a word.'"

Gibson told him, "There's somebody in Hong Kong, says he's a spy and wants to leak documents."

They both laughed.

When MacAskill returned from lunch, Poitras and Greenwald were in the office. They showed him some documents. "Snowden had sent to Laura a sort of introduction package," MacAskill recalled. In it "were the Verizon documents, the PRISM documents, and some others. . . . It went totally over my head. . . . I didn't understand why they were so excited about it. . . . After that, Glenn and Laura left, and Glenn told Laura that I was going with them to Hong Kong."

By their second meeting with Snowden, Poitras and Greenwald were beginning to trust MacAskill. They took him along. MacAskill, like the others, was surprised at Snowden's youth: "He sort of misled a little bit on exactly on what he was."

Tuesday morning, the journalists visited Snowden at his hotel. "I said, 'I've got an iPhone. Do you mind if I record this?'" asked MacAskill. Snowden panicked.

"You've got to get that phone out of here," he replied.

"Okay. Where do you want me to put it?" asked MacAskill.

"Put it in Laura's room."

As MacAskill, recalled, Snowden said, "You've got to put it in the freezer compartment."

MacAskill was baffled: "I thought, 'That's slightly odd behavior.' In his room, he had cushions up the side of the doors so people couldn't eavesdrop. He put a bottle of soy sauce behind the door. He was telling us that if somebody came in the room, knocked over the soy bottle, you'd get a different stain. I looked at Glenn as if to say, 'This guy is nuts.'"

That Wednesday, the group reconvened and reviewed Snowden's story. He told them he had been deeply affected by 9/11 and decided to join the military. "He was training in the Special Forces. As soon as I heard him say that," recalled MacAskill "I thought, 'Shit. This guy is a fantasist.' [But] everything he told us was true."

From the outset, recalled MacAskill, Snowden "wanted the stories to be about surveillance" and had no intention of revealing operational secrets. He told the journalists he trusted their judgment about what should be printed and what withheld.

MacAskill asked about GCHQ, the British intelligence organization. Snowden told him, "Their behavior is worse than the NSA" and promised to provide evidence. "The next day he gave me two thumb drives. And I said to him, 'What's on that?' It was 60,000 documents, and that's when I realized this . . . wasn't like any other story I'd ever done."

The information Snowden provided led to a *Guardian* article that asserted GCHQ "is able to drink from the same trough" as the NSA. GCHQ had had access to PRISM since "at least June 2010," reported the *Guardian*. As a result, the organization had radically increased the number of intelligence reports it generated.

On July 7, the *Guardian* editorialized, "Few Americans believe that they live in a police state. . . . Yet the everyday fact that the police have the right to monitor the communications of all its citizens—in secret—is a classic hallmark of a state that fears freedom as well."

The stories generated by Snowden were not limited to those in the *Guardian* and *Washington Post*. Snowden's documents spawned thousands of news stories and televised commentary around the globe—in outlets ranging from MSNBC, to Canada's *Globe and Mail*, to *The Observer* in London, which editorialized, "we should not allow a cabal of grave-faced, middle-aged politicians and spies to bury this scandal with the usual national security response."

Meanwhile, the *Post* and *Guardian* continued to publish blockbuster revelations. The *Guardian* reported, "Barack Obama has ordered his senior national security and intelligence officials to draw up a list of potential overseas targets for US cyber-attacks." The "Offensive Cyber Effects Operations," revealed the *Guardian*, offered "unique and unconventional capabilities to advance US national objectives around the world with little or no warning to the adversary or target and with potential effects ranging from subtle to severely damaging.'"

The *Guardian* followed up with an expose on "Boundless Informant," a powerful NSA-developed tool "for recording and analysing where its intelligence comes from, raising questions about its repeated assurances to Congress that it cannot keep track of all the surveillance it performs on American communications."

On Monday, June 10, the *Guardian* ran a photo of the bespectacled, dark-haired Snowden, posed against a dark background. "The whistleblower: I can't allow the US government to destroy privacy and basic liberties," read the headline.

The story revealed the "individual responsible for one of the most significant leaks in US political history" to be "a 29-year-old former technical assistant for the CIA and current employee of . . . Booz Allen Hamilton."

The newspaper was "revealing his identity at his request." Snowden explained, "I have no intention of hiding who I am because I know I have done nothing wrong."

The *Guardian* predicted that Snowden would "go down in history as one of America's most consequential whistleblowers, alongside Daniel Ellsberg and Bradley Manning."

In the Q&A conducted by Greenwald and MacAskill, Snowden says, "I do not want to live in a world where everything I do and say is recorded."

Asked whether his actions were criminal, he responds, "We have seen enough criminality on the part of government. It is hypocritical to make this allegation against me."

What did he expect to happen to him? "Nothing good . . . The only thing I can do is sit here and hope the Hong Kong government does not deport me." He doubted he had "committed a crime outside the domain of the US." He was inclined "to seek asylum in a country with shared values."

That Monday, the *Post* ran its profile of Snowden. The article, by Barton and two other reporters, reported that Snowden was "willing to face the consequences of exposure." In an accompanying article, Barton described his interactions with Snowden. "Verax was the name he chose for himself, 'truth teller' in Latin," wrote Barton, who added that Snowden "knew full well the risks he had undertaken and the awesome powers that would soon be arrayed to hunt for him."

That June 12, MacAskill published yet another profile of Snowden. In the short time he had spent with Snowden, much had changed, Mac-Askill observed. Snowden had become "the world's most famous spy, whistleblower and fugitive, responsible for the biggest intelligence breach in recent US history."

MacAskill wrestled with whether Snowden was a "whistleblower or traitor" and ultimately left the question unanswered. Instead, he offered Snowden's critique of Obama's argument that security and privacy were in conflict.

Snowden "disputed that there had to be a trade-off between security and privacy, describing the very idea of such a trade-off as a fundamental assault on the US constitution."

MacAskill closed with Snowden's paraphrase of Benjamin Franklin's observation that, "Those who would give up essential Liberty, to purchase a little temporary Safety, deserve neither Liberty nor Safety." (Snowden's version was, "Those who surrender freedom for security will not have, nor do they deserve, either one.")

Snowden, MacAskill concluded, "has gone underground, for now. But this saga is far from over."

In many respects, Snowden's journey was just beginning. He was in a foreign country, sought by U.S. authorities, with no plan of escape. At that point, Greenwald ran into Gill Phillips, the *Guardian*'s chief lawyer, who, as Greenwald tells it, "had stopped in Hong Kong on her way from Australia to London to provide Ewen and me with legal counsel." Working with a couple of local attorneys, the group came up with a plan to get Snowden out of his hotel. Dodging reporters who were swarming in hopes of spotting the now famous fugitive, the lawyers spirited him away and stashed him in what Snowden called a "safe house."

Desperate for an exit option, Snowden called WikiLeaks founder Julian Assange, who had taken refuge in the Ecuadorian embassy in London. Assange advised him to seek asylum in Russia and arranged for an associate, Sarah Harrison, to fly to Hong Kong from Australia. She arrived on June 11 and immediately went to work, setting up decoy flights to Beijing, New Delhi, and other cities to mask his real destination, which was Moscow. She booked him on a June 23 flight to Russia, with a connecting flight to Havana, Cuba.[4] Meanwhile, the U.S., government filed a criminal complaint and demanded Snowden's extradition.

On June 23, the *Telegraph* reported that Snowden had "boarded an Aeroflot jet to Moscow's Sheremetyevo airport, which landed just after 2 p.m. UK time." Russia's Interfax news agency "quoted a source within Aeroflot who claimed there was a ticket in his name for a flight onward to Cuba," added the *Telegraph*.

Hong Kong authorities were claiming they'd had no legal basis for holding Snowden. Assange's people were tweeting that WikiLeaks had provided Snowden with travel papers and an exit from Hong Kong and was working on getting him asylum in a democratic country.

Meanwhile, a CNN correspondent in Moscow's Sheremetyevo airport reported that a black car had pulled up to a plane on the tarmac and a man had left the plane: "We presume at this stage this was Snowden." Anchor Candy Crowley speculated that he might be bound for Iceland, Havana, or Venezuela.

That Monday, reporters who had flown from Russia to Cuba in hopes of finding Snowden reported that he was not on their flight. The United States expressed "deep disappointment" with Hong Kong's decision to let Snowden go and demanded that Moscow hand him over.

CNN's Wolf Blitzer summed up the state of confusion: "Edward Snowden has been on the move from Hong Kong to Moscow and maybe— maybe, we just don't know—beyond."

On June 25, an Aeroflot flight from Moscow landed in Havana. When the captain emerged, photographers surrounded him, prompting him to pull out his own camera and take pictures of them. "No Snowden," he said.

In early 2012, Wizner had been promoted to direct the newly created Speech, Privacy, and Technology Project. The new job offered in-depth exposure to technologies at the center of complex constitutional questions regarding speech and privacy—issues that were central to the Edward Snowden saga.

"The irony is that I was making this decision to step back from the spotlight a little bit, and then Snowden fell out of the sky," said Wizner.

Wizner had been friendly with both Greenwald and Poitras for some time. As a regular guest on Greenwald's podcast, and as someone Greenwald occasionally interviewed when writing about civil liberties, he considered Greenwald a "long-distance friend." He had met Poitras while she was making *The Oath*, a documentary film released in 2010 that followed the interconnected stories of two former employees of Osama bin Laden. One, after being arrested in Afghanistan and declared an enemy combatant, won a U.S. Supreme Court case that forced reforms on the military's tribunal system.

Wizner met Poitras while she was making the film. Her travel for that project apparently brought her to the attention of federal authorities, who repeatedly stopped and interrogated her when she was returning from abroad. "It got to the point where she just traveled with a pile of my business cards," said Wizner. Instead of answering officers' question, she "would just hand them my card."

In January of 2013, Poitras stopped by his office.

"She said, 'Can we put our phones here in your drawer and then go talk somewhere else?'"

"I thought, 'This sounds a little paranoid, but sure.'"

They went to a coffeeshop where Poitras showed him an email from someone calling himself "Citizenfour." He described himself as a senior intelligence official with important information to share.

"She wanted my advice about whether . . . this was a crazy person."

The email, he concluded, "didn't seem delusional."

Wizner advised her that, if she wished to proceed, she should involve an established national security journalist. Not only would such a journalist provide needed expertise but she would gain "the legal protection that person's institution might be able to provide." He recommended Gellman, a former *Post* staff writer who sometimes still wrote for the newspaper.

In late May, Poitras asked Wizner to meet her in a small restaurant in her office building. Citizenfour had asked her to meet him in Hong Kong, which made her "very nervous."

"As I heard the story, the *Post*'s lawyers balked at Hong Kong," pointing out that talking to a source in Hong Kong could subject the journalists to Chinese surveillance and even result in espionage charges against the newspaper. Gellman stayed behind.

Wizner knew a story was in the works but had no idea how big it would be. "I actually got a call from Greenwald from Hong Kong before the first story appeared. He said, 'I'm calling you because I need you to talk me out of something.'"

At that point, the *Guardian* seemed to be dragging its feet, and Greenwald was considering taking the stories elsewhere, or perhaps just publishing them on a specially created website. Wizner advised Greenwald that publishing on his own would be dangerous and also would likely lessen the story's impact.

Soon thereafter, "Greenwald and Poitras began sort of pitching to me the idea of me and the ACLU coming on as Snowden's counsel," said Wizner. Nothing was decided. Meanwhile, Snowden fled to Moscow.

In early July, the press reported that Snowden had simultaneously applied for asylum to twenty-one countries.

The Times of London observed on July 3, "at the time of writing, seven have rejected these applications. . . . Others look likely to follow suit. . . . Mr. Snowden is running out of options." *The Times* advised Snowden to "Go home. . . . In truth, he never should have left."

Snowden was living in the transit zone of Sheremetyevo Airport. Greenwald and Poitras encouraged him to engage a lawyer, recommending Wizner.

That July 4 weekend, Wizner was on vacation in Honolulu. He had anxiously followed the Snowden coverage. "I didn't know Snowden's name before anyone else did. I saw him for the first time in that video on *The Guardian* website." Greenwald and Poitras arranged for the two to talk during Wizner's vacation.

Greenwald was able to put them in touch and verify their respective identities to each other. They talked using "sort of an encrypted form of GChat. . . . The first thing that we needed to get clear is that he wanted me and the ACLU to act on his behalf."

Wizner told Snowden there might at times be a conflict "between what's best for you and what's best for the ACLU."

Asked what he meant, Wizner explained, "it might be in our interest for certain things to be published that might increase your criminal jeopardy." Wizner was not sure how likely such a scenario might be but felt duty-bound to make the point.

Snowden replied, "The whole reason why I did what I did was to empower groups like the ACLU to be able to get into the courts, go to Congress and seek reform, seek accountability. I can't imagine a situation in which what I want and what the ACLU wants will diverge. And if that happens . . . you will find me another lawyer and keep doing what the ACLU needs to do."

Snowden also asked whether, as a result of his actions, the ACLU now had "standing."

"I wasn't expecting to hear [that] from someone who had just turned 30, who had probably never spoken to lawyers before," Wizner recalled. "But he had been very focused on our litigation and . . . and wanted to know had he given us the ticket . . . to get into federal court."

Wizner responded, "Honestly, I don't know. They're going to continue to try to argue that we don't have standing. They're going to say the fact that these documents are public doesn't mean that they're not classified still. . . . But we have a much better argument now to get over those standing barriers than we ever had."

By the end of the conversation, Wizner was deeply impressed. "It was clear from the video on *The Guardian* website that he was thoughtful. . . . But it wasn't at all clear . . . that this would be someone thinking about the sort of specific reasons why our litigation had been unsuccessful in the past."

"We did turn out to have standing," said Wizner. "Two years later we got a hundred-page decision from the Second Circuit Court of Appeals saying not only that we had standing but that the program that we challenged had been illegal from the outset and not even authorized by Congress. That was *ACLU v. Clapper*," which challenged the legality of the NSA surveillance programs.

Not everyone at the ACLU was an easy sell when it came to Snowden. Nor did Wizner expect them to be. He did expect Romero, whom he considered a risk taker, to welcome working with the whistleblower. Romero "has always believed that the capital that the ACLU has accrued . . . is not to be hoarded; it's to be spent at times," said Wizner.

On the other hand, as Wizner recalls the conversations, "both Steve Shapiro, who was our legal director, and Laura Murphy, who at that time was the director of our Washington legislative office, were adamantly opposed to the ACLU representing Snowden."

Both pointed out, he said, that the ACLU would inevitably be involved in whatever legislation and litigation came out of the Snowden revelations. "Why should we saddle ourselves with somebody who is viewed as toxic by members of Congress because he went to China and now he's in Russia?" he recalls Murphy saying. "Steve had a sort of instinctual hesitation bordering on dislike for the way that Snowden had gone about it, the way that he [Snowden] spoke. It sounded grandiose to him."

Murphy doesn't remember being opposed to Snowden, "but I do remember being concerned about the communications strategy and how representing him would be perceived on Capitol Hill and in the White House. I wanted them to be smart about the possible implications."

Certainly, once Snowden became the ACLU's client, she was fully supportive. "I think it would be very helpful for us to have snappy retorts to those who would find it convenient to smear Snowden," she emailed Romero several months after Snowden came aboard.

She also suggested pushing back with a blog post against the Defense Department's "unsubstantiated claims" that Snowden had harmed national security. He had caused "more embarrassment than harm," she argued.

She advised her colleagues to make the argument that the "real threat to national security" were the activities Snowden had exposed: "[All] this data in the government's hands chills dissent, suppresses cooperation from communities, breeds distrust and gives hackers and terrorists a one-stop shop for deeply personal information that can harm all Americans. Fidelity to the Bill of Rights makes us stronger, not invasions of our privacy by our own government."

Shapiro declined to discuss his initial take on Snowden. "I don't think it's appropriate, honestly, to discuss internal deliberations about the representation of somebody who remains an ACLU client. I view those as confidential," said Shapiro. "But what I will say is . . . that one of the ways I viewed my role as legal director was to ask a series of hard questions whenever we were thinking about undertaking a high-profile case or a high-profile client. . . . . So there were certainly questions that I thought we needed to think about both for our internal vetting and in order to be able to respond if people raised objections afterwards."

"It was clear from the beginning that he was potentially facing very serious criminal charges," added Shapiro. "We are not criminal lawyers. And

I just thought that we needed to think . . . through what that meant to take him on as a client."

In retrospect, said Shapiro, "I am very comfortable saying that it was the right decision for the ACLU to make. I think that Snowden's revelations triggered a . . . worldwide discussion about the depth and scope and consequences of the surveillance state that has grown up around us . . . and I think that that conversation has been a beneficial one in the United States and globally."

Wizner acknowledges feeling less than total confidence in what he was doing. "Many times during those first months and really the whole first year, I had feelings that could be described as fear," he said. "But it wasn't fear that someone was going to . . . say, 'You crossed this line. What you're doing now isn't lawyering. [It's] just aiding and abetting in a conspiracy.' I really did feel protected by the ACLU from that kind of attack. But there was a lot of fear that I might be doing it wrong, and that there might be avenues that should be pursued that I wasn't pursuing."

He couldn't help realizing that his was a rather bizarre assignment: "What does it even mean to say that I've been his lawyer when the whole purpose of our engagement was to keep him away from any kind of legal encounter with the United States? The only court we were dealing with was the court of public opinion."

In January 2014, Wizner finally met Snowden in person. Wizner and Romero traveled to Russia together. "I thought it was important for Anthony to meet him face to face at that time . . . because of how invested he was and how much of the ACLU capital had been invested and risked," said Wizner. "I assumed that the face to face meeting would introduce an entire new dimension to the way that we connected; and that turned out not to be true. He was so comfortable communicating through the internet, had been doing it since he was a teenager, had been talking to people around the world." It turned out that the person Wizner met in Russia was the exact same man he had met earlier on the internet.

"Some of the biggest decisions I have regretted around here are the decisions I didn't make, or choices I didn't make," confided Romero during an interview. One of those was the decision not to lead the battle on behalf of the Guantánamo Bay detainees. Instead, he listened to colleagues who told him, "we're not focused on Guantánamo, we're focusing on the domestic immigrants who are being detained and deported."

"Give credit to where credit is due," said Romero. The Center for Constitutional Rights "was making some very big decisions that we demurred on Gitmo."

Ultimately, Guantánamo Bay became one of the ACLU's signature issues. The ACLU fought tirelessly for the so-called 9/11 mastermind Khalid Sheikh Mohammed and his alleged confederates to be tried in a civilian court as opposed to by a military commission. But Romero could not shake his regret that the ACLU had not done more early on.

He had no intention of repeating that mistake with Snowden. "When Snowden came up, I was kind of really playing that in the back of my head. . . . We had litigated the NSA surveillance effort through the Supreme Court. Jameel Jaffer had litigated the case. . . . We got to the court and got kicked out because we could not prove anyone was under this type of surveillance."

Then suddenly Snowden appears, documenting things the ACLU previously had been unable to prove. When Romero walked into the office the Monday following Snowden's first revelations, "I knew that the lawyers would be thinking, 'How do we find the new case, the new clients? We had brought [the cases] on behalf of Amnesty [International] the first time around. And since I sign all the contracts, I knew I was a client of Verizon Business Network. I knew where [the ACLU litigators] were going to be: the Brooklyn Bridge Conference Room."

Romero walked into the conference room and announced, "I have a client for you."

"Who do you have?" someone asked.

"Us, because we are clients of Verizon Business Network, and our data has been therefore seized by the United States Government," Romero replied.

In *ACLU v. Clapper*, filed June 11, 2013, in the U.S. District Court of the Southern District of New York, the ACLU argued that the NSA's metadata collection program violated the Fourth Amendment prohibition against an illegal search as well as the First Amendment right to free speech and association. The ACLU also claimed that the program illegally exceeded the provisions of the USA Patriot Act.

The government's actions were "akin to snatching every American's address book—with annotations detailing whom we spoke to, when we talked, for how long, and from where," argued the ACLU complaint.

That "mass call tracking," said the ACLU, "allows the government to learn sensitive and privileged information about [the Plaintiffs'] work and clients, and it is likely to have a chilling effect on whistleblowers and others who would otherwise contact Plaintiffs for legal assistance."

On October 29, 2013, Senator Patrick Leahy and Congressman Jim Sensenbrenner introduced what they called the USA Freedom Act. It was a direct response to the brouhaha set off by Ed Snowden, and its objective was to claw back for Americans some of the privacy Snowden revealed had been stripped away.

It took aim at two problems. One was with FISA, the Foreign Intelligence Surveillance Act, which Leahy argued had allowed "government surveillance programs . . . far broader than the American people previously understood." The other was the USA Patriot Act, which had "for years been secretly interpreted to authorize the dragnet collection of Americans' phone records on an unprecedented scale, regardless of whether those Americans have any connection to terrorist activities or groups."

"Somewhere along the way," said Sensenbrenner, "the balance between security and privacy was lost." The new law, they declared, "would end the dragnet collection of Americans' phone records" and provide safeguards against warrantless surveillance under FISA.

The ACLU issued a statement calling the proposed legislation "a true reform bill that rejects the false and dangerous notion that privacy and our fundamental freedoms are incompatible with security."

The bill cleared the House Judiciary Committee on May 7, 2014, by a vote of 32 to 0. The ACLU's Laura Murphy called it "a historic turn of events" and "a direct result" of Snowden's revelations. The full House passed the measure, 303 to 121, on May 22; but it had been altered, at the request of intelligence agencies, to allow for a broader range of searches, leading some former supporters to disassociate themselves from the bill.

Congresswoman Carol Shea-Porter complained about the changes in the bill made during private negotiations between House leadership and the White House. "The final version was available for less than 48 hours before the vote," she said. Congressman Jared Polis also objected to the changes, arguing that a loophole had been introduced that would allow uncomfortably vague terms to identity the target of surveillance. That version of the bill failed to pass the Senate.

A revised version, dubbed the Freedom Act of 2015, passed the House (338 to 88) in May, amidst objections from the left that it was too oppressive and from the right that it left America too vulnerable.

The Senate passed the bill June 2 by a vote of 67 to 32. President Obama, who signed it late that night, declared: "It protects civil liberties and our national security." The ACLU's deputy legal director Jaffer called it "the most important surveillance reform bill since 1978, and its passage is an indication that Americans are no longer willing to give the intelligence agencies a blank check." It was, he added, "a testament to the significance of the Snowden disclosures."

In December 2013, in two separate decision, federal district courts reached essentially opposite conclusions on the questions raised by *ACLU v. Clapper*.

On December 16, in *Klayman v. Obama*, Judge Richard Leon of the District Court for the District of Columbia found that the NSA's data sweep program violated the Fourth Amendment prohibition against unreasonable search and seizures. "I cannot imagine a more 'indiscriminate' and 'arbitrary invasion' than this systematic and high-tech collection and retention of personal data on virtually every single citizen," declared Leon. He stayed enforcement, allowing time for the government to appeal.

Larry Klayman, a former Justice Department prosecutor and founder of Judicial Watch and Freedom Watch, called Leon's ruling "the biggest decision in the context of the government in my lifetime."

On December 27, Judge William Pauley III of the U.S. District Court for the Southern District of New York, dismissed *ACLU v. Clapper*. The "question for this Court is whether the Government's bulk telephony metadata program is lawful. This Court finds it is. But the question of whether that program should be conducted is for the other two coordinate branches of Government to decide," wrote Pauley in a fifty-four-page decision.

"No doubt, the bulk telephony metadata collection program vacuums up information about virtually every telephone call to, from, or within the

United States," conceded Pauley. "Technology allowed al-Qaeda to operate decentralized and plot international terrorist attacks remotely. The bulk
telephony metadata collection program represents the Government's
counter-punch: connecting fragmented and fleeting communications to re-
construct and eliminate al-Qaeda's terror network."

Deputy legal director Jaffer denounced the decision, "which misinterprets
the relevant statutes, understates the privacy implications of the government's surveillance and misapplies a narrow and outdated precedent to read
away core constitutional protections." He promised to appeal.

The *New York Times* also attacked the decision, pointing out that a study
by experts appointed by Obama found the NSA's mass data collection program had not helped to prevent terrorist attacks. "Yet in a ruling issued on
Friday, Judge William Pauley III . . . came to the opposite conclusion. . . .
The ruling . . . demonstrates once more the importance of fixing the law at
its source, rather than waiting for further interpretations by higher courts."

On May 7, 2015, Pauley was reversed by the U.S. Circuit Court of Appeals for the Second Circuit. Judge Gerard E. Lynch, writing for the three-
judge panel, rejected the government's assertion that the information
obtained was "relevant" to counterterrorism investigations.

Congress, he added, "cannot reasonably be said to have ratified a program of which many members of Congress—and all members of the
public—were not aware. The statutes to which the government points have
never been interpreted to authorize anything approaching the breadth of
the sweeping surveillance at issue here."

"If Congress chooses to authorize such a far-reaching and unprecedented
program, it has every opportunity to do so, and to do so unambiguously,"
he wrote. ACLU staff lawyer Alex Abdo, who argued the case, called the
decision a victory for the rule of law. Jaffer said, "it underscores once again
the need for truly systemic reform." "The current reform proposals from
Congress look anemic in light of the serious issues raised by the Second
Circuit," added Romero.

Without Snowden's admittedly illegal act, *ACLU v. Clapper* would never
have been filed; and even some of Snowden's harshest critics concede that
he launched a much-needed discussion on the necessity and ethics of mass
surveillance. But from the beginning of his public journey, he has been

hounded by the accusation that he lacked the courage of, say, a Daniel Ells-berg, who took a stand and was willing to accept the consequences of his actions, and that, worse, he fled into the arms of an enemy state.

"What we know of the information that Snowden has released has been known for a while," the *Washington Post*'s Jonathan Capehart dubiously as-serted before getting to the heart of his argument: "Unlike Snowden, Ellsberg went to senior members of Congress with his concerns about the secret policy toward Vietnam. He went to the press when it looked like Congress would do nothing." But he "turned himself in at the federal court-house in Boston."

Rupert Cornwell, writing in the *Independent* of London in August 2013 also compares Snowden unfavorably to Ellsberg, writing, "Mr. Ellsberg didn't run. He turned himself in to federal prosecutors in Massachusetts, admitting that he was the leaker."

Daniel Ellsberg, in an "as told to" piece in the *Daily Beast* in June 10, 2013, when Snowden's fate was unknown, emphatically disagreed with all those using him as a club to bash Snowden.

"I think there has not been a more significant or helpful leak or unau-thorized disclosure in American history ever than what Edward Snowden shared with the Guardian about the NSA—and that definitely includes the Pentagon Papers," he declared.

Ellsberg also tore into the notion that he was somehow superior for bravely facing the music. In fact, said Ellsberg, he had no idea of how brutal his government could be or what was potentially in store. And he emphatically rejected the idea that Snowden's was a coward's risk-free route.

"The White House sent people with orders 'to incapacitate me totally.' I was subject to a White House death squad that fortunately backed off and aborted the mission," said Ellsberg.

Snowden, Ellsberg added, "could be kidnapped, he could be sent to Guantánamo, he could be executed. Certainly slandered. You can count on that. A lot of people will surely call him a traitor, but they're mistaken."

Ellsberg concluded, "I definitely have a new hero in Edward Snowden. . . . People who respect or admire what I did, they may not realize it right now, but before this is over, they'll recognize that he deserves great admiration. And people who hate what I did, can hate."

Ben Wizner imagined what would have happened had Snowden chosen to leave his fate to the Obama administration. "If he had walked into prison, he would have been under 'special administrative measures.' I would have had to sign a nondisclosure agreement just to be able to go and talk to him. He wouldn't be able to look at newspapers, and he certainly wouldn't be able to be online and be part of these conversations. . . . He pretty clearly is more comfortable with the prospects that he faces right now than with the notion that he would be a convicted felon."

Snowden's Russian residency, added Wizner, "is renewable every three years. The status is roughly equivalent to a green card. . . . I'm sure if he wanted to be a citizen, they would let him be one, but he has no interest in being a citizen of any country other than the United States. . . . I have a hard time believing that he's going to live out his days there. . . . He said over and over that he would accept a guilty plea to a misdemeanor, with whatever that might entail."

From Wizner's perspective, "the worst part about his being in Russia as opposed to anywhere else . . . is just that it has created political headwind."

One of Wizner's low points occurred in 2014: "I was offline for a few days . . . in Japan. I came back online to one of the worst inboxes of my life." Snowden, at the invitation of his Russian lawyer, had agreed to participate in Vladimir Putin's annually televised question and answer session. Snowden planned to ask Putin a version of the question Senator Ron Wyden had famously asked James Clapper, director of national intelligence, before the Senate Intelligence Committee in March 2013.

"Does the NSA collect any type of data at all, on millions or hundreds of millions of Americans?" Wyden asked.

"No, sir," said Clapper.

"It does not?" asked Wyden.

"Not wittingly," Clapper replied.

Snowden's revelations subsequently proved that Clapper had lied—or at least had not spoken the truth. Wyden later called Clapper's response "flagrantly inaccurate" and attributed it to a "culture of misinformation."

Snowden's idea was to similarly trap Putin. As Snowden later explained in an article he penned for the *Guardian*, he saw the event as a "rare opportunity to lift a taboo on discussion of state surveillance before an audience," which would "provide opportunities for serious journalists and civil society to push the discussion further." He hoped to pin Putin down with a question that "cannot credibly be answered in the negative by any leader who runs a modern, intrusive surveillance programme." Thus, he would force Putin to make an "important concession" or engage in a transparently "clear evasion."

Instead, when Snowden (in a pre-recorded video) asked whether Russia intercepted, analyzed, or stored millions of individual's communications, Putin—addressing Snowden as a "fellow former spy"—responded with pre-baked propaganda. Russian "intelligence efforts are strictly regulated by our law" and are directed at "criminals and terrorists," he said, adding that Russia had no "mass-scale uncontrollable efforts."

Snowden's press reviews were savage. Anthony Hall, writing for McClatchy-Tribune Business News, griped, "like the useful idiot I predicted he would become, Snowden duly played his part." "Snowden looked to some like he was participating in a Soviet-style propaganda play," wrote Eli Lake in the *Daily Beast*.

Washington Post national security writer Walter Pincus suggested that Snowden should have asked Putin, "would you please describe how the three versions of SORM [Russia's System for Operative Investigative Activities] operate and what is done with the intercepted phone, email and other electronic media those systems collect?" Another *Post* writer, Stephen Stromberg, argued that by appearing at the event and asking his "timid question" Snowden had "surrendered any remaining shred of dignity."

"I regret that my question could be misinterpreted, and that it enabled many to ignore the substance of the question—and Putin's evasive response—in order to speculate, wildly and incorrectly, about my motives for asking it," wrote Snowden, in his *Guardian* article.

Wizner was dismayed at the international ruckus raised by Snowden's appearance: "Of course, his participating in that was viewed as a propaganda victory for Russia. It made it seem like he was in a gilded cage, when in fact he has been living quite independently and freely there and did this because he thought it would be politically helpful. . . . People in Russia in civil society have said that it actually was helpful to push that conversation out. But the audience that I was worried about wasn't Russia. The audience that I was worried about was the U.S. and the rest of the world where it made our work a lot harder."

Despite such frustrations, "we're never going to stop being involved in trying to bring him home with dignity, get him a better outcome for himself, given the sacrifices that he made for the issues that we care about," said Wizner.

When I asked Snowden about his motivation, he said the seeds of protest were planted during the Bush administration; but he arrived at his ultimate decision gradually. In the beginning, he was "very much the true believer." He "signed up for the Iraq War because I bought . . . what was the propaganda of the time," that it was a just war "to free the oppressed."

After washing out of the military and going to work for the CIA, he was exposed to dark truths involving torture, drone programs, and the weak case for going to war. At the CIA, "I started to see points of friction where the public statements were not aligning with the private realities."

Gradually, he began to question his original presumptions. "And then we see Barack Obama. I wasn't supporting him directly as a voter, although Lindsay [Mills], my long-term partner, was."

Obama's candidacy, said Snowden, "created a space" to criticize certain aspects of American policy. It seemed okay to discuss American misbehavior—such as torture and renditions—since Obama was saying, "That's not who we are. That's not what we do."

But after Obama took office, Snowden was disappointed at the "extremely rapid retreat from the kinds of things that he sort of campaigned on. . . . I think within sixty days of taking office, he said, 'We need to look forward, not backwards.' But that's fundamentally a sort of betrayal, not just of his campaign promises but really the idea of justice to begin with, because every investigation is necessarily retroactive looking. . . . And suddenly I learn not only did he not stop warrantless wiretapping, he actually embraced, expanded, and entrenched it. Or at least these were the policies that came to happen during his administration."

Snowden had not yet given up on Obama. "I had a belief that if Obama had the platform, if he had the controversy, if he had the scandal, he would do the right thing." Under pressure from the courts, Obama might acknowledge some of the surveillance programs were plainly unconstitutional and might be motivated to act. But "then the Congress changed the law to prevent [the controversial programs] from going to the Supreme Court . . .

because they really wanted to avoid having that become a formal precedent."

Snowden had extraordinary access to information. And he used that access to "figure out the extent of the surveillance that was going on. . . . It wasn't just affecting phones . . . it was affecting the Internet . . . in secret, without public debate, without even the majority of members of Congress understanding what was [happening]."

Eventually Snowden became convinced that people in all three branches of government "were sort of party to this wrongdoing, at different levels . . . and that's what drove me forward beyond the point of no return."

How did he choose which journalists to recruit?

"Glenn Greenwald I picked because he was a pretty ferocious civil libertarian, which is kind of consistent with the ACLU." He shied away from approaching the *New York Times* and even the *Washington Post* out of fear that those institutions ultimately might defer to government officials and delay or even spike the story. He knew *Times* reporter James Risen's exposé on a domestic spying program called Stellar Wind had been delayed more than a year by cautious editors deferring to government officials.

"The idea was we needed people who were independent," said Snowden, "and it couldn't just be one person."

Early in 2013, when he reached out to journalists, "I was actually not committed yet. I was talking to these people, I was telling them, sort of hinting them along, but I hadn't given them documents yet. They didn't actually have anything that would land me in jail. I'd probably lose my job, lose my clearance, but nothing worse than that. And I was just sort of telling them where to look. I tried to vet them and make it all work out."

At the end of February 2013, as Snowden was thinking things through, the Supreme Court decided *Clapper v. Amnesty*: the case brought by the ACLU on behalf of Amnesty International and other groups challenging part of the Foreign Intelligence Surveillance Act. The decision, written by Samuel Alito, pointed out that the plaintiffs did not have "standing" because even though they feared they had been monitored, they did not have actual proof.

Stephen Breyer attacked that reasoning in his dissent: "The plaintiffs' standing depends upon the likelihood that the Government . . . will harm them by intercepting at least some of their private, foreign, telephone, or email conversations. In my view, this harm is not 'speculative.' Indeed it is as likely to take place as are most future events that commonsense inference and ordinary knowledge of human nature tell us will happen."

As Snowden interpreted the decision, "the Supreme Court says, 'All right, this is a reasonable allegation. It's a serious concern. It could have constitutional implications; but your argument's too speculative. You can't prove that you have been spied on. You can't prove that Americans are being spied on in a similar manner.' The government is asserting the state secrets privilege, basically, and saying, 'You don't have the right to these documents. You can't see them. Therefore, the court has no role in this controversy. You can't establish standing.'" With that ruling, Snowden's mission became clear.

Snowden reached out to Laura Poitras shortly after the Supreme Court handed down that decision, which coincided with James Clapper telling Senator Ron Wyden "No, sir. . . . Not wittingly."

That Supreme Court decision and Clapper's blatant lie "drove me . . . to actually give documents for the first time to Laura Poitras," said Snowden, who had seen Wyden, in his role on the intelligence committee, as "the last watchdog."

Wyden, in his view, was "supposed to prevent this from happening," but Clapper was denying him information. What this meant, believed Snowden, was that "two branches of our system of checks and balances had basically had their roles removed or amputated." And no one was doing anything about it.

"The ACLU was trying. They were doing the right thing. They were absolutely on the right track. They were arguing the right case." But what did that really mean if, in the end, the ACLU couldn't prove its case? "The idea was . . . I could provide the public evidence of these facts that would then provide the ACLU standing to get into the courts and to decide this sort of question. The first time I talked to Ben Wizner, the very first communication we ever had, I think the very first question I ever asked him, was, 'Do you have standing now?'"

Previously, he had not thought of ACLU representation. "I didn't even actually consider [it]. But Laura Poitras had talked to them . . . and she talked to me and mentioned she was in contact with Ben and . . . could sort of arrange a conversation with us."

The secrets he revealed, said Snowden, were not random. They were selected with the aim of bolstering the ACLU's work: "The very first story that was ever published [focused on] Section 215, the secret FISA court order. And this was directly related to the *Amnesty v. Clapper* kind of case the ACLU had just been flushed out of for lack of standing. . . . I'm not gonna pretend that I have this incredible level of insight to know that the ACLU happened to be a Verizon business customer. . . . But I did realize that was a class broad enough that they would be able to find a plaintiff that would get them back in. The fact that they could represent themselves was just sort of [a bonus]."

Why didn't he take his documents to Assange and WikiLeaks?

"I had been thinking about this for quite some time. I had seen how the government went after [Chelsea] Manning [who leaked military secrets to WikiLeaks in 2010]. I had seen how the government went after Thomas Drake," an NSA official prosecuted in 2010 for violating the Espionage Act of 1917 for revealing government wrongdoing in connection with a failed surveillance project named Trailblazer.

Snowden wanted to minimize the risk of being credibly accused of harming American interests. He therefore wanted a process with more checks and balances than WikiLeaks offered. He decided that journalists he trusted would become his system of checks and balances.

If he could recruit principled journalists to play that role, he thought he could "maximize the public benefit while minimizing the potential risks. And so I would gather information that I thought was material that journalists needed to know, both [to] investigate and report and also to check the government's claims."

All the information he collected was not meant to become public. Part of it was to provide the journalists with context. "I wasn't calling the shots on what they should and shouldn't publish." As a condition of access, they were required to agree they would only publish stories they believed it was "in the public interest to know."

Also, they promised that prior to running a story, they would alert the government: "They didn't provide the government the actual draft text, but they provided them details of the documents to allow the government to argue against publication. . . . So, when you ask, why didn't I go to WikiLeaks? I saw what had happened to the people before, and I wanted to be more careful. . . . And in both cases, now that we've had both the WikiLeaks model and mine, we haven't seen harm as a result; but I think we have seen the public benefit served."

His "big regret," said Snowden, "is that it took me so long to really understand what was going on. I should have come forward sooner. . . . The longer you let these programs go uncontested, the more entrenched they become."

As for returning to the United States: "Since the very beginning, I have had a single condition, and that is that I have, basically, the right to make my argument to the jury of why I did what I did. . . . I think that is fundamentally the entire purpose of a trial, for the jury to decide, 'Was this right?' You know, it's not simply a question of, 'Was this legal?' It's a question of, 'Was this right?' Because what happens when the law is wrong? . . . Anybody charged under the Espionage Act is denied the right to tell the jury why they did it. You can't even breathe it. . . . The prosecutor will say, 'Objection!' And the judge will say, 'Sustained.'

"And so the question . . . for me is not what conditions do I require; it's, 'What does it mean if I return without having access to a fair trial? What does that [mean for] the next whistleblower? Because there are going to be more."

Anthony Romero has no doubt that taking on Snowden as a client was the right decision: "I mean, he was iconic. Even before he became an icon, he was going to become iconic, like Ellsberg with the Pentagon Papers. It didn't take a lot to figure out that the plight of this young man would become inextricably tied to the policy and legal issues that were going to play out for us."

Romero had declined to assist Julian Assange in part because he believed the WikiLeaks approach put human rights workers in harm's way. An Egyptian friend of Romero's had to flee his country because the release of WikiLeaks cables outed him as someone "providing information to the U.S. State Department. So, I was not an Assange advocate. I was more than glad when CCR [the Center for Constitutional Rights] took him up as a client. That was not a client I wanted. But with Snowden . . . we were already beginning to understand that he wasn't self-publishing any of the data, that he was giving it to journalists whose editors and publishers were making the editorial decisions over what was released and in what order. I think it was really quite different."

Once Snowden was safely ensconced, Romero flew to Moscow to meet him and "take the measure of the man." They spent a few days together in the winter cold, getting to know one another.

"I asked him a bunch of questions. I put him on the hot seat about, 'How can we be sure that you're not working for the Russians or the Chinese? . . . Why should I trust you? . . . I was convinced that he really did steal and release the documents with the interest of trying to promulgate the public debate that we wanted around surveillance."

He recalls Snowden telling him, "Look, if there's a way for me to come back to the U.S., I'd like to come back. And I need someone to help me think through a legal team and the parameters for what might be a plea bargain. . . . I trust your organization, and I trust you to help me identify U.S.-based lawyers to represent me in conversations with the U.S. government. . . . That's all I want, and I want to be able to help you."

"I wasn't really worried after I met him," said Romero. "There were many people who thought of him as a traitor, and many people, some people, within the organization were squeamish about it. And I wanted to make sure that I wasn't just doing it out of benevolence."

Romero decided to trust his instincts and to focus on the upside: "It's great for us to have a relationship with someone who is going to turn out to be the twenty-first century Ellsberg . . . kind of the digital Mandela. It's hard to compare anyone to Mandela; but to say someone is iconically identified with a cause and reviled at the beginning and then is seen to have subsequently done a service, it's not that far a stretch."

14

The Rise of Trump, the Decline of Truth

On November 9, 2016, the morning Donald Trump learned he would be the forty-fifth president of the United States, the American Civil Liberties Union posted a warning: "President-elect Trump, as you assume the nation's highest office, we urge you to reconsider and change course on certain campaign promises you have made. These include your plan to amass a deportation force to remove 11 million undocumented immigrants; ban the entry of Muslims into our country and aggressively surveil them; punish women for accessing abortion; reauthorize waterboarding and other forms of torture; and change our nation's libel laws and restrict freedom of expression," wrote Anthony Romero on the ACLU blog.

The following Friday, in a full-page ad in the *New York Times*, the ACLU reaffirmed the message: "As you assume the nation's highest office, we must ask you now as president-elect to reconsider and change course." The ad listed several of his controversial campaign promises and pronounced them "un-America . . . wrong-headed . . . unlawful and unconstitutional."

"If you . . . endeavor to make these campaign promises a reality, you will have to contend with the full firepower of the ACLU . . . Our staff of litigators and activists in every state, thousands of volunteers, and millions of supporters stand ready to fight against any encroachment on our cherished freedoms and rights," concluded the ACLU.

The ACLU had opposed previous presidents. It had taken out ads attacking Barack Obama and called for Richard Nixon's impeachment. But never previously, in its nearly one-hundred-year history, had it effectively declared war on a president before he took office.

The foundation had been laid in February 2016 at the ACLU leadership retreat in Glen Cove, New York. That annual meeting between Romero and leaders of the ACLU's largest affiliates is an occasion for unfiltered conversation about issues and challenges facing the country and the ACLU. "If Donald Trump becomes the presidential candidate, do you think it's time for us to revisit our policy that we don't oppose or support any candidate for office?" asked Romero.

"It was a serious question," Romero later explained, but he was also playing "a little bit of the provocateur."

The directors in attendance, all from "blue" states, unanimously agreed that targeting Trump would be a huge mistake, that the ACLU had never opposed or supported a candidate for elective office and should not do so now. Romero agreed but couldn't shake the feeling that Trump represented a "level of danger" higher than he had seen from any previous presidential candidate. He "insisted that we do an analysis of his promises on the stump and then outline how we would fight them."

The project was more challenging than expected. "With Hillary Clinton, you could just go on her website and download her position papers. With Trump, you had nothing. So we literally had to hire an opposition research firm to follow him on the stump, collect all the goddamn statements, synthesize them," said Romero. "We had the report in July."

That report, later published as "Donald Trump: A One-Man Constitutional Crisis," detailed some of the controversies Trump had sparked on immigration, torture, Muslims, and free speech. His "statements and policy proposals would blatantly violate the inalienable rights guaranteed by the Constitution, federal and international law, and the basic norms of a free and decent society," concluded the ACLU, which pointed out he had promised "to deport over 11 million undocumented immigrants, to ban Muslims from entering the United States, to surveil American Muslims . . . [and] to revise libel laws." Taken together, those proposals would encroach upon the First, Fourth, Fifth, and Eighth Amendments.

"We actually had the game plan" for how to "fight the Muslim ban," said Romero.

Romero spend part of election evening at the home of philanthropist George Soros, where, as the returns came in, the party became "more like a wake." "I turned around at one point to my partner . . . and I'm like, 'Come on, honey, we've got to get out of this before the curtain falls.'"

The next morning, as he sat in his office, Romero wondered, what words of "reassurance, comfort, guidance, defiance," he could share with his deflated colleagues. Instead of words of comfort, Romero composed a call to battle, drafting what became the Trump challenge ad in the *New York Times*.

David Cole, a constitutional law professor at Georgetown University scheduled to become the ACLU's legal director in January, had stopped by to meet the national staff. Much of that morning, he recalled, was spent reviewing the ad: "We just essentially put [Trump] on notice. 'Look, if you do these things, we'll see you in court. That's what we do.'"

In his inaugural address, Trump drew a dark portrait of an isolated, ramshackle nation. It was an America whose citizens hungered for "great schools for their children, safe neighborhoods for their families and good jobs for themselves" but had to contend with "rusted-out factories scattered like tombstones across the landscape."

Following his speech, Trump ignited a controversy that was both petty and absurd. He insisted that his inauguration crowd was bigger than President Obama's and sent out his press secretary to make the case.

The doubling down on false so-called facts and anger at the press for calling him on such lies quickly became touchstones of Trump's presidency. So did Trump's insistence that the key to America's lost greatness was to wall itself off from the world and fight off an "infestation" of dark-skinned immigrants, some of them wearing turbans and singing the praises of Allah.

On January 27, Trump signed an executive order barring most natives of seven predominantly Muslim countries from America. As he issued the order, Trump declared his intention to "keep radical Islamic terrorists out of the United States of America. We don't want them here. . . . We will never forget the lessons of 9/11, nor the heroes who lost their lives at the Pentagon."

The order suspended all refugee admissions for 120 days, indefinitely blocked refugees from Syria, and put a 90-day hold on visitors from the seven targeted Muslim-majority countries: Iran, Iraq, Libya, Syria, Somali, the Sudan, and Yemen. The Department of Homeland Security said the order applied even to those who already had green cards. If they were outside the country, they would be re-admitted on a case-by-case basis.

One of the first casualties was Acting Attorney General Sally Yates, an Obama-administration holdover who was fired for refusing to defend the order after concluding it was likely illegal. Stephen Miller, Trump's senior policy adviser, called her behavior "reckless, irresponsible and improper." But Yates was far from alone in her doubts about the policy.

Critics immediately pointed out that the targeted countries had nothing to do with 9/11. Most of the hijackers hailed from Saudi Arabia (whose subjects were not among those banned). The other hijackers were citizens of Lebanon, Egypt, and the United Arab Emirates. Indeed, some of the refugees Trump would bar had risked their lives to keep America safe.

Donna Lieberman, executive director of the New York Civil Liberties Union, issued a statement noting that immediately after Trump's order took effect, people were detained at JFK International Airport. The ACLU and NYCLU, she said, were working to get a count on the numbers affected. In the interim, the ACLU had challenged the executive order in a Brooklyn federal court.

As images of stranded travelers and asylum-seekers flooded TV screens, Americans responded powerfully. Thousands showed up at airports to support the very people Trump had condemned. Meanwhile, attorneys general from states across America banded together to file a lawsuit that successfully halted enforcement of key provisions of Trump's order. Celebrities flocked to the cause.

Upon accepting her award for best actress from the Screen Actors Guild that Sunday, January 29, Sarah Paulson asked the audience to donate "any money you have to spare . . . to the ACLU." At the Producers Guild of America Awards ceremony, singer-songwriter John Legend announced that he and his wife Chrissy Teigen had "made a donation to the ACLU and other organizations who are committed to fighting for freedom in the land of the free." A host of celebrities went online—including comedian Rosie O'Donnell, singer Sia, actor Zach Braff, and musician Jack Antonoff—to pledge money to the ACLU.

Such an outpouring of celebrity support would have been unimaginable seventy-five years earlier, when—weeks after the Pearl Harbor attack—President Franklin Roosevelt issued an executive order paving the way for the internment of more than 100,000 American residents of Japanese descent.

Equally unimaginable, in the wake of Pearl Harbor, would have been the spectacle of civil society and state governments standing up against an American president in support of values of inclusion and religious toler-ance. Legal challenges were brought not only by the ACLU but by a host of other organizations, including the International Refugee Assistance Project, the Council on American-Islamic Relations, the National Immi-gration Law Center, and the Northwest Immigrant Rights Project.

The various organizations sent attorneys to airports throughout the coun-try, where they aided a variety of travelers—refugees, musicians, students, businesspeople, family members, and others—who suddenly found their lives turned upside down.

"There is no evidence that refugees—the most thoroughly vetted of all people entering our nation—are a threat to national security. This is an or-der that is based on bigotry, not reality," commented Lena Masri, litiga-tion director of the Council on American-Islamic Relations.

In Virginia, a federal judge issued a weeklong stay against removing people detained under Trump's order at Dulles Airport. In Brooklyn, Fed-eral Judge Ann M. Donnelly, at the ACLU's request, intervened to stop a traveler about to be deported to Syria—citing probable violations of the rights to due process and equal protection."

The Saturday after Trump signed the order, some three thousand pro-testors showed up at Seattle-Tacoma International Airport chanting "no hatred, no fear, immigrants are welcome here." Responding to a suit filed by the ACLU and the Northwest Immigrant Rights Project, U.S. District Judge Thomas Zilly in Seattle granted an emergency stay, preventing the deportation of two travelers. One of the men, from Sudan, was headed to an engineering conference in Los Vegas. The other, from Yemen, was try-ing to reunite with his family.

That Sunday, Trump declared, "to be clear, this is not a Muslim ban, as the media is falsely reporting. . . . This is about terror and keeping our coun-try safe."

The same weekend, U.S. District Judge Allison Burroughs and Magistrate Judge Judith Dein in Boston issued a seven-day restraining order on behalf of two Iranian-born associate professors at the University of Massachusetts Dartmouth. The order prevented authorities from detaining travelers arriving at Logan International Airport.

Massachusetts attorney general Maura Healey announced that her staff was working on a challenge to the Trump edict; and New York attorney general Eric Schneiderman said he and colleagues in fifteen other states were planning to challenge Trump. He was confident "that the executive order will ultimately be struck down by the courts."

On February 3, District Court Judge James Robart in Seattle issued an order temporarily blocking Trump's Muslim ban nationwide. The ban violated the Establishment Clause of the First Amendment, said Robart, a George W. Bush appointee who had done pro bono work on behalf of refugees before becoming a judge.

The Saturday after the ruling, Trump tweeted that the "ridiculous" decision by a "so-called judge" was certain to be overturned. "Because the ban was lifted by a judge, many very bad and dangerous people may be pouring into our country," he added.

On February 7, in a class action filed in the Western District of Washington, the ACLU argued that Trump's order violated both the Constitution and federal law.

On February 9, a three-judge panel of the U.S. Court of Appeals for the Ninth Circuit in San Francisco agreed to put Trump's travel ban on hold. "The government has not shown that the executive order provides what due process requires, such as notice and a hearing prior to restricting an individual's ability to travel," wrote the panel, in response to a suit against the ban brought by the states of Washington and Minnesota. As for the government's position that "the president's decisions about immigration policy . . . are unreviewable," the judges agreed it was "beyond question that the federal judiciary retains the authority to adjudicate constitutional challenges to executive action."

Within minutes of the ruling, Trump angrily told reporters he would appeal to the Supreme Court. "THE SECURITY OF OUR NATION IS AT STAKE!" he tweeted.

The following month, on March 6, Trump issued a second executive order that attempted to repair the flaws in the first.

Trump restricted entry for ninety days from six countries: Iran, Libya, Somalia, Sudan, Syria, and Yemen—not because they were majority Muslim, but supposedly because each "is a state sponsor of terrorism, has been significantly compromised by terrorist organizations, or contains active conflict zones." Iraq was no longer on the list.

The *Wall Street Journal* noted the appearance of protestors in front of the White House carrying signs, one of which read, "We are all Muslim now."

The bad legal news for Trump continued. On March 15, U.S. District Judge Derrick Watson in Hawaii cited "questionable evidence supporting the government's national security motivation" and pointed to "significant and unrebutted evidence of religious animus" behind the revised travel ban. Watson concluded that a "reasonable, objective observer" would view even the new order as "issued with a purpose to disfavor a particular religion, in spite of its stated, religiously neutral purpose."

Watson flatly rejected the government's argument that it could not deduce religious animus absent investigating Trump's "veiled psyche." Among other things, he cited a press release from Trump calling for "a total and complete shutdown of Muslims entering the United States." Watson granted a nationwide temporary restraining order barring enforcement of the ban.

U.S. District Judge Theodore Chuang in Maryland also rejected the administration's arguments. "The history of public statements continues to provide a convincing case that the purpose of the second executive order remains the realization of the long-envisioned Muslim ban," wrote Chuang, in blocking enforcement of certain sections of the new ban.

Lee Gelernt, an ACLU lawyer representing clients in the Maryland case, thought it significant that "two judges have looked at the revised order, and both have come to the same conclusion that it continues to be a Muslim ban."

Meanwhile, the administration got encouragement from five Republican-appointed judges on the Ninth Circuit Court of Appeals in San Francisco. That March, the judges issued a statement expressing disagreement with the decision of a three-judge panel that had rejected the travel ban in February. Judge Jay Bybee, writing for the Republican dissenters, called the panel's errors "many and obvious" and said its decision "stands contrary to well-established separation-of-powers principles." Two days later, the conservative judges doubled down with a statement, authored by Judge Alex Kozinski (and signed by Bybee and three other conservative judges), criticizing his more liberal colleague's "hasty opinion" and its "sea of insults and hyperbole."

Fellow circuit court judge Stephen Reinhardt responded, "Judge Kozinski's diatribe, filed today, confirms that a small group of judges, having failed in their effort to undo this court's decision with respect to President Trump's first Executive Order, now seek on their own, under the guise of a dissent . . . to decide the constitutionality of a second Executive Order that is not before this court."

Former President Jimmy Carter observed, "that is hardly the way the judiciary functions. Peculiar indeed!" reported Politico.

On May 25, Virginia's Fourth Circuit Court of Appeals upheld, by a vote of 10 to 3, the decision by Judge Theodore Chuang of Maryland staying the Muslim Ban. Chief Judge Roger Gregory, who wrote the sixty-eight-page opinion, rejected Trump's national security argument as "a post hoc, secondary justification for an executive action rooted in religious animus and intended to bar Muslims from this country."

The majority conceded that the president had broad power to deny people entry to the United States, but "that power is not absolute" and "cannot go unchecked when, as here, the president wields it through an executive edict that stands to cause irreparable harm to individuals across this nation."

Judge Dennis Shedd, dissenting, argued, "at the end of the day, the real losers in this case are the millions of individual Americans whose security is threatened on a daily basis by those who seek to do us harm."

Over the next several weeks, President Trump continued to tweet away, accusing the courts of being "slow and political." "The Justice Department should have stayed with the original Travel Ban, not the scaled-down version that is now before the high court," he groused.

On September 24, Trump came up with a third version of the ban, placing travel restrictions on citizens of eight countries whose systems for identifying "public safety threats" were deemed insufficient: Chad, Iran, Iraq, Libya, North Korea, Syria, Venezuela, and Yemen.

In mid-October, federal judges in both Maryland and Hawaii blocked the new ban. Federal immigration laws "do not afford the President unbridled discretion to do as he pleases," concluded U.S. District Judge

Derrick Kahala Watson in Honolulu. Trump had failed, he said, to show that the entry of nationals from the designated countries "would be detrimental to the United States."

Appearing before Judge Chuang in Maryland, the ACLU's Omar Jadwat called the new ban "a bigger, tougher version" of the old ban. "It excludes over 100 million people, and it actually makes it worse by extending the ban indefinitely," he argued. Chuang agreed, ruling that the new ban "plainly discriminates based on nationality."

In an interview with Bloomberg Wire Service, Jadwat said, "as long as the government tries to enact the same core policy over and over again, it should not be surprised that it ends up with the same result over and over again."

On December 4, the U.S. Supreme Court temporarily lifted the injunctions issued in Maryland and Hawaii. Jadwat reacted to the order with both consternation and optimism. "It's unfortunate that the full ban can move forward for now, but this order does not address the merits of our claims," he said.

The Supreme Court held oral arguments on April 25, 2018, during which Justice Elena Kagan posed a hypothetical about a virulently anti-Semitic president who requested that his cabinet officers make recommendations allowing him to bar natives of Israel.

Solicitor General Noel Francisco responded by acknowledging the quandary posed by the "tough" hypothetical but said that if the cabinet agreed the visitors posed "a national security risk," the president could follow their advice "even if in his private heart of hearts he also harbored animus."

Justice Sonia Sotomayor followed up: "If we take Justice Kagan's hypothetical president . . . who basically says to his review committee, I want to keep out Jews . . . why would the actions of the committee . . . not be subject to great suspicion and to thorough review?"

Francisco said he assumed "that if any cabinet member were given that order, that cabinet member would refuse to comply or resign in the face of a plainly unconstitutional order. Also, a president making such extreme statements "would undermine the facial legitimacy of the action."

He added: "Here, however, you don't have anything like that. Rather, you have the cabinet doing its job through the agencies . . . to construct and apply this neutral standard to every country in the world, including every Muslim country."

Trump v. Hawaii was decided two months later, on June 26. The 5 to 4 decision authored by Roberts ruled that Trump had followed the law and reversed the court of appeals. The Immigration and Nationality Act "vests the President with authority to restrict the entry of aliens whenever he finds that their entry 'would be detrimental to the interests of the United States,'" wrote Roberts. The law "exudes deference to the President in every clause" he continued.

Yes, conceded Roberts, "five of the seven nations currently included in the Proclamation have Muslim-majority populations. Yet that fact alone does not support an inference of religious hostility."

As to Japanese American internment camps and that disgraceful chapter of American history, "*Korematsu* has nothing to do with this case," declared Roberts. "The forcible relocation of U.S. citizens to concentration camps, solely and explicitly on the basis of race, is objectively unlawful and outside the scope of Presidential authority. But it is wholly inapt to liken that morally repugnant order to a facially neutral policy denying certain foreign nationals the privilege of admission."

In a sharp dissent, Sotomayor, joined by Ruth Bader Ginsburg, wrote: "The United States of America is a Nation built upon the promise of religious liberty. . . . The Court's decision today fails to safeguard that fundamental principle." A policy of exclusion of Muslims, she added, "now masquerades behind a façade of national-security concerns."

She suggested that the government administrative review process was a sham, pointing out that the analysis "was a mere 17 pages." Moreover, "the government remains wholly unable to articulate any credible national security interest that would go unaddressed by the current statutory scheme absent the Proclamation."

In a withering rebuke to Roberts, she pointedly compared the current decision to *Korematsu v. United States*: "As here, the Government was unwilling to reveal its own intelligence agencies' views of the alleged security concerns to the very citizens it purported to protect. . . . By blindly accepting the Government's misguided invitation to sanction a discriminatory policy motivated by animosity toward a disfavored group, all in the name of a superficial claim of national security, the Court redeploys the same dangerous logic underlying *Korematsu* and merely replaces one 'gravely wrong' decision with another."

In response to the court's decision, Senator Mazie Hirono of Hawaii tweeted, "By ignoring the President's clear intent to discriminate against Muslims, the Court handed the President unfettered power to continue to target minorities."

David Cole, the ACLU's newly minted legal director, wrote an op-ed in the *Washington Post* asserting that Trump's travel ban "is likely to be judged by history as one of the court's greatest failures—in a league with *Dred Scott v. Sandford*, which helped bring on the Civil War, and *Korematsu v. United States.*"

When Romero had recruited Cole for the ACLU in 2016, Cole had not envisioned himself writing such a piece. "Anthony came down to Washington . . . took me to lunch and said basically, 'How can you not do this work?' . . . He said, 'You've been doing constitutional litigation and teaching constitutional law, writing about the Constitution for your entire thirty-plus-year career under a conservative Supreme Court. Just think what it would be like to lead the ACLU under the first liberal Supreme Court since 1972.'"

At the time, recalled Cole, "We knew Hillary was going to win. We knew she would appoint Justice Scalia's successor, and indeed for the first time in forty years, forty-plus years, we would have a majority liberal Supreme Court. Of course, I signed on the bottom line. I didn't put any conditional 'what if' in because there wasn't any what if. We all knew what was going to happen."

As the so-called Muslim ban made its way through the courts, Charlottesville, Virginia, coped with an influx of angry racists and anti-Semites. In May 2017, a band of white supremacists, led by professional provocateur Richard Spencer, mounted two marches to protest the planned removal of a statue of Confederate Army commander Robert E. Lee. The demonstrators were also annoyed that Lee Park, which housed the statue, was scheduled that June to be renamed Emancipation Park.

Participants in the marches, which took place on Saturday, May 13, carried flaming torches and confederate flags while chanting such things as "we will not be replaced," "blood and soil," and "Russia is our friend." "What brings us together," Spencer told his fellow white supremacists, "is that we are white, we are a people, we will not be replaced."

That same year, on July 8, a group of between thirty and fifty members of the Loyal White Knights of the Ku Klux Klan came to Charlottesville to protest the removal of the same statute. The KKK group was confronted by a much larger group of counter-protestors.

The Klansmen shouted "white power," and the counter-protestors shouted "racists go home." Fears of gun violence (Virginia is an "open carry" state) did not materialize, but fights broke out. Police ordered the crowd to disperse, eventually arresting twenty-two people.

The week following the KKK rally, local alt-right blogger and white supremacist Jason Kessler held a press conference during which he defended the KKK and attacked Black Lives Matter and other groups, whom he blamed for the violence. He announced that on August 12, he was holding a "Unite the Right" rally in Emancipation Park to protest the planned removal of the notorious Lee statute.

Charlottesville Mayor Mike Signer attributed all the attention to Charlottesville's attempt to foster a racial dialogue. "Charlottesville has kind of been put on the map recently. We want to change the narrative by telling the true story of race through public spaces. That has made us a target for groups that hate that change and want to stay in the past, but we will not be intimidated," he told CNN.

Nihad Awad, executive director of the Council on American-Islamic Relations, predicted that the planned "Unite the Right" rally "may be the largest gathering of racists and bigots in recent history. Spooked by all the warnings and negative attention, the city endeavored to move the rally to a more remote venue. The planned demonstration "is incompatible with the dense and urban location of Emancipation Park, which is right next to our Downtown Mall," explained Mayor Signer.

University of Virginia president Teresa Sullivan, among others, thought violence might erupt. In early August, she sent a letter to members of the university community advising them to stay away. "One may stand up for one's beliefs without physical confrontation. I urge students and all UVA community members to avoid the August 12 rally and avoid physical confrontation generally. There is a credible risk of violence at this event, and your safety is my foremost concern," wrote Sullivan.

She asked students to instead attend more positively themed UVA-sponsored activities: "With the Aug. 12 rally coming just a few weeks after the KKK rally in July and amid the continued divisive rancor in our national discourse, we are reminded that the struggle for equality, inclusion and civility requires a prolonged and persistent effort."

Several businesses announced that they would close rather than expose customers to the potential violence. One restaurant tweeted, "Due to the chaos (and) violent threat of the Nazi rally, and for the safety of our customers and employees, Brazos Tacos will be closed Aug. 12."

"From information that . . . groups are presenting and sharing online, we have concluded that there is an extremely high potential for physical violence and brutality directed at our community" a clergy group called Congregate Charlottesville warned its members.

On the Monday before the planned march, Charlottesville announced that the city would grant a permit for the neo-Nazis to meet at McIntire Park instead of Emancipation Park. The proposed alternative site was larger but also a mile away from the Lee statute and the city center.

During a news conference, the mayor and city manager explained that the event was likely to attract more than the four hundred persons estimated in the permit application submitted by Kessler. To balance the competing imperatives of free speech and community safety, they were offering a different venue. McIntire Park, they argued, could better accommodate the overflow crowd and would be easier for the police to patrol.

At this point, the ACLU and a local civil liberties organization called the Rutherford Institute stepped in. On August 8, the organizations sent a letter to city official warning that moving the rally to McIntire Park would violate Kessler's free speech rights.

"Both the timing and justification for the demand that organizers accept a move to McIntire Park show a callous disrespect for the rights of free speech and assembly, forcing an 11th-hour relocation of the rally from the place chosen specifically because of its importance to the message of the rally organizers," said the letter. It demanded the city "act in accordance with the law, even if doing so is distasteful to members of the community." The city was told to respond by noon the next day.

City Attorney S. Craig Brown denied that the proposed move had anything to do with denial of free speech but with the best use of city resources. John Whitehead, president of the Rutherford Institute, rejected the explanation that the projected drain on city resources was a justifiable reason to move the event. "You can't do that under the First Amendment," he told the *Cavalier Daily*, UVA's student newspaper.

That Thursday, the ACLU of Virginia issued a press release saying that, in collaboration with the Rutherford Institute, it had filed a federal lawsuit against the City of Charlottesville on Kessler's behalf "claiming his 1st and 14th Amendment rights are being denied by the city's refusal to allow him and supporters to access Emancipation Park on Aug. 12 for a previously approved demonstration."

The ACLU argued before District Court Judge Glen Conrad that Charlottesville's actions were based on animosity toward Kessler's views and asked that the city be compelled to allow the protest as originally planned. As Conrad deliberated that Friday, scores of protestors carrying torches marched onto the University of Virginia campus. They chanted "blood and soil," "white lives matter," and "Jews will not replace us." School was in hiatus between summer and fall semesters, but a group of counter-protestors had surrounded a statue of university founder Thomas Jefferson. A brawl broke out between the two groups. The police intervened.

"People are angry, they're scared, they're hurt, they're confused," the Reverend Seth Wispelwey of United Church of Christ told the *New York Times*. "White supremacists rallying in our town is an act of violence."

That same night, Judge Conrad granted a preliminary injunction against the city. The city announced it would allow the protest to go on as originally planned.

The protest in Charlottesville that Saturday was as toxic as predicted. Some of the protestors dressed for battle, carrying shields, clubs, and helmets. Many flaunted swastikas and confederate flags. Repeated clashes between hate-mongers and counter-protestors led Governor Terry McAuliffe to declare a state of emergency. Police forced the mob to disperse. The protest, scheduled for noon, ended before it began.

Shortly after 2 p.m., James Fields Jr. plowed his car into a group of counter-protestors. The impact killed Heather Heyer, a thirty-two-year-old paralegal and Virginia native. The official cause of death was blunt force injury to the chest. Another thirty-five bystanders were injured.

Charlottesville resident Brennan Gilmore was among the anti–white supremacist protestors. Fields's vehicle, he told the press, "came down a street where no traffic was passing. [Fields] clearly saw what was going on,

accelerated into the crowd . . . sending bodies flying. The car stopped, reversed fast back up the street and disappeared."

It turned out that Fields, described in press accounts as a twenty-year-old
former teacher from Maumee, Ohio, was enamored of the Nazi era in Germany. He also apparently suffered from schizoid personality disorder. Fields
was arrested and charged with second-degree murder and various other crimes.

Later that Saturday, President Trump addressed the Charlottesville tragedy at a press conference originally scheduled to deal with the Veterans Administration. He quickly went off script.

"We condemn in the strongest possible terms this egregious display of
hatred, bigotry and violence on many sides, on many sides. It's been going
on for a long time in our country. Not Donald Trump, not Barack
Obama. . . . No citizen should ever fear for their safety and security in our
society. And no child should ever be afraid to go outside and play or be
with their parents and have a good time," he said.

On Monday, after vociferous criticism for his blaming of "many sides"
for the tragic events in Charlottesville, Trump read a prepared statement:
"To anyone who acted criminally in this weekend's racist violence. You will
be held fully accountable. . . . Racism is evil. And those who cause violence
in its name are criminals and thugs, including the KKK, neo-Nazis, white
supremacists and other hate groups that are repugnant to everything we
hold dear as Americans."

On Tuesday, Trump again weighed in. During an impromptu press conference at Trump Tower, he told reporters, "I watched that very closely,
much more closely than you people watched it. You had a group on one
side that was bad. You had a group on the other side that was also very violent. Nobody wants to say that. I'll say it right now. . . . You look at both
sides . . . not all of those people were neo-Nazis, believe me. You also had
some very fine people on both sides."

Trump's comments moved former Ku Klux Klan grand wizard David
Duke to tweet, "Thank you President Trump for your honesty & courage
to tell the truth."

The comments also moved business leaders to distance themselves from
Trump. Several executives exited his American Manufacturing Council,
including the CEOs of Under Armour, Intel, and Merck. As the execu-

tives peeled away, Trump announced he was disbanding the AMC and the Strategic and Policy Forum.

But the groups had already apparently decided to dissolve on their own, reported the *Washington Post*: "JP Morgan Chase chief executive Jamie Dimon, a member of the Strategic and Policy Forum, told employees in a note on Wednesday that his group decided to disband following Trump's news conference . . . in which he appeared to show sympathy for some of the people who marched alongside the neo-Nazis and white supremacists in Charlottesville."

Dimon told his employees: "It is a leader's role, in business or government, to bring people together, not tear them apart."

Given the ACLU's role as the neo-Nazis' attorney and the (not altogether unanticipated) violence that ensued, soul searching followed. The ACLU was long accustomed to fallout from defending the rights of the outrageously bigoted and temperamentally cruel, but this time someone had died. And this time, at least some of the criticism was coming from within the ACLU itself.

In "Shall We Defend Free Speech for Nazis in America?"—the old ACLU pamphlet—the ACLU had explained why an organization fighting for social good and bias-free justice would defend architects of evil. The argument, first rehearsed in the 1930s, was essentially the same argument used in the David Goldberger letter some forty years later explaining why the ACLU would defend Nazis determined to march in Skokie: in order to defend the free speech rights of the virtuous, the ACLU also had to defend the rights of the wicked.

K-Sue Park, a Harvard Law School graduate and former ACLU volunteer, argued in a *New York Times* op-ed that the ACLU had no business defending racist zealots: "The danger that communities face because of their speech isn't equal. The A.C.L.U.'s decision to offer legal support to a right-wing cause, then a left-wing cause, won't make it so. Rather, it perpetuates a misguided theory that all radical views are equal," wrote Park.

The ACLU, she insisted, must acknowledge that by "insisting on a narrow reading of the First Amendment, the organization provides free legal support to hate-based causes" that are at war with marginalized communities whose "power of expression is impoverished."

For the ACLU, which has made a practice of periodically defending odious people and odious speech, the options had always been rather simple: defend speech, irrespective of the views represented by the speaker, or risk being labeled a hypocrite.

No one at the ACLU, for instance, believed that Redskins was a proper name for a football team. But in 2015, after the U.S. Patent and Trademark Office tried to cancel the trademark registration for the Washington Redskins (on the grounds that the name was offensive to the very Native Americans it was supposedly meant to honor), the ACLU came down on the side (and filed an amicus brief on behalf) of the team. "The government doesn't get to withhold a benefit because it disagrees with the content of someone's speech," explained ACLU legal director Steven Shapiro.

The ACLU also represented a rock band that named itself The Slants after the Patent and Trademark office refused to register the name because it seemed disrespectful of Asians. The band, comprised of four Asian Americans based in Portland, Oregon, saw things differently. "Asian Americans have been using the term slant in a self-referential, empowering way for decades now," explained the band's founder, Simon Tam. He compared his appropriation of "slants" to the way certain African Americans had appropriated the so-called N-word.

In 2017, the Supreme Court ruled, 8 to 0, in the band's favor. "Speech that demeans on the basis of race, ethnicity, gender, religion, age, disability, or any other similar ground is hateful; but the proudest boast of our free speech jurisprudence is that we protect the freedom to express 'the thought that we hate,'" wrote Justice Samuel Alito for the court.

"The Slants chose their name to reappropriate a racial slur used against their community, with the goal of deflating the word's hurtful power. The government's misguided effort to protect minorities from disparagement instead hurt members of that very community by hindering their right to compete in the marketplace of ideas," commented ACLU attorney Lee Roland.

The Supreme Court victory was noted by Redskins owner Daniel Snyder, who declared, "I am THRILLED! Hail to the Redskins" in an email sent out by his public relations team.

Leslie Mehta was the ACLU of Virginia's legal director when the affiliate office took Jason Kessler's case. A North Carolina native, Mehta had attended Howard University School of Law largely because of its reputation for training social justice warriors. She had worked for a San Francisco law firm that specialized in civil and prisoners' rights before joining the ACLU of Virginia roughly a year and a half before the Charlottesville tragedy. At the ACLU, she "felt a sense of pride to be participating, even if in a small way, in what I considered to be taking a stance for the Constitution against a president who at times seemed as though he didn't seem interested in doing so."

The decision to accept the Kessler case was not controversial, but there certainly was an awareness of the potential for backlash. The Virginia affiliate kept the national office informed as things proceeded. But never was there any doubt that the ACLU would take the case.

"There were a lot of revisions back and forth with briefs and . . . discussions about potential implications, but nobody has a crystal ball," said Mehta. "At the time it was my understanding, and . . . is still my understanding now, that there was no evidence that there would be violence."

"When I read the papers in response to our pleadings, I was thinking, 'I see that [Charlottesville city officials] don't like it, but where is the information that says that they're dangerous? . . . I didn't see it. Obviously, the judge ultimately agreed."

Given the presumption that the Unite the Right rally would be peaceful, Mehta saw no rationale for rejecting the case: "I can understand the other point of view. . . . I'm an African American woman. This was not an easy decision.

"But if you're fighting for the rights of people, you have to fight for rights even when you disagree with the underlying message," Mehta said. The "comfortable decision," she added, would have been simply to ignore Kessler's request, to pretend that "we just didn't see the intake when it came in."

Still, Mehta felt "a certain kind of responsibility . . . to explain myself. And maybe that wasn't because of what other people felt. Maybe that was me personally. . . . I spoke to my mother about this often during that time period, and I spoke to my ninety-two-year-old grandmother [who] lives back in my hometown in Woodland, North Carolina . . . because I wanted to get her real perspective. . . . She never said that she fully agreed or disagreed, but she did not think that I was wrong. . . . She understood why I did what I did. My mother was okay. My grandmother was okay. And so I was okay with the decision."

Even as Mehta was talking to her grandmother, reassuring herself that she had had done the right thing, the ACLU, institutionally, was going through a similar process. People within the organization were openly asking, "Why, in God's name, was the ACLU in Charlottesville defending neo-Nazis?"

That simmering disgruntlement eventually resulted in a letter (addressed to Romero and "other members of ACLU Leadership") from 334 staffers begging that the ACLU "create space" and make time to sort out what it had done. They promised to keep the contents of the letter "within the ACLU."

The signatories affirmed their collective belief in "the fundamental rights to freedom of speech and peaceful protest" even for white supremacists—along with racists' right to representation. But they did not believe "that the ACLU must always represent white supremacists when they seek our assistance in free speech cases." They also supported racial equality and justice, to which "white supremacy presents a grave, and growing, threat." They believed "the speech of white supremacist groups arises . . . in the context of an individually, institutionally, and structurally racist country in which existing power structures already amplify the voices of some and not others."

The letter requested a discussion of the decision-making process for representing white supremacists. The process, it argued, "should involve a weighing of the competing constitutional concerns involved, including both the effect on racial equality and the effect on others' ability to speak." The signatories flatly rejected the notion that "the antidote for repugnant speech is more speech."

As the letter banged around the ACLU universe, the *New York Review of Books* published an article by legal director David Cole that some staffers saw as a rebuttal of their letter and also as a betrayal.

In the article, Cole cites a poll indicating that 40 percent of millennials believe the government should be able to suppress hate speech. "Young people today voice far less faith in free speech than do their grandparents," he observes.

"People who oppose the protection of racist speech make several arguments, all ultimately resting on a claim that speech rights conflict with equality, and that equality should prevail in the balance," he writes. "They contend that the 'marketplace of ideas' assumes a mythical level playing field. . . . They argue that the history of mob and state violence targeting African-Americans makes racist speech directed at them especially indefensible. . . . And still others argue that while it might have made sense to tolerate Nazis marching in Skokie in 1978, now, when white supremacists have a friend in the president himself, the power and influence they wield justify a different approach."

Cole dismisses the relevance of the power differential argument. "The right to free speech does not rest on the presumption of a level playing field. Virtually all rights—speech included—are enjoyed unequally, and can reinforce inequality." He concedes that there are times and places when the goal of equality trumps free speech, but argues such exceptions "do not extend to the public sphere, where ideas must be open to full and free contestation, and those who disagree can turn away or talk back."

He focuses on Charlottesville, pointing out that there "the ACLU's client swore under oath that he intended only a peaceful protest." And he notes that, "in light of Charlottesville and the risk of violence at future protests, the ACLU will not represent marchers who seek to brandish weapons while protesting."

"If we defended speech only when we agreed with it, on what ground would we ask others to tolerate speech they oppose?" Cole asks, and concludes with a ringing defense of free speech: "We protect the First Amendment not only because it is the lifeblood of democracy and an indispensable element of freedom, but because it is the guarantor of civil society itself. It protects the press, the academy, religion, political parties, and nonprofit associations like ours. In the era of Donald Trump, the importance of preserving these avenues for advancing justice and preserving democracy should be more evident than ever."

Inside the ACLU, the article landed with a resounding thud.

Shortly thereafter, a second staff letter appeared. Dated August 27, 2017, and addressed to Romero, the letter expressed "deep concern" about Cole's essay. The article "misrepresents our substantive concerns," complained the staffers. "It reduces those concerns to the strawman that 'it would be much easier for the ACLU to represent only those with whom we agree.' But the problem with representing white supremacists is not that we disagree with them. It is that doing so advances their racist agenda in a country where they have great strength, and where institutional and structural racism continue to give some speakers greater power than others."

The staffers accused the ACLU of violating its own plea to keep the dispute within the family. The communications department, they noted, had sent out a directive: "Debate, analysis and reflection is standard practice at the ACLU. We engage in it with our staff directly. We don't have those conversations in the press."

"We are left wondering," said the signatories, "to whom that directive applies. If airing the substance of our disagreements is not good for the organization, surely that is not less true when the person who airs them is the legal director."

The aggrieved staffers asked leadership to cease its aggressive defense of the ACLU's traditional policy and to spell out the steps the organization would take to reestablish trust.

Dorothy Ehrlich, the ACLU's deputy director, believes the staffers misunderstood Cole's role. "Putting aside the content of what [Cole] said, and whether some people might've felt mischaracterized . . . when David published [that] article, they felt like, 'What are you doing? We were told we can't. . . . Why are you publishing it outside?'"

What the annoyed staffers missed, she said, is "that David was [writing] on behalf of the institution." They didn't understand, in other words, that Cole was not violating the agreement by arguing his case outside the ACLU family, but was simply explaining the position the institution had always held. "So it was seen as this incredible betrayal, that they had followed the rules and he hadn't."

As for the dialogue the critics requested, "that is something we've actually engaged in," said Ehrlich, who is co-chair of the Equity Diversity Inclusion Council. "We added sort of a task force. It was given the role of dealing with that request. We added some people from affiliates.

"It's a hard-enough conversation to have with the five hundred people here, but when you add the twelve hundred people outside, it's really unwieldy. And so we . . . orchestrated small group conversations among the entire national staff, and people were sort of assigned different groups. . . .

We had twenty-six separate conversations here, and about half of the affiliates also had their own day. . . . And then we actually had make-up sessions."

As a result, Ehrlich said, the ACLU developed a "tool kit, so that if someday the ACLU were to decide to take such a controversial case again, we would at least have in place a number of recommended actions that affiliates or the national office would take."

She acknowledged it "has been a genuinely vexing issue for the organization. . . . And for me, . . . it was very painful . . . as somebody who got a lot of pushback in the very early stages, in the eighties, of really trying to push the organization in the direction of doing more racial justice work, and ensuring that that be a priority in the organization."

As head of the Northern California ACLU affiliate, which she headed for a quarter of a century, Ehrlich "started the first racial justice program. I hired Michelle Alexander, who was our first director. . . . A lot of really kind of remarkable leaders came through our office, and kind of really made major contributions to moving the organization to really embrace racial justice as not only a core part of the program but a real priority. . . . All of those years, we had the only full-time police practices program, which remains one of the single most important areas for the ACLU."

Ehrlich discovered that the racial justice work "never, in any way, diminished the First Amendment activity. . . . I'm not saying we did a Klan case every year, but we definitely represented [them]. We did . . . those sort of controversial First Amendment cases. It was something that we saw as part of our mandate. And so, it was a real rude awakening, and sort of a personal failure, seeing that . . . people couldn't hold those two concepts together at the same time."

It was the ACLU's racial justice work that attracted Dennis Parker. A native of Mount Vernon, New York, and a graduate of Middlebury and Harvard Law School, Parker was deeply influenced by Derrick Bell, Harvard's first black law professor. Bell left the law school in 1990 in protest against its failure to hire a black female in a tenure track position. "I cannot continue to urge students to take risks for what they believe if I do not practice my own precepts," said Bell.

Parker's first summer job in law school was with the NAACP Legal Defense Fund (LDF). He spent his second year at a legal services office and after graduation joined the Legal Aid Society and worked as a criminal defense lawyer in Brooklyn. From there he joined the civil rights bureau of the New York Attorney General's office, which he became head of before returning to the LDF. He joined the ACLU in 2006, where he was charged with starting up the racial justice program: "There were people who did racial justice work [at the ACLU, but] . . . when they reached out to me, what they said is we want to create a program that is going to be thinking about race all the time."

That suited Parker fine: "I was glad that someone was doing the free speech cases. I didn't know whether I would necessarily have to be the person to do them. I thought about what that meant. At LDF . . . we were advocating on behalf of black people. There may have been questions about what would be best for black people, but it was not a question of should we be representing the Klan because that would just never occur. . . . You didn't have to explain [to colleagues] the way race works. I think one of the biggest shocks of leaving LDF . . . is how much that's not true for everywhere else in the world."

Nonetheless, Parker found the prospect of working for the ACLU exciting: "What appealed to me was the fact that you could build a project from scratch, determine which cases you would bring and [tackle them]. Even at its most difficult time, the resources here are quite good."

His first week on the job gave him pause. "There was something on the legal listserv. Somebody had sent something out saying . . . 'We have a sheriff who is the founder of the Posse Comitatus in our region. What should we do about it?'"

A black ACLU staff attorney responded with, "It's kind of problematic that the person who is in charge of law enforcement is a member of a white supremacist group." Parker was amazed at the feedback engendered by that comment. "There was this email . . . this uncivil email" sent to the black staffer whose gist was, "Don't you understand the First Amendment? He has the right to associate with whomever he wants." The tone, recalls Dennis, was "condescending and nasty." Upon reading the email, he recalls thinking, "'Oh my God! What did I walk into here.' Because to me, it *is* problematic that the head law enforcement person is the head of a white nationalist group."

"That wouldn't happen now," Parker quickly added. "We still have huge issues to deal with [but] there is more of a recognition that the Bill of Rights doesn't end with the First Amendment."

At the ACLU's biennial leadership conference in Denver that September, the tragic events at Charlottesville were very much on people's minds. During a panel discussion set up to explore the implications of that episode, Charles Lawrence, a law professor at the University of Hawaii, challenged the ACLU's commitment to representing racists. He argued that the speech of the alt-right should not be legitimized by the ACLU's representation and seemed to question whether the ravings of such a group were worthy of any protection at all. "Is this a protest or a mob?" he asked.

Lawrence answered his own question: "The white supremacists in Charlottesville felt like a mob to me. I know what it feels like when people take to the streets to push hard with their political views, to persuade me that their vision or values would better serve our democracy. I also know what threat feels like. I know the bully, the mob that believes my life is worthless. Yes, the mob has a message that contains content. The content is my body, my person and its worthlessness. The content is also a notice, a reminder, a promise that violence accompanies this speech—that [violence] always has."

"Are there reasons to treat white supremacy differently from other ideas? he asked. "I believe that we should defend the expression of all ideas, even those with which we disagree. . . . But what if this particular idea, white supremacy, Nazism, negates my humanity, asserts my non-citizenship, excludes me from democracy's conversation, calls for my extermination, makes possible and then justifies the murder of my son or daughter?"

When, he wondered, "do Nazi marches become a paramilitary arm of the state? The white supremacist march in Virginia felt no different than a Trump campaign rally to me. The Make America Great signs were replaced by swastikas and chants of 'blood and soil' but the message was the same."

He concluded with, "those of us who know racism as the objects of racism's dehumanization know the injuries of Charlottesville differently than those of you who choose to ally yourself with us because you believe in the principle of racial equality."

ACLU board president Susan Herman suggested that "part of the purpose of having the panel with Chuck Lawrence" was to help people understand "that it's painful to people to hear this [hate] speech. But . . . we're asking people to take the pain and understand that we believe that there will be more pain in the future if we don't manage to find a way to talk back to these people instead of silencing them."

During the meeting at which Lawrence spoke, David Goldberger received the Norman Dorsen Presidential Prize, bestowed on academics for "outstanding lifetime contributions to civil liberties."

In accepting the award, Goldberger expressed pride in being a lawyer "identified with an organization whose commitment to the First Amendment extends from defense of the First Amendment rights of the Nazis in Skokie, to the Communist Party seeking a place on the ballot, to Dr. Benjamin Spock leading the charge against the war in Vietnam, to the white supremacists in Charlottesville."

When I asked him about Lawrence's comment, Goldberger rejected the view that the "pain experienced by racial minorities when white nationalists exercise their right to freedom of speech" meant the ACLU shouldn't represent them. He found Lawrence's comments "hurtful because they seemed indifferent to the pain that I and other Jews feel when racists make bigoted public statements about us. . . . The Jews who continued in their support for the ACLU during Skokie and after—and there were many— knew that the pain had to be tolerated because protection of freedom of speech in a democracy was more important."

He likewise rejected the notion that advocating on behalf of racist speakers made them stronger: "The Nazis in the Skokie case promptly disappeared after their fifteen minutes of fame. And the national revulsion at the conduct of the white nationalists in Charlottesville has been anything but helpful to their movement. Sure, they picked up a few folks on the fringe who are looking for fellow haters. However, the general response to the white nationalists and their spokesman Richard Spencer has been so violent that they cannot make public speeches anywhere without significant police protection."

Romero is sympathetic to the view that hate speech doesn't deserve the ACLU's protection: "I think that's a perfectly legitimate viewpoint for staff members to have, and the answer can't be, 'You're not one of us. Get out!' . . . At the same time, you can't run the work of the organization through kind of a focus group [where] everyone gets to decide, and everyone has a veto power. . . . Ultimately, the organization's got to stand for something [even] when people within the organization don't agree. I actually think there's no other organization that's trying to do both and trying to straddle . . . both sets of issues, saying, 'Both of them are equally important to us.'"

If he were head of the Puerto Rican Legal Defense Fund, added Romero, "I wouldn't bring a Nazi case. If I were the head of the First Amendment Center, I would bring every Nazi case and not worry about the racial justice implications. I think part of what is magical and different and kind of vexing is . . . trying to accomplish both and . . . to have a conversation that allows that."

David Cole doesn't believe the hullabaloo around Charlottesville will make for a major change in how the ACLU operates. "I think we will always find ourselves on occasion, and it's only on occasion, defending people whose views we find deeply antithetical to other values we believe in."

Although the ACLU is the "premier defender of the First Amendment," it is also a civil rights organization, said Cole. "In fact, we spend more of our time and more of our resources on civil rights than on civil liberties." One reason the ACLU felt obligated to take on Jason Kessler and his rally was that there was "not another attorney or organization with experience that was ready to represent this."

"Let's imagine—I think it's actually unthinkable—but let's imagine the board came together and said, 'You know what? We're not going to defend white supremacists' speech rights anymore.' I think that would be deeply harmful to the ACLU, to its reputation, to its credibility, and in the long run, to the First Amendment."

Lee Rowland, a senior attorney for the ACLU who resigned in the wake of the Charlottesville controversy, notes that potential ACLU cases don't all exist in the same reality. High-impact cases, of the sort typically tried by the national office, go through an extremely rigorous vetting process. And racial justice cases often fit in that category: "We never plan a big suit without thinking, 'Hey, are these the right plaintiffs for public education value, for winning the case?' 'Are they going to be in a position where we can put them through litigation for two years?' There are all kinds of sensitive considerations about building the perfect case."

Cases like the Charlottesville neo-Nazi case are typically picked up by affiliates and handled very differently. A rally or other event is looming, and attorneys are under pressure to intervene. "When you're in a reactive posture, that [intense vetting] doesn't happen. And I see that distinction . . . between the kind of constructed nature of an impact litigation suit that you proactively file, and a very, very, very time-sensitive response to a government saying 'no permit for tomorrow.' You either go to court in the next twenty-four hours or you don't."

She doesn't believe there's "a lot of value in rethinking whether we extend our resources to people based on their point of view. . . . I have very little sympathy for that argument, because it is antithetical to how free speech rights are defended.

"Nonetheless, I have some sympathy for the view that says, 'Hey, it kind of looks to me like we take almost every First Amendment case that walks in the door, when it's a Nazi being told they can't march. But then when it comes to people with racial justice issues, we meticulously select one out of every thirty to bring the big case. . . . I think it's totally fair to have an organizational conversation about the ways in which we take the subject matter of different cases."

But the more interesting issue, in her mind, is almost incidental to whether the ACLU represents Nazis. "I think the ACLU's most important role is to protect speech from levers of power. And usually those levers of power are the government, sometimes they can be corporations. We want to think very carefully and make sure we are maintaining our traditional role in protecting vulnerable voices from [abuses of] power."

The widely shared anguish in the wake of the Charlottesville fiasco ultimately resulted in a memo that spelled out "case selection guidelines" in the event of "conflicts between competing values or priorities." The memo was the work of a group chaired by legal director Cole. The guidelines were meant to be binding on the national office but advisory for affiliates. Decision makers are asked to consider some fourteen factors.

Among those factors are the merits of the case, the potential impact of the litigation, the likelihood of prevailing, the potential impact on ACLU credibility, the availability of other competent counsel, the potential drain on resources, and the likely harm to important ACLU relationships. In considering free speech cases, ACLU lawyers are asked to determine whether the speakers intend to engage in or promote violence (which automatically disqualifies prospective clients); whether speakers intend to carry weapons (which also is an automatic disqualifier); the impact of the proposed speech or its suppression on social justice work; the ACLU's ability to distance itself from the message of the speakers; and the ACLU's ability to mitigate harm associated with the speech.

The policy memo acknowledges that the impact of the guidelines will be limited: "The guidelines do not seek to resolve the conflicts, because resolution will virtually always turn on factors specific to each case. Nor do they change ACLU policy, which is set by the Board. Rather, consistent with Board policy, they attempt to identify the kinds of questions that ought to be considered, the processes for their consideration, and the measures that can help mitigate the harms to competing interests."

Even under the new guidelines, the affiliate would not necessarily have rejected Charlottesville's neo-Nazis. Never mind that the guidelines are not binding on affiliates at any rate. As a practical matter, it seems unlikely that the guidelines will cause any significant change. The larger impact is likely to come from memories of the chaos in Charlottesville, the loss of a life, and the organizational distress that ensued. Affiliates will be more likely to ask themselves whether defending a particular hatemonger advances social welfare or not.

In December 2017, the charge against James Fields, the Charlottesville killer, was upgraded from second-degree to first-degree murder. He was also charged with "aggravated wounding" and crimes in connection with the thirty-five individuals injured by his car.

A UVA psychologist who evaluated Fields testified he had been diagnosed, at fourteen, with schizoid personality disorder. "Mr. Fields did not come to Charlottesville in good mental health. In fact, he came to Charlottesville not having taken medication in two years," argued his defense attorney. Nonetheless, Field was deemed legally sane at the time of the attack and therefore competent to stand trial.

His trial began on November 26, 2018. The defense argued that Fields was in fear for his life. Senior Assistant Commonwealth's Attorney Nina-Alice Antony refuted that in her closing argument: "He said he was scared of people attacking him, but . . . there was no evidence that shows he is credible." Fields was convicted of the murder charge, eight counts of malicious wounding, and leaving the scene after killing Heyer. He subsequently also pled guilty to federal hate crime charges.

In June 2019, before sentencing by the federal judge, Fields apologized to his mother "for putting her through all of this. Every day I think about how things could have gone differently, and how I regret my actions. I am sorry," he said. Fields received a life sentence.

In July 2019, he was again sentenced to life—this time by the Virginia state judge—with his sentences to run consecutively.

Even as the ACLU maneuvered through the morass of the Charlottesville controversy, it was dealing with the Trump administration's provocations on the southern border.

The separation of families crisis leapt into the headlines on May 7, 2018, when Attorney General Jeff Sessions announced that people crossing the border illegally would be charged and their children taken: "If you are smuggling a child then we will prosecute you, and that child will be separated from you as required by law. If you don't like that, then don't smuggle children over our border."

Sessions did not address the human cost on families fleeing danger or the monumentally unready state of the court system to adjudicate their claims. Nor did he describe the hellish state of detention centers.

Within days, the press was filled with reports of overcrowded courtrooms. Stories poured forth of children effectively imprisoned in foul, chaotic, crowded facilities ill-equipped to care for them. It also became clear—Trump administration claims notwithstanding—that there was no plan to reunite families ripped apart by the American government.

The child separation program, it turned out, was not as new as the Trump administration was claiming. The pilot program had launched in 2017, shortly after Trump took office. The only thing new was that it was now being openly acknowledged by the administration.

Using the Department of Homeland Security's own figures, news organizations in May 2018 reported that at least 1,768 children had been separated from their families between October 2016 and February 2018. The total number acknowledged by the administration in May 2018 was over four thousand. And the shelter situation was worsening.

On May 30, 2018, the *Los Angeles Times* reported, "As of Wednesday, 10,852 migrant children were being held at shelters run by the Department of Health and Human Services, compared with 8,886 at the end of last month. . . . The average time such children spent at government shelters has also increased, from 51 to 56 days."

The courts were straining under the weight. "The crowded courtroom reeked of stale sweat, and 92 immigrants filled all five benches, leaving standing room only for visitors and court personnel," reported the *Los Angeles Times* from Texas.

In May 2018, information obtained from an open records lawsuit filed by the ACLU suggested that the phenomenon of children mistreated at the border had occurred under the Obama administration. As the *Washington Post* reported, sourcing the ACLU's data, "unaccompanied minors who crossed the U.S.-Mexico border during a historic wave of migration earlier this decade were repeatedly beaten, sexually abused, and deprived of food and medical care by federal border agents."

The huge difference from current policy was that the earlier report concerned children who had arrived unaccompanied; the new horror was children systematically and intentionally ripped from their parents.

The ACLU filed a series of lawsuits. One of the most consequential, filed in June 2018, named two mothers as plaintiffs. Both had been separated from their children (a Brazilian arrested at the border with her fourteen-year-old son and a Congolese woman with a six-year-old daughter).

On June 7, Judge Dana Sabraw, of the U.S. District Court for the Southern District of California in San Diego, rejected a motion to dismiss the ACLU lawsuit. "At a minimum, the facts alleged are sufficient to show the government conduct at issue 'shocks the conscience' and violates Plaintiffs' constitutional right to family integrity," said the judge.

Bardis Vakili, an ACLU attorney in San Diego, commented, "the judge stated what is obvious to everyone except our own government: that the forcible separation of asylum-seeking parents and their traumatized children is a brutal act, comparable to the very persecution these parents hoped to protect their children from in the first place."

On June 26, Judge Sabraw again ruled in the ACLU's favor, ordering the Trump administration to stop separating children from their parents and to reunite those already separated within thirty days. Judge Sabraw declared the situation at a "crisis level."

Lee Gelernt, of the ACLU, called the ruling "an enormous victory." It soon became clear, however, that the government had no idea how to reunite many of the separated children. It also became clear that thousands more children than originally had been assumed might have been separated.

In August 2018, the *New York Times* reported: "The government was supposed to submit a plan to a federal judge in California on Thursday to reunite the families, but instead it told the ACLU to come up with its own plan."

The ACLU filed yet another suit in U.S. District Court in the District of Columbia in another immigration-related matter. This time, the ACLU was objecting to the new "expedited removal" policies of the Trump administration. Those policies essentially asked federal officials to summarily reject claims of asylum seekers fleeing horrors at home and to immediately send them back. The new approach, argued the ACLU, violated the Constitution, U.S. immigration law, and international refugee law. "Without an injunction, Plaintiffs and thousands of other immigrants . . . will be unlawfully deported to places where they fear they will be raped, kidnapped, beaten and killed," argued the ACLU.

On August 9, U.S. District Court Judge Emmet Sullivan demanded the immediate return of two Salvadoran asylum seekers deported to El Salvador despite the U.S. government's promise that they would not be removed. Sullivan threatened to hold Attorney General Sessions and Secretary of Homeland Security Kirstjen Nielsen in contempt. "This is pretty outrageous that someone seeking justice in U.S. court is spirited away while her attorneys are arguing for justice for her. I'm not happy about this at all," said Sullivan.

Following the 2018 midterm elections, Trump again turned his attention to the southern border. On November 9, he issued a presidential proclamation targeting so-called caravans of asylum seekers. The proclamation claimed that "a substantial number of aliens primarily from Central

America" were "traveling in large, organized groups through Mexico and reportedly intend to enter the United States unlawfully."

In order "to protect the national interest," Trump was suspending "the entry of certain aliens . . . traveling through Mexico to enter our country unlawfully or without proper documentation." Such aliens, he declared, "will be ineligible to be granted asylum." In addition, the "entry of any alien into the United States across the international boundary between the United States and Mexico is hereby suspended and limited."

He ordered the secretaries of state and homeland security to "consult with the Government of Mexico regarding appropriate steps."

In March 2019, Judge Sabraw again intervened at the ACLU's request and ordered that the children previously separated be reunited. "The court made clear that potentially thousands of children's lives are at stake and that the Trump administration cannot simply ignore the devastation it has caused," said the ACLU's Gelernt.

That April, in response to Judge Sabraw's demand, federal officials said the process of reuniting families might take as long as two years—in part because many of the children were effectively lost. A report that January from the Inspector General of the Department of Health and Human Services made clear that the government had never put an effective program in place to track the children once they were separated.

In the following months, the ACLU and other nonprofits struggled to reunite children, even as the Trump administration announced, and then delayed, a massive roundup of undocumented immigrants in the United States. The government also announced plans to hold migrant children at an army base in Oklahoma used during World War II for Japanese internment.

One particularly disturbing aspect of the Trump border policies was a rise in the number of deaths in detention. "Two children have died in US border custody this month. Before that, none in a decade. Why now?" asked *USA Today* in a December 2018 headline. The story did not provide a conclusive answer, but it noted facilities lacked adequate medical supplies and equipment. A CNN wire service story in July 2019 similarly pointed out that a thirty-year-old Honduran man was the eleventh person to die in Immigration and Customs Enforcement (ICE) custody since the previous September.

In September 2019, the House Homeland Security Subcommittee released the testimony of Katherine Hawkins, an analyst for the Project on Government Oversight, which Hawkins described as a "nonpartisan independent watchdog that investigates and exposes waste, corruption and abuse of power."

In investigating conditions at ICE detention centers, said Hawkins, her team had found "serious flaws in ICE's inspection and oversight system and inhumane conditions in ICE detention centers." Government documents "reveal inadequate medical care, inadequate mental health care, and overuse of solitary confinement." The problems, she added, "are chronic, but they have grown worse with the rapid expansion of ICE detention over the last two and a half years." Those problems were compounded, she added, by an inadequate and often unaccountable inspection system and by ICE's own unresponsiveness. As a result, she concluded, "inhumane and unsafe conditions persist . . . sometimes with fatal consequences."

On July 9, 2018, President Trump nominated Brett Kavanaugh (a judge on the U.S. Court of Appeals for the District of Columbia) for the Supreme Court. The ACLU's leadership was disturbed by aspects of his judicial record, but there was no plan to actively oppose him. That changed after the special Senate Judiciary Committee hearings held in late September explored the issue of his possible guilt in the sexual assault of psychology professor Christine Blasey Ford.

The week of September 23 was particularly brutal for the Supreme Court nominee. That Sunday, Deborah Ramirez, a Yale classmate, accused Kavanaugh of shoving his penis in her face when both were freshmen at Yale. Monday found Kavanaugh declaring in an interview on Fox News, "I've never sexually assaulted anyone. I did not have sexual intercourse or anything close to sexual intercourse in high school or for many years thereafter." That Wednesday, on the eve of Ford's testimony before the Senate committee, a woman named Julie Swetnick accused Kavanaugh of sexual misconduct as a teen.

In her appearance that Thursday before the Senate Judiciary Committee, Ford said she was "one hundred percent certain" that Kavanaugh was "the boy who sexually assaulted me." She feared he "was going to rape me." Ford accused Kavanaugh of "having fun" at her expense.

A visibly angry Kavanaugh called the confirmation process "a national disgrace" and accused vengeful Democrats of plotting against him. "You tried hard," he told the Democrats. "You've given it your all. . . . You may defeat me in the final vote, but you'll never get me to quit."

Previously, Ehrlich recalled, the board had decided to remain neutral on the Kavanaugh nomination. "We were basically staying out of it." After the hearing, the board had a three-hour meeting by telephone and voted to oppose the nominee.

That Saturday, September 29, the ACLU posted an article authored by board president Susan Herman announcing the decision:

"The ACLU's board of directors, deeply concerned by the allegations raised in recent weeks, has made a rare exception to its longstanding policy [of neutrality] and voted to oppose the nomination of Brett Kavanaugh to the Supreme Court."

Herman's article quoted the board resolution noting the "credible allegations that Judge Kavanaugh has engaged in serious misconduct that have not been adequately investigated by the Senate."

"We cannot remain silent under these extraordinary circumstances about a lifetime appointment to the highest court of the land. The standard for such an appointment should be high, and the burden is on the nominee. That burden is not met as long as there are unresolved questions regarding the credible allegations of sexual assault," read the resolution.

The ACLU announced it was allocating more than a million dollars to back its anti-Kavanaugh campaign. Shortly thereafter, a TV ad appeared in selected markets. It began with pictures of accused sexual offenders Matt Lauer, Harvey Weinstein and Charlie Rose, as a female intoned, "We've seen this before. Denials from powerful men." Then, Bill Clinton, Bill Cosby and Kavanaugh appear, in turn, denying allegations of sexual misconduct. The female voice returns, "America is watching; and as we choose a lifetime seat on our highest court, integrity matters, and we cannot have any doubt."

On October 6, by a 50 to 48 vote, the Senate confirmed Kavanaugh's nomination. It was the closest vote for a Supreme Court justice in well over a century.

The Trump presidency was something virtually no one saw coming. And it has profound implications, not just for the Supreme Court but for the nation and the world. For the ACLU, it has brought unprecedented growth, fueled largely by donors alarmed that such a man became the Leader of the Free World.

In a message to ACLU members in February 2017, Romero described the Trump effect as "agonizing but also exhilarating." Since the Trump age dawned, reported Romero, contributions to ACLU had soared: "Almost one million people have made online donations to the ACLU. Our membership has now more than doubled since the election." And he pledged an ambitious new set of initiatives to take on the threat to constitutional liberties that Trump represents.

Indeed, the money pouring into the ACLU with the ascent of Trump easily dwarfs what came in in the wake of the call for Nixon's impeachment—or in the aftermath of the attack on the World Trade Center. In early 2019, the ACLU claimed 1.85 million "card-carrying" members, more than four times the 400,000 it claimed in 2016. It also claimed annual revenue approaching $400 million, roughly double what it had seen in 2016. Its national staff had grown from 335 to 550. Its affiliate staff had grown from 774 to 1,180.

That surge in resources has been fueled by one Trump outrage after another. "I don't think we've ever had as dangerous a president as President Trump, and I don't think we've ever had one as either ignorant or just dismissive of not just constitutional law but constitutional norms. . . . I think he is a unique challenge to people who believe in civil rights and civil liberties," said David Cole. "But I think that I have never seen before in this country the level of citizen engagement in defense of civil rights and civil liberties."

15

Reflections

Since its origins, the ACLU has stood—more than anything else—for the protection of America's Bill of Rights. In particular, it has stood for safeguarding the First Amendment. The ACLU assumed, as did America's founders, that America was made stronger by free speech. Only through free speech could virtuous arguments triumph over meritless arguments and could truth triumph over propaganda. So what happens when the assumption is shown to be false? Or at least, to be extremely questionable?

In his famous concurring opinion in the case of Charlotte Whitney (1927's *Whitney v. California*), Supreme Court Justice Louis Brandeis (see Chapter 5) made an eloquent argument for the virtue of free speech. In what is perhaps the most famous passage, he wrote, "If there be time to expose through discussion the falsehood and fallacies, to avert the evil by the processes of education, the remedy to be applied is more speech, not enforced silence."

As legal scholar Vincent Blasi observed, "Brandeis sounds almost like a dewy-eyed idealist in the way he articulates the argument for a strong principle of freedom of speech. It is, I believe, the idealism that permeates his Whitney opinion that makes it arguably the most important essay ever written, on or off the bench, on the meaning of the first amendment."[1]

Roger Baldwin agreed with Brandeis that good ideas will drive out bad ideas—as people rationally decide what's in society's best interest. In other words, the remedy to bad speech is more speech—presumably of a higher, more enlightening variety.

Back in those days, when the modern notion of civil liberties was being born, there was a faith in the proposition that shining a light on truth would inevitably benefit those on the side of justice; that a free speech movement on the side of the angels, arguing on behalf of unions, minorities, women's liberationists, and social equality, would lead to a society that held those things dear.

Baldwin's view of the First Amendment and of civil liberties was not so much rooted in constitutional history as in a certain brand of progressive activism—and that view ultimately became inextricably intertwined with how Americans viewed free speech. To quote Laura Weinrib, author of *The Taming of Free Speech*, "when the ACLU was founded in the aftermath of the First World War, it declared itself an adjunct of the radical labor movement. Its defense of free speech was motivated by a deep-seated distrust of state institutions stemming from decades of hostile treatment of unions in the courts as well as the political branches; the rights it championed were the rights to picket, boycott, and strike."[2]

Given that history, it stood to reason that the ACLU became deeply involved in the case of Benjamin Gitlow, the Communist Labor Party member convicted of violating New York State's criminal anarchy law (see Chapter 4). Even though the Supreme Court found Gitlow guilty, it also found that "freedom of speech and of the press are among the fundamental personal rights and 'liberties' protected by the due process clause of the Fourteenth Amendment from impairment by the States."

But despite Roger Baldwin's fervent beliefs, there is nothing inherently liberal, progressive, or radical in free speech. At some point, the wealthy class, the class of industrialists and union breakers, was bound to realize that, just as they would realize that truth will not necessarily emerge from untrammeled speech.

To be blunt, neither the nation's founders, Brandeis, or Baldwin ever envisioned anything remotely like the situation we have today—in which made-up facts are widely deemed to be more credible than the truth, and in which it is all but impossible to "avert the evil by the processes of education" that "falsehoods and fallacies" can wreak on society.

Since the beginning of the Trump presidency, the *Washington Post* (among others) has made tracking Donald Trump's misstatements and falsehoods a spectator's sport. In October 2019, the *Post* reported, "as President Trump approaches his 1,000th day in office Wednesday, he has significantly stepped up his pace of spouting exaggerated numbers, unwarranted boasts and outright falsehoods." He had made 13,435 "false or misleading claims," according to the *Post* database, "an average of almost 22 claims a day since our last update 65 days ago."

There is something amusing but also profoundly disturbing about this— if for no other reason than that democracy becomes increasingly difficult as the value placed on truth diminishes. And no major politician in American history has a more cavalier attitude toward truth than does Donald Trump.

Trump, of course, rose to political prominence through endless repetition of an easily provable lie—that Barack Obama was not American. But undergirding the slander of "birtherism" was an even more potent lie: that real Americans are not black or brown. That lie, that myth, was the wind behind his sails as he glided down Trump Tower's golden escalator on June 16, 2015. That lie, that myth, is the reason why, as he stood before eight American flags and announced his candidacy for the presidency, he lashed out at Mexican immigrants: "When Mexico sends its people, they're not sending their best. . . . They're sending people that have lots of problems and they're bringing those problems with us. They're bringing drugs. They're bringing crime. They're rapists."

His objective was to gain victory through race-based polarization, to win by further dividing the country. And he succeeded magnificently—with, as we now know, a little help from his (Russian) friends.

The report of the Senate Select Committee on Intelligence, released in October 2019, observed that the St. Petersburg–based Internet Research Agency (IRA) "sought to influence the 2016 U.S. presidential election by harming Hillary Clinton's chances of success and supporting Donald Trump at the direction of the Kremlin." That "information warfare campaign," reported the senate committee, "was broad in scope and entailed objectives beyond the result of the 2016 presidential election."

The committee also found that, "by far, race and related issues were the preferred target of the information warfare campaign designed to divide the country in 2016. . . . [In] the IRA's Facebook advertising over 66 percent contained a term related to race." Five of the IRA's ten best performing Instagram accounts "were focused on African-American issues

and audiences." And its Twitter content and YouTube activity "heavily focused on hot-button issues with racial undertones, such as the NFL kneel-
ing protests" and police brutality.

Trump was not the first candidate to realize that bigotry could be wielded
as a political weapon. Nor was he the first genius to understand that once
you embrace racism, you are set free from the truth. Decades ago, Richard
Nixon had similar insights, and he convinced his party to make a deal with
the Devil when it sided with Southern segregationists in return for political power. But for that marriage to work, the party had to embrace a lie—
that Southern segregationists were not anti-democratic, that they were not
even racist. They were just believers in states' rights.

Even then, thoughtful critics saw beyond the con. Civil rights activist
Bayard Rustin denounced Nixon's "insidious strategy to win the Wallace
vote in the South and to organize an electoral majority on the basis of hostility to Negroes." The hostility, these days, is not just to blacks, but to
Muslims and poor Latinos.

Reflecting on the role of race in today's politics, the Ford Foundation's
Darren Walker observed, "the backlash to Barack Obama's presidency is
something we never anticipated. I think for many of us, we naively believed
that the election of a black president would unleash a new era of understanding and reconciliation. And I think in fact in some ways it did that . . .
but it actually caused the opposite with a significant number of Americans."

No one could have anticipated that a foreign power would seize upon
that bigotry as a perfect weapon against the United States. Just as no one
could have anticipated that so many Americans would be so eager to reject
truth and sense for lies—and to abandon the oft-declared virtues of their
own nation to imbibe the toxins of intolerance and ignorance.

So we have a White House that dismisses its own national climate assessment and gives short shrift to America's intelligence chiefs and their
global threat assessment.

There is a danger in this beyond having a president garner a reputation
as a chronic liar. As Margaret Sullivan, media columnist for the *Washington Post* put it: "When news organizations hand a megaphone to lies—or
liars—they do actual harm."

Deborah Lipstadt, author of *Denying the Holocaust*, recalls the day that
David Irving, a notorious Holocaust denier, burst into her classroom and

promised $1,000 to anyone who could prove Hitler had ordered the final solution. As she recounted in an interview with *The Guardian*, "I was a deer in the headlights. I didn't know what to do. If I started debating with him it would suggest to students that there were two sides. If I didn't debate it suggested I was afraid."

Lipstadt compared Irving's gambit to Trump's frequently repeated yarn that he had witnessed thousands of Muslims dancing on the night of the 9/11 attack. "You would have thought some evidence would have emerged. . . . And he says, 'Oh, no. I know it. It's true. 100 people called me and said the same thing.' There is no need to provide the evidence. Opinion becomes fact," she observed.

In present-day America, we have brought the slick, intentional deceptions of advertising into the political sphere and wedded those practices to long-established tactics of political propaganda, even as our political class has learned to use social media to spread disinformation that propagates at a breath-taking rate. And we are learning how much everyday thinking is influenced by things that have nothing to do with either logic or reality. We have learned that if you have the money—or social media expertise—to constantly push an idea, or a slur, forward, it gains traction.

We are also learning—researchers Brendan Nyhan and Jason Reifler call this the "backfire effect"—that fact-checking may have the precise opposite result of its intended effect. In other words, if the fact-checking is telling people things they don't want to hear, they don't just tune it out, they double-down on their original misconception. As Nyhan and Reifler put it, "If people counterargue unwelcome information vigorously enough, they may end up with more 'attitudinally congruent information in mind than before the debate,' which in turn leads them to report opinions that are more extreme than they otherwise would have had.[3]

Interestingly—and relevantly—when politicians (in one experiment) were told that they would be exposed if they made false statements, they seemed to become more honest. As the researchers described it, legislators warned about making "questionable" claims "were substantially less likely to receive a negative fact-checking rating . . . when it poses a salient threat."[4]

Post-Truth author Lee McIntyre points out, "Experimental evidence has shown that the fear-based amygdala tends to be larger in conservatives than in liberals. Some have speculated that this is why the lion's share of fake news stories during the 2016 election were targeted toward a conservative audience."[5]

None of this provides evidence of good ideas pushing out bad, or, quoting Thomas Jefferson, free speech giving "the will of the people the influence it ought to have." So, instead of the Brandeisian model of rational decision-making, we are left with a model in which preconceptions, repetition, fear, and skillfully presented propaganda pretty much trump everything—and also leave us frightfully open to foreign manipulation. And then there is the impact of money.

In his review of Adam Winkler's *We the Corporations: How American Businesses Won Their Civil Rights*, David Cole points out that *Citizens United v. Federal Election Commission*, decided in 2010, was one of the most unpopular Supreme Court decisions ever. The problem, many say, is that the court wrongly extended constitutional rights to corporations. But Cole rejects that criticism, pointing out that the Supreme Court has a long history of doing that.

In his book, Winkler tells the story of Roscoe Conkling, a former senator who, in an 1882 case involving the Southern Pacific Railroad, tried to show that the drafters of the Fourteenth Amendment wanted corporations to be treated as human beings. Conkling was wrong, but that did not stop corporations from pushing the argument.

Winkler points out that "between 1868, when the amendment was ratified, and 1912, when a scholar set out to identify every Fourteenth Amendment case heard by the Supreme Court, the justices decided 28 cases dealing with the rights of African Americans—and an astonishing 312 cases dealing with the rights of corporations."

Citizens United, it turns out, was only a dramatic development in a long-established trend. And that trend has been extended, with the court deciding that chain stores have religious liberty rights and can refuse service to same-sex couples, and that big companies don't have to include birth control in health plans.

David Cole argues, "the problem with *Citizens United* is . . . not in its protection of corporate rights or its view of money as speech, but in its inability to recognize a broader set of justifications for limiting the distorting effects of concentrated wealth."

Whether one agrees or not with Cole's analysis, there is no reason, in the Constitution or law, why justices should feel compelled to recognize that broader set of justifications. And meanwhile, the forces of corporatism and regressive chauvinism—who are locked in an unholy alliance—will take full advantage of their free speech rights to argue for regressive policies aimed at benefitting the wealthy and small-minded.

When I mentioned Cole's position to john powell, a former ACLU legal director (who deliberately lowercases his name), he strongly pushed back. Professor powell, who teaches at UC Berkeley Law School, pointed out that all ACLU legal directors prior to Steven Shapiro believe *Citizens United* "was wrongly decided."

He points to Justice John Paul Stevens's dissent in the case, which he praises as "a very beautiful [treatise on] corporations and speech going back to the Founding Fathers.

"The whole of idea of having a Bill of Rights," argues powell, "was to protect people from the state. Protect people from the consolidation of power. And that's what corporations are, consolidation of power. . . . *Citizens United* is a break [with tradition]. . . . When you have courts that protect corporate rights, they actually eviscerate individual rights."

Justice Stevens's partial dissent in *Citizens United* makes it very clear, as powell argues, that in another universe, with a less corporate court, the outcome would have been different. The majority's decision, argues Stevens, was too broad, appallingly dismissive of established precedent, and ignored the fundamental fact that corporations are not human. "They cannot vote or run for office," he points out. Nor is it clear "'who' is even speaking when a business corporation places an advertisement that endorses or attacks a particular candidate."

Stevens also accuses the majority of misreading history: "Those few corporations that existed at the founding were authorized by grant of a special legislative charter. . . . It was 'assumed that [they] were legally privileged organizations that had to be closely scrutinized by the legislature because their purposes had to be made consistent with public welfare.'"

Stevens concludes, "at bottom, the Court's opinion is thus a rejection of the common sense of the American people, who have recognized a need to prevent corporations from undermining self-government since the founding, and who have fought against the distinctive corrupting potential of corporate electioneering since the days of Theodore Roosevelt."

In 2018, 28 percent of respondents to a survey by The Democracy Project rated "big money in politics" as one of their top two issues of concern among eleven possibilities offered—putting it in a statistical tie with "racism and discrimination." In addition, a large majority (80 percent) believed that the "influence of money in politics" is getting worse rather than better.

In today's America, the ability to speak and reach a receptive audience has a lot to do with wealth. One of the largest tax cuts in American history was sold as a boon to working-class people. That positioning was possible because the people making the argument were able to message their way into the hearts of people whose economic interests they do not serve.

The First Amendment guarantee of freedom of speech was not just rooted in the idea that good ideas crowd out bad ideas; it was rooted in the notion that dialogue is dominated by real people with an interest in ideas, not by corporations and wealthy individuals hiding behind PACs and other creations and using trickery, appeals to base prejudice, and outright lies to gather gullible people to their side in the interest of commerce.

"In my moments of reflection and worry, I keep thinking, 'Well, how much are [we at the ACLU] adding to the acrimony [of] the political process?" confided Romero. "I mean we are being vigorous, vehement defenders of our issues. And in a moment like this, it certainly can feel like you're throwing more wood onto this fire that seems to be burning the basic infrastructure of democracy. . . . Is the solution for me to pull my punches? Is a solution for me to not advocate for that which we're here to advocate?'

Certainly, the ACLU is doing a lot of things these days that it did a lot less of in the past. During the midterm elections of 2018, it supported a wide array of ballot initiatives. In Florida, it successfully lobbied for Amendment 4, which restored the right to vote to people convicted of felonies (excluding murder and sexual assault) who had served their time. It also supported Proposition 3 in Michigan, which provided for same-day voter registration; Question 5, in Nevada, which provided automatic voter registration for Nevadans when they get a driver's license or officially change their address; Proposition 4, an anti-gerrymandering provision in Utah; Question 3, an anti-transgender-bias measure in Massachusetts; Amendment 2, requiring a unanimous verdict for felony convictions in Louisiana; and the list goes on.

The Trump era has seen the ACLU file an unprecedented number of anti-administration lawsuits. As of early 2019, the ACLU had initiated 186 legal actions against the Trump administration, including 92 lawsuits.

The ACLU has also ramped up various get-out-the-vote initiatives and even gotten involved in individual political races. In Kansas, where Secretary of State Kris Kobach was running for governor, the ACLU distributed fliers reading, "Kris Kobach wants to be governor of Kansas but has violated our civil liberties."

It took out ads in Arizona reminding voters that Senate candidate Joseph Arpaio, when he was Maricopa County sheriff, had a record of discriminating against Latinos: "For years, Joe Arpaio broke the law to humiliate and terrorize Latinos and immigrants," intoned the narrator. "Martha McSally and Kelli Ward have joined Arpaio's anti-immigrant bandwagon. . . . For those seeking Arizona's Senate seat, Democrat or Republican, we have one question: Will you defend everyone's rights?" And in Georgia, where Stacey Abrams was running for governor, the ACLU took out ads reminding voters that Abrams had championed reforms to help low-level offenders and that she intended to end the use of private prisons.

Although the ACLU claims its activities do not cross a partisan line, critics are not so sure. The ACLU has been publicly skewered by writers across the ideological spectrum for wandering far afield of its jurisprudential roots—and even further from its pledge of nonpartisanship.

After the ACLU ran its anti-Kavanaugh ad, many ACLU watchers protested. "It's a violation of everything we believe in as civil libertarians," said Michael Meyers. Wendy Kaminer said, "I think the ad is appalling and one more example of progressive political sentiment trumping civil liberty concerns at ACLU. You should ask National Legal Director David Cole how he feels about arguing a case before a Justice Kavanaugh who the ACLU has labelled a [Bill] Cosby-like sexual predator."

In July 2018, the *New Republic* ran an article titled, "The Twilight of Free Speech Liberalism," in which journalist Marin Cogan wonders about the implications of the ACLU morphing from a civil liberties group into, well, something else: "Can a group defined by principled opposition to threats to civil liberties lead a popular movement? Can the ACLU engage in grass-roots activism and still stick to its traditionally nonpartisan approach?"

Deputy Executive Director Ehrlich rejects the criticism that the ACLU is either becoming more partisan or suffering from mission creep: "I see it for the first time having the resources that you could actually invest in this, because even in my day, twenty-five, thirty years ago, we were circulating [fliers] sometimes door to door, [highlighting the] voting records of people. But we couldn't possibly run a television ad. We were saying the same kinds of things [as now], without the resources that allow you to really be heard in an election."

Romero sees the organization as inherently and constantly in flux, both when it comes to activities and scope: "The ACLU is a living, breathing organism. It goes through points of expansion and kind of builds muscle . . . and then there are points when we have to slim it back. But I think one of the things that I learned . . . is that we never go back to the size that we were pre the growth spurt. . . . There were about 280,000 members who were here when I got here . . . then it doubles in the years of Bush to 550,000, then it contracts in the years of Obama to 400,000; but we never went back to 280,000."

With that growth, Romero, argues, have come new initiatives, along with new tools and tactics. The ACLU, he points out, has always been involved in ballot referenda. The only thing new about that, he maintains, is the "breadth and ambition," which with those efforts are undertaken: "We could never have envisioned a world before . . . where we can say we're going to sponsor, create, underwrite, and implement a six-and-a-half million-dollar ballot referendum all-in in Florida, right?"

He also argues that the ACLU has always commented on political candidates: "What is different . . . is that we're trying to do it in real time in a way to effectuate kind of a better understanding [among] the voting public . . . and tying it back to our issues."

The ACLU, he insists, is "not picking races to jump in because we want either a Democrat to get elected or a Republican to get defeated. We're picking races where the civil liberties issues are at such play that they should be a determinant for how people end up voting. . . . When you look at any one ad, you can say, 'Oh, that one is too close to the line.' . . . Whereas

[when] you look at the complete engagement . . . I think the nonpartisanship comes out in much fuller detail."

Nearly a half-century ago, in a lengthy *Human Events* article titled, "Should the American Civil Liberties Be So Political," Harvard Law School professor Joseph W. Bishop wrestled with the very charges of partisanship that the ACLU wrestles with now.

"Within the community of liberals the American Civil Liberties Union—now celebrating its fiftieth anniversary—has long occupied a place comparable to that of Dwight D. Eisenhower among Republicans. For half a century it has done more than any other organization to enforce the 1st, 4th, 5th, 6th and 8th Amendments. . . . It has also labored diligently on the 14th," wrote Bishop.

The "ACLU, spreading the protection of the Constitution to more and more people, has also spread itself like a green bay tree, and flourishes mightily. Its contributing members number 150,000, or 100 times as many as in 1921," added Bishop.

He described the organization as "divided between 'activists' and 'traditionalists.'" The "former believe the union's mission is to crusade for such political causes as find favor in their eyes. The latter have an aggravating habit of pointing out that the union's own constitution provides that its objects 'shall be to maintain and advance civil liberties, including the freedoms of association, press, religion and speech, and rights to the franchise, to due process of law, and to equal protection of the laws . . . wholly without political partisanship.'"

Bishop concludes, "The policies of its present management risk a considerable, and I think undesirable, change in its base of support—from a large number of people having very different political views, but sharing a common belief in the virtues of the Bill of Rights, to a rather smaller and politically homogenous group whose belief in civil liberties for everybody, including old thinkers, is in some cases very dubious."

As Bishop's article makes clear, the battle over defining the proper ACLU mission has been waged since at least 1972. Indeed, as pointed out previously, that argument was taking place even before the ACLU became the ACLU. The *New York Times* (see Chapter 2) greeted the creation of the National Civil Liberties Bureau with, "the freedom of speech wanted by these troublesome folk is that of talking sedition and of lending aid and comfort to our enemies."

In 1929 (see Chapter 5), Baldwin proposed to his national committee "the extension of our field of activity" beyond what the ACLU then embraced.

Pretty much from the beginning, the ACLU has been straying away from its prescribed mission, and one way or another, amicably or angrily, the leadership and membership have worked it out. It is hardly surprising that now—when the very existence of truth seems imperiled in the political sphere, when foreign powers have mastered the art of using our bigotry and polarization against us, and when an American president sees his "exoneration" from impeachment as a license to make war on American patriots and values, while declaring himself America's "chief law enforcement officer"—the ACLU is wrestling with the issue of how to protect not just the First Amendment but democracy itself.

Laying out a plan for the future of America is beyond the scope of this book and beyond the capacity of its author; but it is indisputably clear (by definition) that the way forward cannot lie in the past.

Moving forward means accepting the fact that America has changed. It means fully and finally doing away with nineteenth-century notions of race and identity and with the idea that, in order to become great (again), we must fight another civil war. It means letting go of the dream of remaking the old America and embracing the possibilities of the new. It means providing not just freedom of speech but actual speech to those citizens who have been largely silenced. It means elevating real humans over corporate entities in the hierarchy of political power. And it means awakening to the reality that the decisions we make now will haunt this earth forever.

Acknowledgments

No work of history is a solo act. A number of people were key to the production of this book. Anthony Romero and Dorothy Ehrlich were kind enough to provide unconditional access to the ACLU and its records. Daniel Linke, associate university librarian for special collections, capably guided my journey through the ACLU papers at the Seeley G. Mudd Manuscript Library at Princeton. Snow Zhu, archivist and records manager for the ACLU, provided equally expert help as I made my way through the files at the ACLU.

This book would have been exponentially more difficult if not for the New York Public Library. The NYPL provided me with a residency in its Allen Room and its president, Anthony Marx, was a vital source of advice and support. Melanie Locay, associate manager of the Center for Research in the Humanities, provided inestimable help in navigating the NYPL's formidable array of resources.

I am also grateful to the leadership, staff, and my fellow fellows at the University of California Center for Free Speech and Civic Engagement. The center provided a perfect place to reflect on, and work through, some key issues raised by my research.

Kirkland Vaughans, with whom I share an office, was an invaluable source of support, as were an array of colleagues, including Rick Smith, Jonathan Alter, Diane McWhorter, Tom Watson, Daniel Rose, and Carroll Bogert.

Editor Marc Favreau's unbounded enthusiasm made it clear that The New Press was the only conceivable home for this book; and Don Fehr, my agent at Trident Media Group, provided expert guidance along every step of the way.

To the scores of people who sat for interviews or otherwise shared their thoughts and recollections, please know that I am endlessly appreciative that you took the time.

Finally, to my daughter, Elisa, and my wife, Lee, thank you so much for putting up with my lengthy periods missing in action as I wrestled this book to the ground. I am eternally grateful for your love and support.

I, alone, am responsible for any errors or omissions.

Notes

Introduction

1. Gordon S. Wood, "The Origin of the Bill of Rights," *Proceedings of the American Antiquarian Society* 101, no. 2 (October 1991): 257.

2. Robert and Marilyn Aiken, "The 1798 Sedition Act: President's Party Prosecutes Press," *Litigation* 33, no. 4 (2007): 53–57.

1. Preaching Peace to a World at War

1. Robert Zieger, *America's Great War* (Lanham, MD: Rowman & Littlefield, 2000), 2.

2. Lillian Wald, *Windows on Henry Street* (New York: Little, Brown and Company, 1934), 292–93.

3. G. Peter Winnington, *The Man Who Had Ideas* (Mauborget, Switzerland: The Letterworth Press, 2014), 179.

4. John Whiteclay Chambers, ed., *The Eagle and the Dove* (Syracuse: Syracuse University Press, 1991), 105–6.

2. The War on Dangerous Speech

1. Peggy Lamson, *Roger Baldwin* (Boston: Houghton Mifflin Company, 1976), 69–70.

2. Wald, *Windows on Henry Street*, 305.

3. Ibid., 307.

4. Ibid., 311.

5. James S. Hirsh, *Riot and Remembrance* (Boston: Houghton Mifflin Company, 2002), 63.

6. Curt Gentry, *J. Edgar Hoover: The Man and the Secrets* (New York: W.W. Norton & Co., 1991), 138.

7. Zieger, *America's Great War*, 3.

3. The Year That Shook America and Spawned the ACLU

1. Robert K. Murray, *Red Scare: A Study in National Hysteria* (Minneapolis: University of Minnesota Press, 1955), 67.

2. Ken Armstrong, "The 1919 Race Riots," in *Chicago Days*, ed. Stevenson Swanson (Chicago: Contemporary Books, 1970), 111.

3. Ida Wells-Barnett, *The Arkansas Race Riot* (Chicago: Aquila, 1920), 7.

4. Cameron McWhirter, *Red Summer* (New York: St. Martin's Press, 2011), 12–13.

5. Walter F. White, "Chicago and Its Eight Reasons," *The Crisis*, October 1919, 297.

6. Claude McKay, *A Long Way from Home* (New Brunswick, NJ: Rutgers University Press, 2007), 30.

7. Gentry, *J. Edgar Hoover*, 79.

8. Editorial, "Is Bolshevism in America Becoming a Real Peril?" *Current Opinion*, July 1919, 4–6.

9. William Bayard Hale, "Bolshevism or Free Speech—Is This the Only Alternative?" *Viereck's American Monthly*, July 1919, 135.

10. Murray, *Red Scare*, 155.

11. Lucille Milner, *Education of an American Liberal* (Kindle edition, eBookIt.com., 2011), 1265.

12. Lamson, *Roger Baldwin*, 118–120.

4. Setting Fire to Wisdom and the Origin of Man

1. Milner, *Education of an American Liberal*, 1281.

2. Stanley Coben, *A. Mitchell Palmer: Politician* (New York: Columbia University Press, 1963), 232.

3. Louis F. Post, *The Deportation Delirium of Nineteen-Twenty: A Personal Narrative of an Historic Official Experience* (Chicago: C.H. Kerr, 1923), 28.

4. Ibid., 276.

5. Milner, *Education of an American Liberal*, 1487.

6. Ibid., 1905.

7. Lamson, *Roger Baldwin*, 150.

8. Ibid., 138.

9. International Committee for Political Prisoners, *Letters from Russian Prisons* (London: The C.W. Daniel Company, 1925), xv.

10. Lamson, *Roger Baldwin*, 141.

5. Phony Rapes and a Righteous Purge

1. Alice D. Rinehart, *One Woman Determined to Make a Difference: The Life of Madeleine Zabriskie Doty* (Bethlehem, PA: Lehigh University Press, 2001), 246.

2. Lamson, *Roger Baldwin*, 173–74.

3. Roger N. Baldwin, *Liberty Under the Soviets* (New York: Vanguard Press, 1928), 2–3.

4. Samuel Walker, *In Defense of American Liberties* (New York: Oxford University Press, 1990), 67.

5. Ibid., 34.

6. James Miller, *Remembering Scottsboro* (Princeton, NJ: Princeton University Press, 2009), 17.

7. Walker, *In Defense of American Liberties*, 82.

8. Ibid., 133.

6. A Yellow Menace, Red Fears, White Racism, and Assimilation

1. John W. DeWitt, *Final Report: Japanese Evacuation from the West Coast 1942* (Washington, DC: U.S. Government Printing Office, 1943), vii.

2. Nat Segaloff, *A History of the ACLU of Southern California* (Los Angeles: ACLU Foundation of Southern California, 2015), 19.

3. Judy Kutulas, "In Quest of Autonomy: The Northern California Affiliate of the American Civil Liberties Union and World War II," *Pacific Historical Review* 67, no. 2 (May 1998): 213.

4. Lorraine K. Bannai, *Enduring Conviction* (Seattle: University of Washington Press, 2015), 51.

5. Ibid., 60.

6. Ibid., 142–43.

7. Peter Irons, *Justice at War: The Story of the Japanese-American Internment Cases* (Berkeley: University of California Press, 1993), 100–102.

8. Jerry Kang, "Denying Prejudice: Internment, Redress, and Denial," *UCLA Law Review* 51 (2004): 945–46.

9. Walker, *In Defense of American Liberties*, 179.

10. Andrea G. Hunter and Alethea Rollins, "We Made History: Collective Memory and the Legacy of the Tuskegee Airmen," *Journal of Social Issues* 71, no. 2 (June 2015): 270.

11. John L. Newby II, "The Fight for the Right to Fight and the Forgotten Negro Protest Movement," *Texas Journal on Civil Liberties & Civil Rights*, Winter 2004, 84–86.

7. McCarthy Crosses a Line and Eisenhower Sends Troops to Little Rock

1. Walker, *In Defense of American Liberties*, 208–11.
2. Corliss Lamont, "The Struggle for Civil Liberties," *Science & Society*, Fall 1986, 333–34.
3. Walker, *In Defense of American Liberties*, 207.

8. A Moral Crusade, an Immoral War, and a Forbidden Romance

1. Charles Morgan Jr., *A Time to Speak* (New York: Harper & Row, 1964), 10–14.
2. John Lewis, *Walking with the Wind* (New York: Harcourt Brace & Company, 1998), 337–42.
3. Mary Stanton, "Vindicating Viola Luizzo," *Alabama Heritage* 98 (Fall 2010), 31.
4. Peter Wallenstein, "The Right to Marry: Loving v. Virginia," *OAH Magazine of History* 9, no. 2 (Winter 1995): 37.

9. Resurrecting a Communist as the Nixon Era Ends

1. Lucas A. Powe Jr., *The Warren Court and American Politics* (Cambridge: Harvard University Press, 2000), 1.
2. David Wecht, "Miranda at 50," *Pennsylvania Lawyer*, November/December 2016, 28.

11. Mourning a Founder, Defeating Bork, and Atoning for Internment

1. Mark Gitenstein, *Matters of Principle* (New York: Simon & Schuster, 1992), 261–62.
2. Kang, "Denying Prejudice," 936.

12. Terrorism, Torture and the Pursuit of Justice

1. Daniel Klaidman, *Kill or Capture* (Boston: Houghton Mifflin Harcourt, 2013), 132.
2. Ibid., 134–35.
3. Ibid., 136.

13. Edward Snowden Joins the ACLU

1. Glenn Greenwald, *No Place to Hide* (New York: Metropolitan Books, 2014), 7.

2. Ibid., 18.

3. Ibid., 42–43.

4. Edward Jay Epstein, *How America Lost Its Secrets* (New York: Random House, 2017), 101–102.

15. Reflections

1. Vincent Blasi, "The First Amendment and the Ideal of Civic Courage: The Brandeis Opinion in Whitney v. California," *William and Mary Law Review* 29 (1988), 653–697.

2. Laura Weinrib, *The Taming of Free Speech* (Cambridge, MA: Harvard University Press, 2016), 1.

3. Brendan Nyhan and Jason Reifler, "When Corrections Fail: The Persistence of Political Misperceptions," *Political Behavior* 32, no. 2 (June 2010): 307–8.

4. Brendan Nyhan and Jason Reifler, "The Effect of Fact-Checking on Elites: A Field Experiment on U.S. State Legislators," *American Journal of Political Science* 59, no. 3 (July 2015): 628.

5. Lee C. McIntyre, *Post-Truth* (Cambridge, MA: MIT Press, Kindle edition, 2018), 881.

Index